MS. MARVEL

MONSTER SMASH

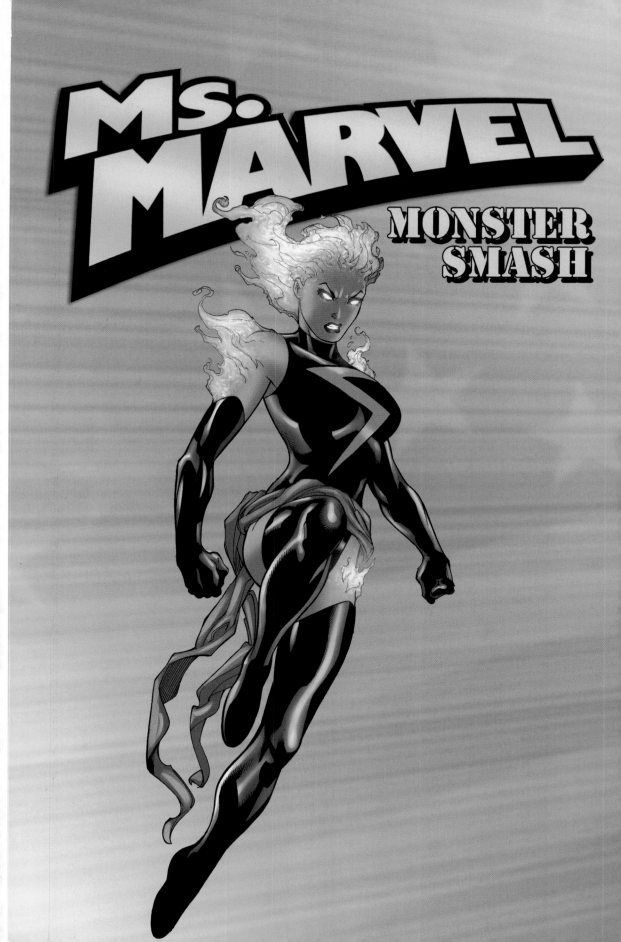

MONSTER SMASH

WRITER: **BRIAN REED**
PENCILS: **AARON LOPRESTI**
WITH GREG TOCCHINI (ISSUE #20)
INKS: **MATT RYAN**
WITH ROLAND PARIS (ISSUE #20)
COLORS: **CHRIS SOTOMAYOR**
LETTERS: **DAVE SHARPE**
COVER ART: **GREG HORN**
ASSISTANT EDITORS: **TOM BRENNAN**
& ALEJANDRO ARBONA
EDITORS: **STEPHEN WACKER**
& BILL ROSEMANN

COLLECTION EDITOR: **JENNIFER GRÜNWALD**
ASSISTANT EDITORS: **CORY LEVINE & JOHN DENNING**
EDITOR, SPECIAL PROJECTS: **MARK D. BEAZLEY**
SENIOR EDITOR, SPECIAL PROJECTS: **JEFF YOUNGQUIST**
SENIOR VICE PRESIDENT OF SALES: **DAVID GABRIEL**
PRODUCTION: **JERRON QUALITY COLOR**
VICE PRESIDENT OF CREATIVE: **TOM MARVELLI**

EDITOR IN CHIEF: **JOE QUESADA**
PUBLISHER: **DAN BUCKLEY**

MS. MARVEL VOL. 4: MONSTER SMASH. Contains material originally published in magazine form as MS. MARVEL #18-24. First printing 2008. Hardcover ISBN# 978-0-7851-3018-5. Softcover ISBN# 978-0-7851-2813-7. Published by MARVEL PUBLISHING, INC., a subsidiary of MARVEL ENTERTAINMENT, INC. OFFICE OF PUBLICATION: 417 5th Avenue, New York, NY 10016. Copyright © 2007 and 2008 Marvel Characters, Inc. All rights reserved. Hardcover: $19.99 per copy in the U.S. and $32.00 in Canada (GST #R127032852). Softcover: $14.99 per copy in the U.S. and $24.00 in Canada (GST #R127032852). Canadian Agreement #40668537. All characters featured in this issue and the distinctive names and likenesses thereof, and all related indicia are trademarks of Marvel Characters, Inc. No similarity between any of the names, characters, persons, and/or institutions in this magazine with those of any living or dead person or institution is intended, and any such similarity which may exist is purely coincidental. **Printed in the U.S.A.** ALAN FINE, CEO Marvel Toys & Publishing Divisions and CMO Marvel Entertainment, Inc.; DAVID GABRIEL, SVP of Publishing Sales & Circulation; DAVID BOGART, SVP of Business Affairs & Talent Management; MICHAEL PASCIULLO, VP of Merchandising & Communications; JIM O'KEEFE, VP of Operations & Logistics; DAN CARR, Executive Director of Publishing Technology; JUSTIN F. GABRIE, Director of Editorial Operations; SUSAN CRESPI, Production Manager; STAN LEE, Chairman Emeritus. For information regarding advertising in Marvel Comics or on Marvel.com, please contact Mitch Dane, Advertising Director, at mdane@marvel.com. For Marvel subscription inquiries, please call 800-217-9158.

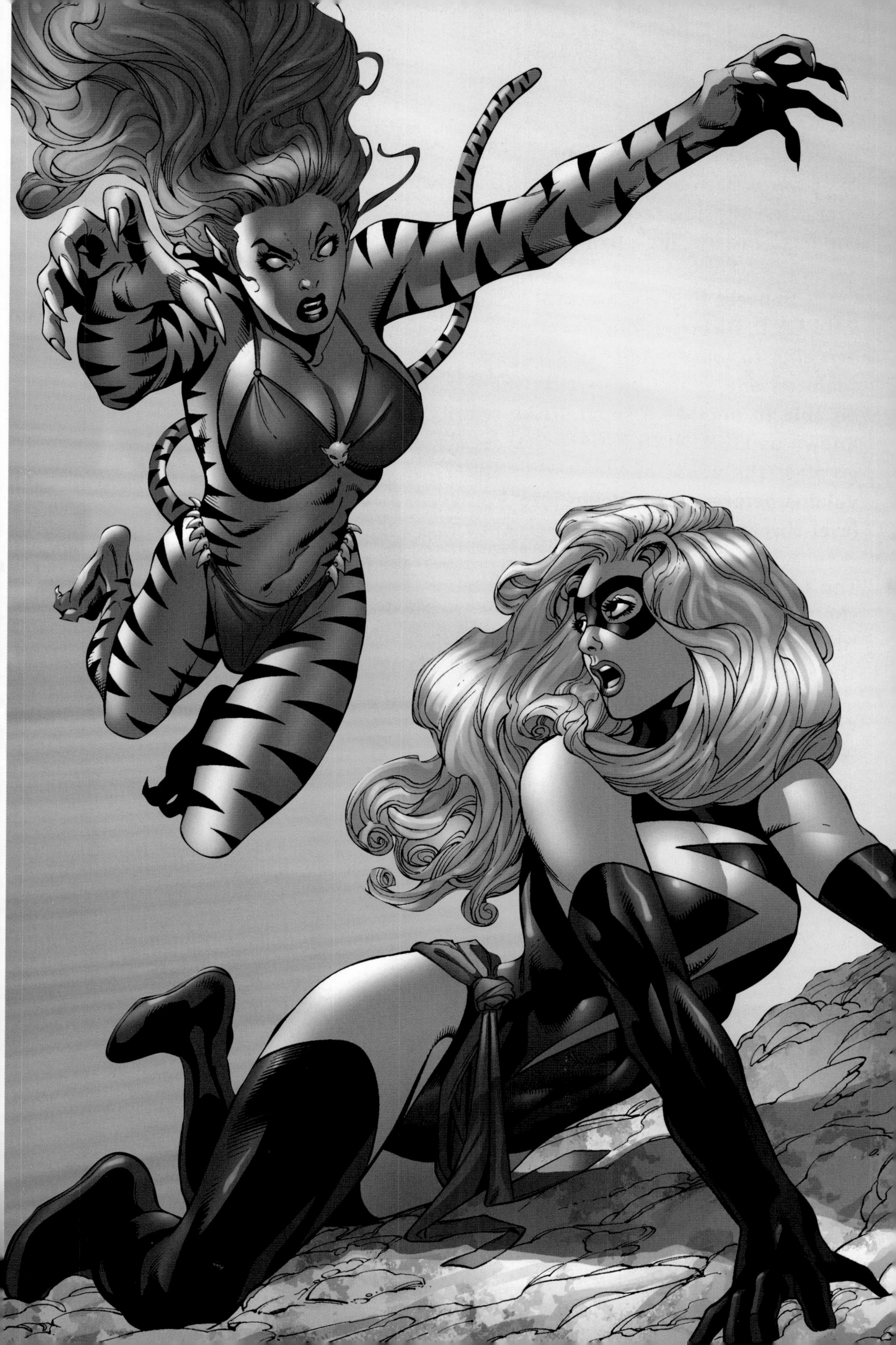

PREVIOUSLY:

In a brilliant flash of light, former U.S. Air Force pilot Carol Danvers was transformed by alien Kree DNA-altering technology, becoming the hard-hitting, high-flying Ms. Marvel!

Carol Danvers has made a deal with S.H.I.E.L.D. Director Tony Stark, agreeing to join his Mighty Avengers team on one condition — that she be able to operate a small strike team known as LIGHTNING STORM that would go after the worst of the world's super-villains before they develop into Avengers-level threats.

The team's first real mission, battling the terrorist organization Advanced Idea Mechanics, ended in chaos and the death of two team members.

Carol also discovered that she is manifesting disturbing new physical developments...

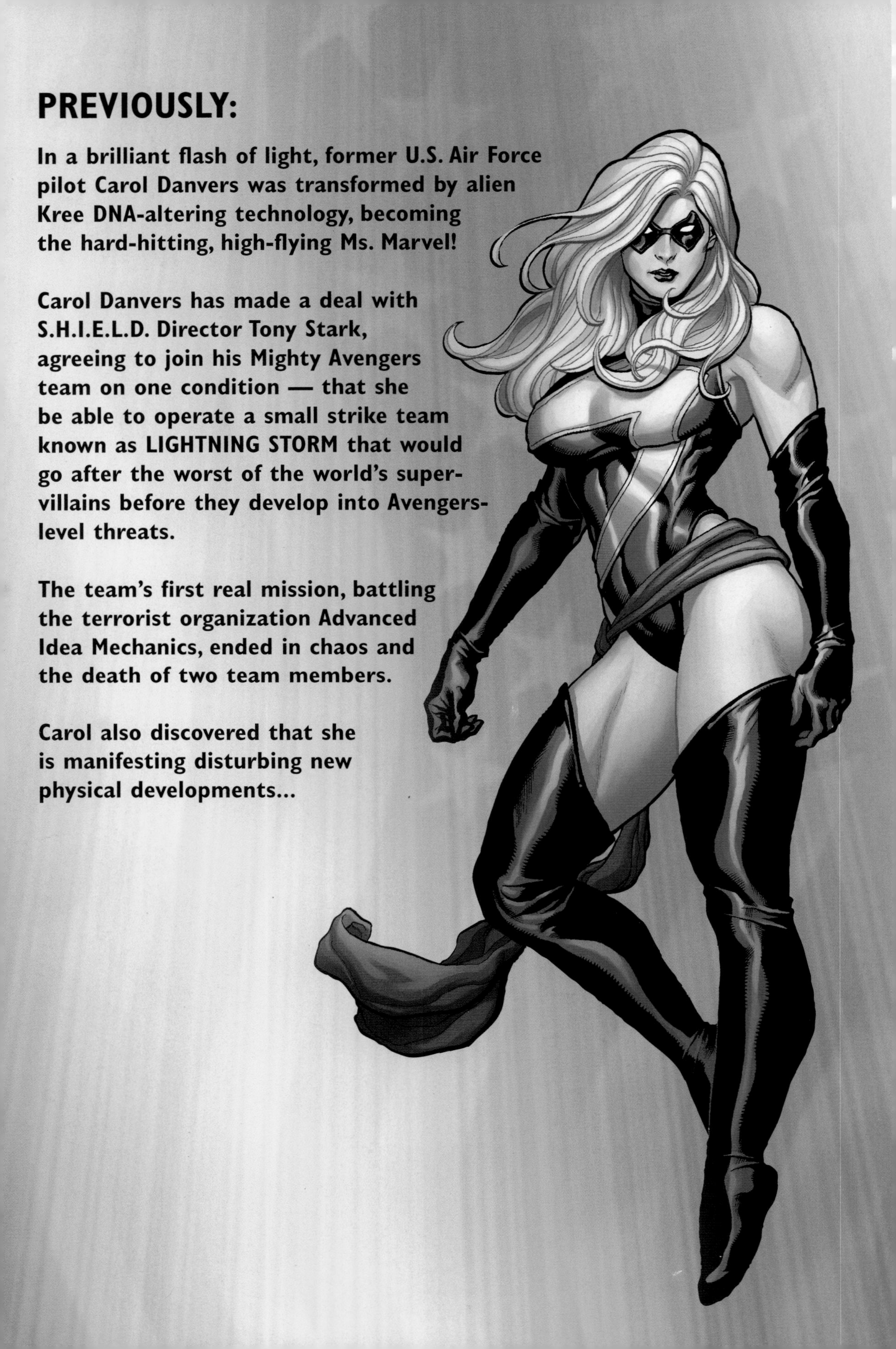

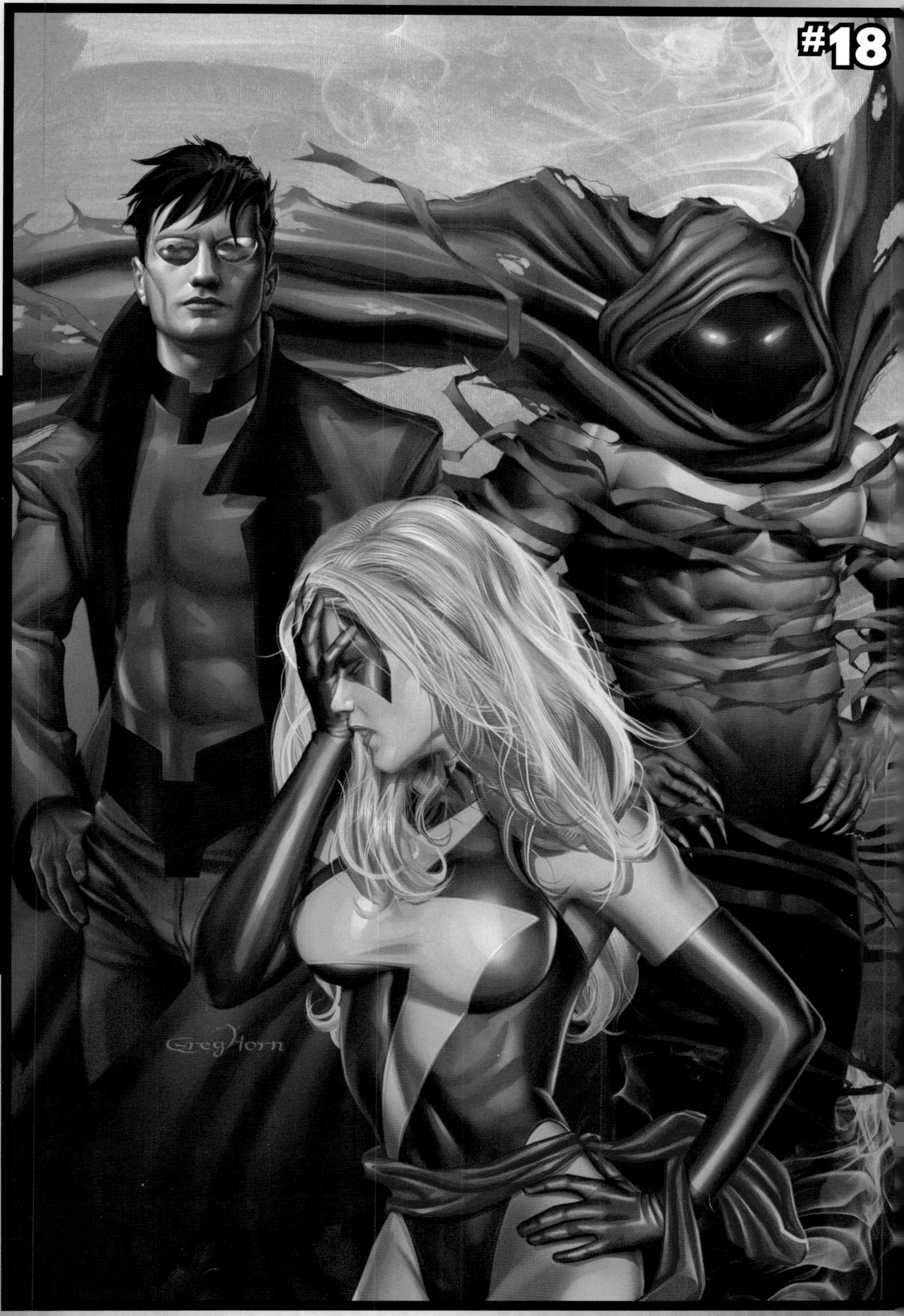
#18
Greg Horn

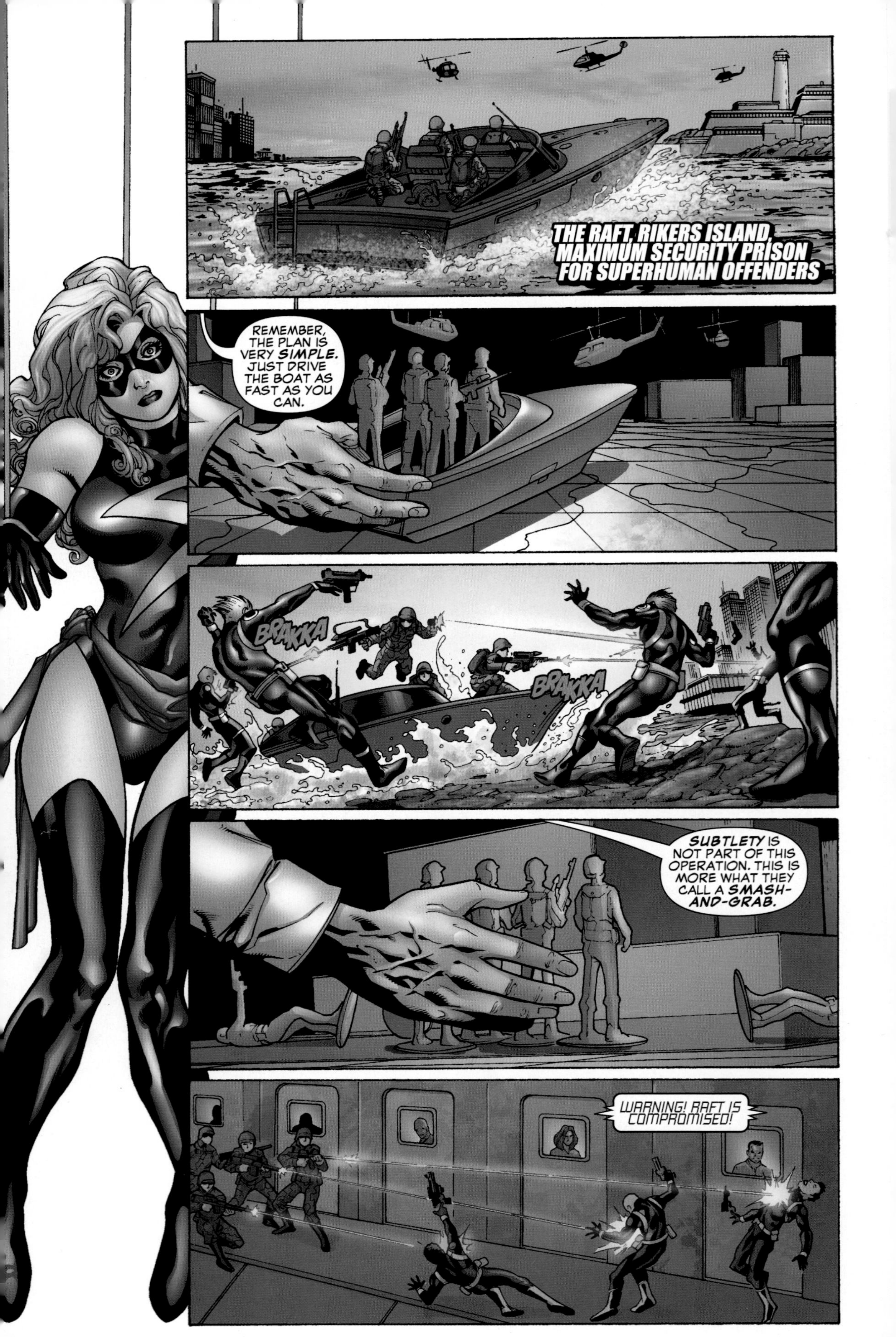
THE RAFT, RIKERS ISLAND, MAXIMUM SECURITY PRISON FOR SUPERHUMAN OFFENDERS
REMEMBER, THE PLAN IS VERY SIMPLE. JUST DRIVE THE BOAT AS FAST AS YOU CAN.
BRAKKA
BRAKKA
SUBTLETY IS NOT PART OF THIS OPERATION. THIS IS MORE WHAT THEY CALL A SMASH-AND-GRAB.
WARNING! RAFT IS COMPROMISED!

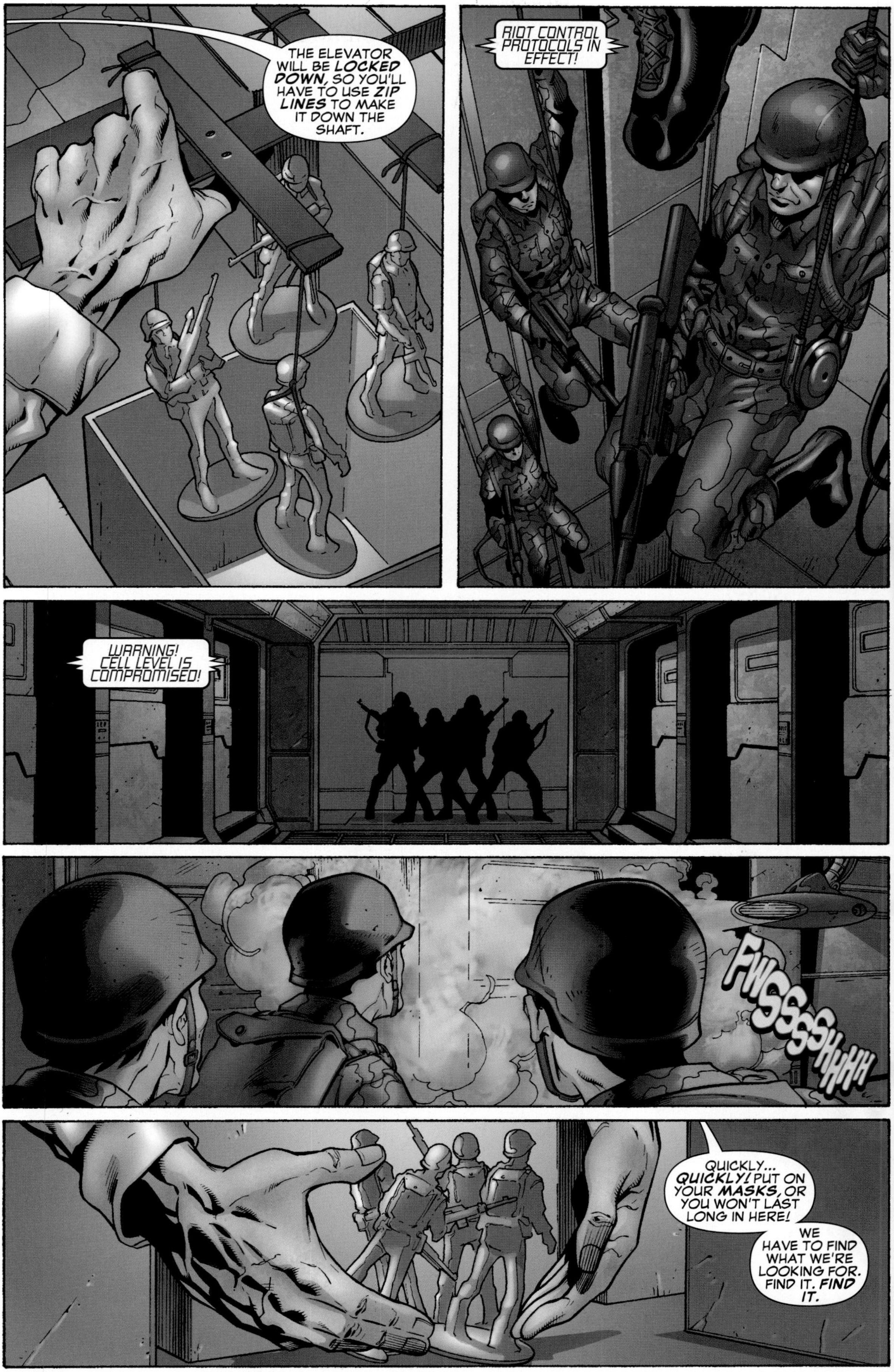
THE ELEVATOR WILL BE LOCKED DOWN, SO YOU'LL HAVE TO USE ZIP LINES TO MAKE IT DOWN THE SHAFT.
RIOT CONTROL PROTOCOLS IN EFFECT!
WARNING! CELL LEVEL IS COMPROMISED!
FWSSSSHHHH
QUICKLY... QUICKLY! PUT ON YOUR MASKS, OR YOU WON'T LAST LONG IN HERE!
WE HAVE TO FIND WHAT WE'RE LOOKING FOR. FIND IT. FIND IT.

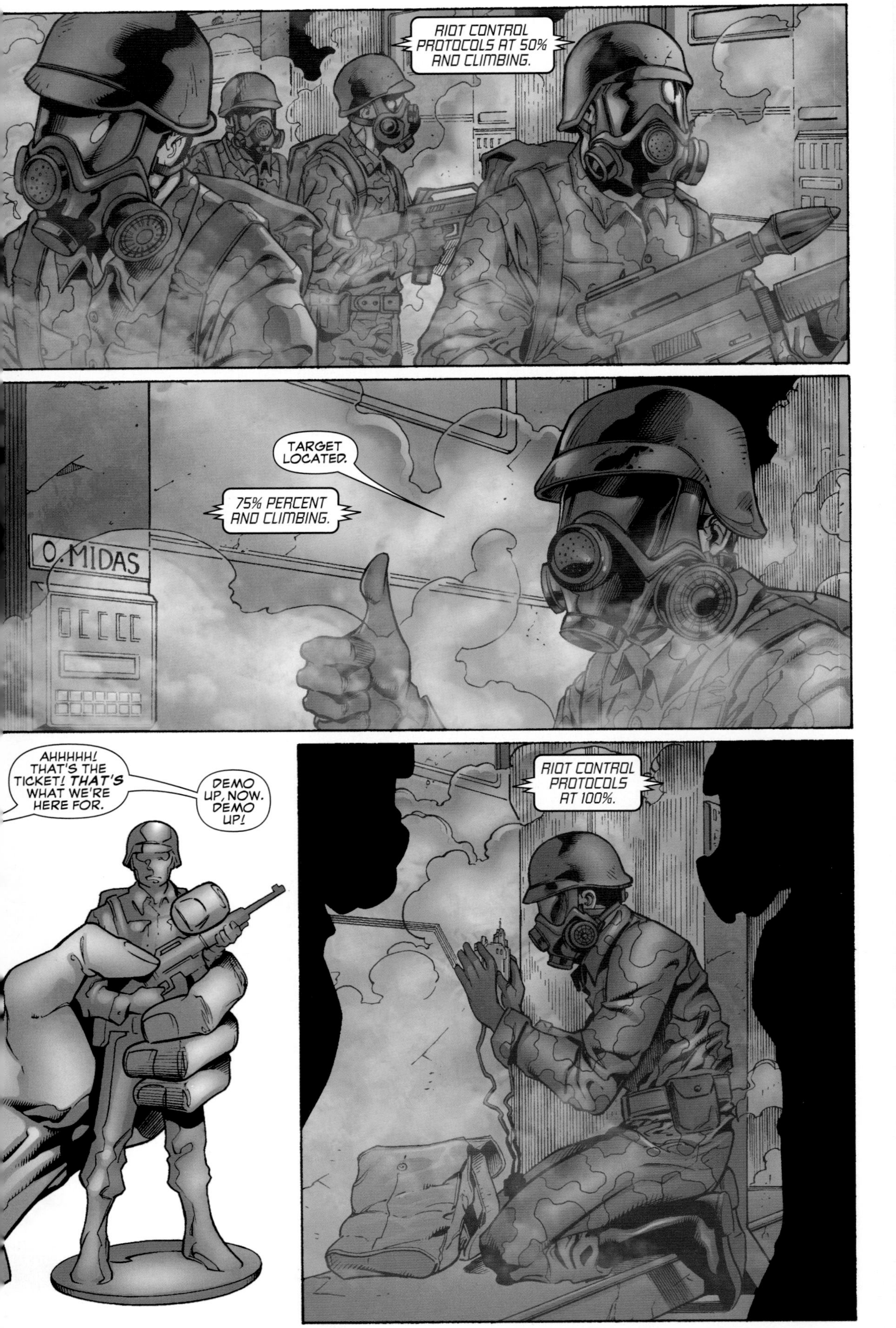
RIOT CONTROL PROTOCOLS AT 50% AND CLIMBING.
TARGET LOCATED.
75% PERCENT AND CLIMBING.
O. MIDAS
AHHHHH! THAT'S THE TICKET! THAT'S WHAT WE'RE HERE FOR.
DEMO UP, NOW. DEMO UP!
RIOT CONTROL PROTOCOLS AT 100%.

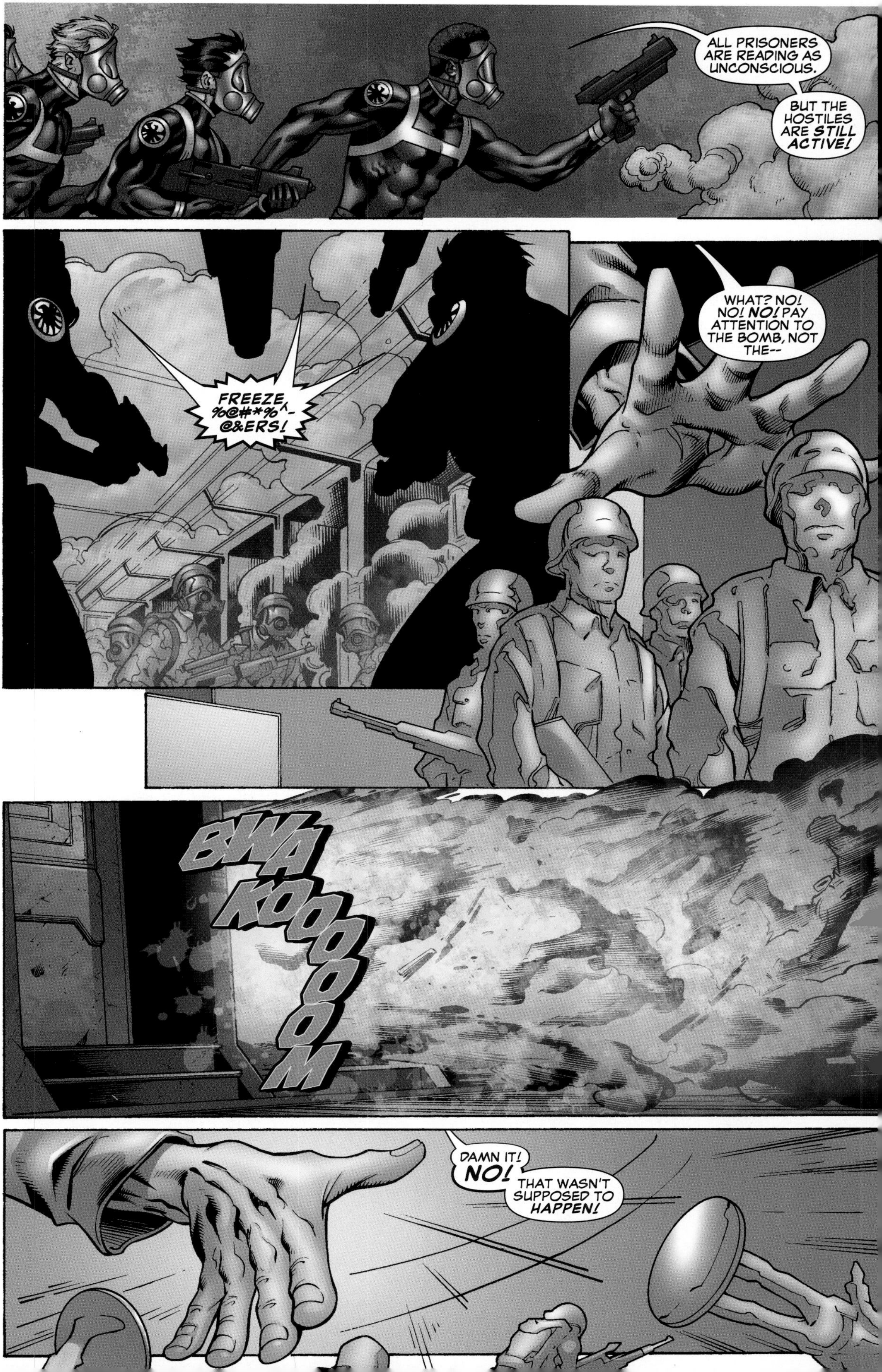
ALL PRISONERS ARE READING AS UNCONSCIOUS.
BUT THE HOSTILES ARE STILL ACTIVE!
FREEZE, %@#*%^-@&ERS!
WHAT? NO! NO! NO! PAY ATTENTION TO THE BOMB, NOT THE--
BWAKOOOOOOM
DAMN IT! NO!
THAT WASN'T SUPPOSED TO HAPPEN!

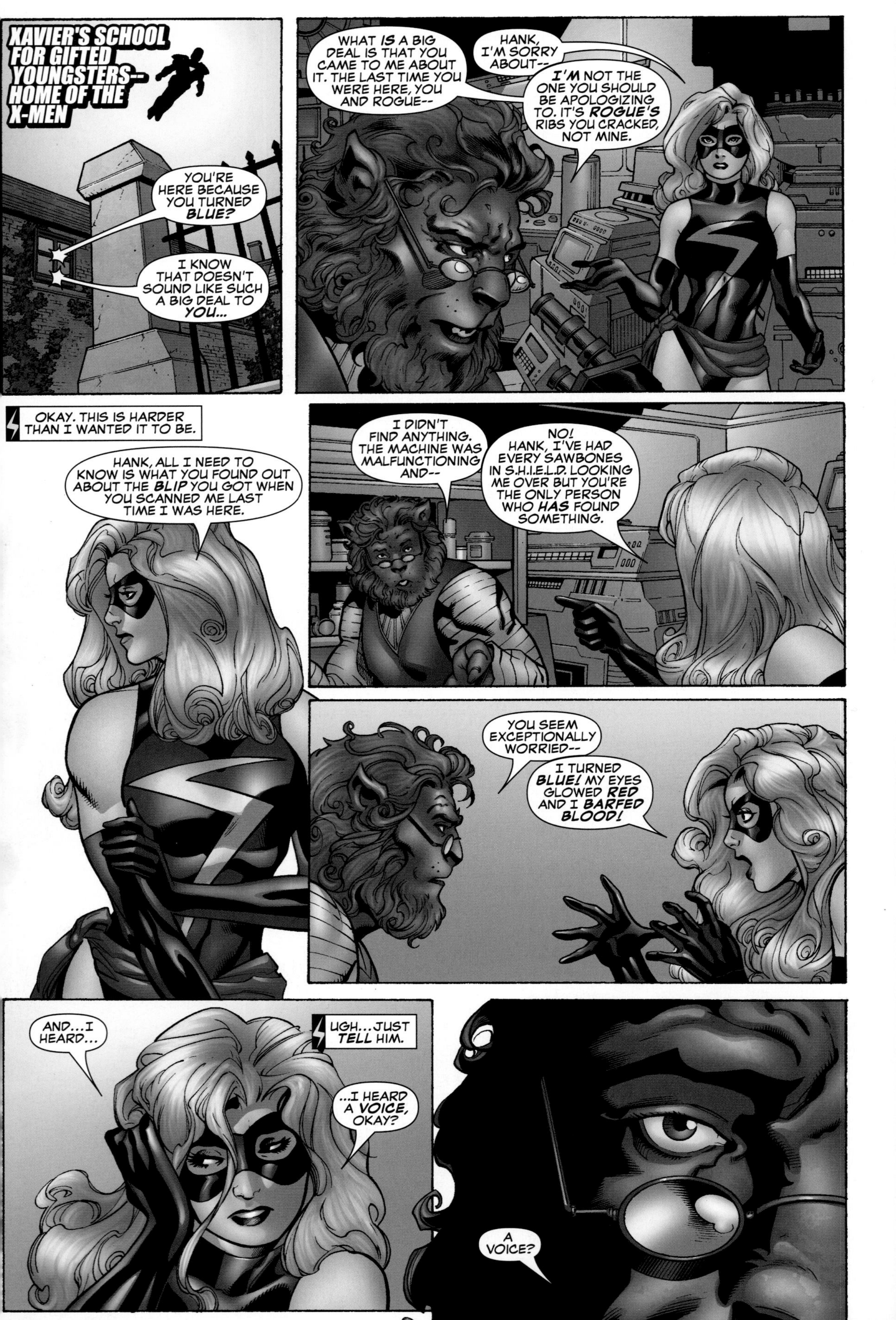
XAVIER'S SCHOOL FOR GIFTED YOUNGSTERS-- HOME OF THE X-MEN
YOU'RE HERE BECAUSE YOU TURNED BLUE?
I KNOW THAT DOESN'T SOUND LIKE SUCH A BIG DEAL TO YOU...
WHAT IS A BIG DEAL IS THAT YOU CAME TO ME ABOUT IT. THE LAST TIME YOU WERE HERE, YOU AND ROGUE--
HANK, I'M SORRY ABOUT--
I'M NOT THE ONE YOU SHOULD BE APOLOGIZING TO. IT'S ROGUE'S RIBS YOU CRACKED, NOT MINE.
OKAY. THIS IS HARDER THAN I WANTED IT TO BE.
HANK, ALL I NEED TO KNOW IS WHAT YOU FOUND OUT ABOUT THE BLIP YOU GOT WHEN YOU SCANNED ME LAST TIME I WAS HERE.
I DIDN'T FIND ANYTHING. THE MACHINE WAS MALFUNCTIONING AND--
NO! HANK, I'VE HAD EVERY SAWBONES IN S.H.I.E.L.D. LOOKING ME OVER BUT YOU'RE THE ONLY PERSON WHO HAS FOUND SOMETHING.
YOU SEEM EXCEPTIONALLY WORRIED--
I TURNED BLUE! MY EYES GLOWED RED AND I BARFED BLOOD!
AND...I HEARD...
UGH...JUST TELL HIM.
...I HEARD A VOICE, OKAY?
A VOICE?

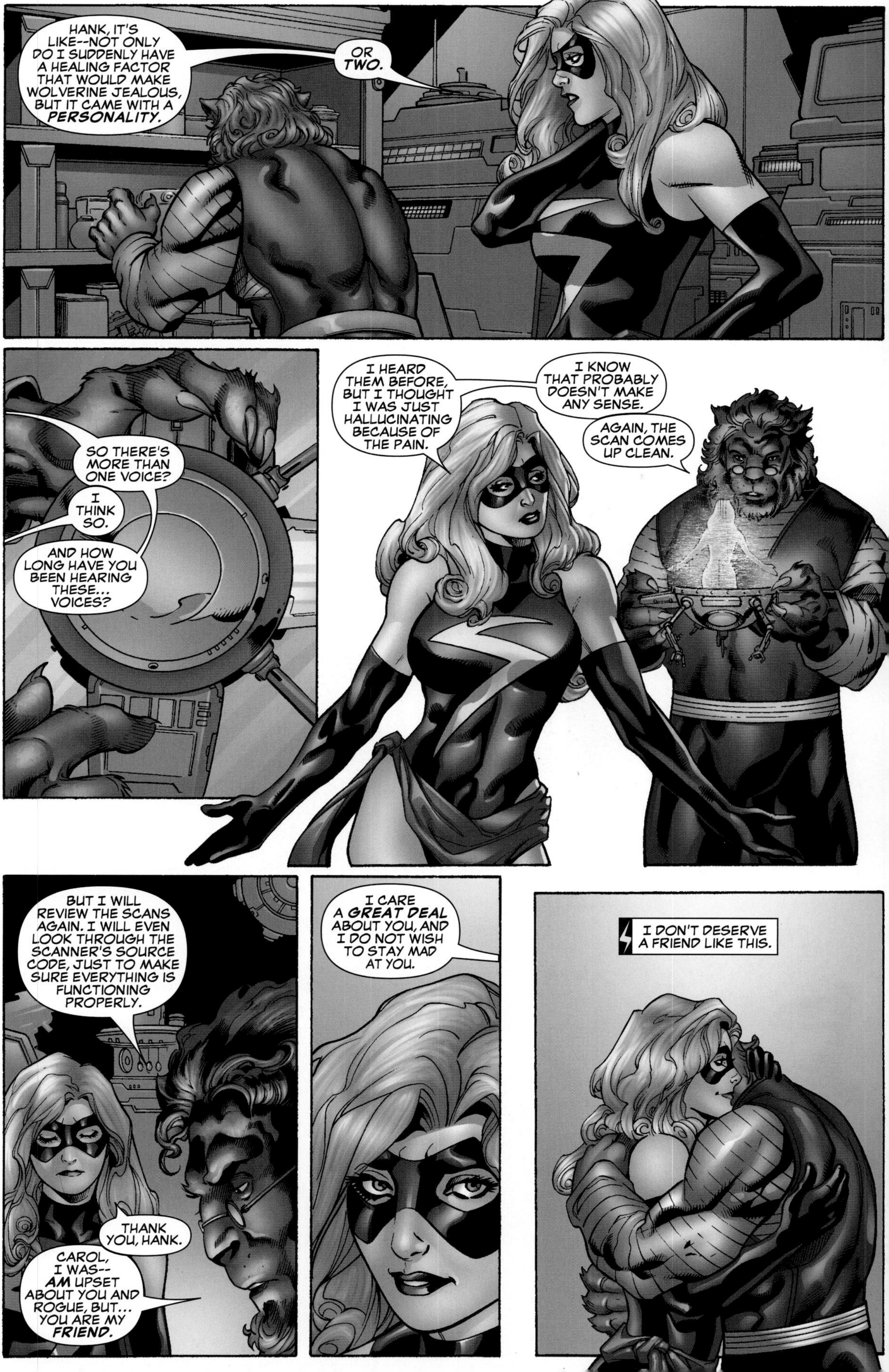
HANK, IT'S LIKE--NOT ONLY DO I SUDDENLY HAVE A HEALING FACTOR THAT WOULD MAKE WOLVERINE JEALOUS, BUT IT CAME WITH A PERSONALITY.
OR TWO.
SO THERE'S MORE THAN ONE VOICE?
I THINK SO.
AND HOW LONG HAVE YOU BEEN HEARING THESE... VOICES?
I HEARD THEM BEFORE, BUT I THOUGHT I WAS JUST HALLUCINATING BECAUSE OF THE PAIN.
I KNOW THAT PROBABLY DOESN'T MAKE ANY SENSE.
AGAIN, THE SCAN COMES UP CLEAN.
BUT I WILL REVIEW THE SCANS AGAIN. I WILL EVEN LOOK THROUGH THE SCANNER'S SOURCE CODE, JUST TO MAKE SURE EVERYTHING IS FUNCTIONING PROPERLY.
THANK YOU, HANK.
CAROL, I WAS-- AM UPSET ABOUT YOU AND ROGUE, BUT... YOU ARE MY FRIEND.
I CARE A GREAT DEAL ABOUT YOU, AND I DO NOT WISH TO STAY MAD AT YOU.
I DON'T DESERVE A FRIEND LIKE THIS.

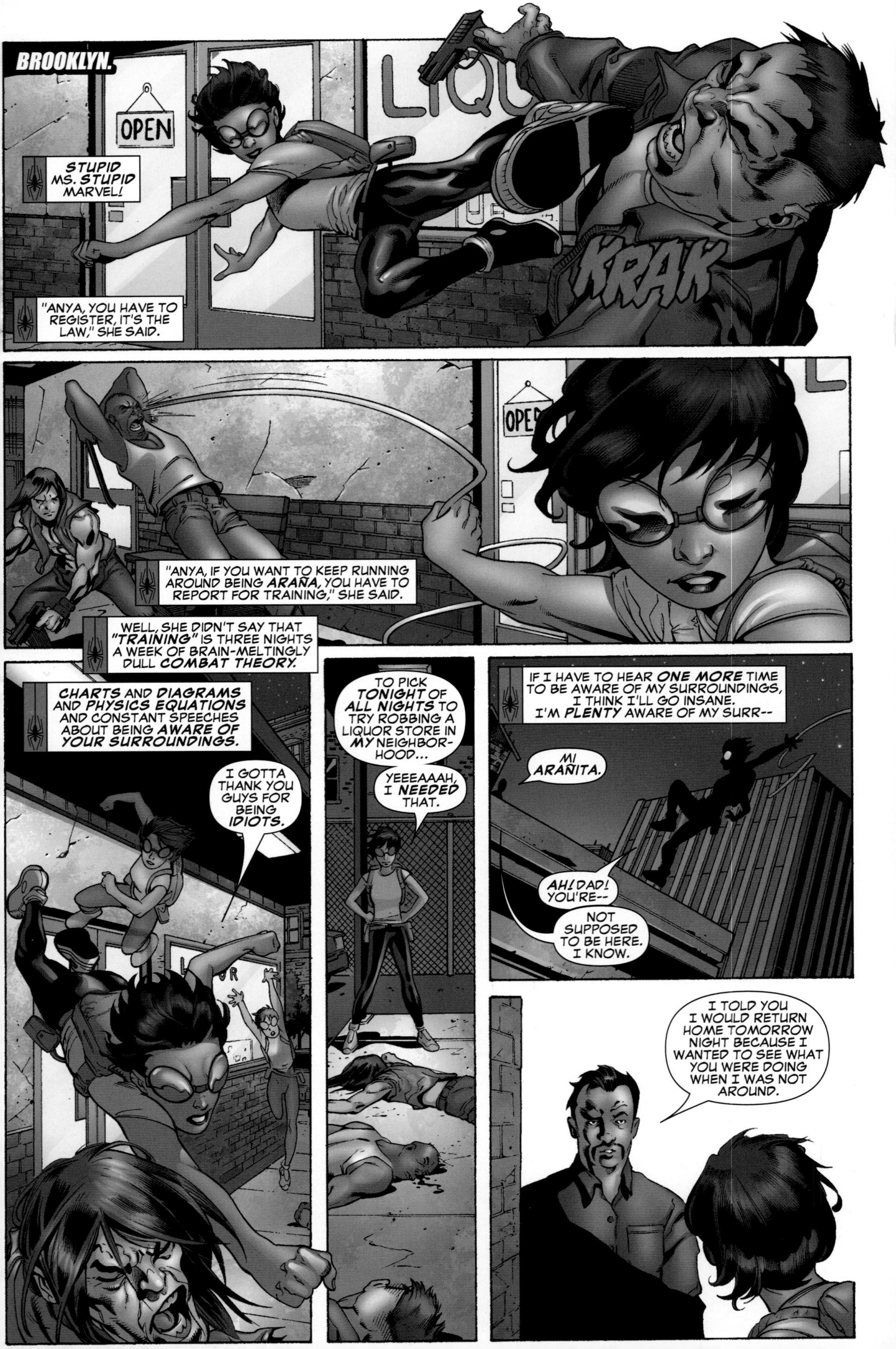

BROOKLYN.
OPEN
STUPID MS. STUPID MARVEL!
KRAK
"ANYA, YOU HAVE TO REGISTER, IT'S THE LAW," SHE SAID.
"ANYA, IF YOU WANT TO KEEP RUNNING AROUND BEING ARAÑA, YOU HAVE TO REPORT FOR TRAINING," SHE SAID.
WELL, SHE DIDN'T SAY THAT "TRAINING" IS THREE NIGHTS A WEEK OF BRAIN-MELTINGLY DULL COMBAT THEORY.
CHARTS AND DIAGRAMS AND PHYSICS EQUATIONS AND CONSTANT SPEECHES ABOUT BEING AWARE OF YOUR SURROUNDINGS.
I GOTTA THANK YOU GUYS FOR BEING IDIOTS.
TO PICK TONIGHT OF ALL NIGHTS TO TRY ROBBING A LIQUOR STORE IN MY NEIGHBOR-HOOD...
YEEEAAAH, I NEEDED THAT.
IF I HAVE TO HEAR ONE MORE TIME TO BE AWARE OF MY SURROUNDINGS, I THINK I'LL GO INSANE. I'M PLENTY AWARE OF MY SURR--
MI ARAÑITA.
AH! DAD! YOU'RE--
NOT SUPPOSED TO BE HERE. I KNOW.
I TOLD YOU I WOULD RETURN HOME TOMORROW NIGHT BECAUSE I WANTED TO SEE WHAT YOU WERE DOING WHEN I WAS NOT AROUND.

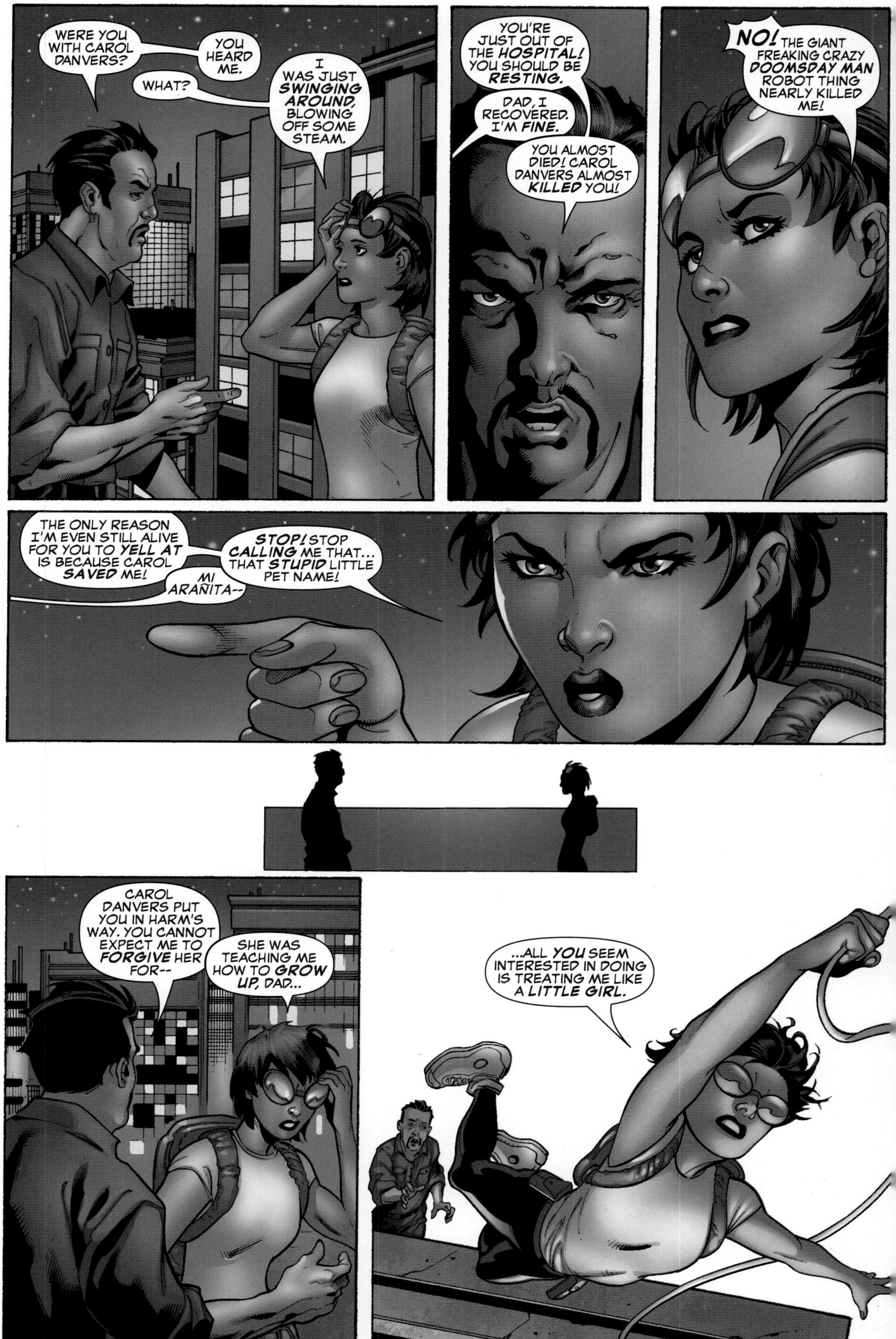
WERE YOU WITH CAROL DANVERS?
WHAT?
YOU HEARD ME.
I WAS JUST SWINGING AROUND, BLOWING OFF SOME STEAM.
YOU'RE JUST OUT OF THE HOSPITAL! YOU SHOULD BE RESTING.
DAD, I RECOVERED. I'M FINE.
YOU ALMOST DIED! CAROL DANVERS ALMOST KILLED YOU!
NO! THE GIANT FREAKING CRAZY DOOMSDAY MAN ROBOT THING NEARLY KILLED ME!
THE ONLY REASON I'M EVEN STILL ALIVE FOR YOU TO YELL AT IS BECAUSE CAROL SAVED ME!
MI ARAÑITA--
STOP! STOP CALLING ME THAT... THAT STUPID LITTLE PET NAME!
CAROL DANVERS PUT YOU IN HARM'S WAY. YOU CANNOT EXPECT ME TO FORGIVE HER FOR--
SHE WAS TEACHING ME HOW TO GROW UP, DAD...
...ALL YOU SEEM INTERESTED IN DOING IS TREATING ME LIKE A LITTLE GIRL.

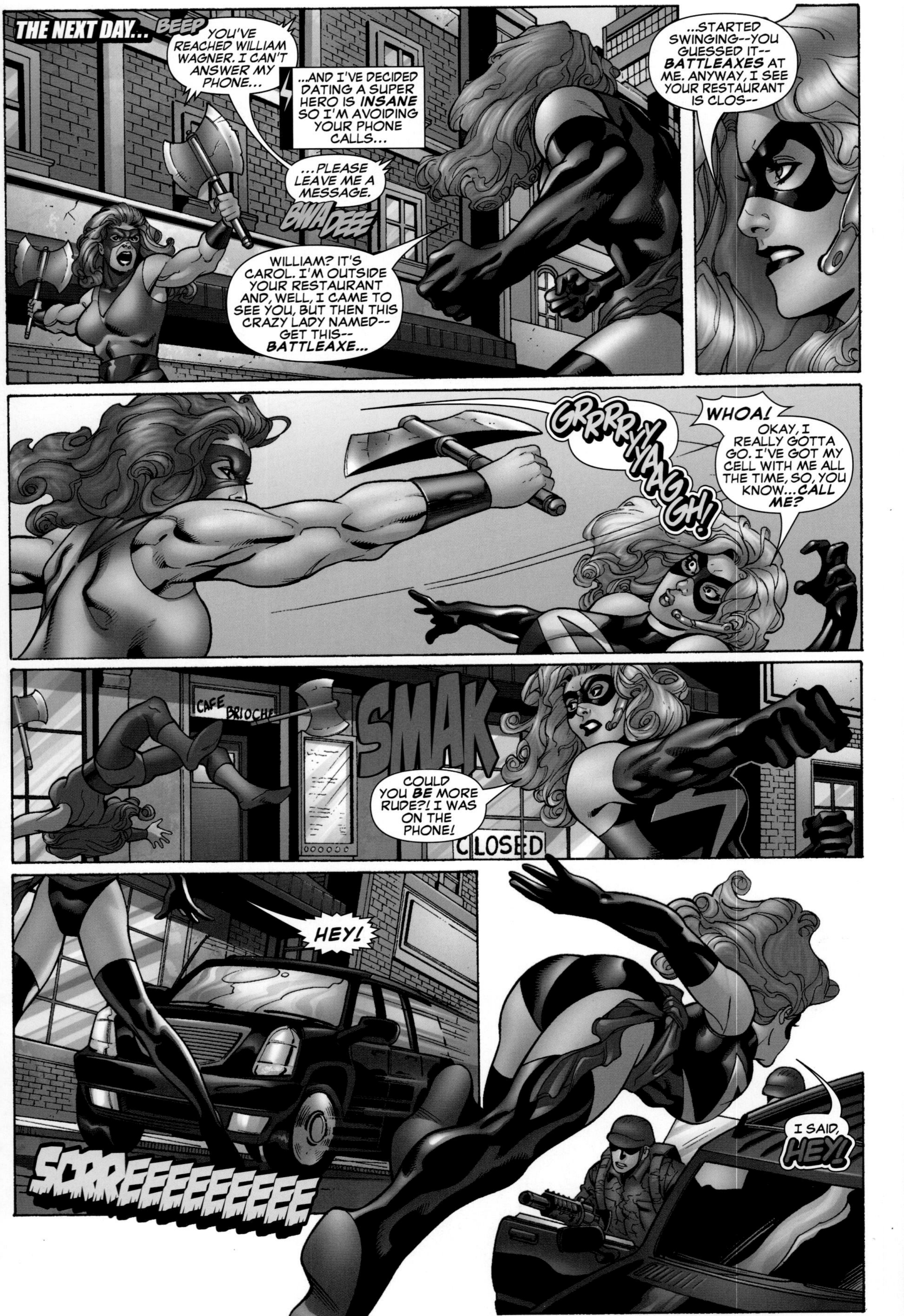
THE NEXT DAY...
BEEP
YOU'VE REACHED WILLIAM WAGNER. I CAN'T ANSWER MY PHONE...
...AND I'VE DECIDED DATING A SUPER HERO IS INSANE SO I'M AVOIDING YOUR PHONE CALLS...
...PLEASE LEAVE ME A MESSAGE.
BWADEEE
WILLIAM? IT'S CAROL. I'M OUTSIDE YOUR RESTAURANT AND, WELL, I CAME TO SEE YOU, BUT THEN THIS CRAZY LADY NAMED-- GET THIS-- BATTLEAXE...
...STARTED SWINGING--YOU GUESSED IT-- BATTLEAXES AT ME. ANYWAY, I SEE YOUR RESTAURANT IS CLOS--
GRRRRYYAAGGH!
WHOA!
OKAY, I REALLY GOTTA GO. I'VE GOT MY CELL WITH ME ALL THE TIME, SO, YOU KNOW...CALL ME?
CAFE BRIOCHE
SMAK
COULD YOU BE MORE RUDE?! I WAS ON THE PHONE!
CLOSED
HEY!
SCRREEEEEEEEEEE
I SAID, HEY!

HOLY--

PUM

FWIP

NYYAAAYAAAA!

HANG ON, GUYS. YOU CLEARLY AREN'T S.H.I.E.L.D. AND UNTIL I SEE SOME I.D. SAYING YOU'RE LICENSED BOUNTY HUNT--

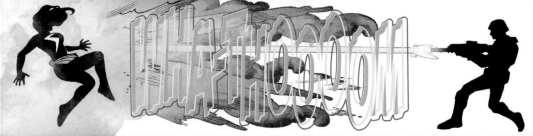

WHATHOOOOM

YEAH, THIS IS AN IMPRESSIVE POSE FOR THE BEST HERO IN THE WORLD.

OKAY, THE GRENADE SURPRISED ME MORE THAN IT HURT--BUT WHO ARE THESE GUYS?

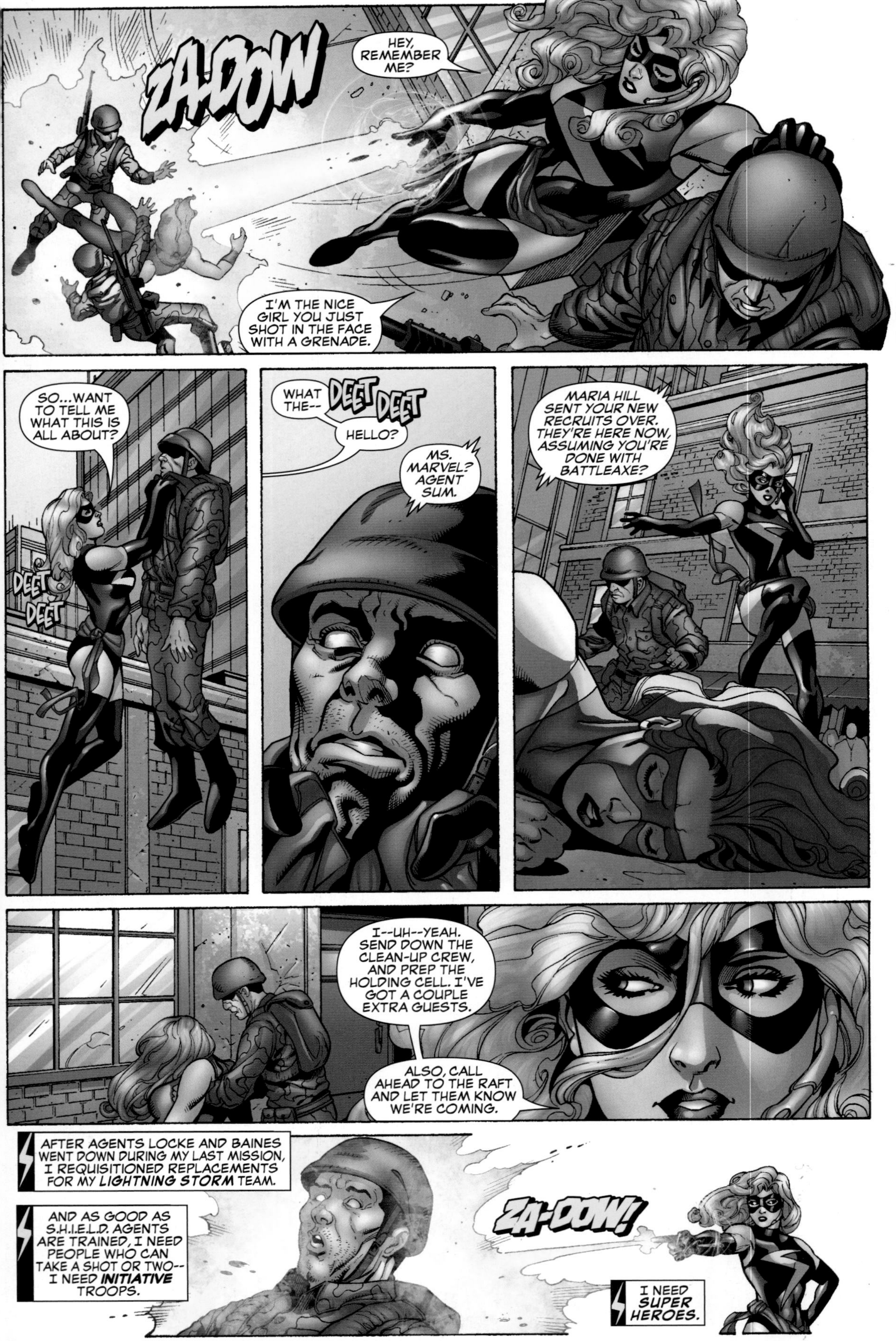
ZA-DOW
HEY, REMEMBER ME?
I'M THE NICE GIRL YOU JUST SHOT IN THE FACE WITH A GRENADE.
SO...WANT TO TELL ME WHAT THIS IS ALL ABOUT?
DEET DEET
WHAT THE--
DEET DEET
HELLO?
MS. MARVEL? AGENT SUM.
MARIA HILL SENT YOUR NEW RECRUITS OVER. THEY'RE HERE NOW, ASSUMING YOU'RE DONE WITH BATTLEAXE?
I--UH--YEAH. SEND DOWN THE CLEAN-UP CREW, AND PREP THE HOLDING CELL. I'VE GOT A COUPLE EXTRA GUESTS.
ALSO, CALL AHEAD TO THE RAFT AND LET THEM KNOW WE'RE COMING.
AFTER AGENTS LOCKE AND BAINES WENT DOWN DURING MY LAST MISSION, I REQUISITIONED REPLACEMENTS FOR MY *LIGHTNING STORM* TEAM.
AND AS GOOD AS S.H.I.E.L.D. AGENTS ARE TRAINED, I NEED PEOPLE WHO CAN TAKE A SHOT OR TWO-- I NEED *INITIATIVE* TROOPS.
ZA-DOW!
I NEED *SUPER HEROES.*

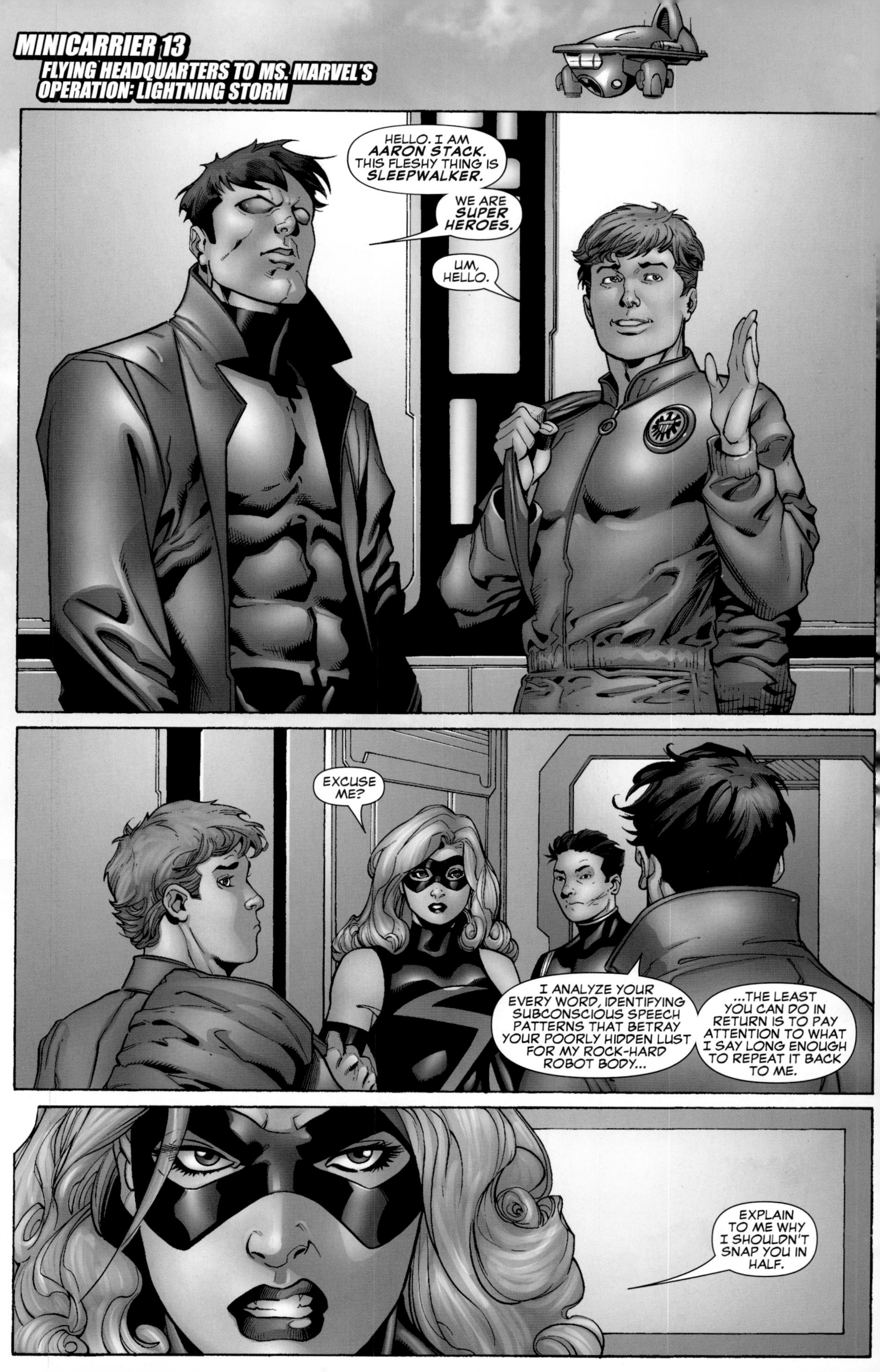
MINICARRIER 13
FLYING HEADQUARTERS TO MS. MARVEL'S OPERATION: LIGHTNING STORM
HELLO. I AM AARON STACK. THIS FLESHY THING IS SLEEPWALKER.
WE ARE SUPER HEROES.
UM, HELLO.
EXCUSE ME?
I ANALYZE YOUR EVERY WORD, IDENTIFYING SUBCONSCIOUS SPEECH PATTERNS THAT BETRAY YOUR POORLY HIDDEN LUST FOR MY ROCK-HARD ROBOT BODY...
...THE LEAST YOU CAN DO IN RETURN IS TO PAY ATTENTION TO WHAT I SAY LONG ENOUGH TO REPEAT IT BACK TO ME.
EXPLAIN TO ME WHY I SHOULDN'T SNAP YOU IN HALF.

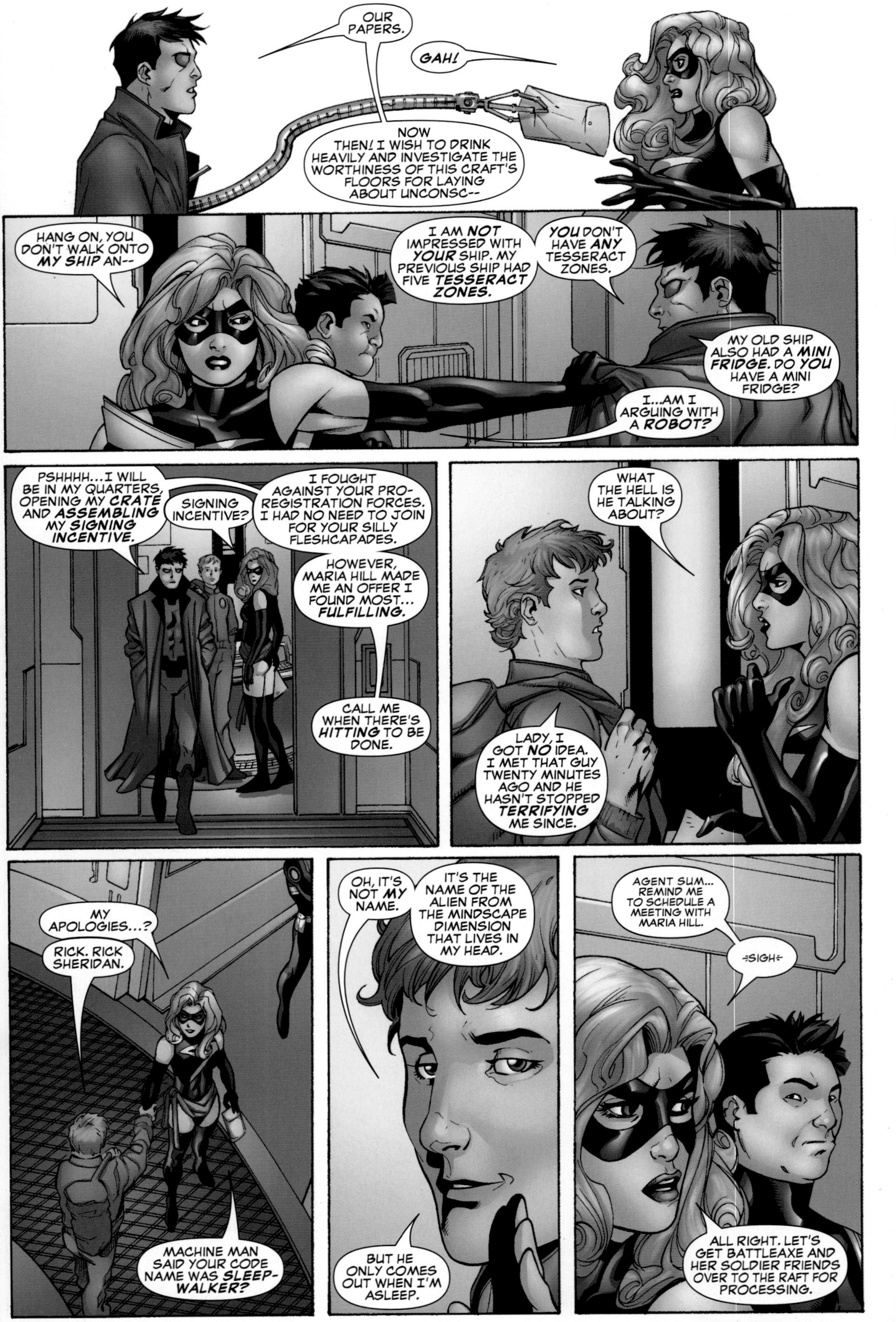
OUR PAPERS.
GAH!
NOW THEN! I WISH TO DRINK HEAVILY AND INVESTIGATE THE WORTHINESS OF THIS CRAFT'S FLOORS FOR LAYING ABOUT UNCONSC--
HANG ON, YOU DON'T WALK ONTO MY SHIP AN--
I AM NOT IMPRESSED WITH YOUR SHIP. MY PREVIOUS SHIP HAD FIVE TESSERACT ZONES.
YOU DON'T HAVE ANY TESSERACT ZONES.
MY OLD SHIP ALSO HAD A MINI FRIDGE. DO YOU HAVE A MINI FRIDGE?
I...AM I ARGUING WITH A ROBOT?
PSHHHH...I WILL BE IN MY QUARTERS, OPENING MY CRATE AND ASSEMBLING MY SIGNING INCENTIVE.
SIGNING INCENTIVE?
I FOUGHT AGAINST YOUR PRO-REGISTRATION FORCES. I HAD NO NEED TO JOIN FOR YOUR SILLY FLESHCAPADES.
HOWEVER, MARIA HILL MADE ME AN OFFER I FOUND MOST... FULFILLING.
CALL ME WHEN THERE'S HITTING TO BE DONE.
WHAT THE HELL IS HE TALKING ABOUT?
LADY, I GOT NO IDEA. I MET THAT GUY TWENTY MINUTES AGO AND HE HASN'T STOPPED TERRIFYING ME SINCE.
MY APOLOGIES...?
RICK. RICK SHERIDAN.
MACHINE MAN SAID YOUR CODE NAME WAS SLEEP-WALKER?
OH, IT'S NOT MY NAME.
IT'S THE NAME OF THE ALIEN FROM THE MINDSCAPE DIMENSION THAT LIVES IN MY HEAD.
BUT HE ONLY COMES OUT WHEN I'M ASLEEP.
AGENT SUM... REMIND ME TO SCHEDULE A MEETING WITH MARIA HILL.
SIGH
ALL RIGHT. LET'S GET BATTLEAXE AND HER SOLDIER FRIENDS OVER TO THE RAFT FOR PROCESSING.

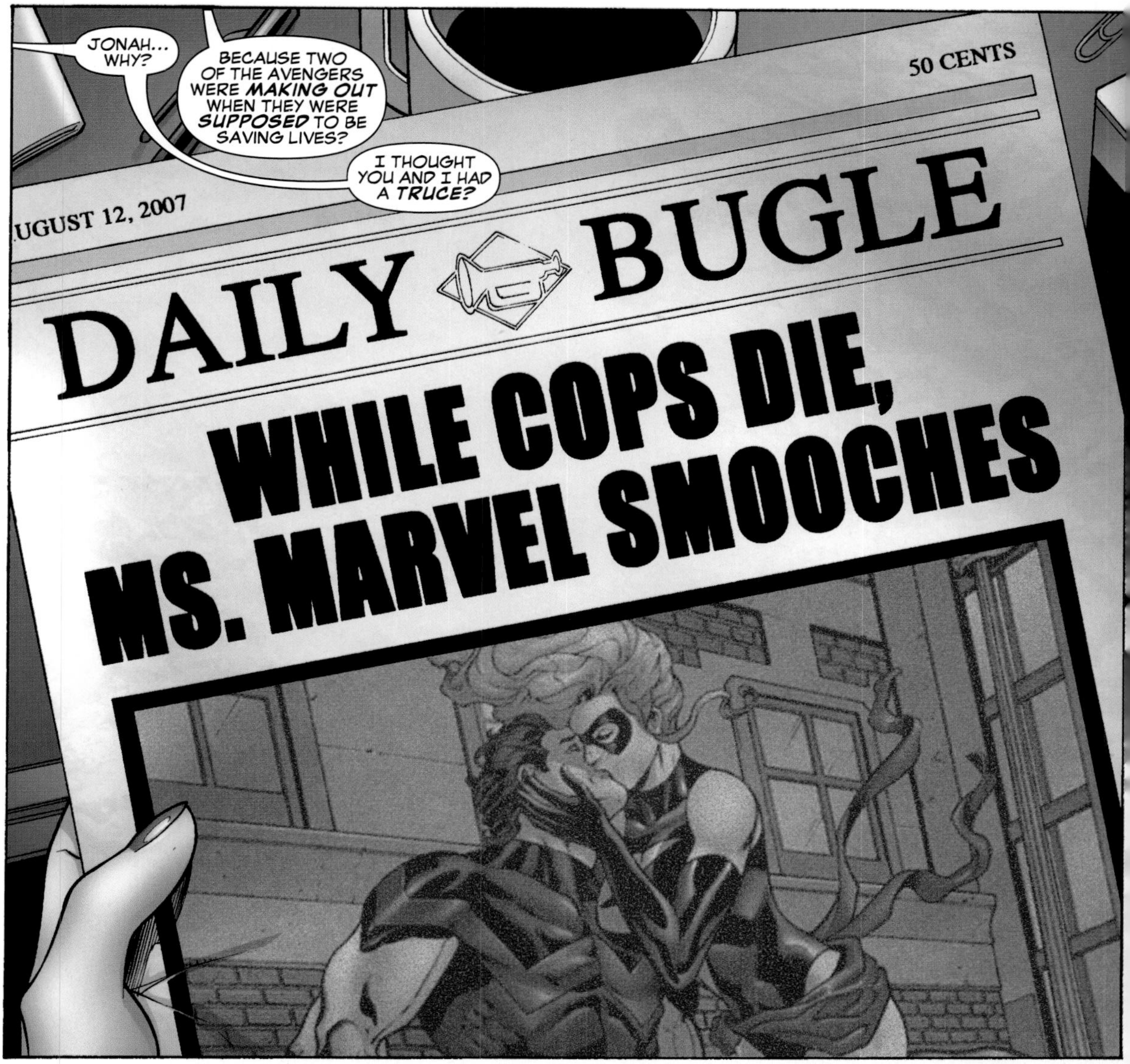
JONAH... WHY?
BECAUSE TWO OF THE AVENGERS WERE MAKING OUT WHEN THEY WERE SUPPOSED TO BE SAVING LIVES?
I THOUGHT YOU AND I HAD A TRUCE?
50 CENTS
UGUST 12, 2007
DAILY BUGLE
WHILE COPS DIE, MS. MARVEL SMOOCHES

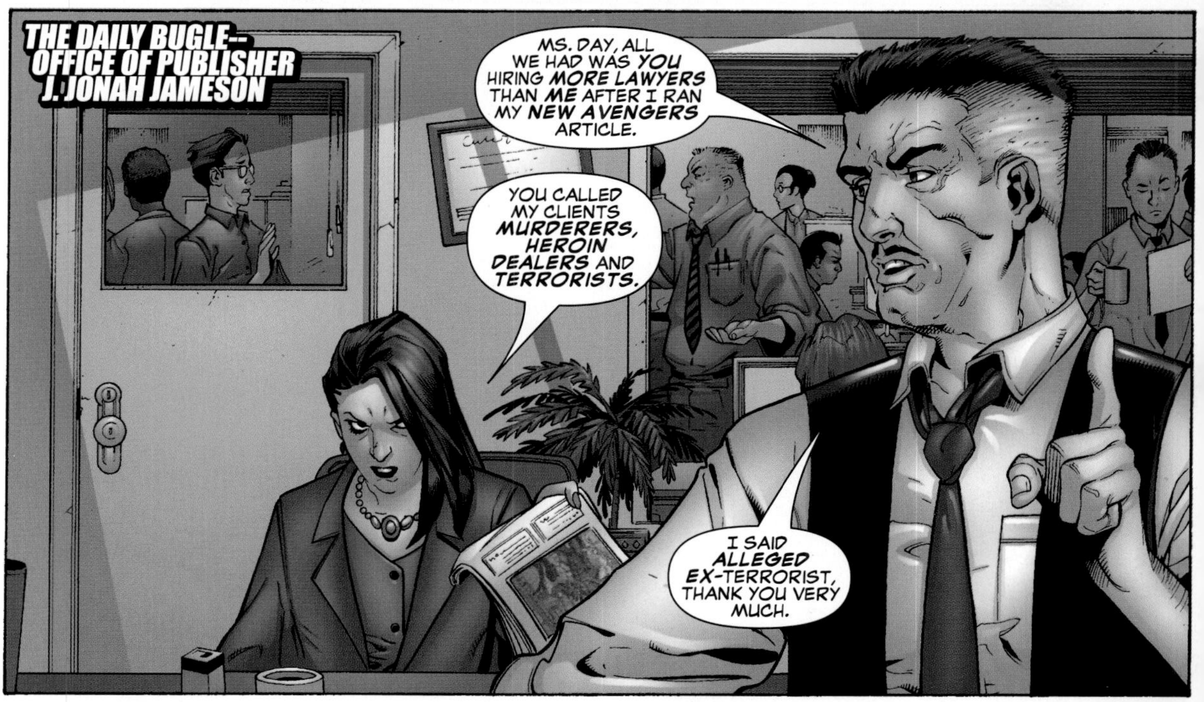
THE DAILY BUGLE-- OFFICE OF PUBLISHER J. JONAH JAMESON
MS. DAY, ALL WE HAD WAS YOU HIRING MORE LAWYERS THAN ME AFTER I RAN MY NEW AVENGERS ARTICLE.
YOU CALLED MY CLIENTS MURDERERS, HEROIN DEALERS AND TERRORISTS.
I SAID ALLEGED EX-TERRORIST, THANK YOU VERY MUCH.

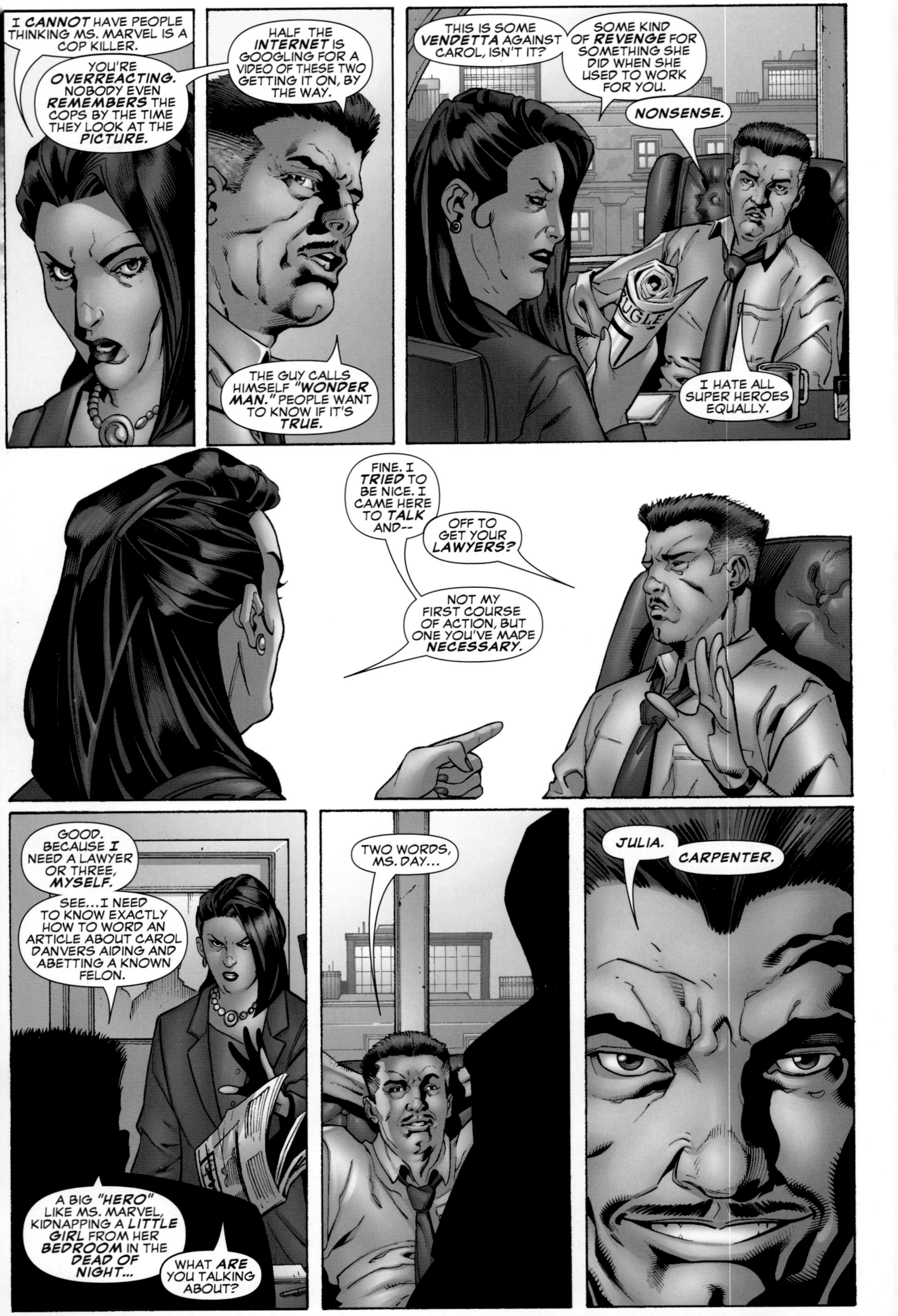
I CANNOT HAVE PEOPLE THINKING MS. MARVEL IS A COP KILLER.
YOU'RE OVERREACTING. NOBODY EVEN REMEMBERS THE COPS BY THE TIME THEY LOOK AT THE PICTURE.
HALF THE INTERNET IS GOOGLING FOR A VIDEO OF THESE TWO GETTING IT ON, BY THE WAY.
THE GUY CALLS HIMSELF "WONDER MAN." PEOPLE WANT TO KNOW IF IT'S TRUE.
THIS IS SOME VENDETTA AGAINST CAROL, ISN'T IT?
SOME KIND OF REVENGE FOR SOMETHING SHE DID WHEN SHE USED TO WORK FOR YOU.
NONSENSE.
I HATE ALL SUPER HEROES EQUALLY.
FINE. I TRIED TO BE NICE. I CAME HERE TO TALK AND--
OFF TO GET YOUR LAWYERS?
NOT MY FIRST COURSE OF ACTION, BUT ONE YOU'VE MADE NECESSARY.
GOOD. BECAUSE I NEED A LAWYER OR THREE, MYSELF.
SEE...I NEED TO KNOW EXACTLY HOW TO WORD AN ARTICLE ABOUT CAROL DANVERS AIDING AND ABETTING A KNOWN FELON.
A BIG "HERO" LIKE MS. MARVEL, KIDNAPPING A LITTLE GIRL FROM HER BEDROOM IN THE DEAD OF NIGHT...
WHAT ARE YOU TALKING ABOUT?
TWO WORDS, MS. DAY...
JULIA.
CARPENTER.

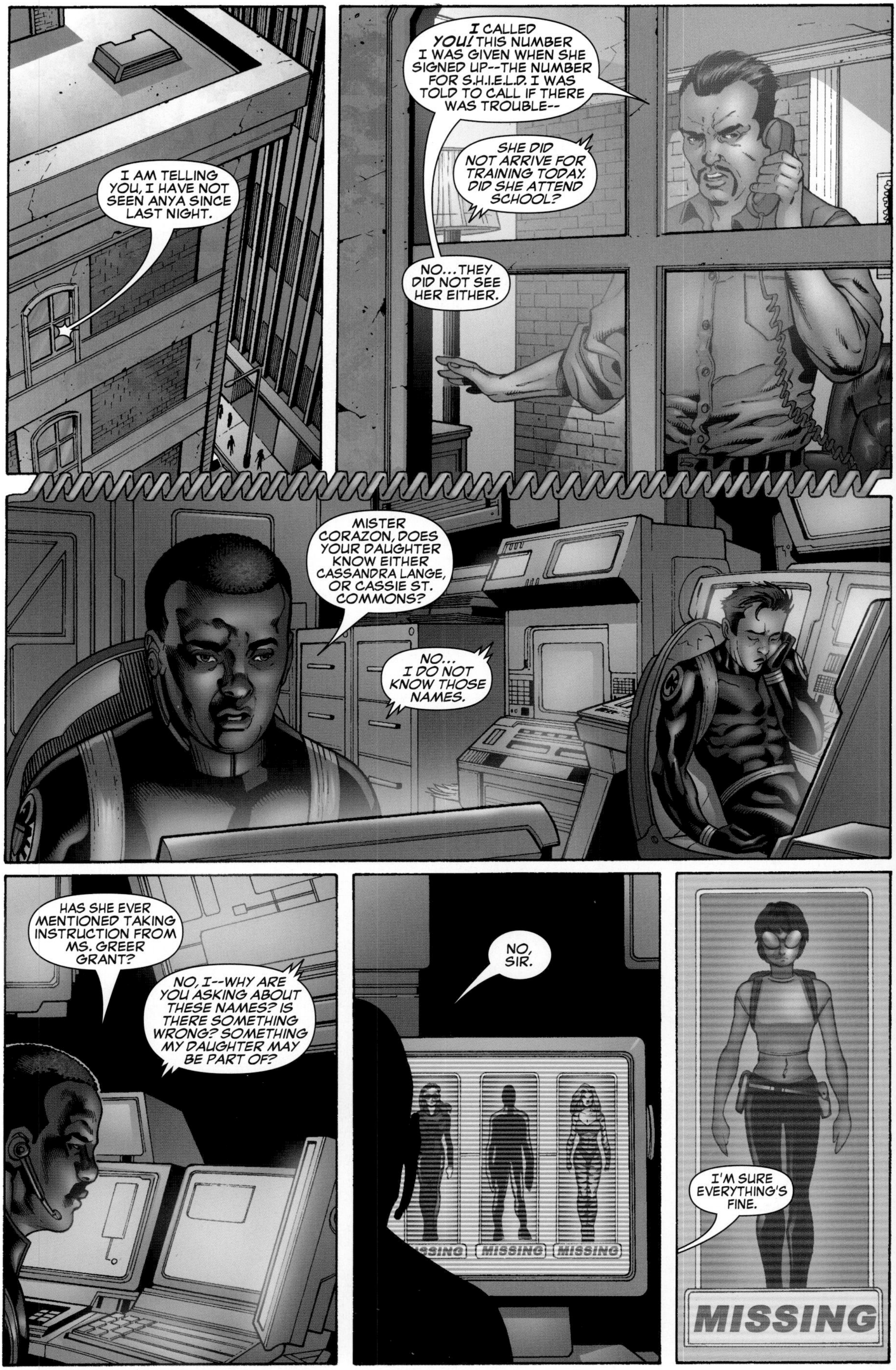
I AM TELLING YOU, I HAVE NOT SEEN ANYA SINCE LAST NIGHT.
I CALLED YOU! THIS NUMBER I WAS GIVEN WHEN SHE SIGNED UP--THE NUMBER FOR S.H.I.E.L.D. I WAS TOLD TO CALL IF THERE WAS TROUBLE--
SHE DID NOT ARRIVE FOR TRAINING TODAY. DID SHE ATTEND SCHOOL?
NO... THEY DID NOT SEE HER EITHER.
MISTER CORAZON, DOES YOUR DAUGHTER KNOW EITHER CASSANDRA LANGE, OR CASSIE ST. COMMONS?
NO... I DO NOT KNOW THOSE NAMES.
HAS SHE EVER MENTIONED TAKING INSTRUCTION FROM MS. GREER GRANT?
NO, I--WHY ARE YOU ASKING ABOUT THESE NAMES? IS THERE SOMETHING WRONG? SOMETHING MY DAUGHTER MAY BE PART OF?
NO, SIR.
MISSING
MISSING
MISSING
I'M SURE EVERYTHING'S FINE.
MISSING

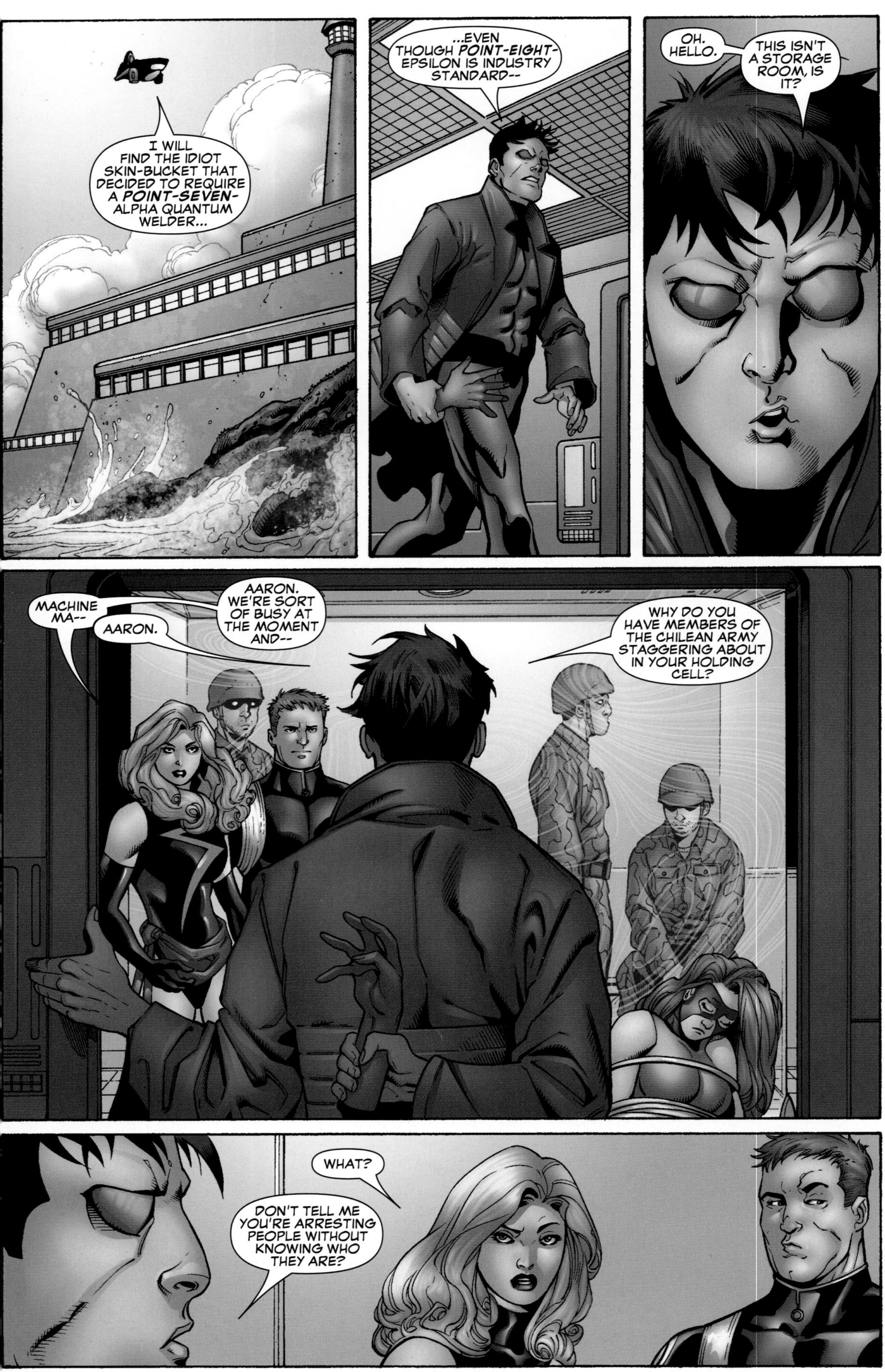
I WILL FIND THE IDIOT SKIN-BUCKET THAT DECIDED TO REQUIRE A POINT-SEVEN-ALPHA QUANTUM WELDER...
...EVEN THOUGH POINT-EIGHT-EPSILON IS INDUSTRY STANDARD--
OH. HELLO.
THIS ISN'T A STORAGE ROOM, IS IT?
MACHINE MA--
AARON. WE'RE SORT OF BUSY AT THE MOMENT AND--
AARON.
WHY DO YOU HAVE MEMBERS OF THE CHILEAN ARMY STAGGERING ABOUT IN YOUR HOLDING CELL?
WHAT?
DON'T TELL ME YOU'RE ARRESTING PEOPLE WITHOUT KNOWING WHO THEY ARE?

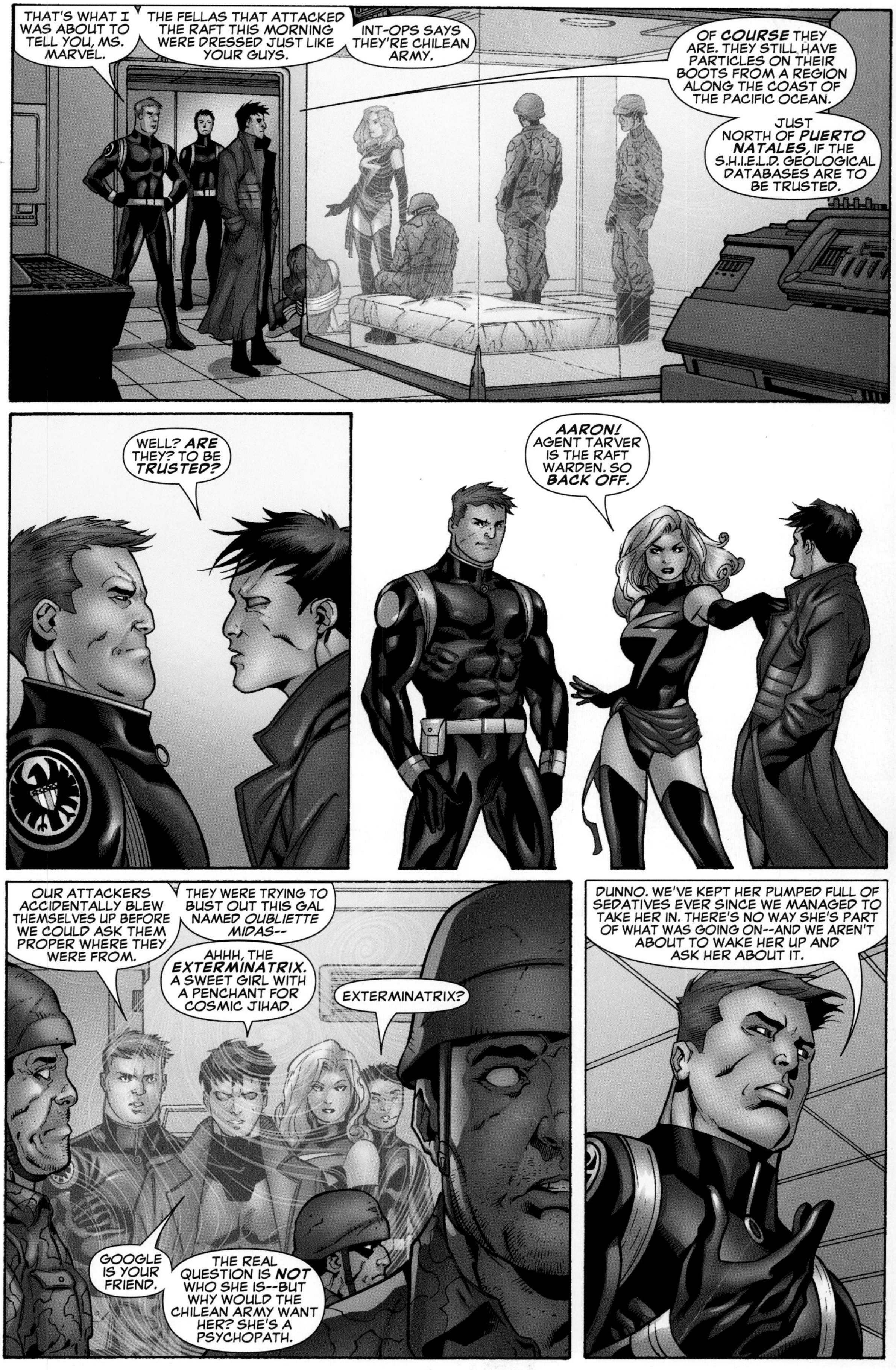

THAT'S WHAT I WAS ABOUT TO TELL YOU, MS. MARVEL.
THE FELLAS THAT ATTACKED THE RAFT THIS MORNING WERE DRESSED JUST LIKE YOUR GUYS.
INT-OPS SAYS THEY'RE CHILEAN ARMY.
OF COURSE THEY ARE. THEY STILL HAVE PARTICLES ON THEIR BOOTS FROM A REGION ALONG THE COAST OF THE PACIFIC OCEAN.
JUST NORTH OF PUERTO NATALES, IF THE S.H.I.E.L.D. GEOLOGICAL DATABASES ARE TO BE TRUSTED.
WELL? ARE THEY? TO BE TRUSTED?
AARON! AGENT TARVER IS THE RAFT WARDEN. SO BACK OFF.
OUR ATTACKERS ACCIDENTALLY BLEW THEMSELVES UP BEFORE WE COULD ASK THEM PROPER WHERE THEY WERE FROM.
THEY WERE TRYING TO BUST OUT THIS GAL NAMED OUBLIETTE MIDAS--
AHHH, THE EXTERMINATRIX. A SWEET GIRL WITH A PENCHANT FOR COSMIC JIHAD.
EXTERMINATRIX?
GOOGLE IS YOUR FRIEND.
THE REAL QUESTION IS NOT WHO SHE IS--BUT WHY WOULD THE CHILEAN ARMY WANT HER? SHE'S A PSYCHOPATH.
DUNNO. WE'VE KEPT HER PUMPED FULL OF SEDATIVES EVER SINCE WE MANAGED TO TAKE HER IN. THERE'S NO WAY SHE'S PART OF WHAT WAS GOING ON--AND WE AREN'T ABOUT TO WAKE HER UP AND ASK HER ABOUT IT.

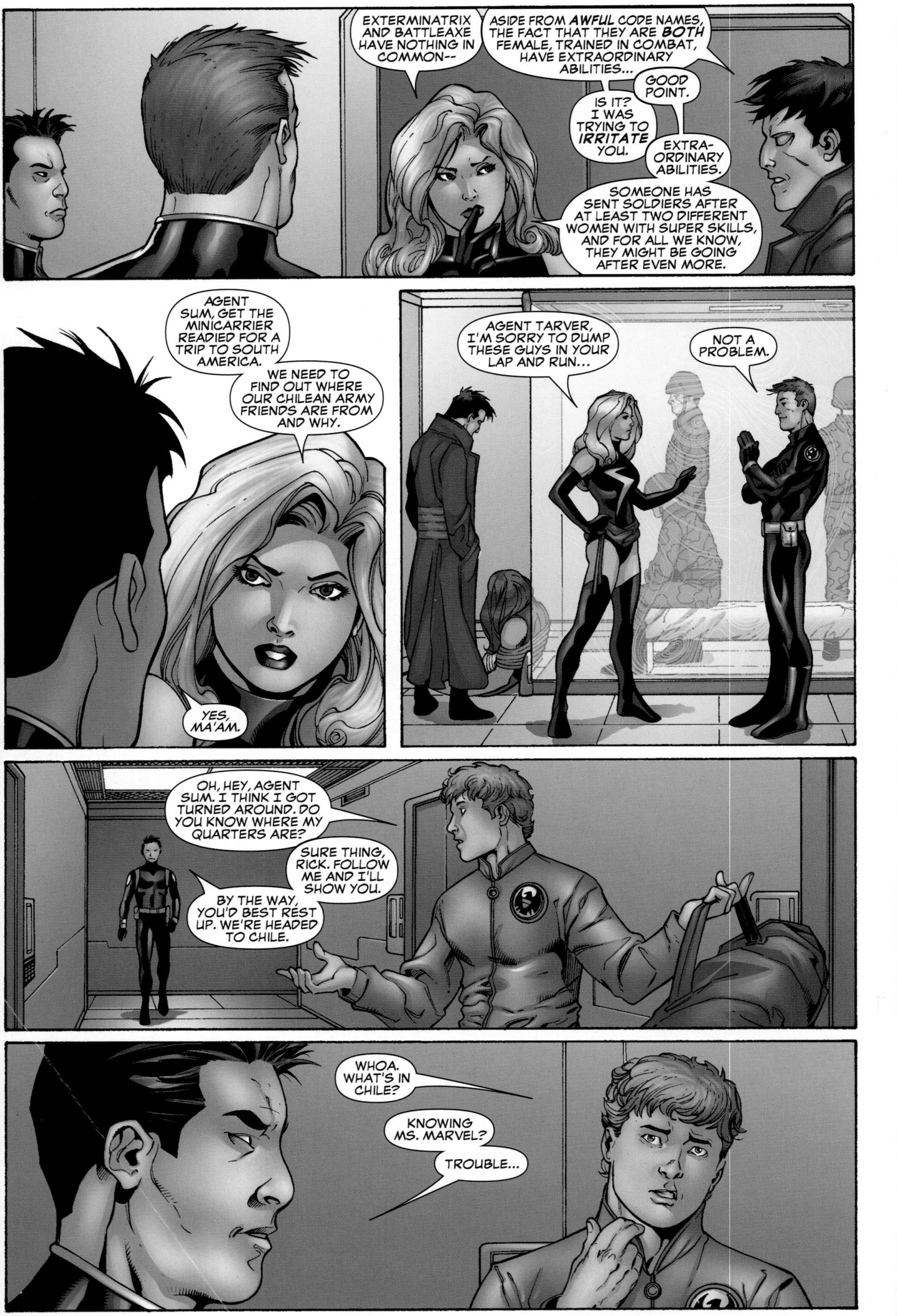
EXTERMINATRIX AND BATTLEAXE HAVE NOTHING IN COMMON--
ASIDE FROM AWFUL CODE NAMES, THE FACT THAT THEY ARE BOTH FEMALE, TRAINED IN COMBAT, HAVE EXTRAORDINARY ABILITIES...
IS IT? I WAS TRYING TO IRRITATE YOU.
GOOD POINT.
EXTRA-ORDINARY ABILITIES.
SOMEONE HAS SENT SOLDIERS AFTER AT LEAST TWO DIFFERENT WOMEN WITH SUPER SKILLS, AND FOR ALL WE KNOW, THEY MIGHT BE GOING AFTER EVEN MORE.
AGENT SUM, GET THE MINICARRIER READIED FOR A TRIP TO SOUTH AMERICA.
WE NEED TO FIND OUT WHERE OUR CHILEAN ARMY FRIENDS ARE FROM AND WHY.
YES, MA'AM.
AGENT TARVER, I'M SORRY TO DUMP THESE GUYS IN YOUR LAP AND RUN...
NOT A PROBLEM.
OH, HEY, AGENT SUM. I THINK I GOT TURNED AROUND. DO YOU KNOW WHERE MY QUARTERS ARE?
SURE THING, RICK. FOLLOW ME AND I'LL SHOW YOU.
BY THE WAY, YOU'D BEST REST UP. WE'RE HEADED TO CHILE.
WHOA. WHAT'S IN CHILE?
KNOWING MS. MARVEL?
TROUBLE...

"...LOTS AND LOTS OF TROUBLE."

PUERTO MARAVILLA-- CHILE

WELCOME TO MY HUMBLE HOME.

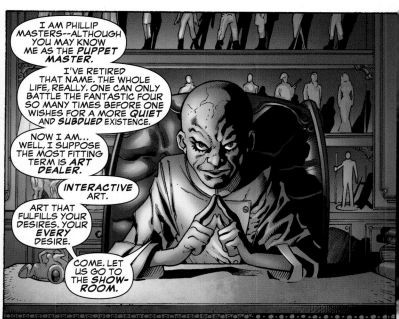

I AM PHILLIP MASTERS--ALTHOUGH YOU MAY KNOW ME AS THE PUPPET MASTER.

I'VE RETIRED THAT NAME. THE WHOLE LIFE, REALLY. ONE CAN ONLY BATTLE THE FANTASTIC FOUR SO MANY TIMES BEFORE ONE WISHES FOR A MORE QUIET AND SUBDUED EXISTENCE.

NOW I AM... WELL, I SUPPOSE THE MOST FITTING TERM IS ART DEALER.

INTERACTIVE ART.

ART THAT FULFILLS YOUR DESIRES. YOUR EVERY DESIRE.

COME. LET US GO TO THE SHOW-ROOM.

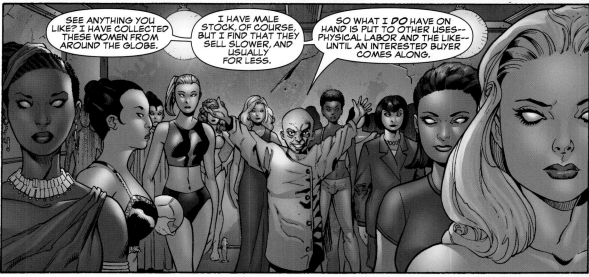

SEE ANYTHING YOU LIKE? I HAVE COLLECTED THESE WOMEN FROM AROUND THE GLOBE.

I HAVE MALE STOCK, OF COURSE, BUT I FIND THAT THEY SELL SLOWER, AND USUALLY FOR LESS.

SO WHAT I DO HAVE ON HAND IS PUT TO OTHER USES--PHYSICAL LABOR AND THE LIKE--UNTIL AN INTERESTED BUYER COMES ALONG.

I DON'T KNOW IF IT WILL INTEREST YOU OR NOT--I SUPPOSE IT DEPENDS ON HOW INTO THE TECHNICAL SIDE OF YOUR NEW HOBBY YOU WANT TO GET--BUT I RECENTLY FOUND ANOTHER SOURCE FOR THE CLAY I'VE USED ALL THESE YEARS.

IT'S STRONGER THAN WHAT I'M USED TO WORKING WITH--

--BUT IT ALLOWS ME A GREATER LEVEL OF CONTROL OVER MY... ART.

OF COURSE, THE FIGURE IS YOURS WITH THE PURCHASE OF ANY MODEL.

SOOO... SEE ANYTHING YOU LIKE?

AHHHH, I KNOW THAT LOOK. YOU'RE THE KIND OF BUYER WHO WANTS SOME-THING MORE, SHALL WE SAY, UNIQUE?

WELL, I CAN SCRATCH THAT ITCH. FOLLOW ME.

BUT BE WARNED. WITH UNIQUENESS COMES A CONSIDERABLE INCREASE IN PRICE.

STILL, WE WOULD NOT BE HAVING THIS CONVERSATION IF MONEY WAS ANY CONCERN TO YOU, WOULD WE?

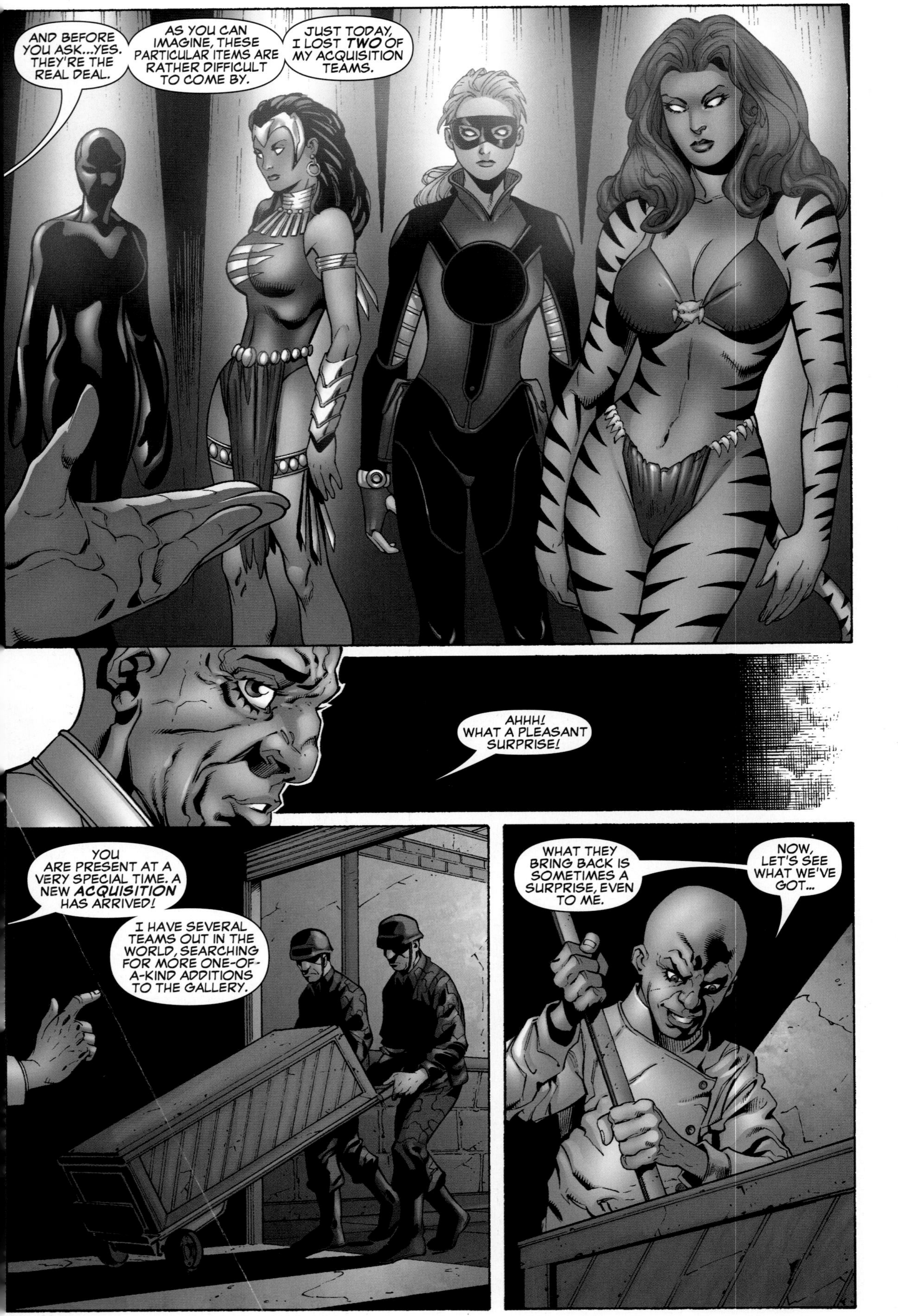
AND BEFORE YOU ASK...YES. THEY'RE THE REAL DEAL.
AS YOU CAN IMAGINE, THESE PARTICULAR ITEMS ARE RATHER DIFFICULT TO COME BY.
JUST TODAY, I LOST TWO OF MY ACQUISITION TEAMS.
AHHH! WHAT A PLEASANT SURPRISE!
YOU ARE PRESENT AT A VERY SPECIAL TIME. A NEW ACQUISITION HAS ARRIVED!
I HAVE SEVERAL TEAMS OUT IN THE WORLD, SEARCHING FOR MORE ONE-OF-A-KIND ADDITIONS TO THE GALLERY.
WHAT THEY BRING BACK IS SOMETIMES A SURPRISE, EVEN TO ME.
NOW, LET'S SEE WHAT WE'VE GOT...

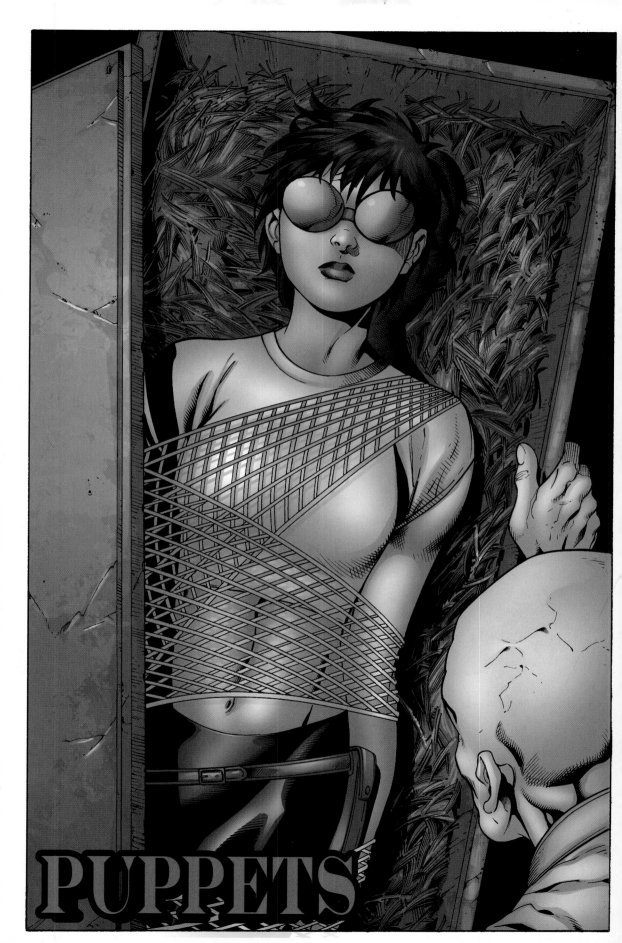

PUPPETS

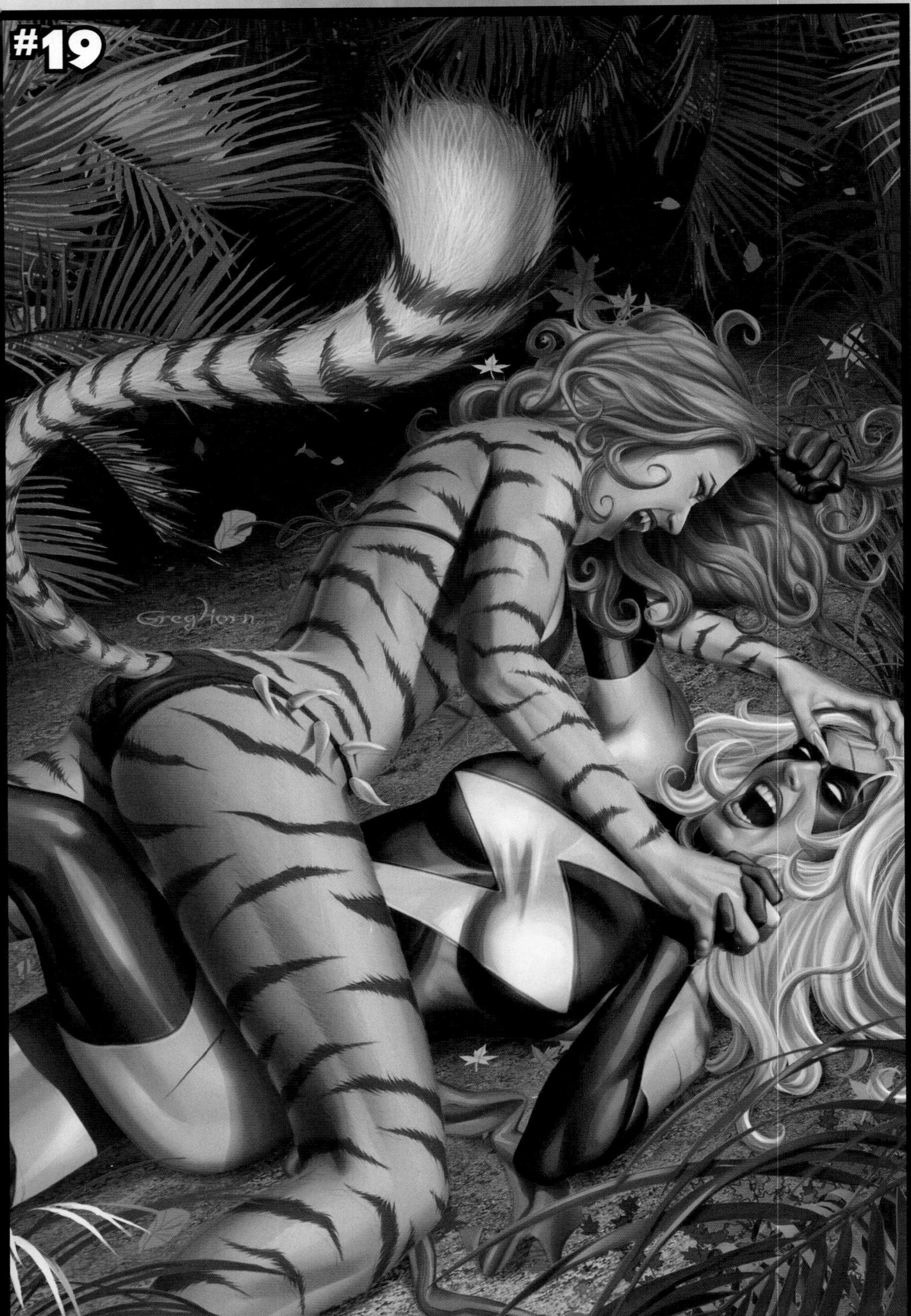
#19
Greg Horn

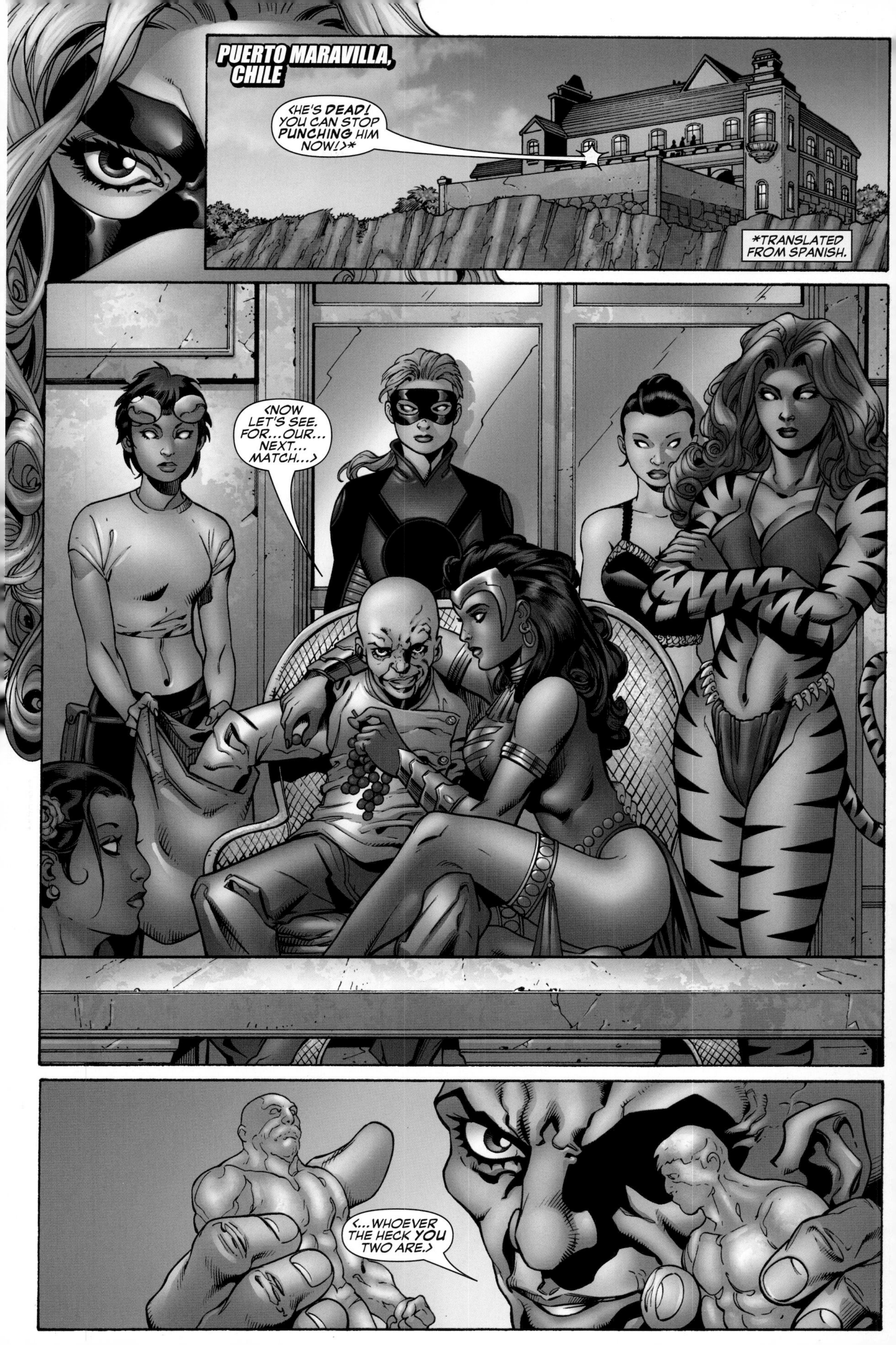
PUERTO MARAVILLA, CHILE
<HE'S DEAD! YOU CAN STOP PUNCHING HIM NOW!>*
*TRANSLATED FROM SPANISH.
<NOW LET'S SEE. FOR...OUR... NEXT... MATCH...>
<...WHOEVER THE HECK YOU TWO ARE.>

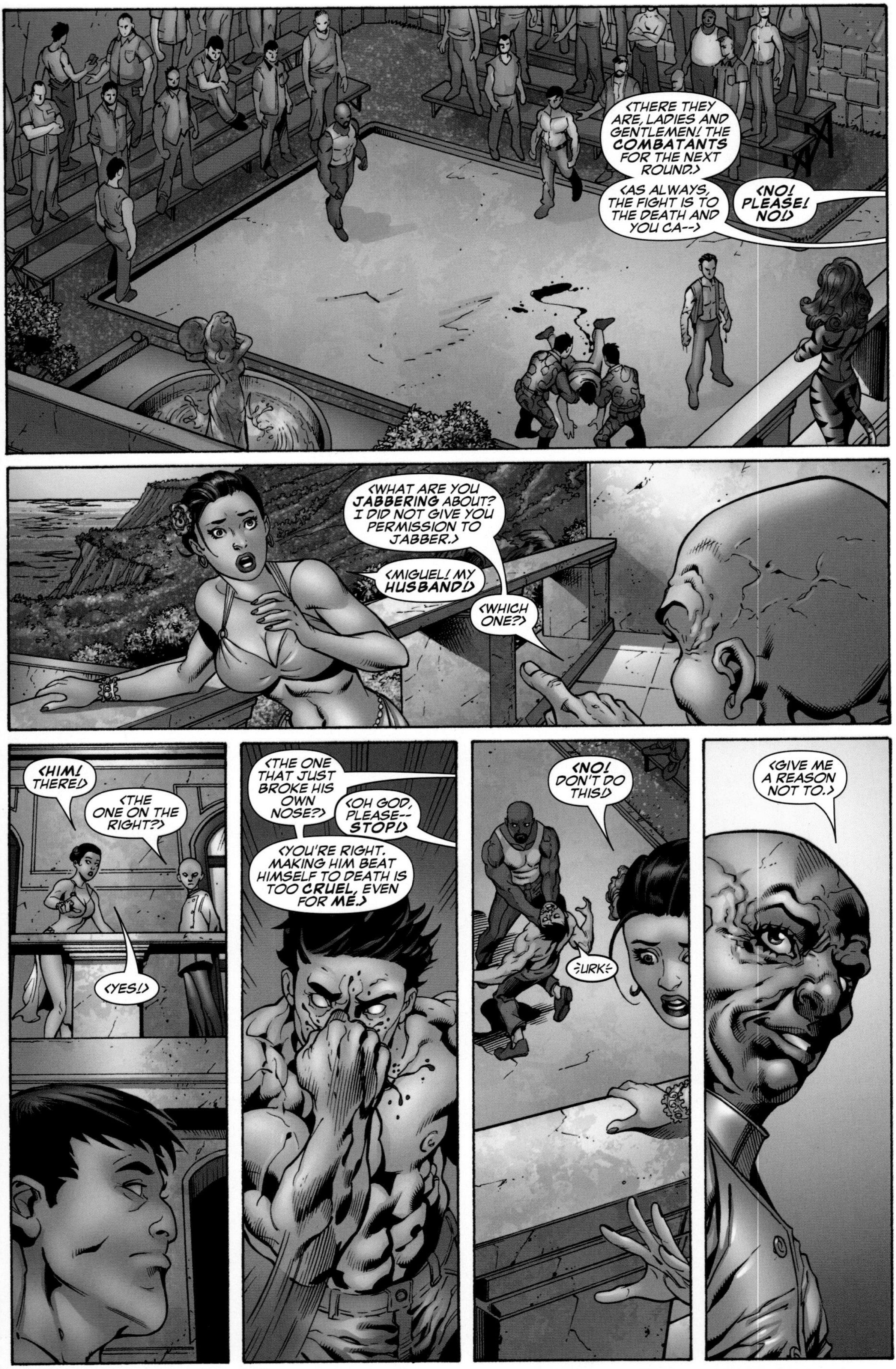

<THERE THEY ARE, LADIES AND GENTLEMEN! THE COMBATANTS FOR THE NEXT ROUND.>
<AS ALWAYS, THE FIGHT IS TO THE DEATH AND YOU CA-->
<NO! PLEASE! NO!>
<WHAT ARE YOU JABBERING ABOUT? I DID NOT GIVE YOU PERMISSION TO JABBER.>
<MIGUEL! MY HUSBAND!>
<WHICH ONE?>
<HIM! THERE!>
<THE ONE ON THE RIGHT?>
<YES!>
<THE ONE THAT JUST BROKE HIS OWN NOSE?>
<OH GOD, PLEASE-- STOP!>
<YOU'RE RIGHT. MAKING HIM BEAT HIMSELF TO DEATH IS TOO CRUEL, EVEN FOR ME.>
<NO! DON'T DO THIS!>
URK
<GIVE ME A REASON NOT TO.>

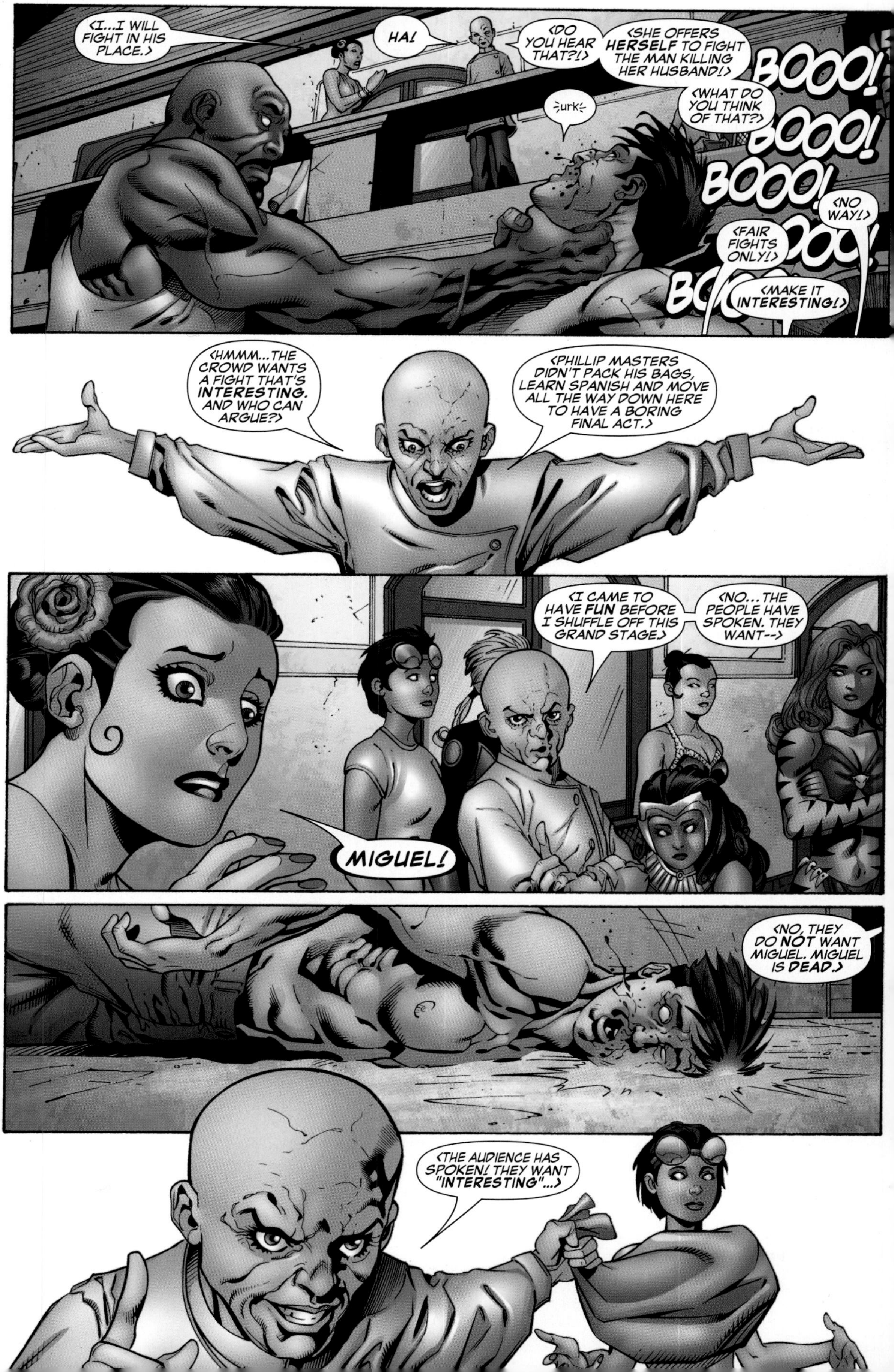
<I...I WILL FIGHT IN HIS PLACE.>
HA!
<DO YOU HEAR THAT?!>
<SHE OFFERS HERSELF TO FIGHT THE MAN KILLING HER HUSBAND!>
<WHAT DO YOU THINK OF THAT?>
<urk<
BOOO! BOOO! BOOO!
<NO WAY!>
<FAIR FIGHTS ONLY!>
<MAKE IT INTERESTING!>
<HMMM...THE CROWD WANTS A FIGHT THAT'S INTERESTING. AND WHO CAN ARGUE?>
<PHILLIP MASTERS DIDN'T PACK HIS BAGS, LEARN SPANISH AND MOVE ALL THE WAY DOWN HERE TO HAVE A BORING FINAL ACT.>
<I CAME TO HAVE FUN BEFORE I SHUFFLE OFF THIS GRAND STAGE.>
<NO... THE PEOPLE HAVE SPOKEN. THEY WANT-->
MIGUEL!
<NO, THEY DO NOT WANT MIGUEL. MIGUEL IS DEAD.>
<THE AUDIENCE HAS SPOKEN! THEY WANT "INTERESTING"...>

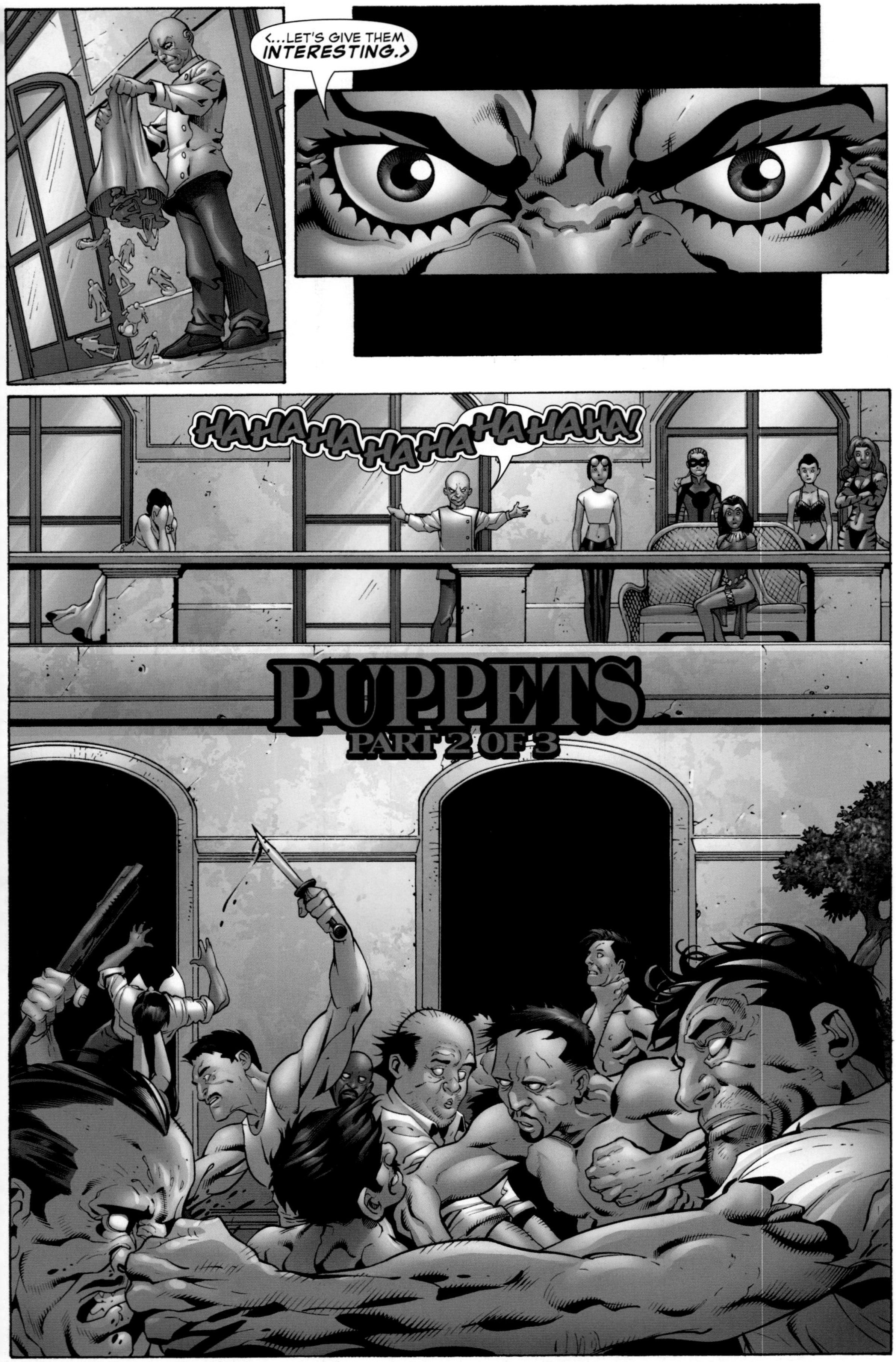
<...LET'S GIVE THEM INTERESTING.>
HAHAHAHAHAHAHAHAHA!
PUPPETS
PART 2 OF 3

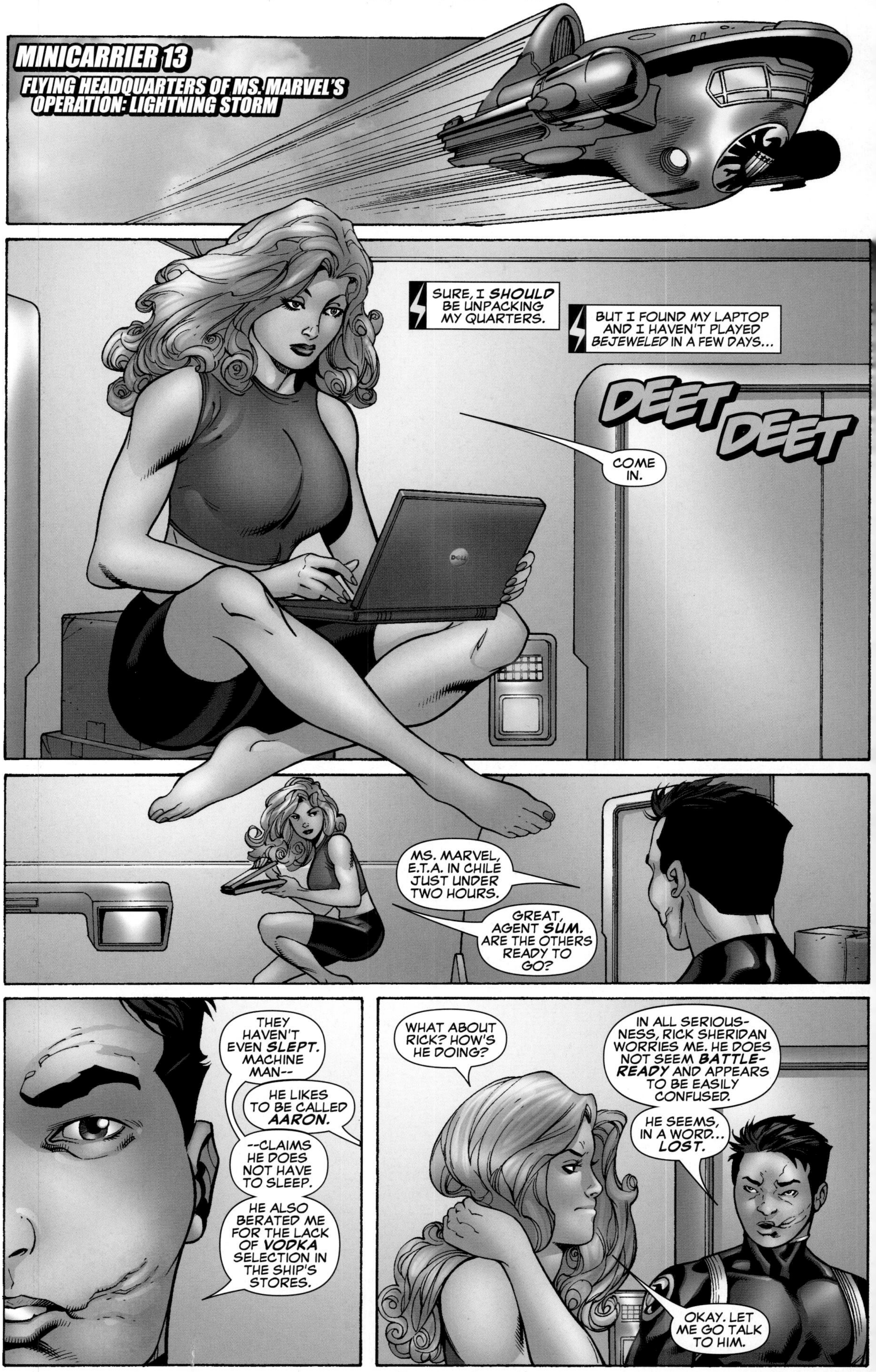
MINICARRIER 13
FLYING HEADQUARTERS OF MS. MARVEL'S OPERATION: LIGHTNING STORM
SURE, I SHOULD BE UNPACKING MY QUARTERS.
BUT I FOUND MY LAPTOP AND I HAVEN'T PLAYED BEJEWELED IN A FEW DAYS...
DEET DEET
COME IN.
MS. MARVEL, E.T.A. IN CHILE JUST UNDER TWO HOURS.
GREAT, AGENT SUM. ARE THE OTHERS READY TO GO?
THEY HAVEN'T EVEN SLEPT. MACHINE MAN--
HE LIKES TO BE CALLED AARON.
--CLAIMS HE DOES NOT HAVE TO SLEEP.
HE ALSO BERATED ME FOR THE LACK OF VODKA SELECTION IN THE SHIP'S STORES.
WHAT ABOUT RICK? HOW'S HE DOING?
IN ALL SERIOUSNESS, RICK SHERIDAN WORRIES ME. HE DOES NOT SEEM BATTLE-READY AND APPEARS TO BE EASILY CONFUSED.
HE SEEMS, IN A WORD... LOST.
OKAY. LET ME GO TALK TO HIM.

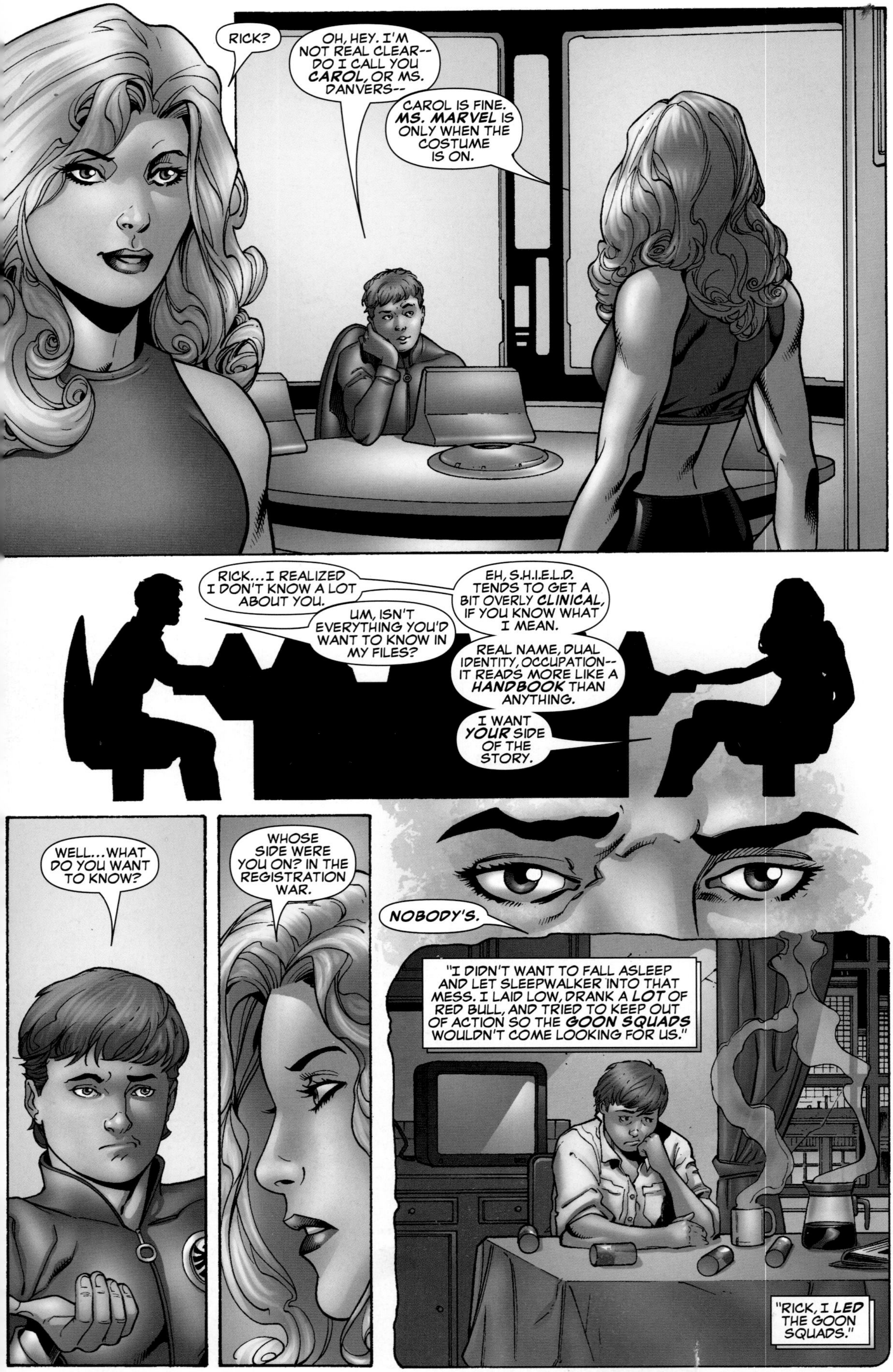
RICK?
OH, HEY. I'M NOT REAL CLEAR-- DO I CALL YOU CAROL, OR MS. DANVERS--
CAROL IS FINE. MS. MARVEL IS ONLY WHEN THE COSTUME IS ON.
RICK...I REALIZED I DON'T KNOW A LOT ABOUT YOU.
UM, ISN'T EVERYTHING YOU'D WANT TO KNOW IN MY FILES?
EH, S.H.I.E.L.D. TENDS TO GET A BIT OVERLY CLINICAL, IF YOU KNOW WHAT I MEAN.
REAL NAME, DUAL IDENTITY, OCCUPATION-- IT READS MORE LIKE A HANDBOOK THAN ANYTHING.
I WANT YOUR SIDE OF THE STORY.
WELL...WHAT DO YOU WANT TO KNOW?
WHOSE SIDE WERE YOU ON? IN THE REGISTRATION WAR.
NOBODY'S.
"I DIDN'T WANT TO FALL ASLEEP AND LET SLEEPWALKER INTO THAT MESS. I LAID LOW, DRANK A LOT OF RED BULL, AND TRIED TO KEEP OUT OF ACTION SO THE GOON SQUADS WOULDN'T COME LOOKING FOR US."
"RICK, I LED THE GOON SQUADS."

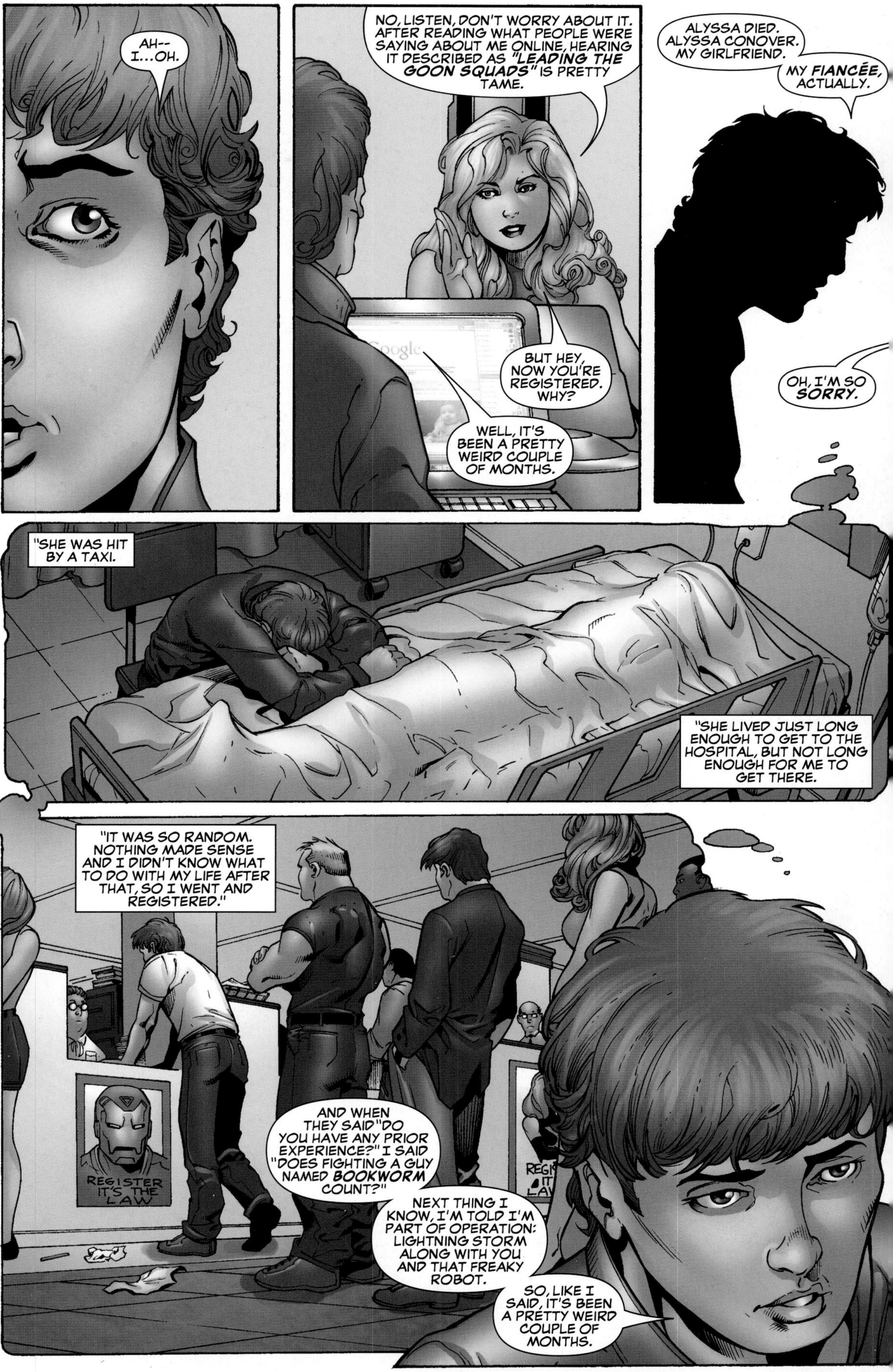
AH-- I...OH.
NO, LISTEN, DON'T WORRY ABOUT IT. AFTER READING WHAT PEOPLE WERE SAYING ABOUT ME ONLINE, HEARING IT DESCRIBED AS "LEADING THE GOON SQUADS" IS PRETTY TAME.
BUT HEY, NOW YOU'RE REGISTERED. WHY?
WELL, IT'S BEEN A PRETTY WEIRD COUPLE OF MONTHS.
ALYSSA DIED. ALYSSA CONOVER. MY GIRLFRIEND.
MY FIANCÉE, ACTUALLY.
OH, I'M SO SORRY.
"SHE WAS HIT BY A TAXI.
"SHE LIVED JUST LONG ENOUGH TO GET TO THE HOSPITAL, BUT NOT LONG ENOUGH FOR ME TO GET THERE.
"IT WAS SO RANDOM. NOTHING MADE SENSE AND I DIDN'T KNOW WHAT TO DO WITH MY LIFE AFTER THAT, SO I WENT AND REGISTERED."
REGISTER IT'S THE LAW
AND WHEN THEY SAID "DO YOU HAVE ANY PRIOR EXPERIENCE?" I SAID "DOES FIGHTING A GUY NAMED BOOKWORM COUNT?"
NEXT THING I KNOW, I'M TOLD I'M PART OF OPERATION: LIGHTNING STORM ALONG WITH YOU AND THAT FREAKY ROBOT.
SO, LIKE I SAID, IT'S BEEN A PRETTY WEIRD COUPLE OF MONTHS.

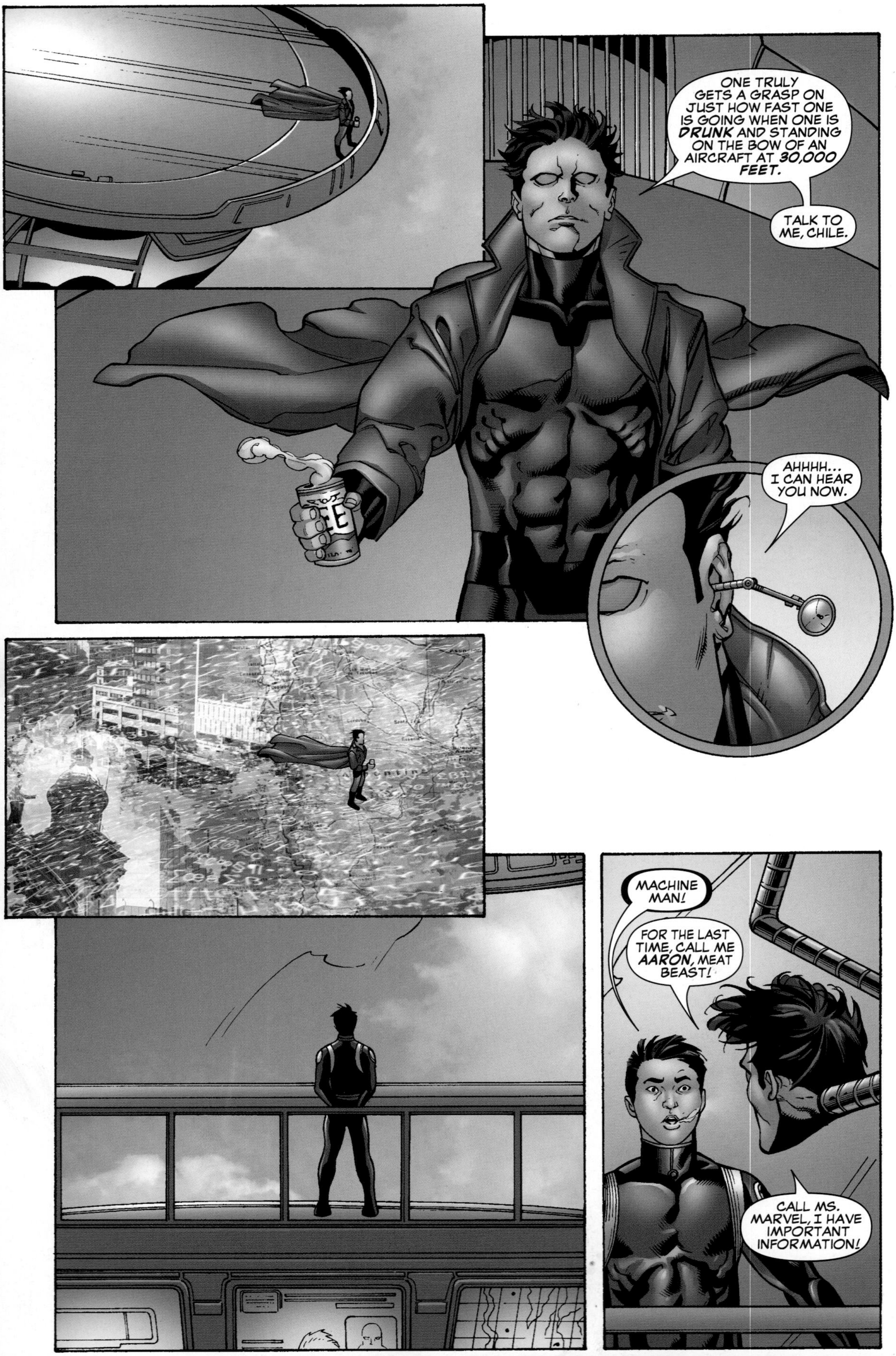
ONE TRULY GETS A GRASP ON JUST HOW FAST ONE IS GOING WHEN ONE IS DRUNK AND STANDING ON THE BOW OF AN AIRCRAFT AT 30,000 FEET.
TALK TO ME, CHILE.
AHHHH... I CAN HEAR YOU NOW.
MACHINE MAN!
FOR THE LAST TIME, CALL ME AARON, MEAT BEAST!
CALL MS. MARVEL, I HAVE IMPORTANT INFORMATION!

CHILE BORDERS THE SOUTH PACIFIC OCEAN, BETWEEN ARGENTINA AND PERU.

WIDESPREAD DEFORESTATION AND MINING THREATEN NATURAL RESOURCES, WHILE WATER POLLUTION FROM RAW SEWAGE IS--

AARON, YOU SAID YOU HAD SOMETHING *IMPORTANT* TO TELL US.

I TALKED TO CHILE. ALL THE DATA THE COUNTRY PRODUCES PASSED THROUGH MY MIGHTY BRAIN AND I LEARNED MUCH.

MARAVILLA

MISSING PERSONS?

THE HIGHEST PER CAPITA RATE IN THE WORLD.

HOW IS THAT POSSIBLE?

JOAQUIN PIÑERA

JOSÉ IBÁÑEZ

EDUARDO INFANTE

MICHELL ROMERO

SALVADOR RODRIGUEZ

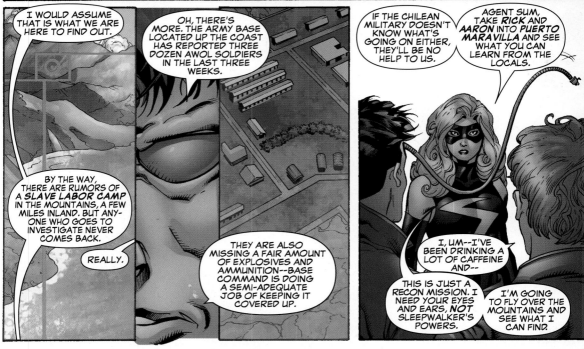

I WOULD ASSUME THAT IS WHAT WE ARE HERE TO FIND OUT.

OH, THERE'S MORE. THE ARMY BASE LOCATED UP THE COAST HAS REPORTED THREE DOZEN AWOL SOLDIERS IN THE LAST THREE WEEKS.

IF THE CHILEAN MILITARY DOESN'T KNOW WHAT'S GOING ON EITHER, THEY'LL BE NO HELP TO US.

AGENT SUM, TAKE *RICK* AND *AARON* INTO *PUERTO MARAVILLA* AND SEE WHAT YOU CAN LEARN FROM THE LOCALS.

BY THE WAY, THERE ARE RUMORS OF A *SLAVE LABOR CAMP* IN THE MOUNTAINS, A FEW MILES INLAND. BUT ANY-ONE WHO GOES TO INVESTIGATE NEVER COMES BACK.

REALLY.

THEY ARE ALSO MISSING A FAIR AMOUNT OF EXPLOSIVES AND AMMUNITION--BASE COMMAND IS DOING A SEMI-ADEQUATE JOB OF KEEPING IT COVERED UP.

I, UM--I'VE BEEN DRINKING A LOT OF CAFFEINE AND--

THIS IS JUST A RECON MISSION. I NEED YOUR EYES AND EARS, *NOT* SLEEPWALKER'S POWERS.

I'M GOING TO FLY OVER THE MOUNTAINS AND SEE WHAT I CAN FIND?

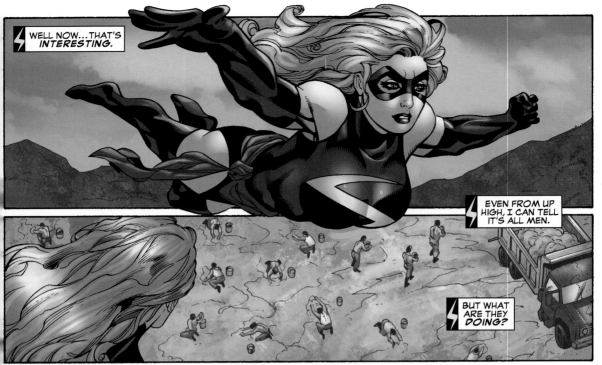

WELL NOW...THAT'S INTERESTING.

EVEN FROM UP HIGH, I CAN TELL IT'S ALL MEN.

BUT WHAT ARE THEY DOING?

GOOD AFTERNOON, GENTLEMEN. I KNOW EVERYBODY HAS TO HAVE THEIR HOBBIES, BUT WHY ARE YOU GUYS OUT HERE DIGGING UP DIRT--

--WITH YOUR BARE HANDS?

I SEE YOUR EYEBALLS ALL ROLLED BACK AND THE FACT THAT THERE'S SOME KIND OF MIND CONTROL GOING ON AROUND HERE SHOULD BE PRETTY OBVIOUS EVEN TO A RAW INITIATIVE RECRUIT BUT--

HANG ON. THIS ISN'T DIRT.

IT'S CLAY.

LET'S SEE...MIND CONTROL...CLAY...

WHO DOES THAT LEAVE US WITH?

AWWWWWW, CRAP. I HATE THAT GUY...HE'S SO CREEPY.

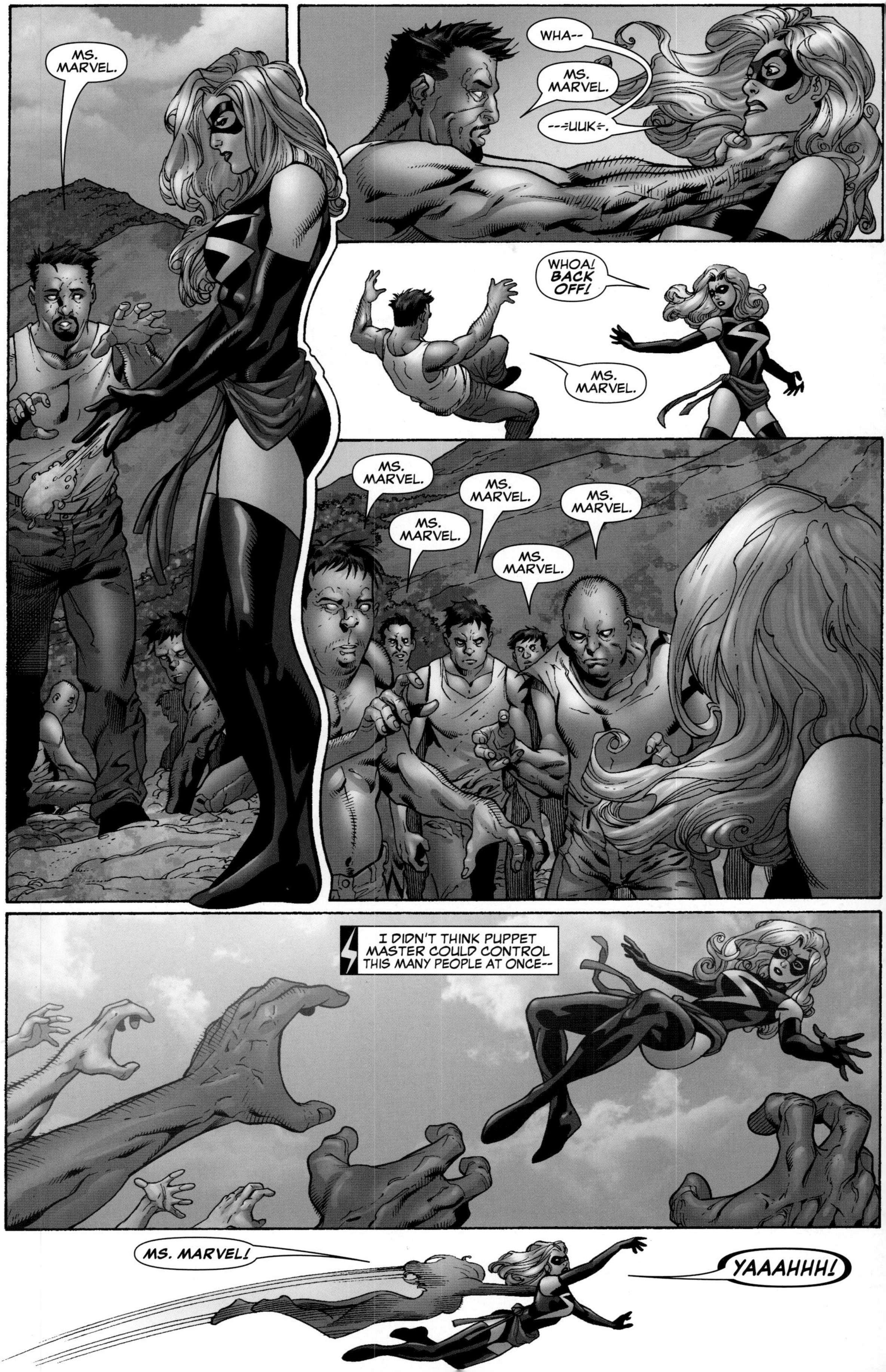
MS. MARVEL.
WHA--
MS. MARVEL.
--=UUK=.
WHOA! BACK OFF!
MS. MARVEL.
MS. MARVEL.
MS. MARVEL.
MS. MARVEL.
MS. MARVEL.
MS. MARVEL.
I DIDN'T THINK PUPPET MASTER COULD CONTROL THIS MANY PEOPLE AT ONCE--
MS. MARVEL!
YAAAHHH!

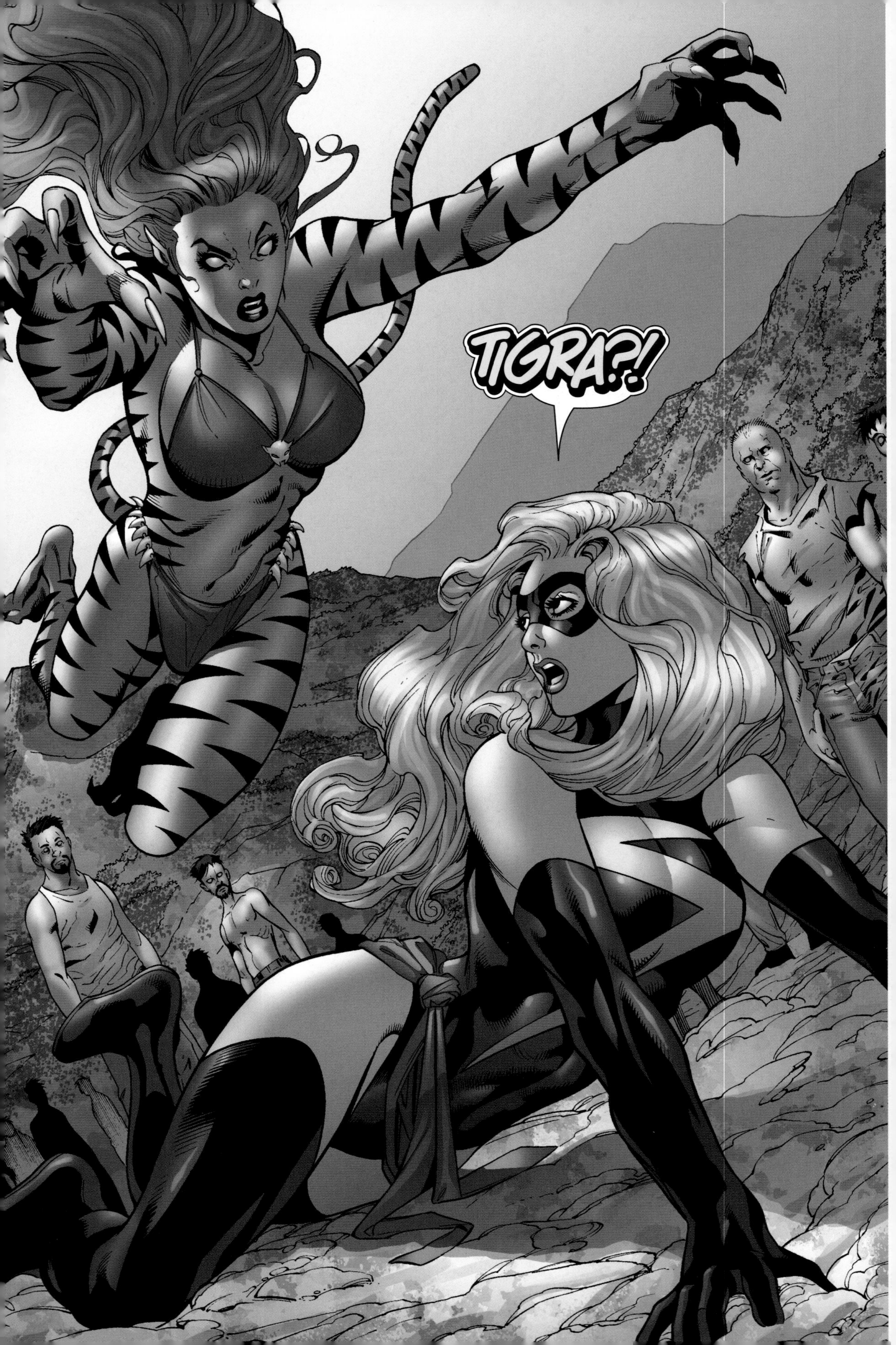
TIGRA?!

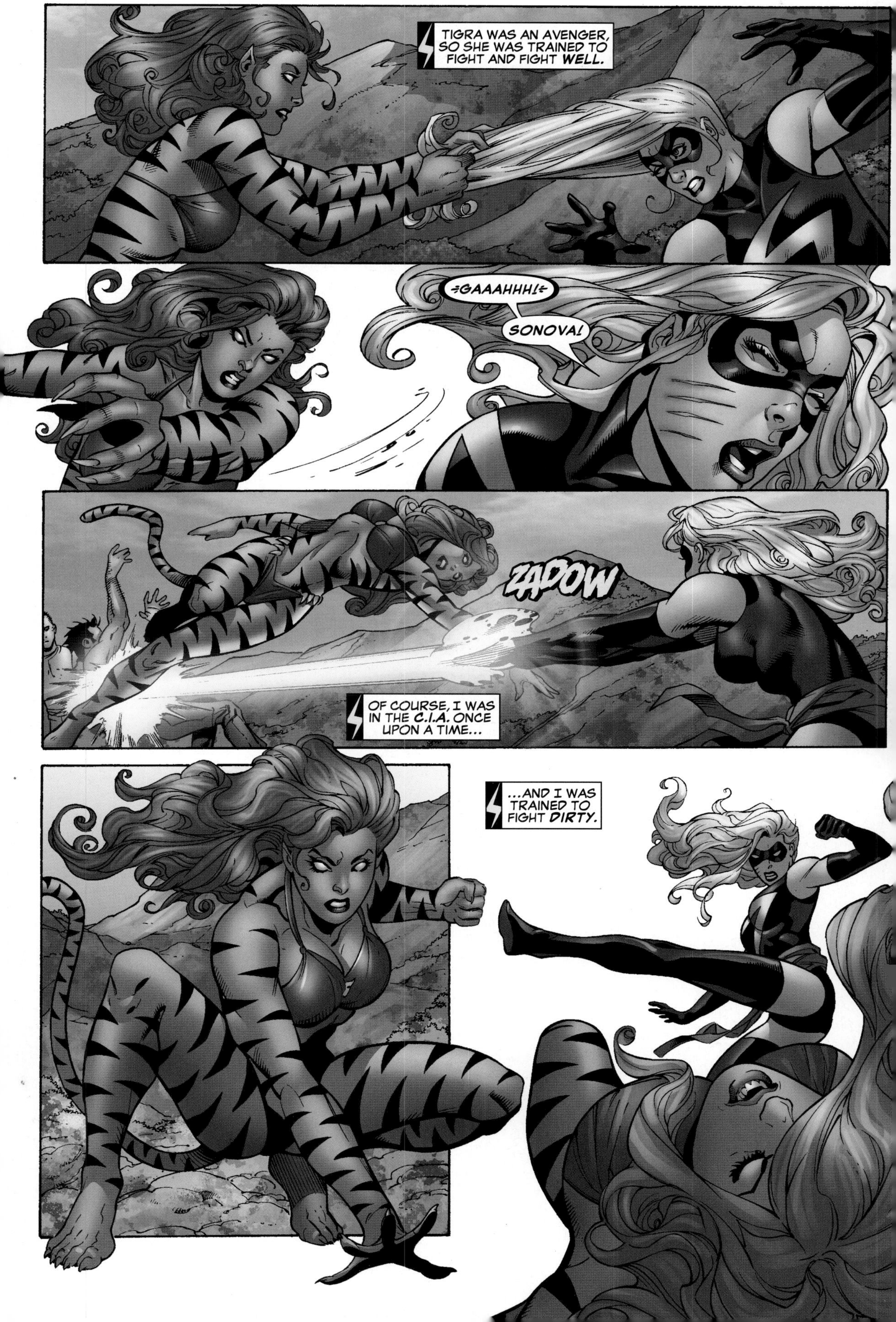
TIGRA WAS AN AVENGER, SO SHE WAS TRAINED TO FIGHT AND FIGHT WELL.
GAAAHHH!
SONOVA!
ZADOW
OF COURSE, I WAS IN THE C.I.A. ONCE UPON A TIME...
...AND I WAS TRAINED TO FIGHT DIRTY.

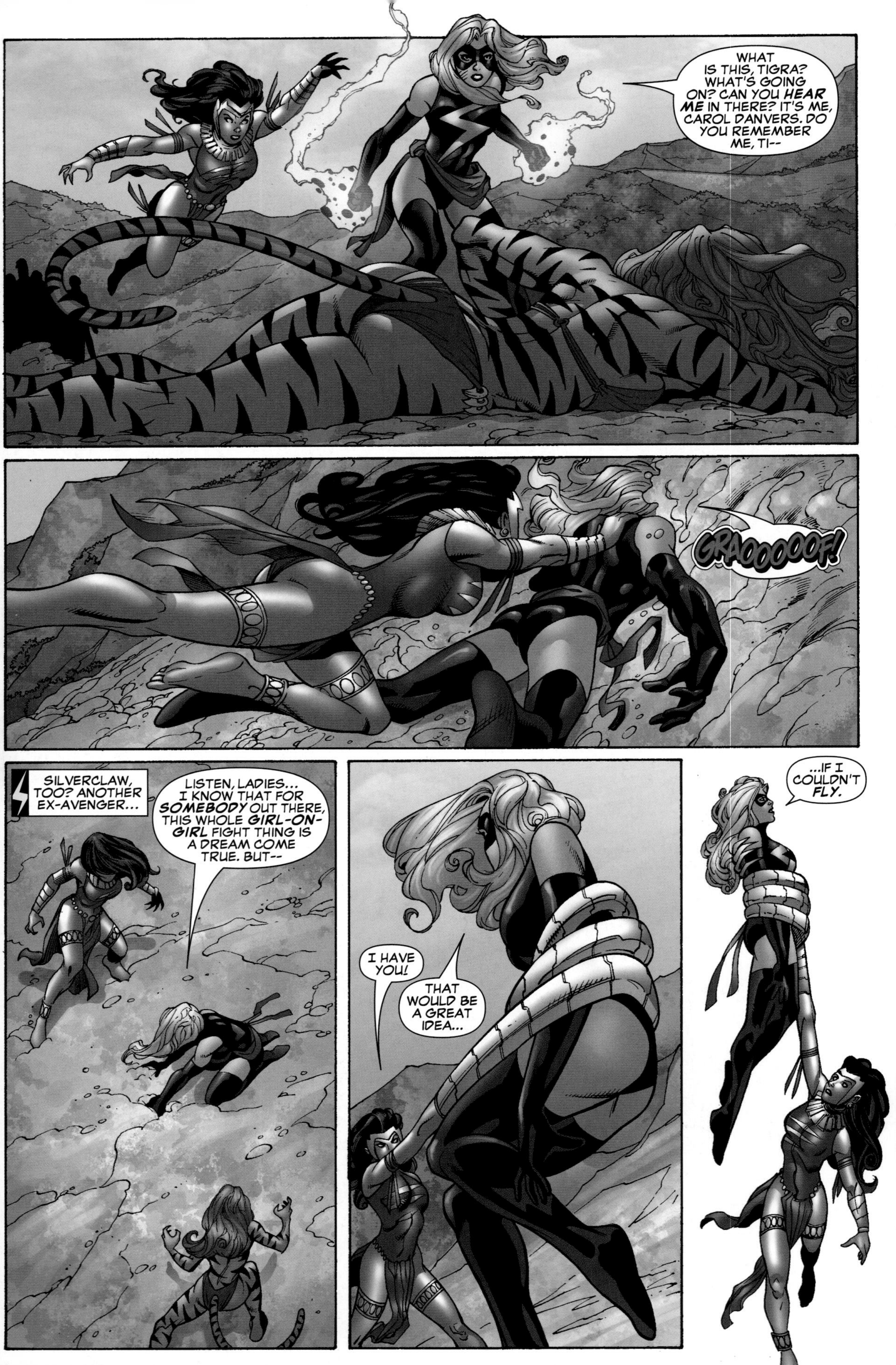
WHAT IS THIS, TIGRA? WHAT'S GOING ON? CAN YOU HEAR ME IN THERE? IT'S ME, CAROL DANVERS. DO YOU REMEMBER ME, TI--
GRAOOOOOF!
SILVERCLAW, TOO? ANOTHER EX-AVENGER...
LISTEN, LADIES... I KNOW THAT FOR SOMEBODY OUT THERE, THIS WHOLE GIRL-ON-GIRL FIGHT THING IS A DREAM COME TRUE. BUT--
I HAVE YOU!
THAT WOULD BE A GREAT IDEA...
...IF I COULDN'T FLY.

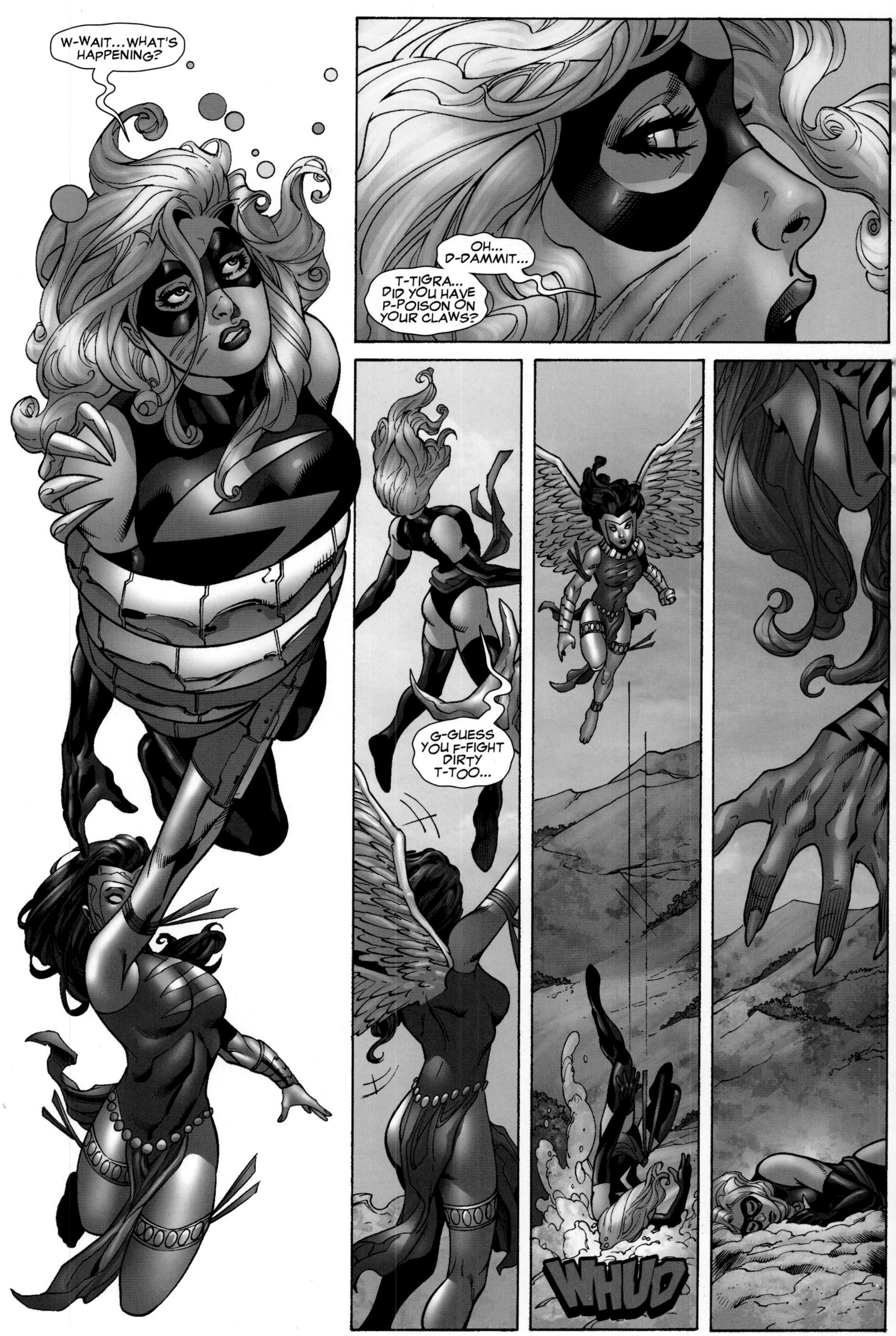
W-WAIT...WHAT'S HAPPENING?
OH... D-DAMMIT...
T-TIGRA... DID YOU HAVE P-POISON ON YOUR CLAWS?
G-GUESS YOU F-FIGHT DIRTY T-TOO...
WHUD

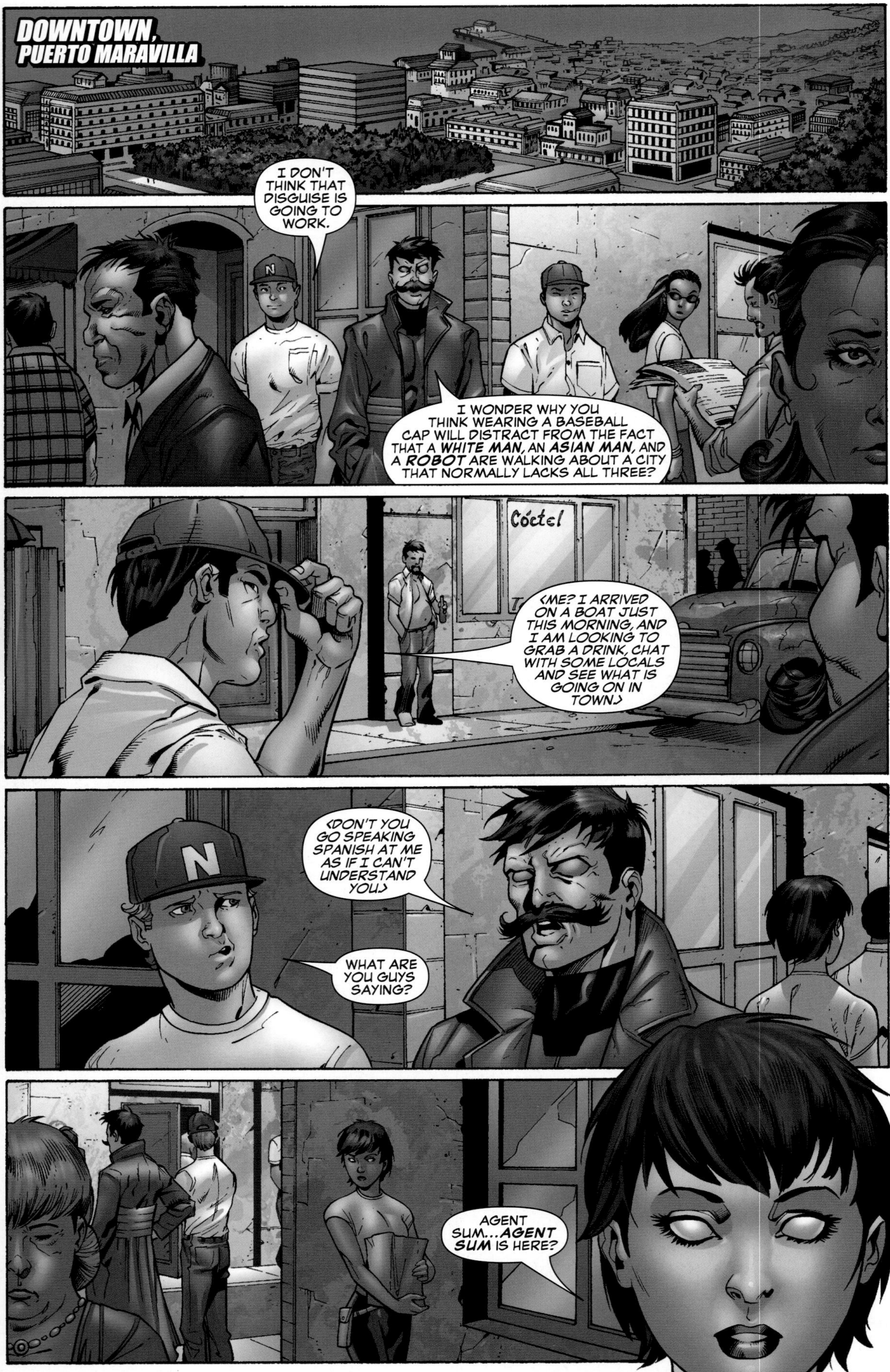
DOWNTOWN, PUERTO MARAVILLA
I DON'T THINK THAT DISGUISE IS GOING TO WORK.
I WONDER WHY YOU THINK WEARING A BASEBALL CAP WILL DISTRACT FROM THE FACT THAT A WHITE MAN, AN ASIAN MAN, AND A ROBOT ARE WALKING ABOUT A CITY THAT NORMALLY LACKS ALL THREE?
Cóctel
<ME? I ARRIVED ON A BOAT JUST THIS MORNING, AND I AM LOOKING TO GRAB A DRINK, CHAT WITH SOME LOCALS AND SEE WHAT IS GOING ON IN TOWN.>
<DON'T YOU GO SPEAKING SPANISH AT ME AS IF I CAN'T UNDERSTAND YOU.>
WHAT ARE YOU GUYS SAYING?
AGENT SUM... AGENT SUM IS HERE?

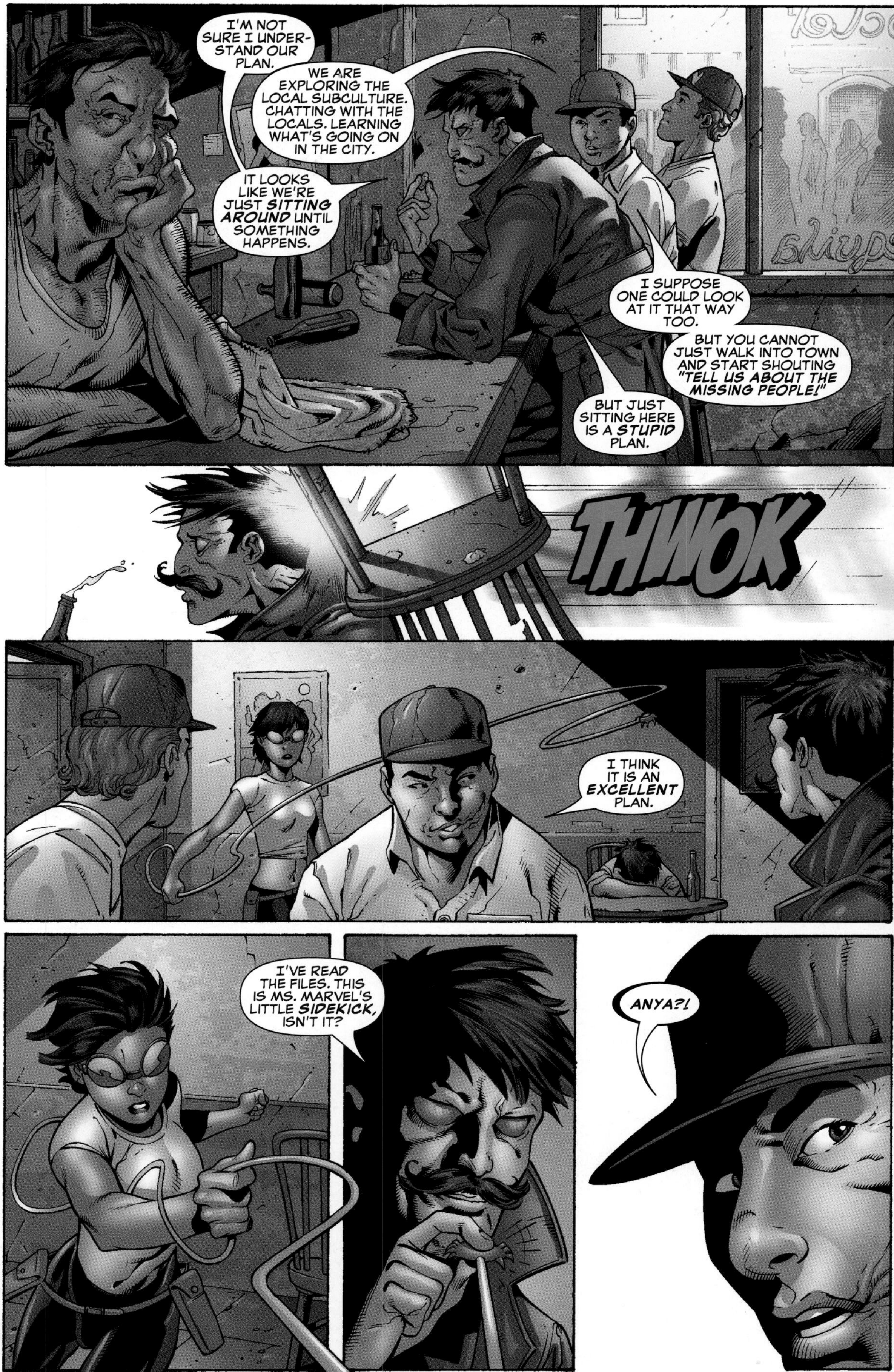
I'M NOT SURE I UNDERSTAND OUR PLAN.
WE ARE EXPLORING THE LOCAL SUBCULTURE. CHATTING WITH THE LOCALS. LEARNING WHAT'S GOING ON IN THE CITY.
IT LOOKS LIKE WE'RE JUST SITTING AROUND UNTIL SOMETHING HAPPENS.
I SUPPOSE ONE COULD LOOK AT IT THAT WAY TOO.
BUT YOU CANNOT JUST WALK INTO TOWN AND START SHOUTING "TELL US ABOUT THE MISSING PEOPLE!"
BUT JUST SITTING HERE IS A STUPID PLAN.
THWOK
I THINK IT IS AN EXCELLENT PLAN.
I'VE READ THE FILES. THIS IS MS. MARVEL'S LITTLE SIDEKICK, ISN'T IT?
ANYA?!

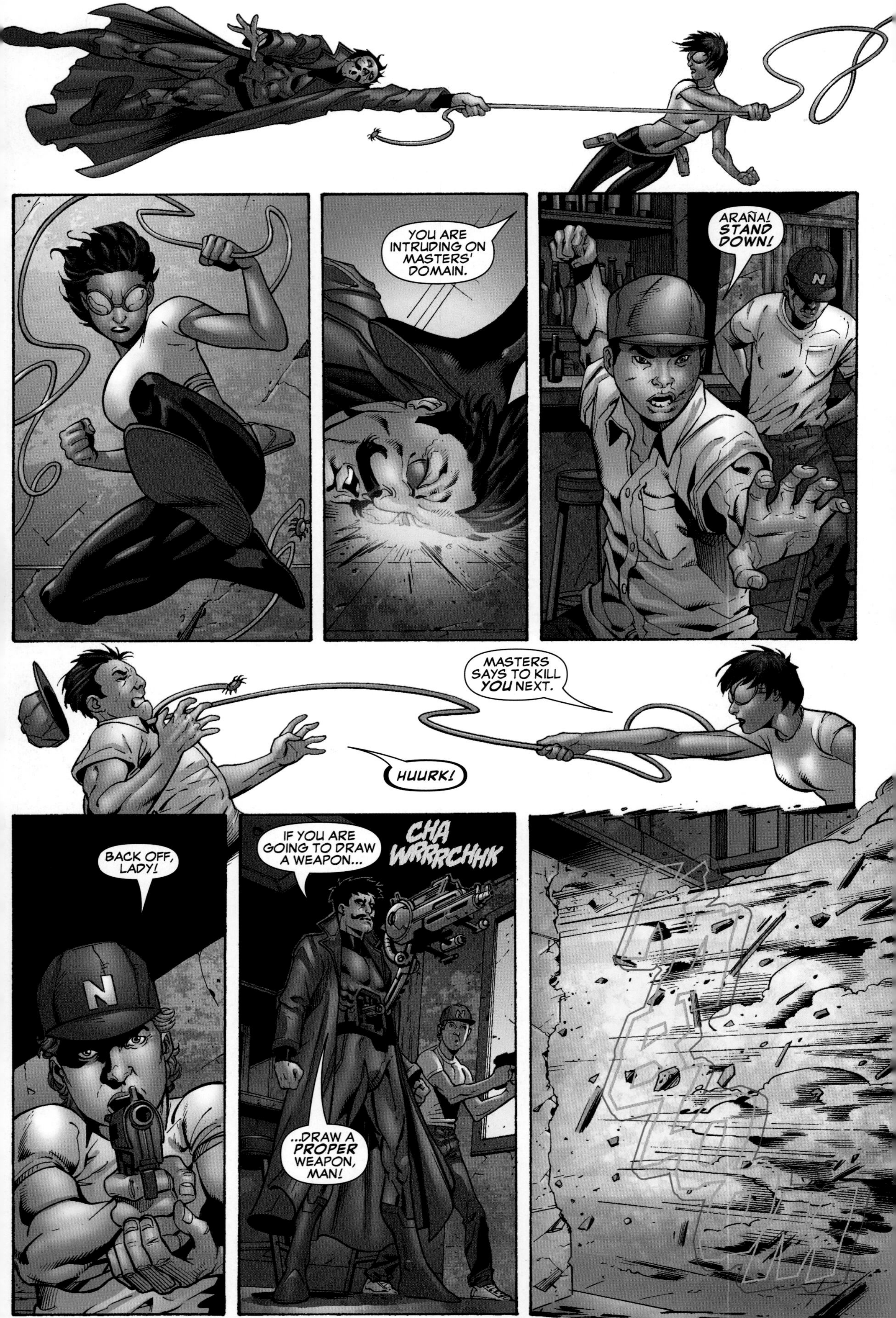

YOU ARE INTRUDING ON MASTERS' DOMAIN.
ARAÑA! STAND DOWN!
MASTERS SAYS TO KILL YOU NEXT.
HUURK!
BACK OFF, LADY!
IF YOU ARE GOING TO DRAW A WEAPON...
CHA WRRRCHHK
...DRAW A PROPER WEAPON, MAN!

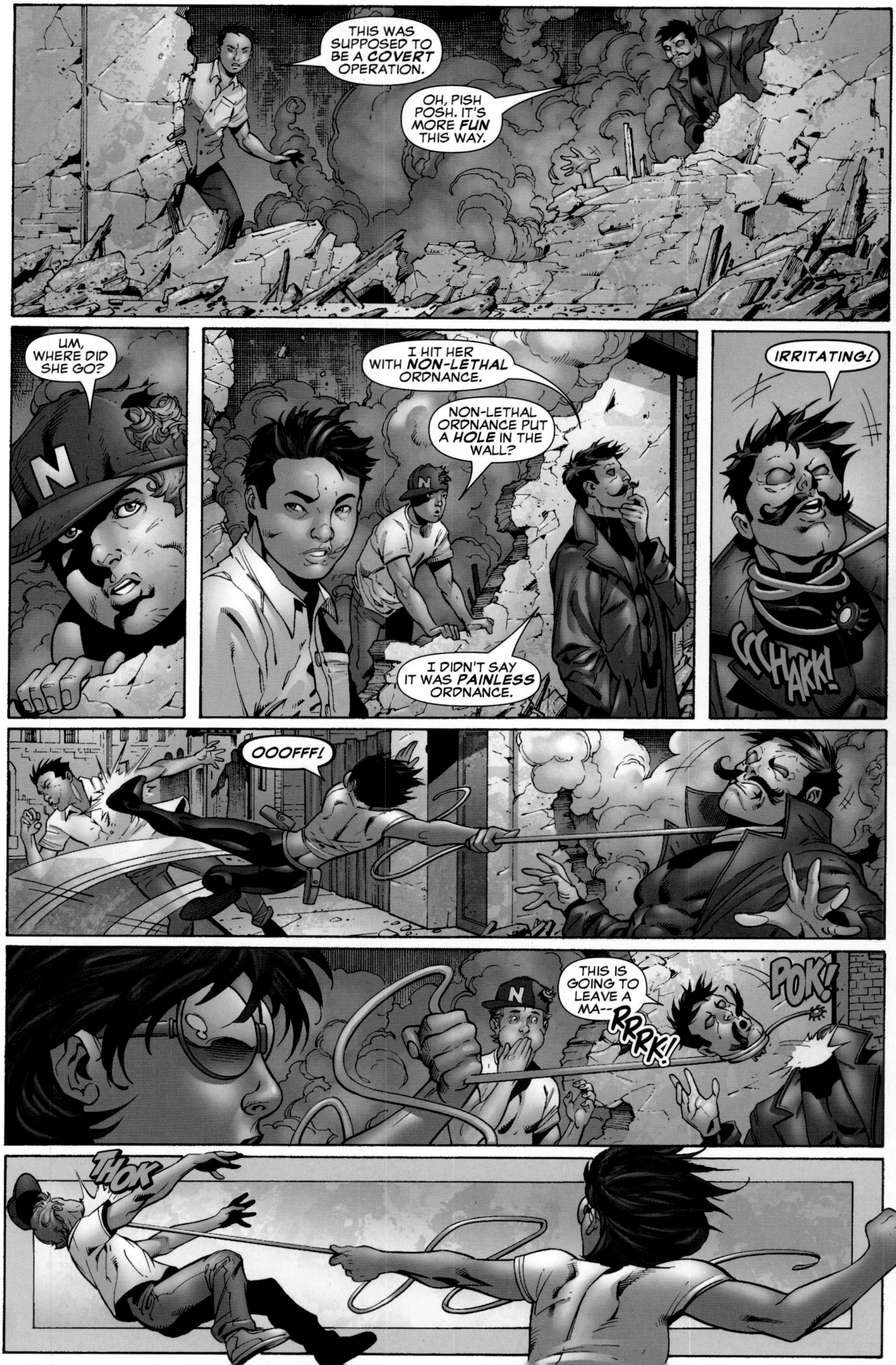
THIS WAS SUPPOSED TO BE A COVERT OPERATION.
OH, PISH POSH. IT'S MORE FUN THIS WAY.
UM, WHERE DID SHE GO?
I HIT HER WITH NON-LETHAL ORDNANCE.
NON-LETHAL ORDNANCE PUT A HOLE IN THE WALL?
I DIDN'T SAY IT WAS PAINLESS ORDNANCE.
IRRITATING!
CCCHAKK!
OOOFFF!
THIS IS GOING TO LEAVE A MA--
RRRK!
POK!
THOK

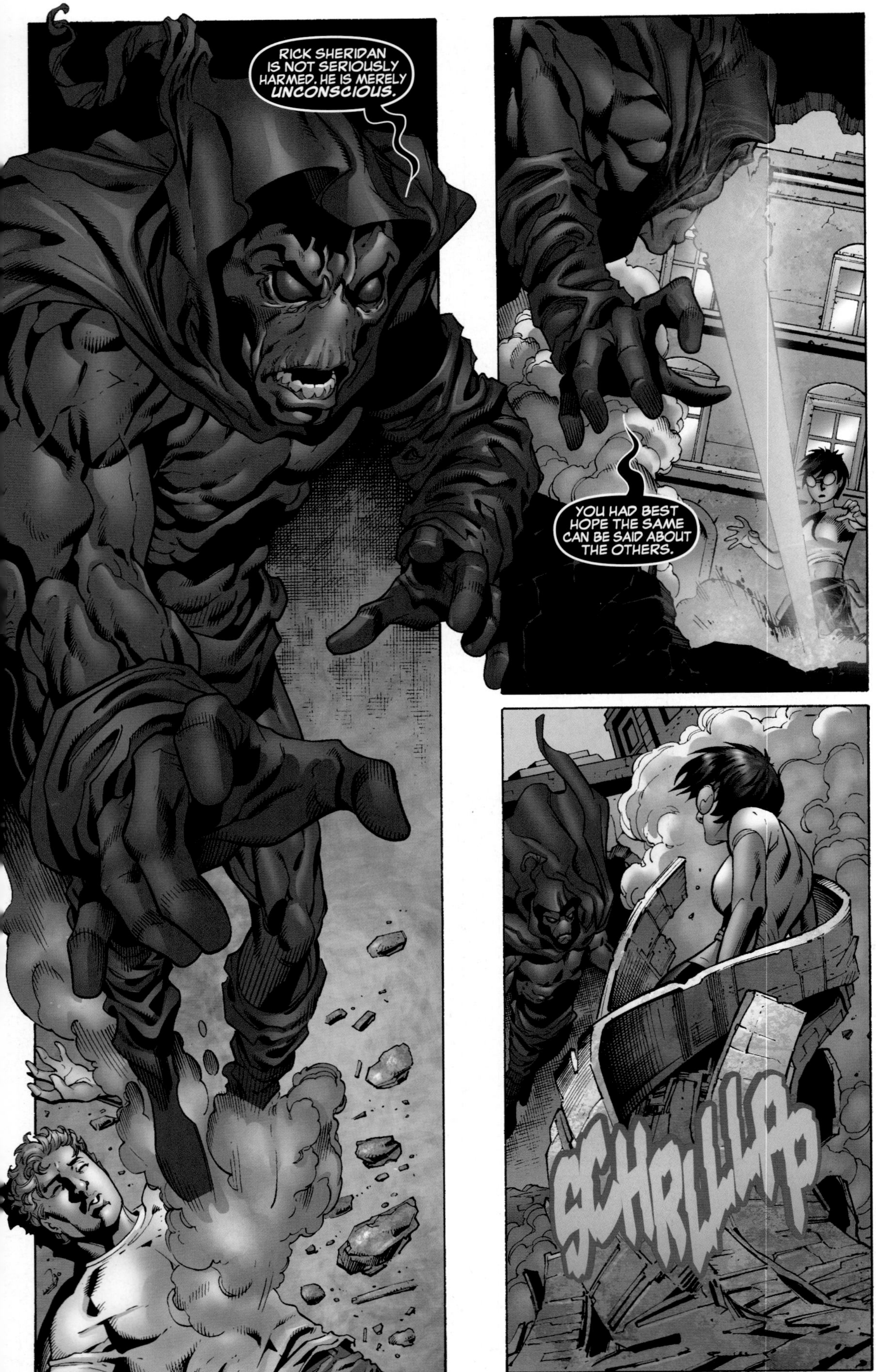
RICK SHERIDAN IS NOT SERIOUSLY HARMED. HE IS MERELY UNCONSCIOUS.
YOU HAD BEST HOPE THE SAME CAN BE SAID ABOUT THE OTHERS.
SCHRUUP

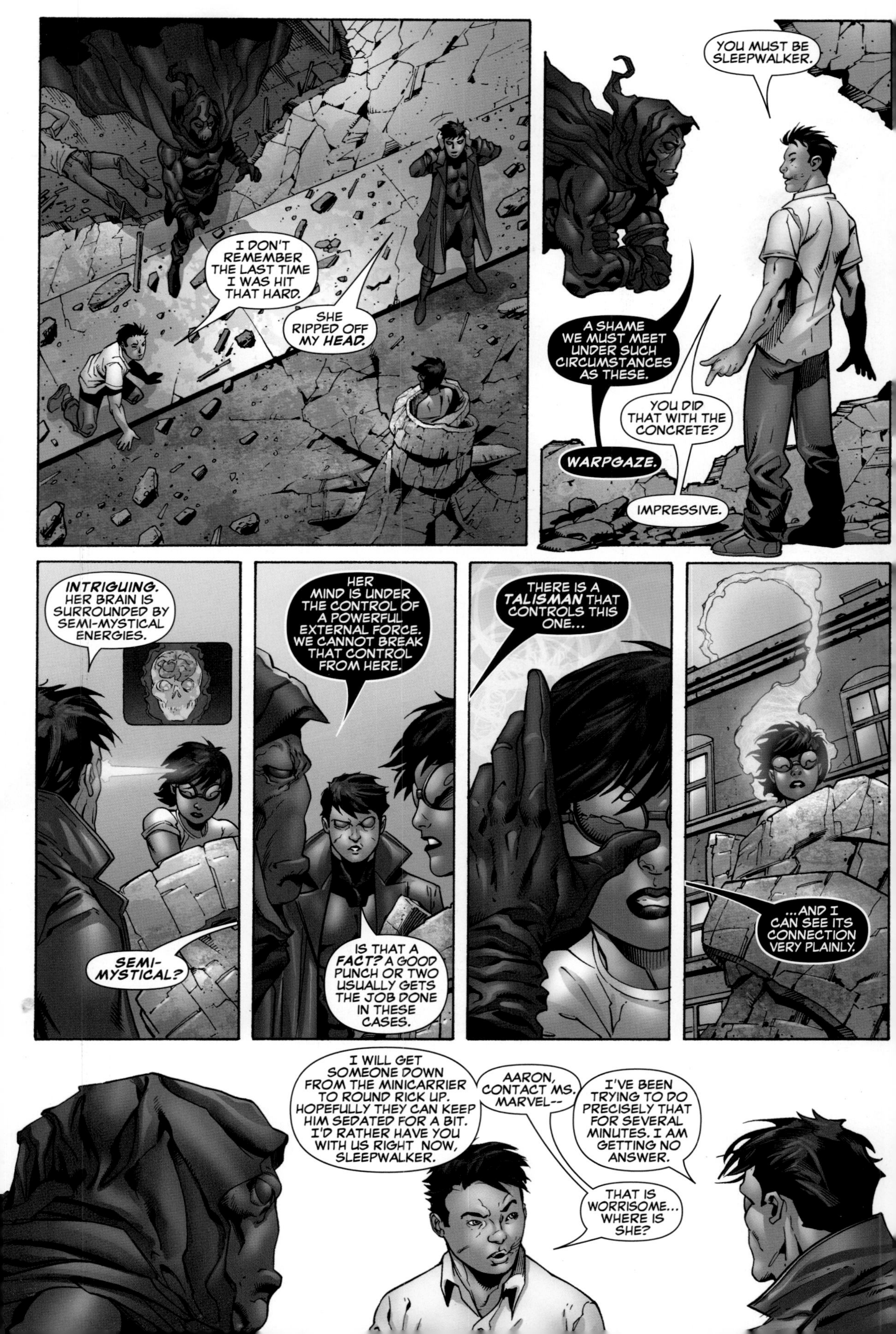
I DON'T REMEMBER THE LAST TIME I WAS HIT THAT HARD.
SHE RIPPED OFF MY HEAD.
YOU MUST BE SLEEPWALKER.
A SHAME WE MUST MEET UNDER SUCH CIRCUMSTANCES AS THESE.
YOU DID THAT WITH THE CONCRETE?
WARPGAZE.
IMPRESSIVE.
INTRIGUING. HER BRAIN IS SURROUNDED BY SEMI-MYSTICAL ENERGIES.
SEMI-MYSTICAL?
HER MIND IS UNDER THE CONTROL OF A POWERFUL EXTERNAL FORCE. WE CANNOT BREAK THAT CONTROL FROM HERE.
IS THAT A FACT? A GOOD PUNCH OR TWO USUALLY GETS THE JOB DONE IN THESE CASES.
THERE IS A TALISMAN THAT CONTROLS THIS ONE...
...AND I CAN SEE ITS CONNECTION VERY PLAINLY.
I WILL GET SOMEONE DOWN FROM THE MINICARRIER TO ROUND RICK UP. HOPEFULLY THEY CAN KEEP HIM SEDATED FOR A BIT. I'D RATHER HAVE YOU WITH US RIGHT NOW, SLEEPWALKER.
AARON, CONTACT MS. MARVEL--
I'VE BEEN TRYING TO DO PRECISELY THAT FOR SEVERAL MINUTES. I AM GETTING NO ANSWER.
THAT IS WORRISOME... WHERE IS SHE?

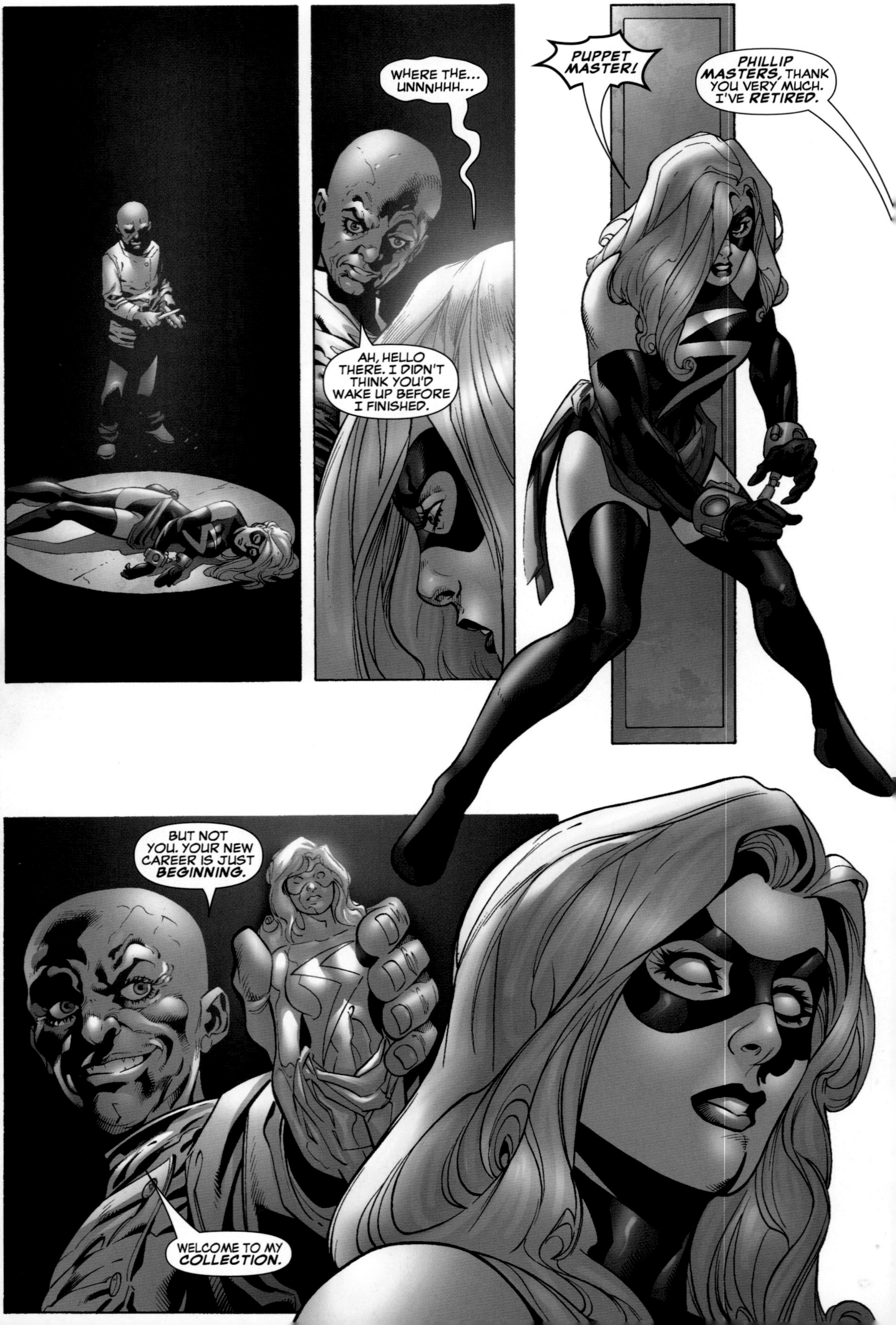
WHERE THE... UNNNHHH...
AH, HELLO THERE. I DIDN'T THINK YOU'D WAKE UP BEFORE I FINISHED.
PUPPET MASTER!
PHILLIP MASTERS, THANK YOU VERY MUCH. I'VE RETIRED.
BUT NOT YOU. YOUR NEW CAREER IS JUST BEGINNING.
WELCOME TO MY COLLECTION.

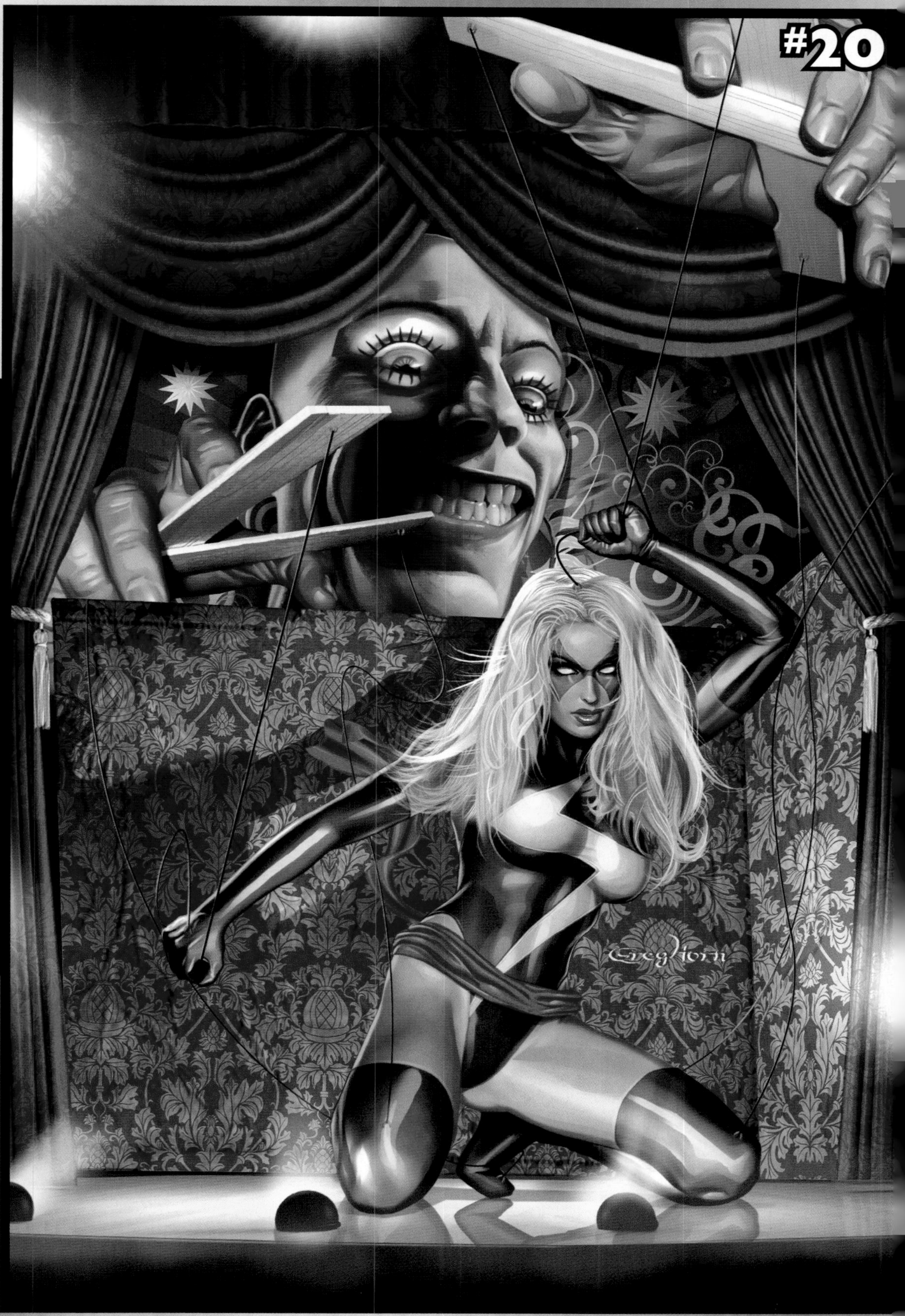
#20
Greg Horn

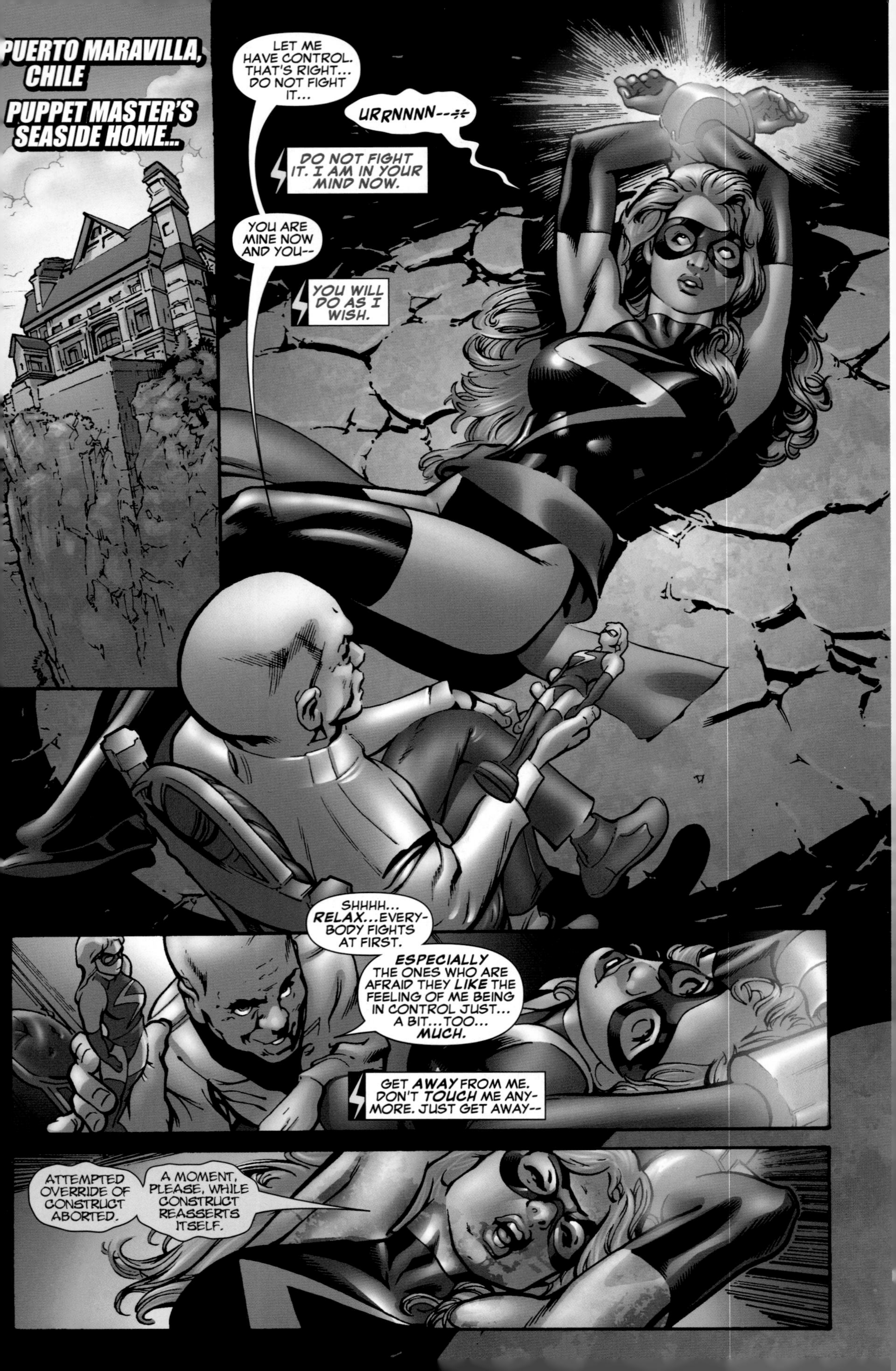
PUERTO MARAVILLA, CHILE
PUPPET MASTER'S SEASIDE HOME...
LET ME HAVE CONTROL. THAT'S RIGHT... DO NOT FIGHT IT...
URRNNNN--
DO NOT FIGHT IT. I AM IN YOUR MIND NOW.
YOU ARE MINE NOW AND YOU--
YOU WILL DO AS I WISH.
SHHHH... RELAX...EVERYBODY FIGHTS AT FIRST.
ESPECIALLY THE ONES WHO ARE AFRAID THEY LIKE THE FEELING OF ME BEING IN CONTROL JUST... A BIT...TOO... MUCH.
GET AWAY FROM ME. DON'T TOUCH ME ANYMORE. JUST GET AWAY--
ATTEMPTED OVERRIDE OF CONSTRUCT ABORTED.
A MOMENT, PLEASE, WHILE CONSTRUCT REASSERTS ITSELF.

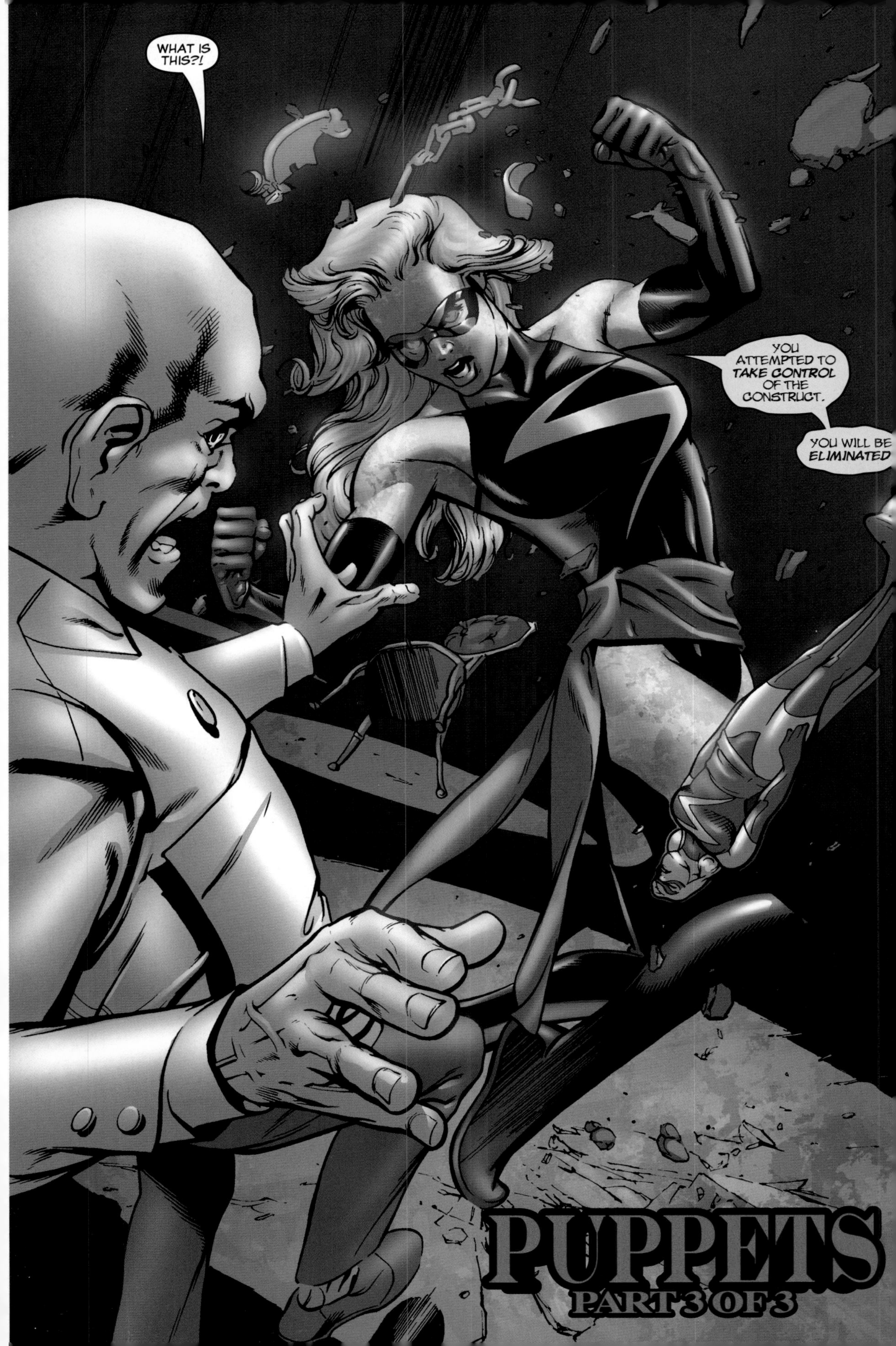
WHAT IS THIS?!
YOU ATTEMPTED TO TAKE CONTROL OF THE CONSTRUCT.
YOU WILL BE ELIMINATED
PUPPETS
PART 3 OF 3

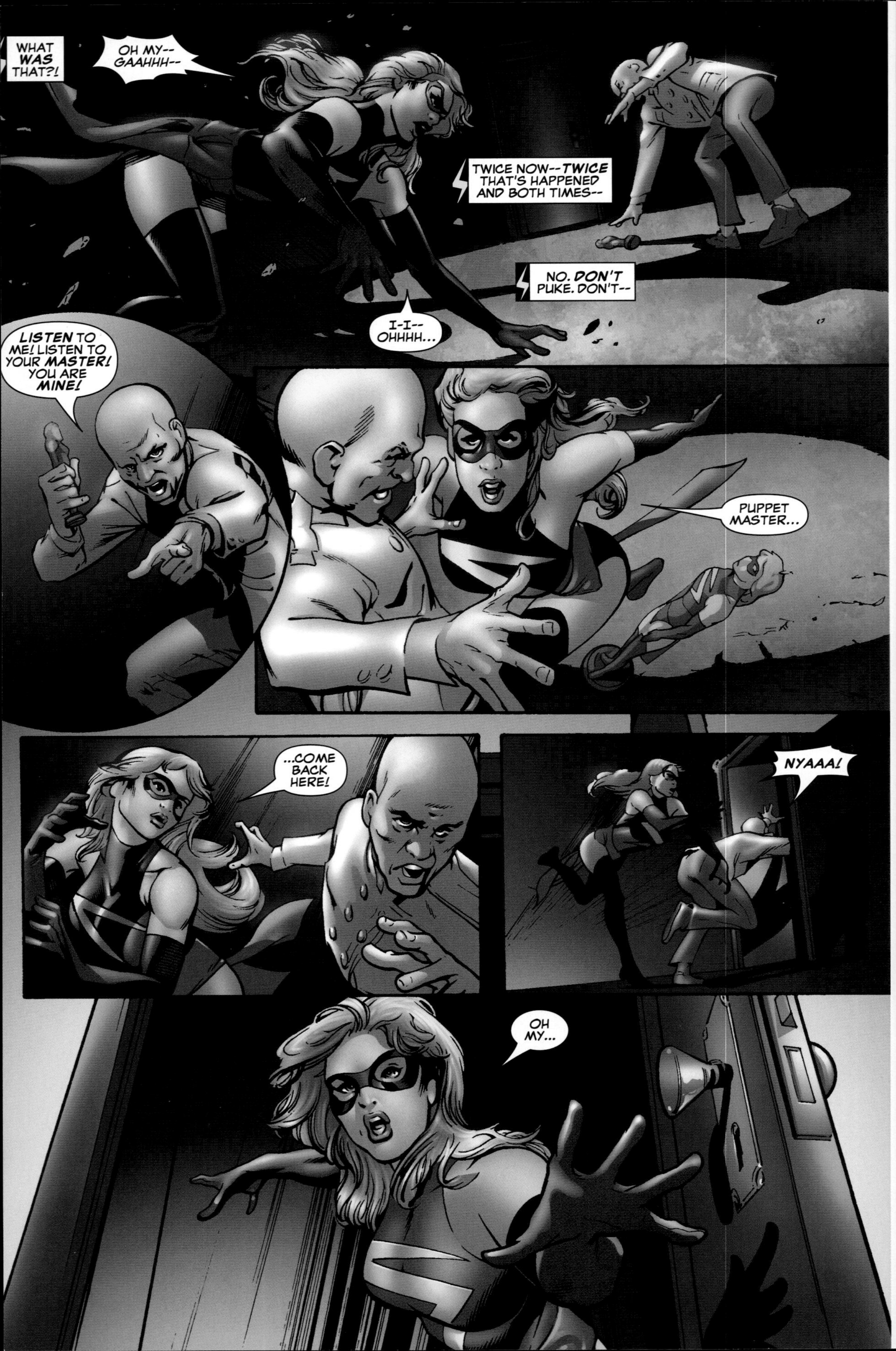
WHAT WAS THAT?!
OH MY-- GAAHHH--
TWICE NOW--TWICE THAT'S HAPPENED AND BOTH TIMES--
NO. DON'T PUKE. DON'T--
I-I-- OHHHH...
LISTEN TO ME! LISTEN TO YOUR MASTER! YOU ARE MINE!
PUPPET MASTER...
...COME BACK HERE!
NYAAA!
OH MY...

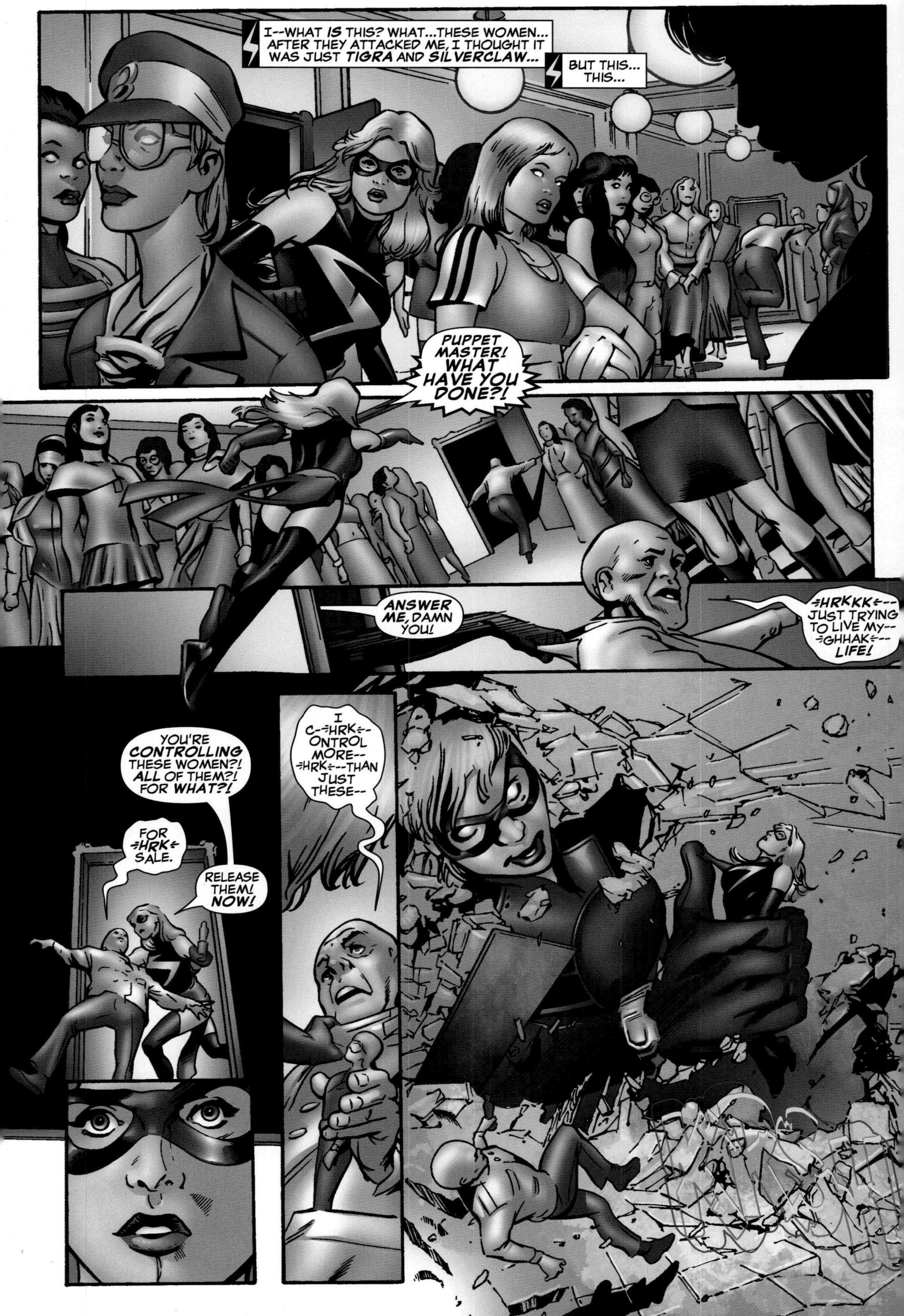
I--WHAT IS THIS? WHAT...THESE WOMEN... AFTER THEY ATTACKED ME, I THOUGHT IT WAS JUST TIGRA AND SILVERCLAW...
BUT THIS... THIS...
PUPPET MASTER! WHAT HAVE YOU DONE?!
ANSWER ME, DAMN YOU!
HRKKK --JUST TRYING TO LIVE MY-- GHHAK-- LIFE!
YOU'RE CONTROLLING THESE WOMEN?! ALL OF THEM?! FOR WHAT?!
FOR HRK SALE.
RELEASE THEM! NOW!
I C-- HRK --ONTROL MORE-- HRK --THAN JUST THESE--

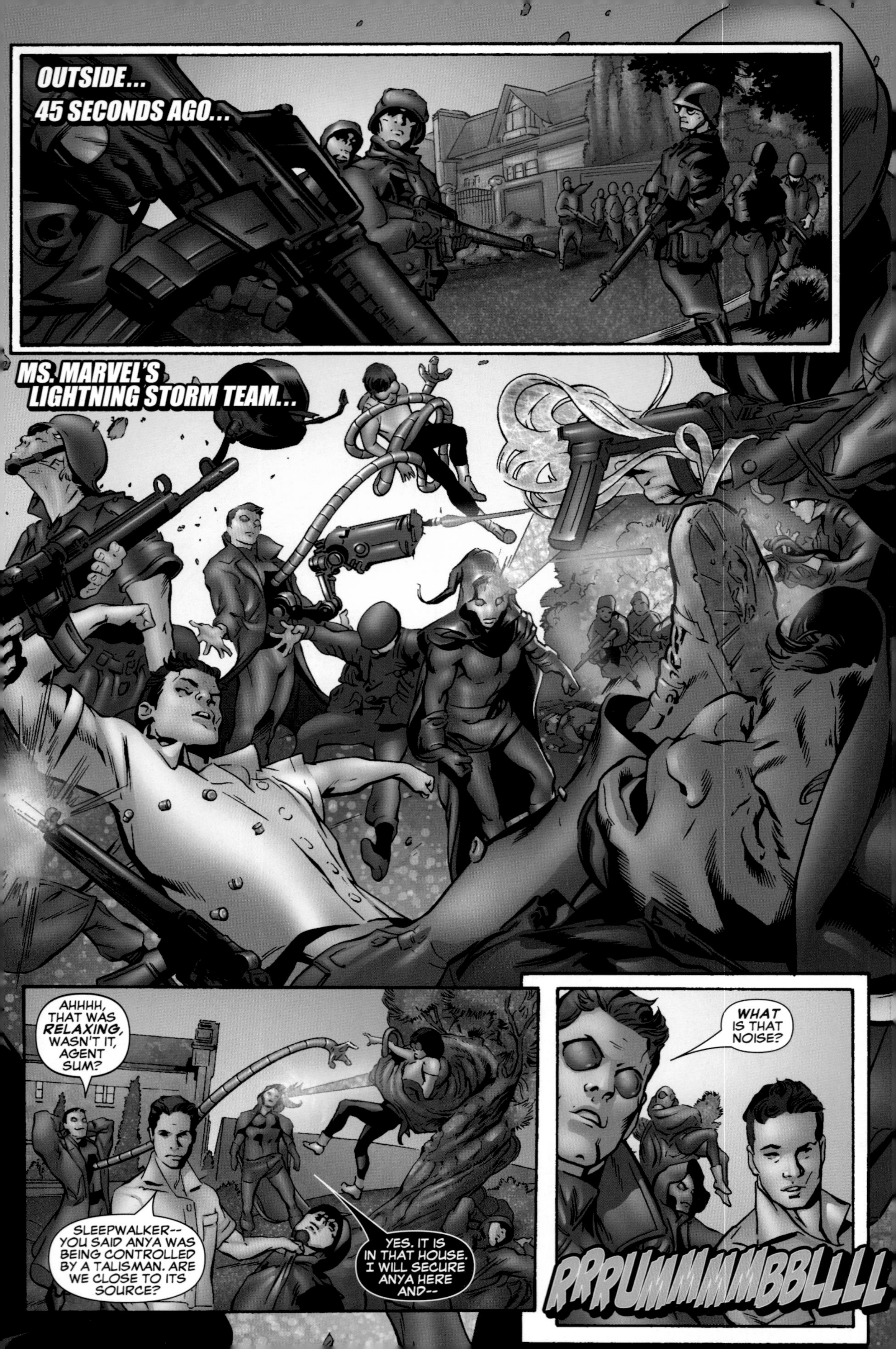
OUTSIDE...
45 SECONDS AGO...
MS. MARVEL'S
LIGHTNING STORM TEAM...
AHHHH, THAT WAS *RELAXING*, WASN'T IT, AGENT SUM?
SLEEPWALKER-- YOU SAID ANYA WAS BEING CONTROLLED BY A TALISMAN. ARE WE CLOSE TO ITS SOURCE?
YES. IT IS IN THAT HOUSE. I WILL SECURE ANYA HERE AND--
WHAT IS THAT NOISE?
RRRUMMMMMBBLLLL

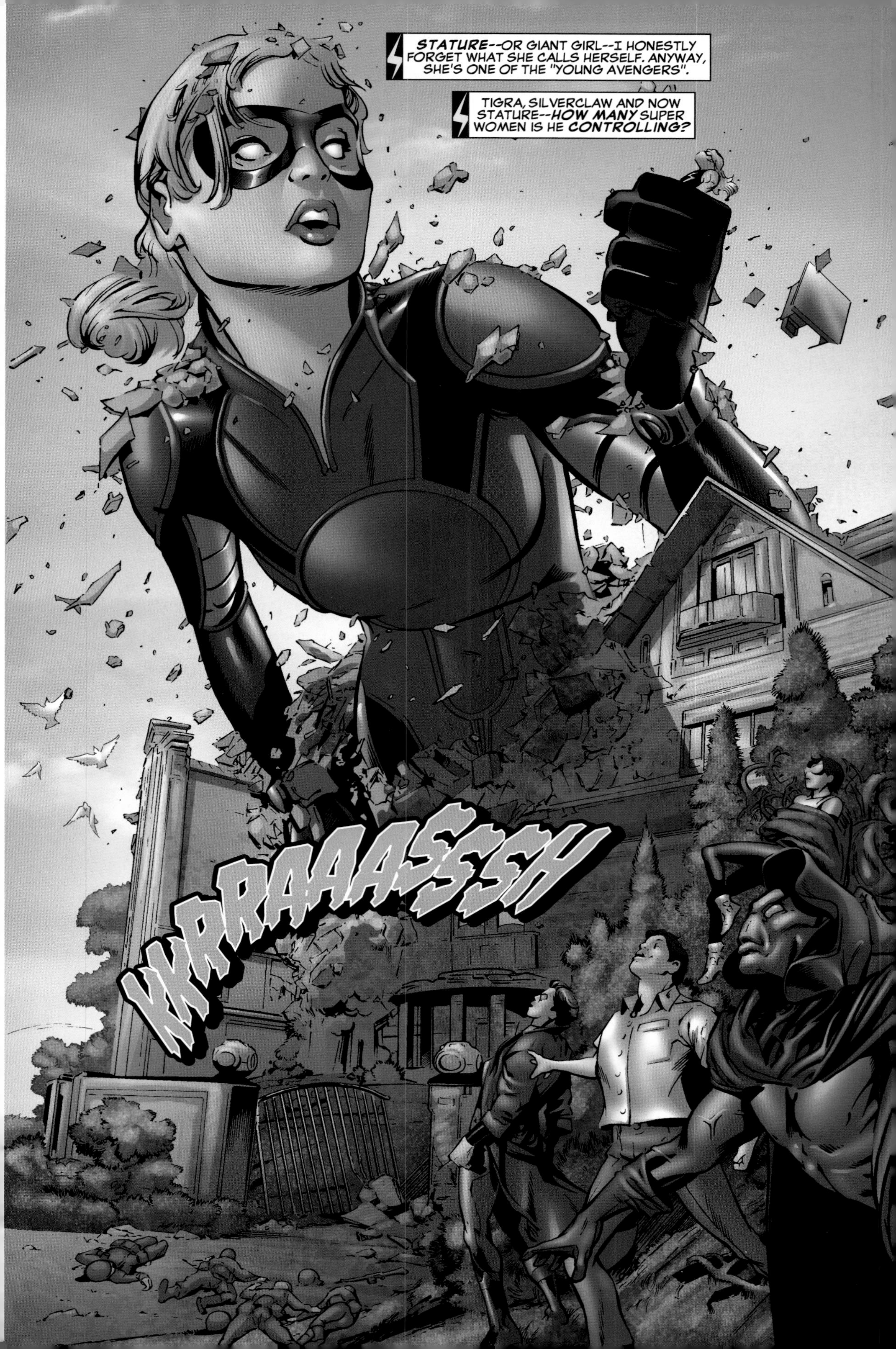
STATURE--OR GIANT GIRL--I HONESTLY FORGET WHAT SHE CALLS HERSELF. ANYWAY, SHE'S ONE OF THE "YOUNG AVENGERS".
TIGRA, SILVERCLAW AND NOW STATURE--HOW MANY SUPER WOMEN IS HE CONTROLLING?
KKRRAAAASSSH

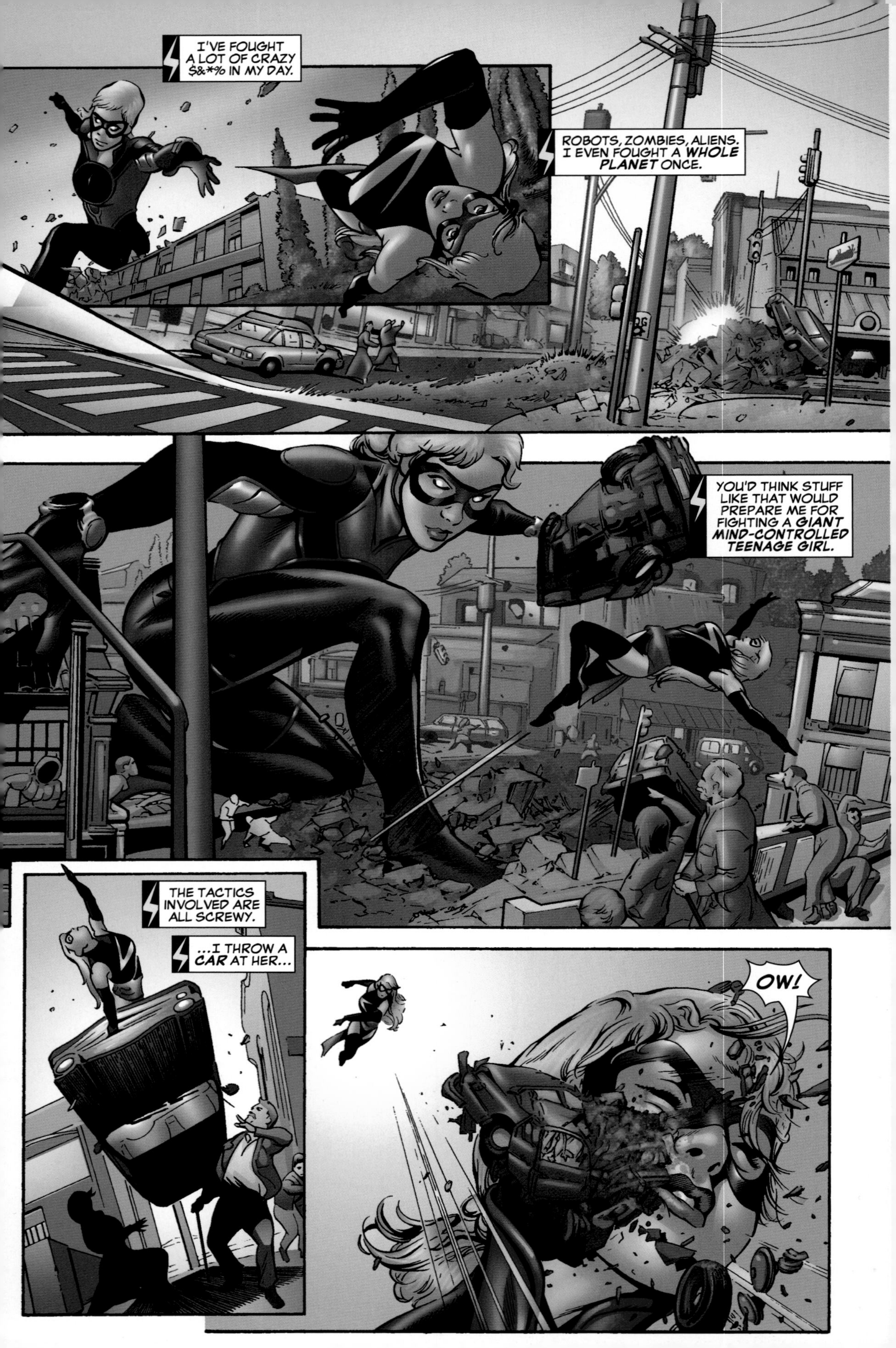
I'VE FOUGHT A LOT OF CRAZY $&*% IN MY DAY.
ROBOTS, ZOMBIES, ALIENS. I EVEN FOUGHT A WHOLE PLANET ONCE.
YOU'D THINK STUFF LIKE THAT WOULD PREPARE ME FOR FIGHTING A GIANT MIND-CONTROLLED TEENAGE GIRL.
THE TACTICS INVOLVED ARE ALL SCREWY.
...I THROW A CAR AT HER...
OW!

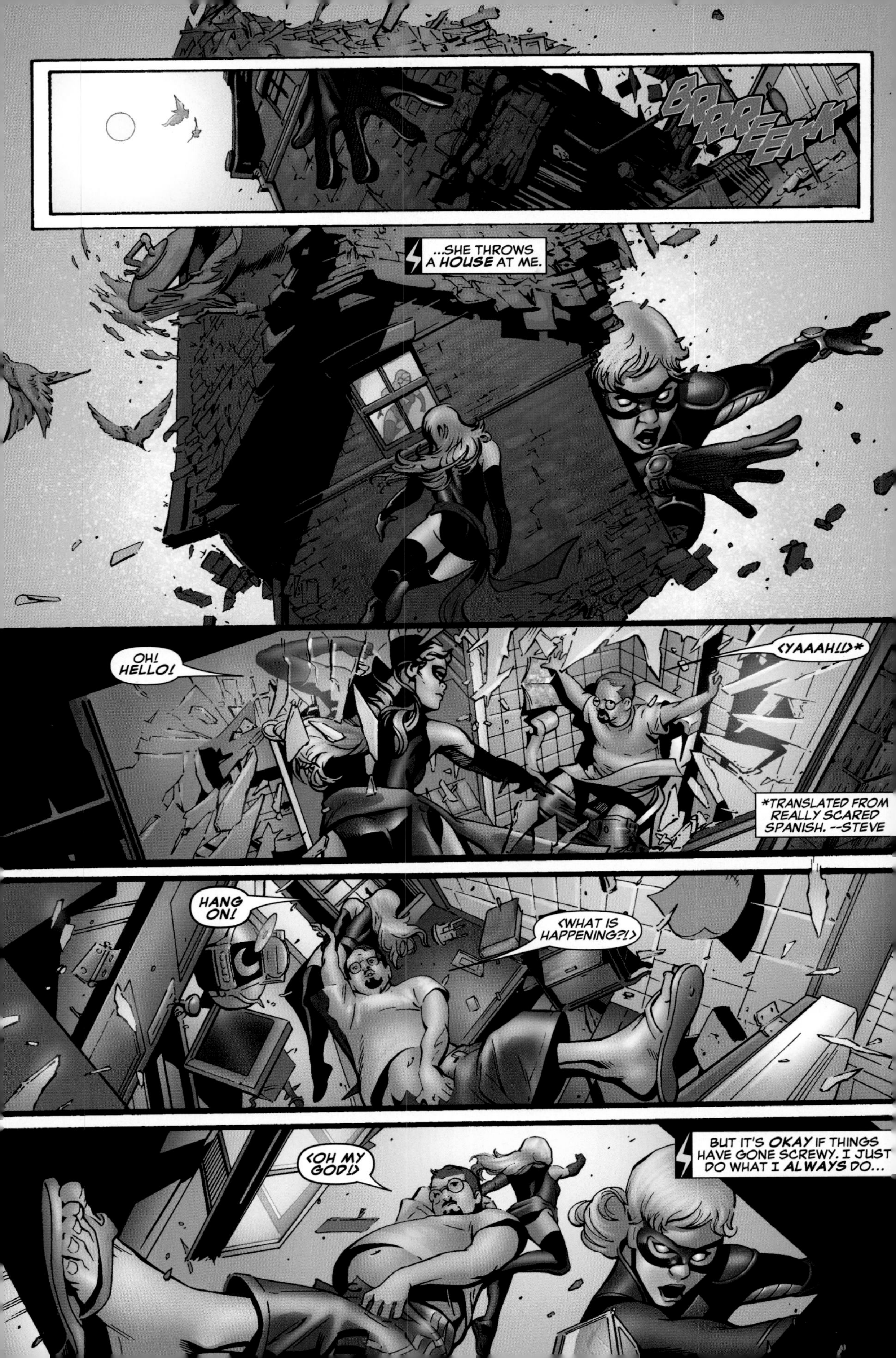
BRRREEKK
...SHE THROWS A HOUSE AT ME.
OH! HELLO!
<YAAAH!!>*
*TRANSLATED FROM REALLY SCARED SPANISH. --STEVE
HANG ON!
<WHAT IS HAPPENING?!>
<OH MY GOD!>
BUT IT'S OKAY IF THINGS HAVE GONE SCREWY. I JUST DO WHAT I ALWAYS DO...

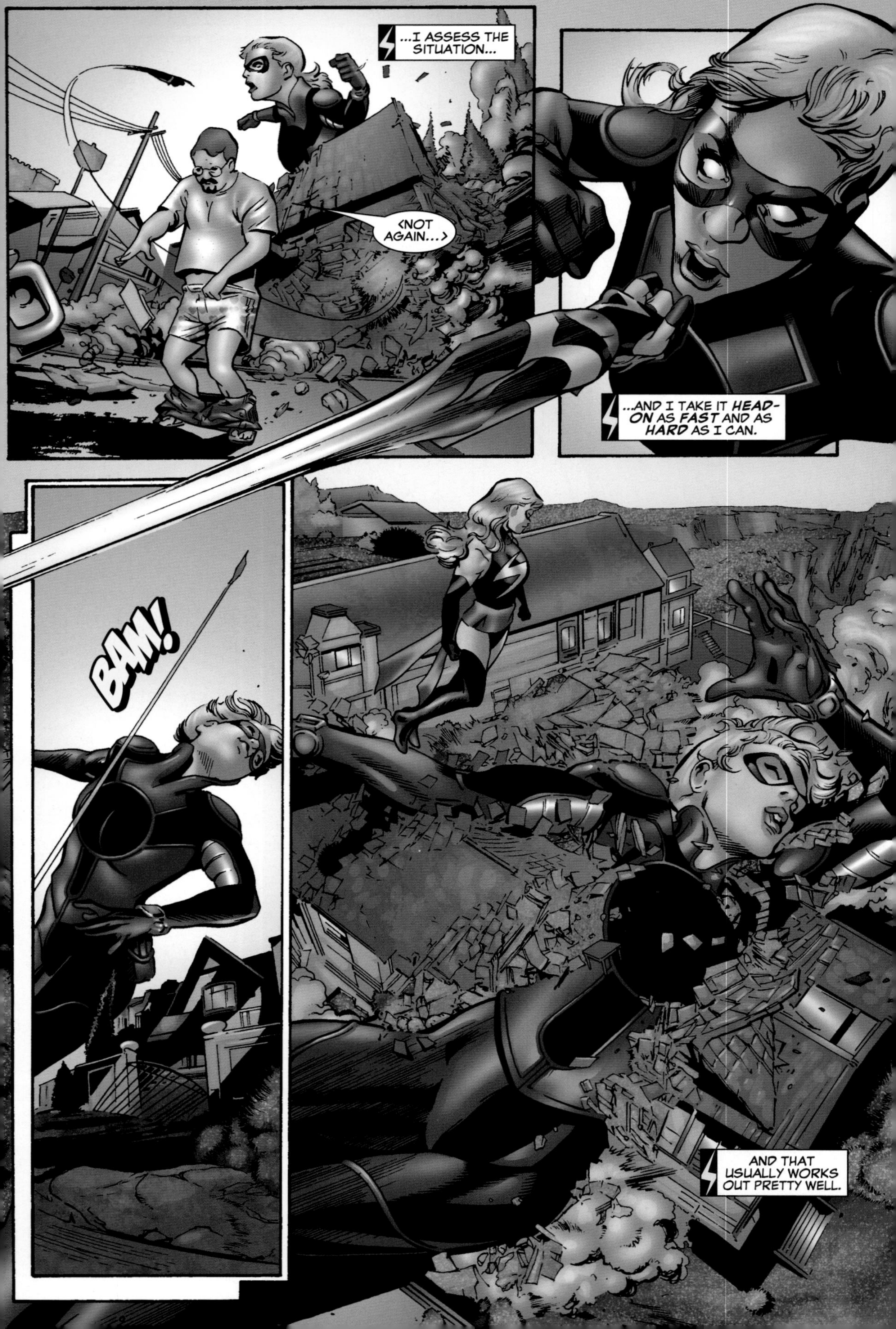
...I ASSESS THE SITUATION...
<NOT AGAIN...>
...AND I TAKE IT HEAD-ON AS FAST AND AS HARD AS I CAN.
BAM!
AND THAT USUALLY WORKS OUT PRETTY WELL.

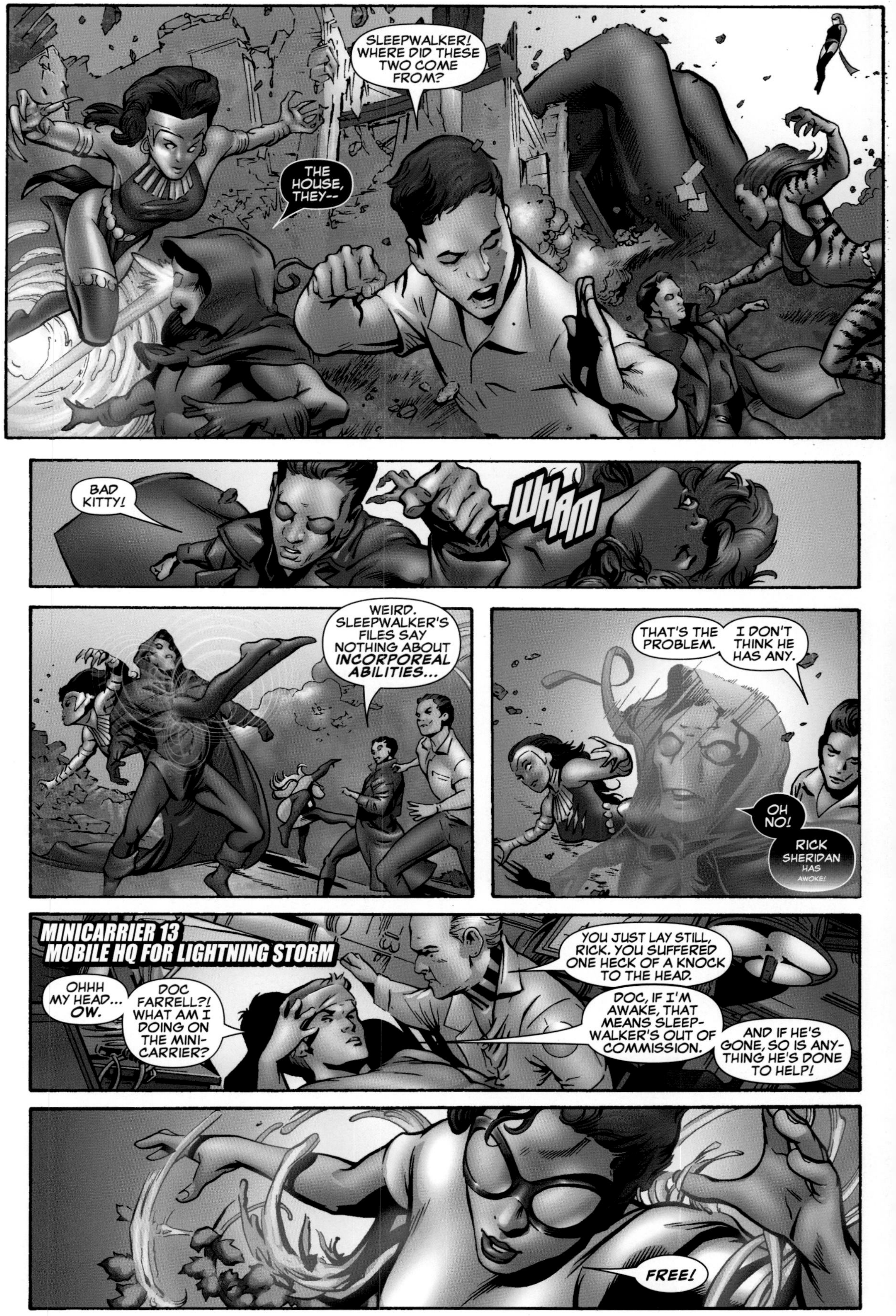
SLEEPWALKER! WHERE DID THESE TWO COME FROM?
THE HOUSE, THEY--
BAD KITTY!
WHAM
WEIRD. SLEEPWALKER'S FILES SAY NOTHING ABOUT INCORPOREAL ABILITIES...
THAT'S THE PROBLEM.
I DON'T THINK HE HAS ANY.
OH NO!
RICK SHERIDAN HAS AWOKE!
MINICARRIER 13
MOBILE HQ FOR LIGHTNING STORM
OHHH MY HEAD... OW.
DOC FARRELL?! WHAT AM I DOING ON THE MINI-CARRIER?
YOU JUST LAY STILL, RICK. YOU SUFFERED ONE HECK OF A KNOCK TO THE HEAD.
DOC, IF I'M AWAKE, THAT MEANS SLEEP-WALKER'S OUT OF COMMISSION.
AND IF HE'S GONE, SO IS ANY-THING HE'S DONE TO HELP!
FREE!

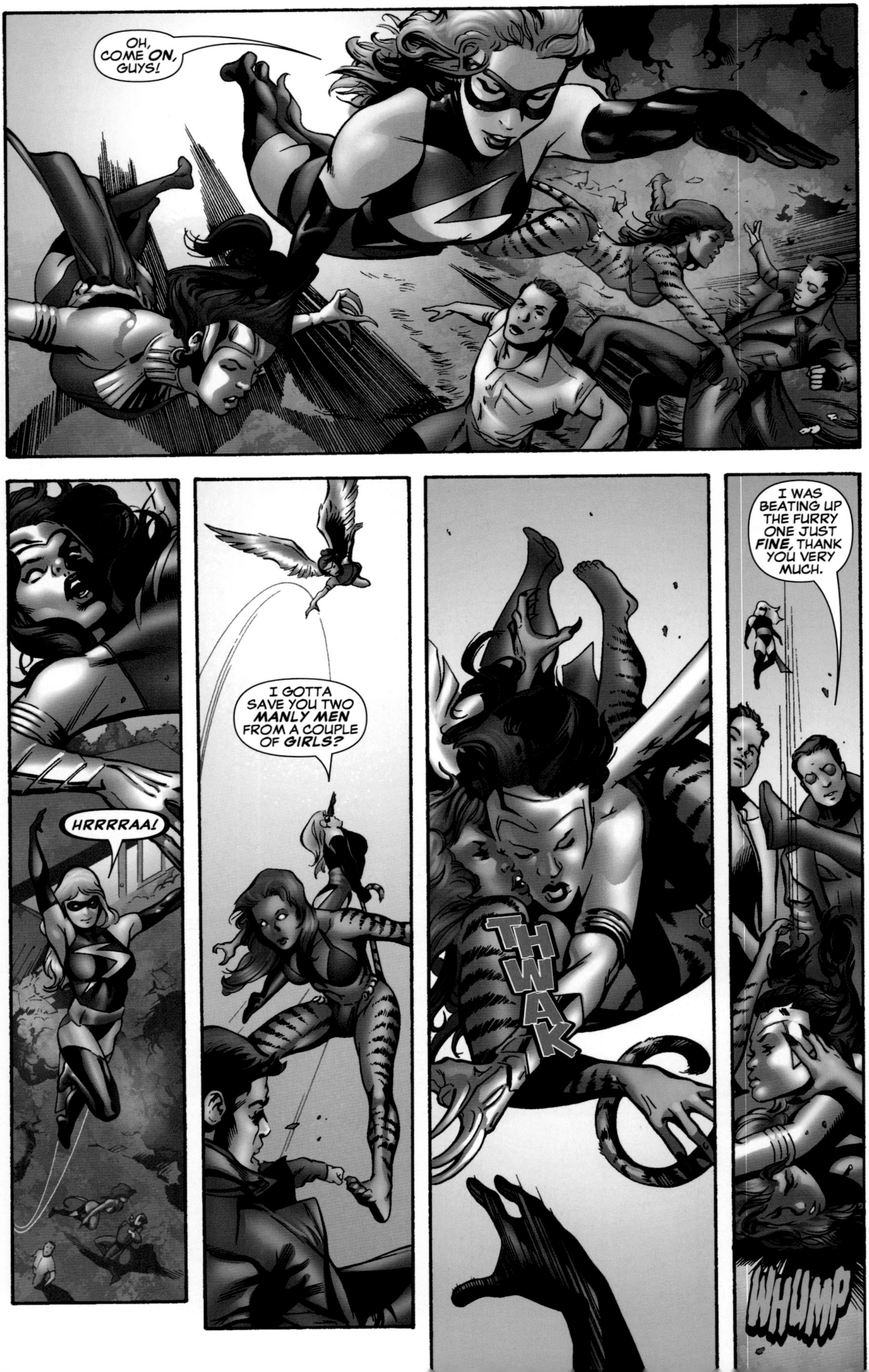
OH, COME ON, GUYS!
HRRRRAA!
I GOTTA SAVE YOU TWO MANLY MEN FROM A COUPLE OF GIRLS?
THWAK
I WAS BEATING UP THE FURRY ONE JUST FINE, THANK YOU VERY MUCH.
WHUMP

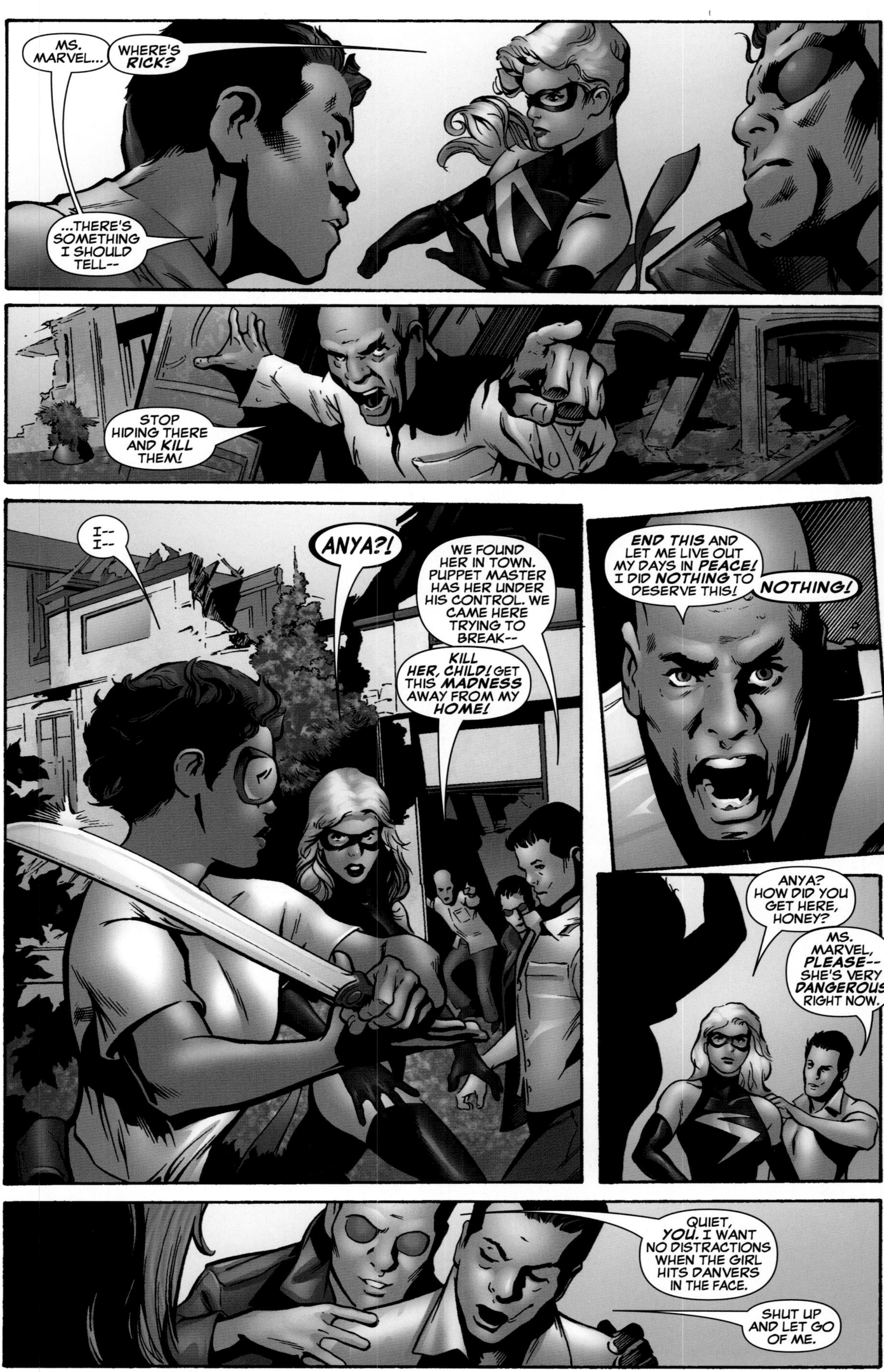
MS. MARVEL...
WHERE'S RICK?
...THERE'S SOMETHING I SHOULD TELL--
STOP HIDING THERE AND KILL THEM!
I-- I--
ANYA?!
WE FOUND HER IN TOWN. PUPPET MASTER HAS HER UNDER HIS CONTROL. WE CAME HERE TRYING TO BREAK--
KILL HER, CHILD! GET THIS MADNESS AWAY FROM MY HOME!
END THIS AND LET ME LIVE OUT MY DAYS IN PEACE! I DID NOTHING TO DESERVE THIS!
NOTHING!
ANYA? HOW DID YOU GET HERE, HONEY?
MS. MARVEL, PLEASE-- SHE'S VERY DANGEROUS RIGHT NOW.
QUIET, YOU. I WANT NO DISTRACTIONS WHEN THE GIRL HITS DANVERS IN THE FACE.
SHUT UP AND LET GO OF ME.

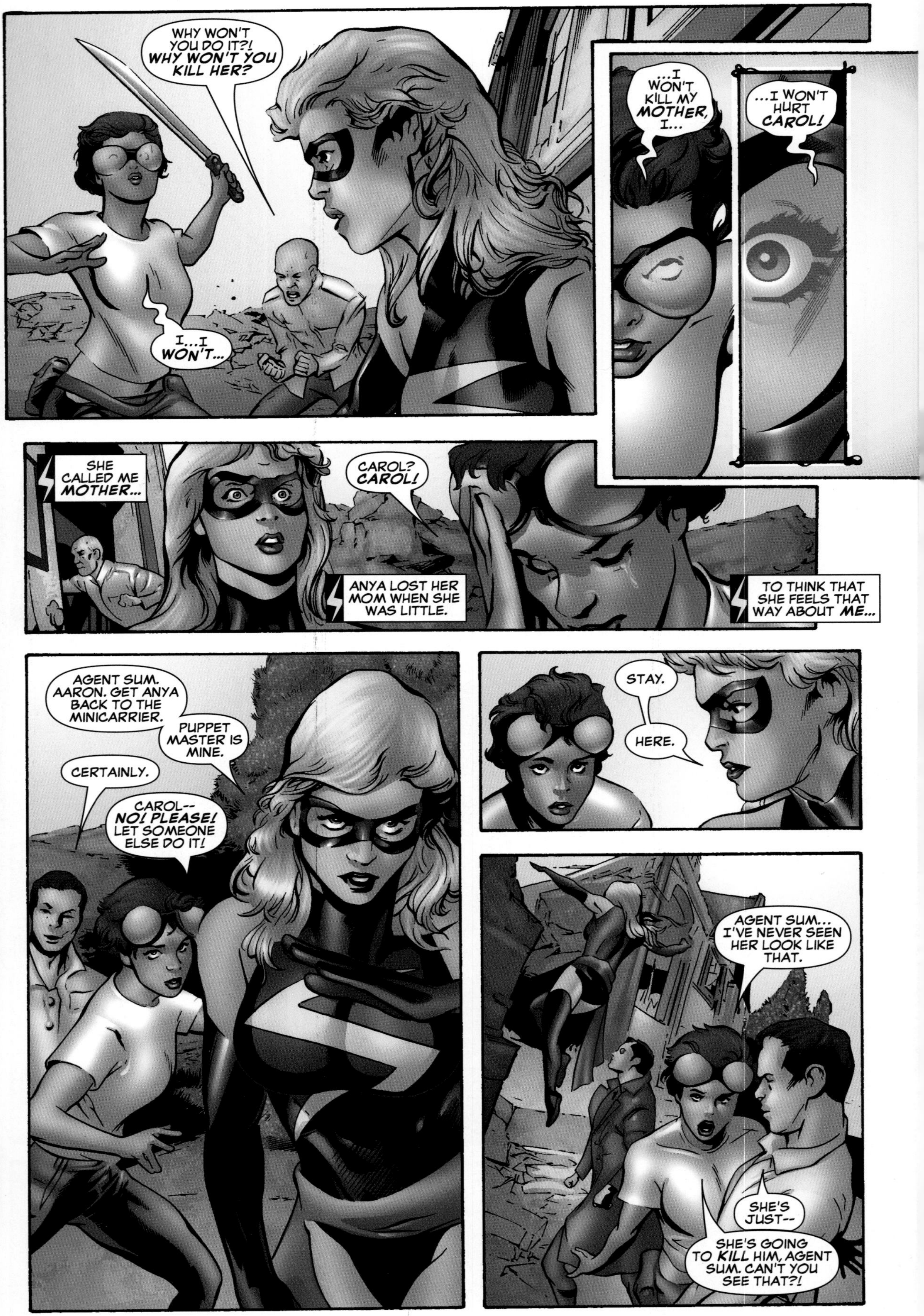
WHY WON'T YOU DO IT?! WHY WON'T YOU KILL HER?
I...I WON'T...
...I WON'T KILL MY MOTHER, I...
...I WON'T HURT CAROL!
SHE CALLED ME MOTHER...
CAROL? CAROL!
ANYA LOST HER MOM WHEN SHE WAS LITTLE.
TO THINK THAT SHE FEELS THAT WAY ABOUT ME...
AGENT SUM. AARON. GET ANYA BACK TO THE MINICARRIER.
PUPPET MASTER IS MINE.
CERTAINLY.
CAROL-- NO! PLEASE! LET SOMEONE ELSE DO IT!
STAY.
HERE.
AGENT SUM... I'VE NEVER SEEN HER LOOK LIKE THAT.
SHE'S JUST--
SHE'S GOING TO KILL HIM, AGENT SUM. CAN'T YOU SEE THAT?!

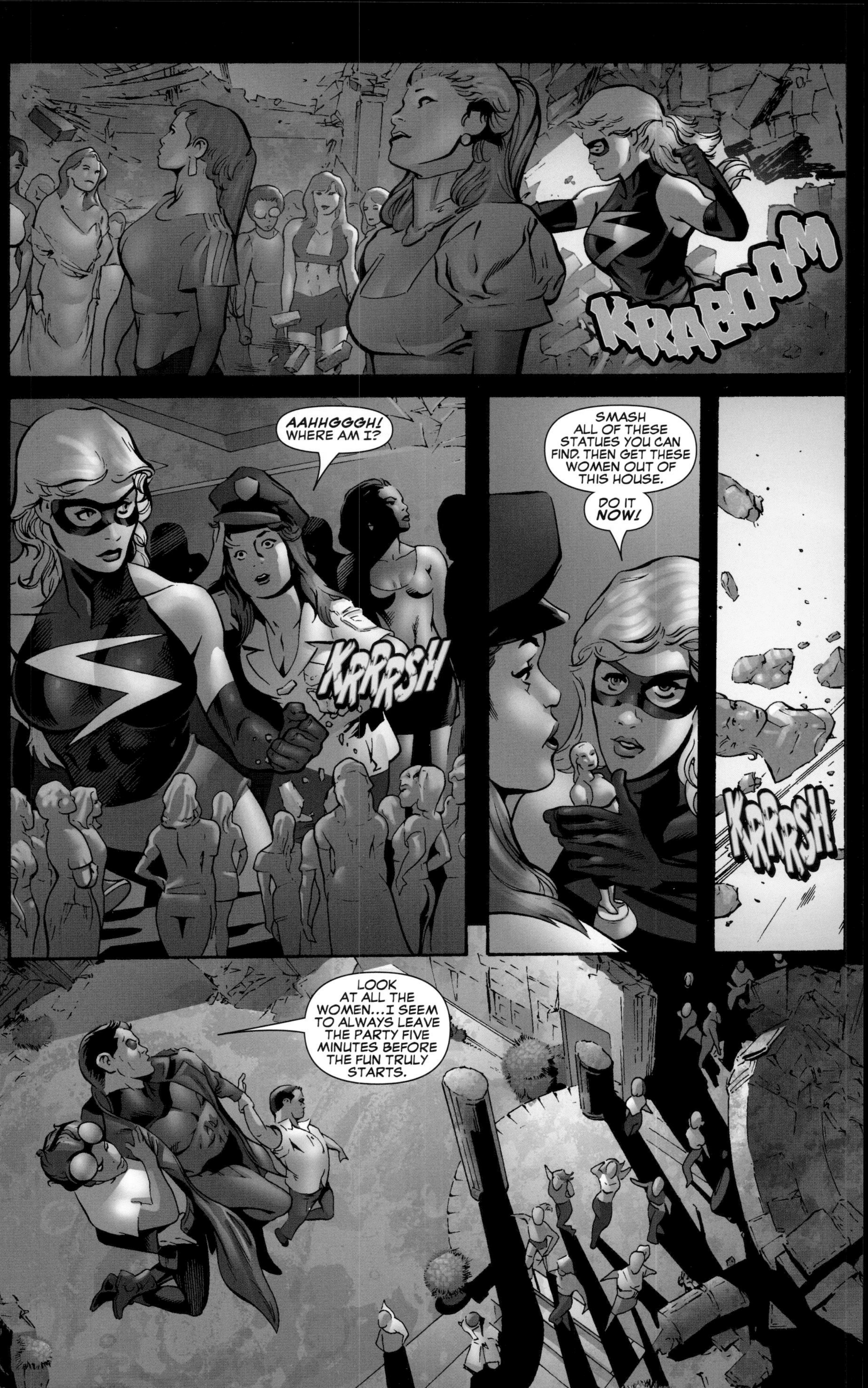
KRABOOM
AAHHGGGH! WHERE AM I?
KRRRSH
SMASH ALL OF THESE STATUES YOU CAN FIND. THEN GET THESE WOMEN OUT OF THIS HOUSE.
DO IT NOW!
KRRRSH
LOOK AT ALL THE WOMEN...I SEEM TO ALWAYS LEAVE THE PARTY FIVE MINUTES BEFORE THE FUN TRULY STARTS.

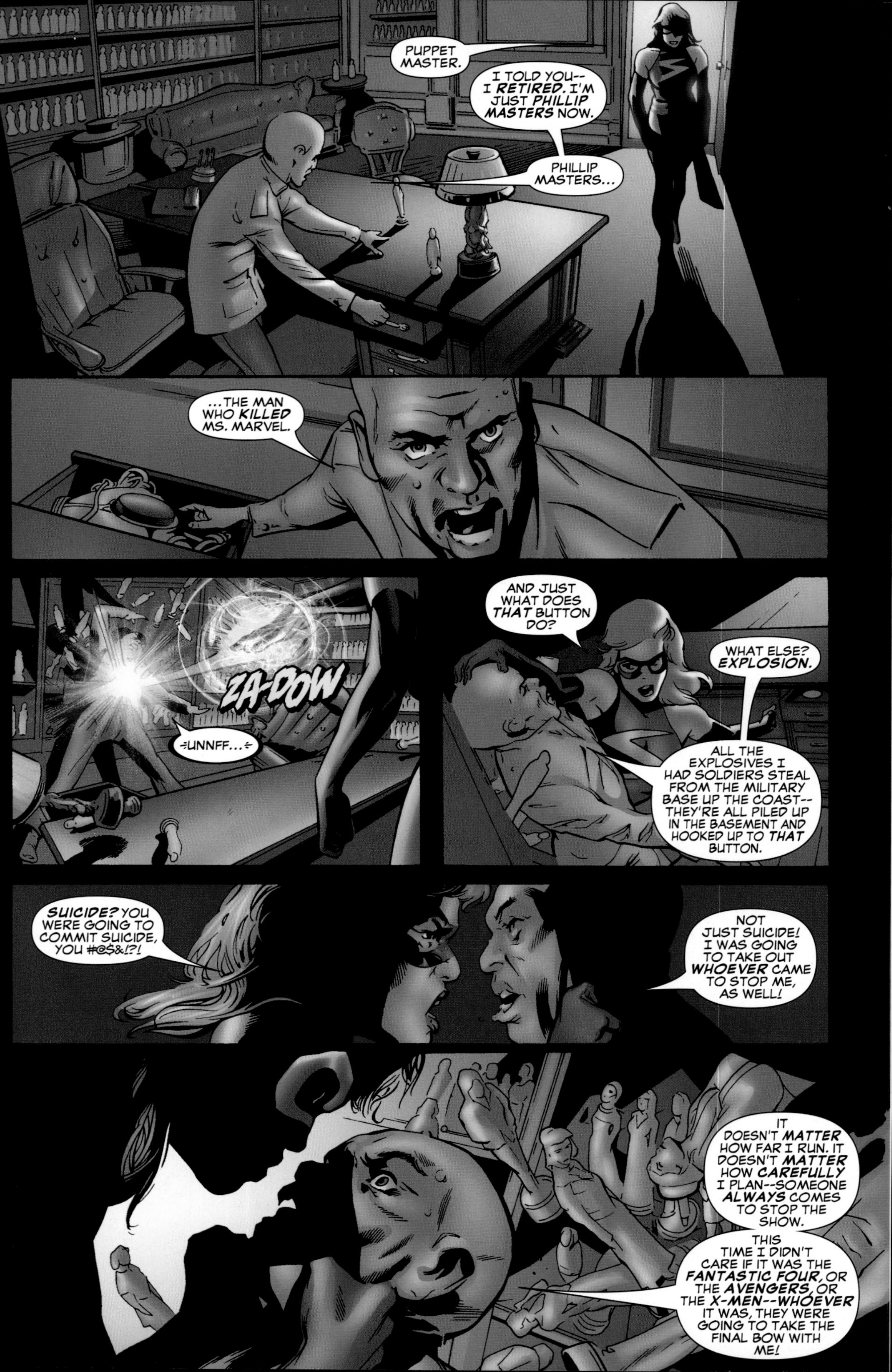
PUPPET MASTER.
I TOLD YOU-- I RETIRED. I'M JUST PHILLIP MASTERS NOW.
PHILLIP MASTERS...
...THE MAN WHO KILLED MS. MARVEL.
ZA-DOW
UNNFF...
AND JUST WHAT DOES THAT BUTTON DO?
WHAT ELSE? EXPLOSION.
ALL THE EXPLOSIVES I HAD SOLDIERS STEAL FROM THE MILITARY BASE UP THE COAST-- THEY'RE ALL PILED UP IN THE BASEMENT AND HOOKED UP TO THAT BUTTON.
SUICIDE? YOU WERE GOING TO COMMIT SUICIDE, YOU #@$&!?!
NOT JUST SUICIDE! I WAS GOING TO TAKE OUT WHOEVER CAME TO STOP ME, AS WELL!
IT DOESN'T MATTER HOW FAR I RUN. IT DOESN'T MATTER HOW CAREFULLY I PLAN--SOMEONE ALWAYS COMES TO STOP THE SHOW.
THIS TIME I DIDN'T CARE IF IT WAS THE FANTASTIC FOUR, OR THE AVENGERS, OR THE X-MEN--WHOEVER IT WAS, THEY WERE GOING TO TAKE THE FINAL BOW WITH ME!

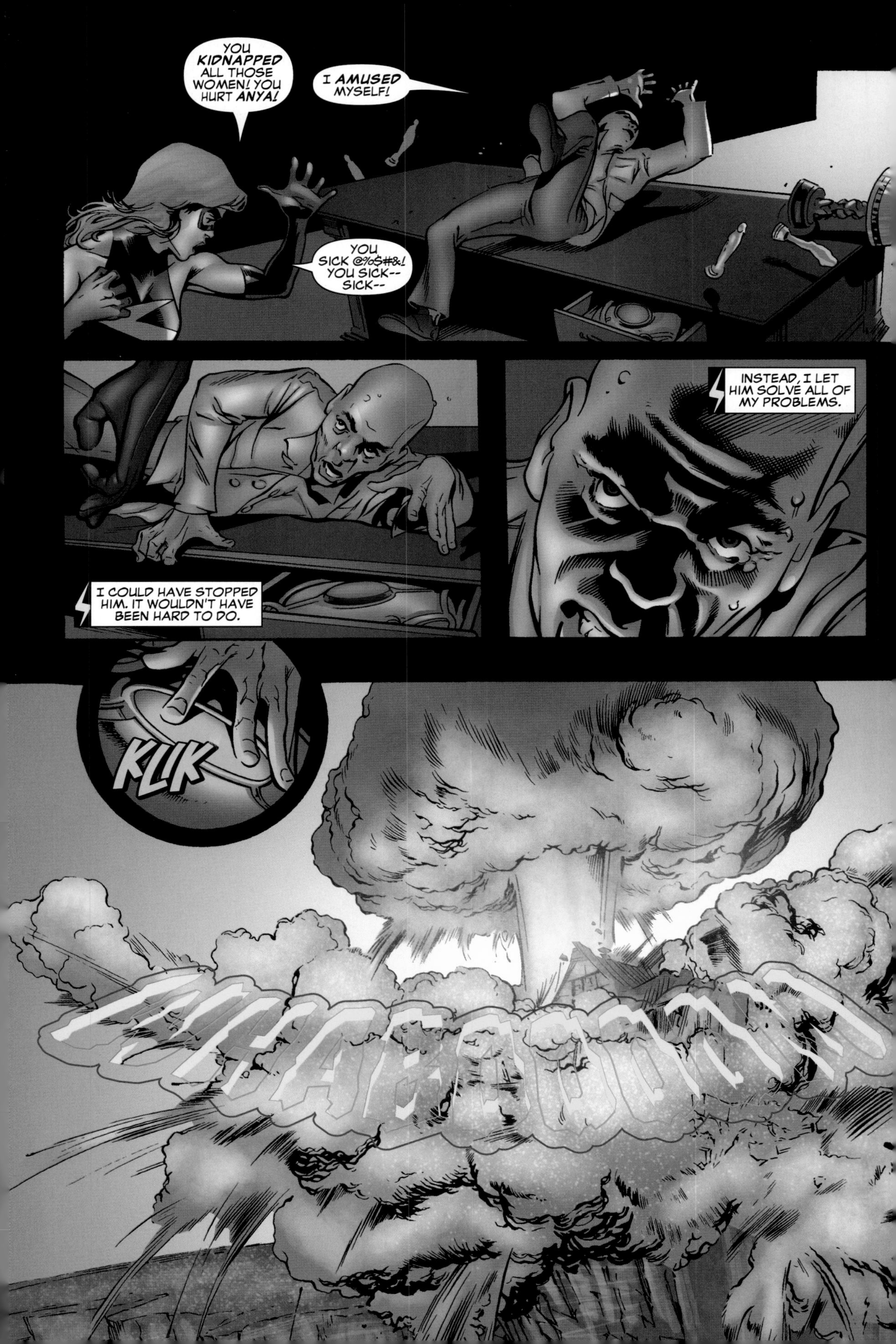

YOU KIDNAPPED ALL THOSE WOMEN! YOU HURT ANYA!
I AMUSED MYSELF!
YOU SICK @%$#&! YOU SICK-- SICK--
I COULD HAVE STOPPED HIM. IT WOULDN'T HAVE BEEN HARD TO DO.
INSTEAD, I LET HIM SOLVE ALL OF MY PROBLEMS.
KLIK

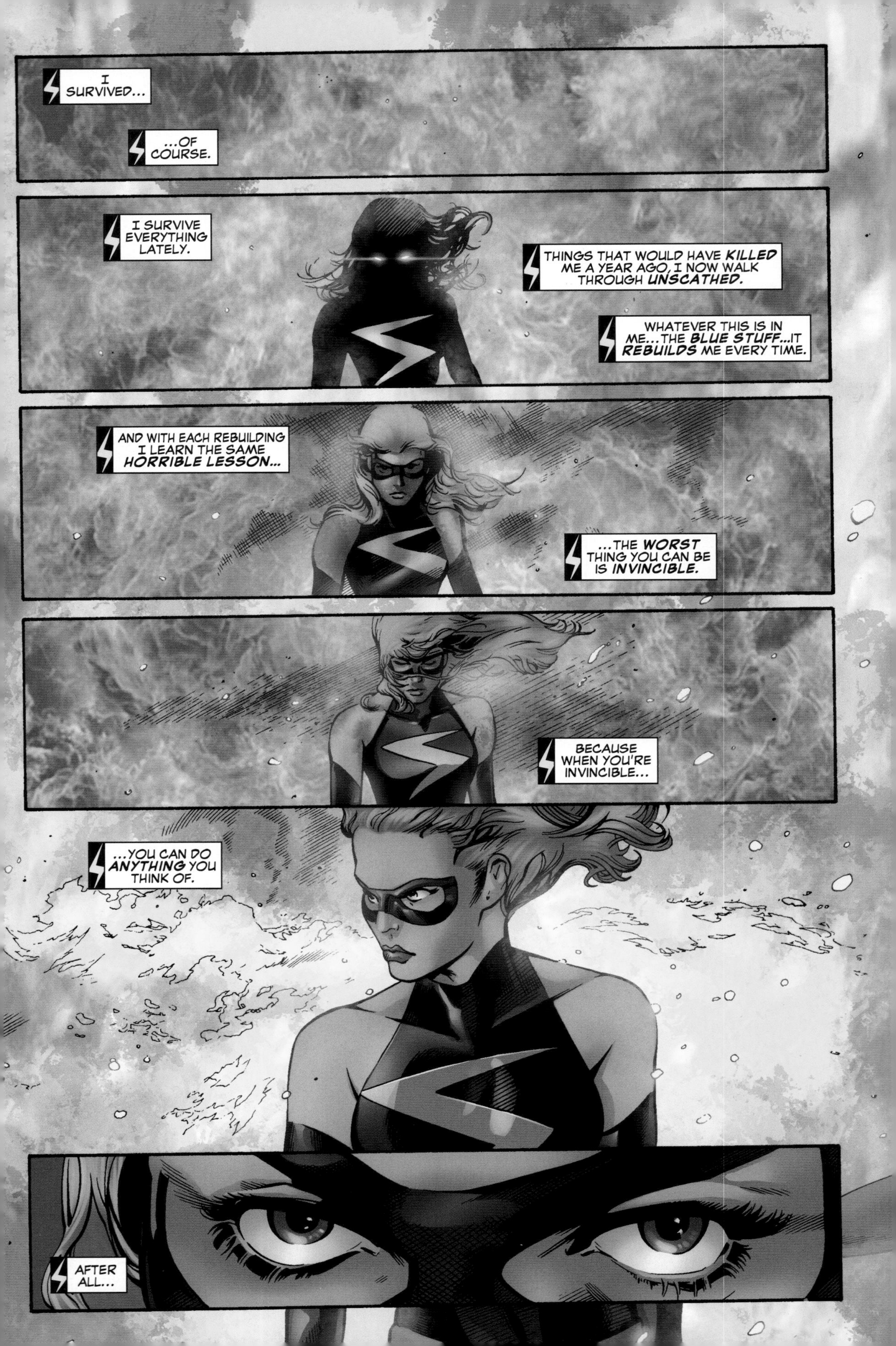

I SURVIVED...
...OF COURSE.
I SURVIVE EVERYTHING LATELY.
THINGS THAT WOULD HAVE KILLED ME A YEAR AGO, I NOW WALK THROUGH UNSCATHED.
WHATEVER THIS IS IN ME...THE BLUE STUFF...IT REBUILDS ME EVERY TIME.
AND WITH EACH REBUILDING I LEARN THE SAME HORRIBLE LESSON...
...THE WORST THING YOU CAN BE IS INVINCIBLE.
BECAUSE WHEN YOU'RE INVINCIBLE...
...YOU CAN DO ANYTHING YOU THINK OF.
AFTER ALL...

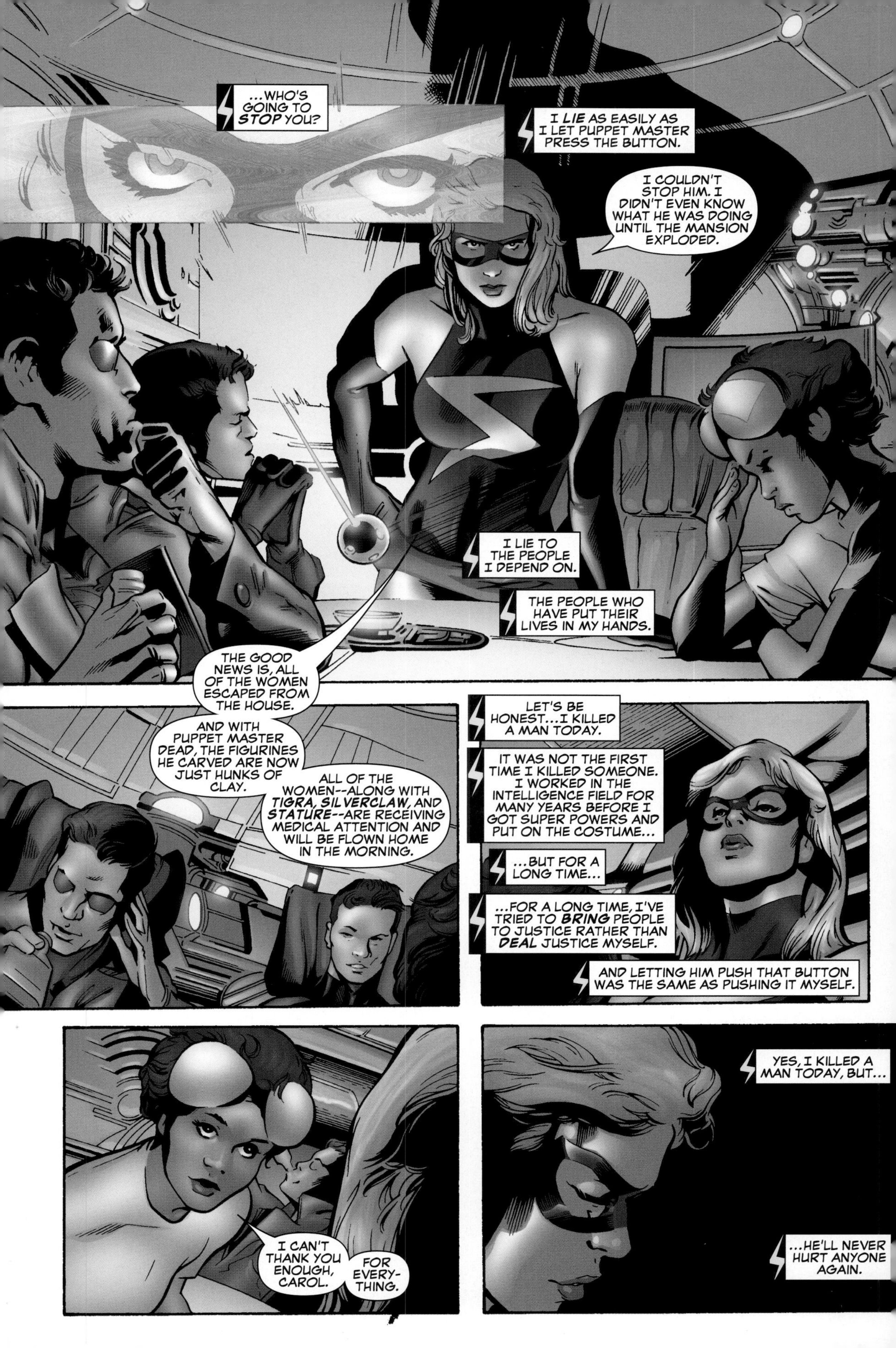

...WHO'S GOING TO STOP YOU?
I LIE AS EASILY AS I LET PUPPET MASTER PRESS THE BUTTON.
I COULDN'T STOP HIM. I DIDN'T EVEN KNOW WHAT HE WAS DOING UNTIL THE MANSION EXPLODED.
I LIE TO THE PEOPLE I DEPEND ON.
THE PEOPLE WHO HAVE PUT THEIR LIVES IN MY HANDS.
THE GOOD NEWS IS, ALL OF THE WOMEN ESCAPED FROM THE HOUSE.
AND WITH PUPPET MASTER DEAD, THE FIGURINES HE CARVED ARE NOW JUST HUNKS OF CLAY.
ALL OF THE WOMEN--ALONG WITH TIGRA, SILVERCLAW, AND STATURE--ARE RECEIVING MEDICAL ATTENTION AND WILL BE FLOWN HOME IN THE MORNING.
LET'S BE HONEST...I KILLED A MAN TODAY.
IT WAS NOT THE FIRST TIME I KILLED SOMEONE. I WORKED IN THE INTELLIGENCE FIELD FOR MANY YEARS BEFORE I GOT SUPER POWERS AND PUT ON THE COSTUME...
...BUT FOR A LONG TIME...
...FOR A LONG TIME, I'VE TRIED TO BRING PEOPLE TO JUSTICE RATHER THAN DEAL JUSTICE MYSELF.
AND LETTING HIM PUSH THAT BUTTON WAS THE SAME AS PUSHING IT MYSELF.
I CAN'T THANK YOU ENOUGH, CAROL.
FOR EVERY-THING.
YES, I KILLED A MAN TODAY, BUT...
...HE'LL NEVER HURT ANYONE AGAIN.

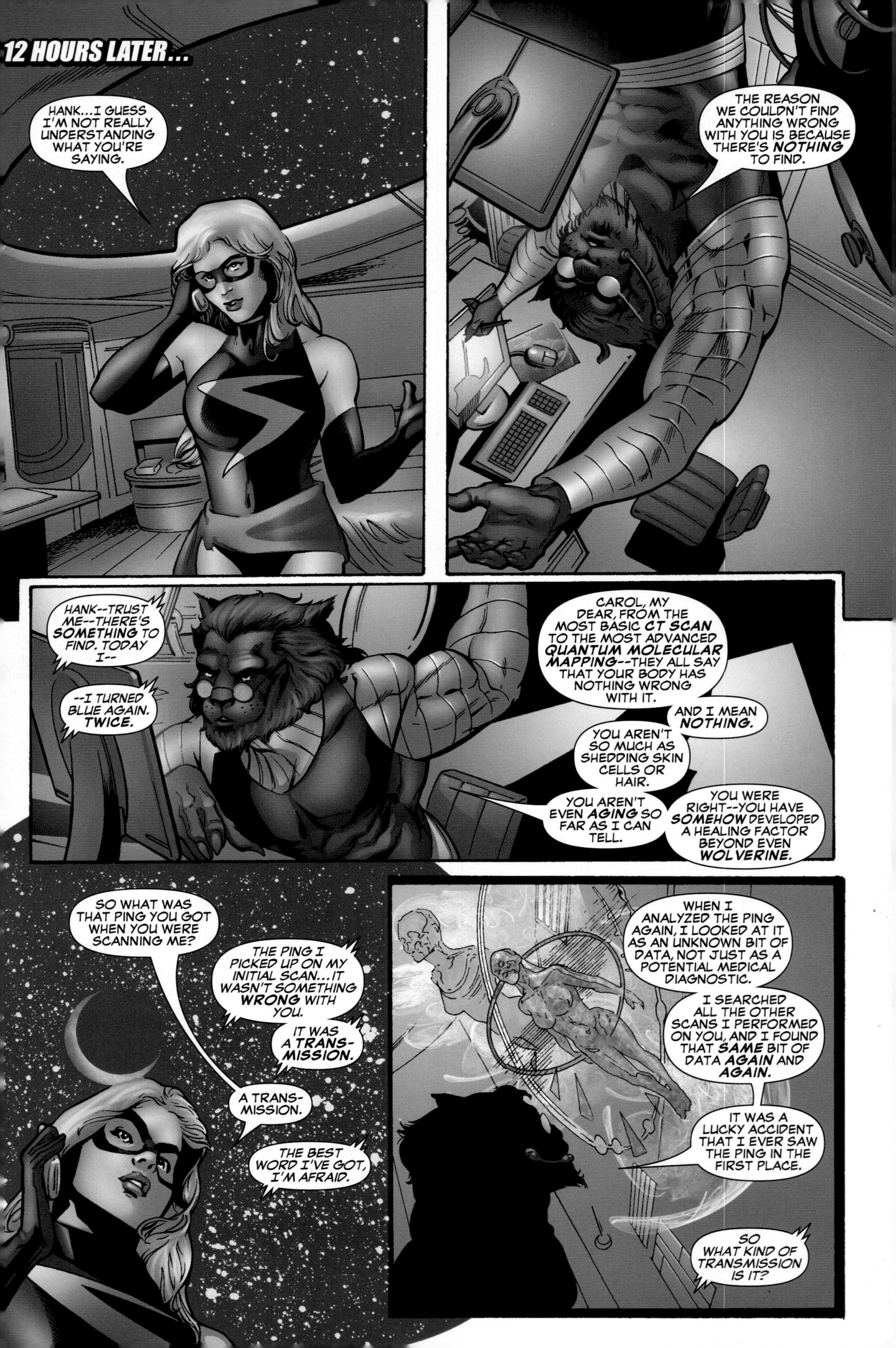
12 HOURS LATER...
HANK...I GUESS I'M NOT REALLY UNDERSTANDING WHAT YOU'RE SAYING.
THE REASON WE COULDN'T FIND ANYTHING WRONG WITH YOU IS BECAUSE THERE'S NOTHING TO FIND.
HANK--TRUST ME--THERE'S SOMETHING TO FIND. TODAY I--
--I TURNED BLUE AGAIN. TWICE.
CAROL, MY DEAR, FROM THE MOST BASIC CT SCAN TO THE MOST ADVANCED QUANTUM MOLECULAR MAPPING--THEY ALL SAY THAT YOUR BODY HAS NOTHING WRONG WITH IT.
AND I MEAN NOTHING.
YOU AREN'T SO MUCH AS SHEDDING SKIN CELLS OR HAIR.
YOU AREN'T EVEN AGING SO FAR AS I CAN TELL.
YOU WERE RIGHT--YOU HAVE SOMEHOW DEVELOPED A HEALING FACTOR BEYOND EVEN WOLVERINE.
SO WHAT WAS THAT PING YOU GOT WHEN YOU WERE SCANNING ME?
THE PING I PICKED UP ON MY INITIAL SCAN...IT WASN'T SOMETHING WRONG WITH YOU.
IT WAS A TRANS-MISSION.
A TRANS-MISSION.
THE BEST WORD I'VE GOT, I'M AFRAID.
WHEN I ANALYZED THE PING AGAIN, I LOOKED AT IT AS AN UNKNOWN BIT OF DATA, NOT JUST AS A POTENTIAL MEDICAL DIAGNOSTIC.
I SEARCHED ALL THE OTHER SCANS I PERFORMED ON YOU, AND I FOUND THAT SAME BIT OF DATA AGAIN AND AGAIN.
IT WAS A LUCKY ACCIDENT THAT I EVER SAW THE PING IN THE FIRST PLACE.
SO WHAT KIND OF TRANSMISSION IS IT?

CAROL, I MUST SAY I DO NOT KNOW.

BUT THE ONLY TIME I CAN THINK OF THAT IT IS USEFUL TO RESEND THE EXACT *SAME DATA* OVER AND OVER AGAIN--

IS A DISTRESS CALL.

OR A LOCATOR BEACON.

MY THOUGHTS EXACTLY.

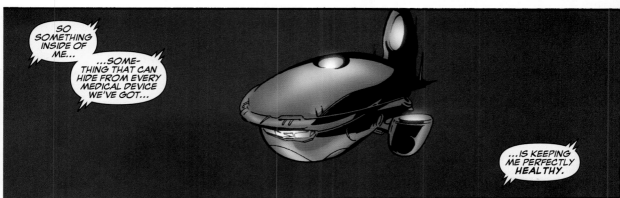

SO SOMETHING INSIDE OF ME...

...SOMETHING THAT CAN HIDE FROM EVERY MEDICAL DEVICE WE'VE GOT...

...IS KEEPING ME PERFECTLY *HEALTHY.*

WHILE ALSO TRYING TO GET BACK *HOME.* I'VE STARTED PICKING UP THE MATCHING VERSION OF THIS TRANSMISSION FROM LOW EARTH ORBIT.

SOMETHING OUT THERE IS RETURNING THE SIGNAL.

THE WHOLE REASON I CALLED JUST NOW IS THAT THE SIGNAL FROM ORBIT HAS BEEN GROWING STRONGER ALL DAY.

GETTING *LOUDER* FOR LACK OF A BETTER WORD. I THINK SOME-THING MIGHT BE--

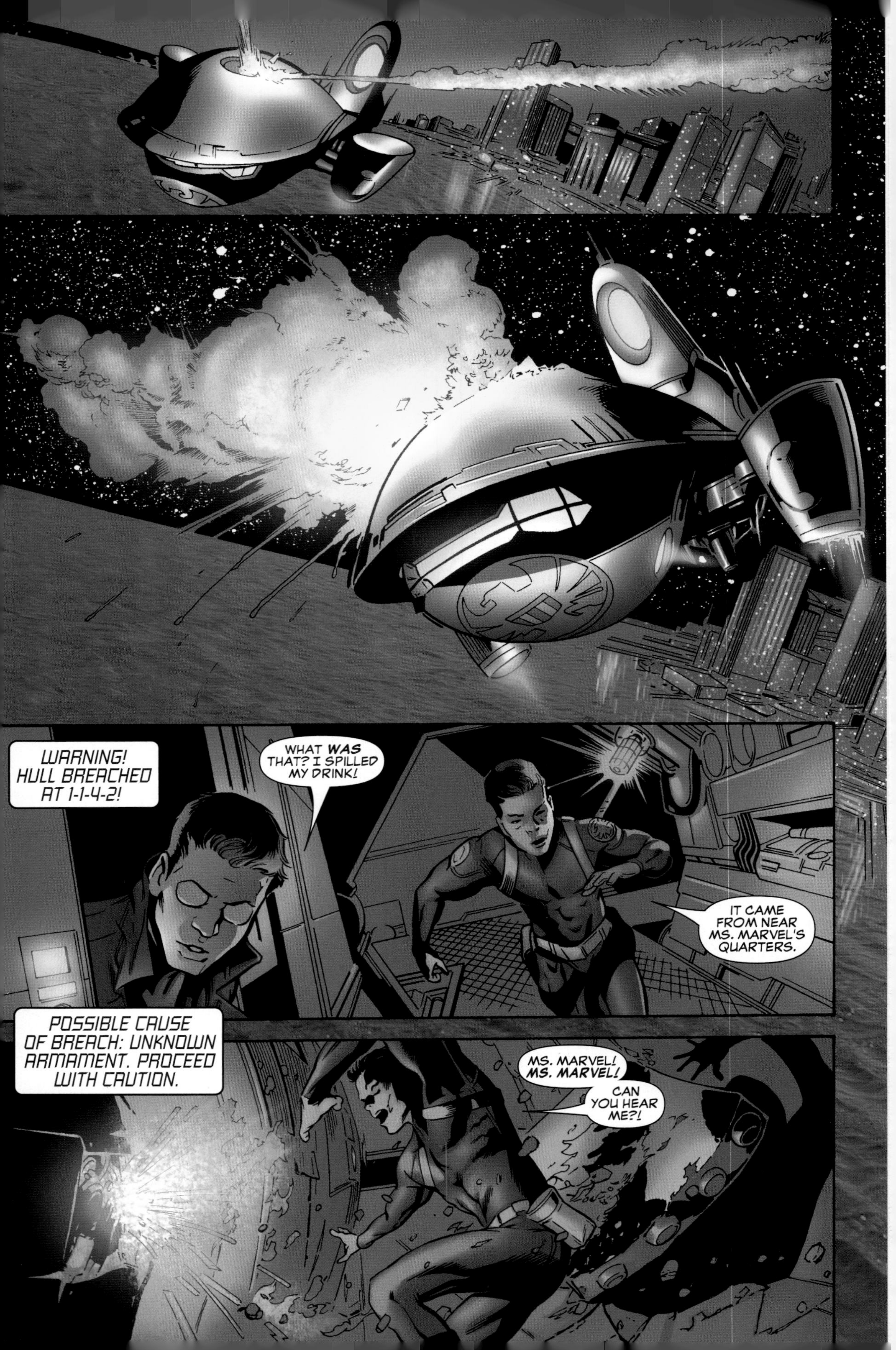

WARNING! HULL BREACHED AT 1-1-4-2!
WHAT WAS THAT? I SPILLED MY DRINK!
IT CAME FROM NEAR MS. MARVEL'S QUARTERS.
POSSIBLE CAUSE OF BREACH: UNKNOWN ARMAMENT. PROCEED WITH CAUTION.
MS. MARVEL! MS. MARVEL!
CAN YOU HEAR ME?!

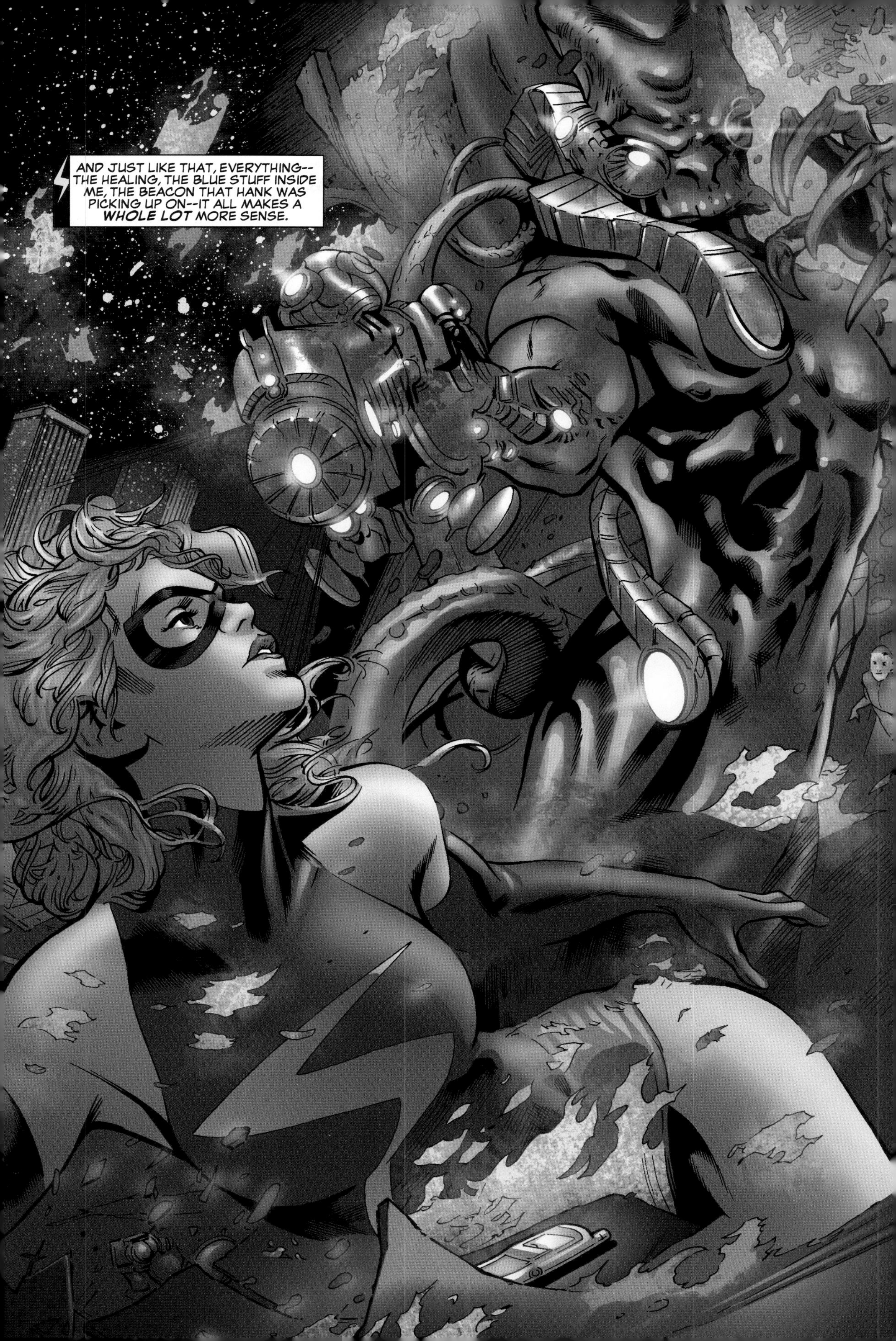
AND JUST LIKE THAT, EVERYTHING--THE HEALING, THE BLUE STUFF INSIDE ME, THE BEACON THAT HANK WAS PICKING UP ON--IT ALL MAKES A WHOLE LOT MORE SENSE.

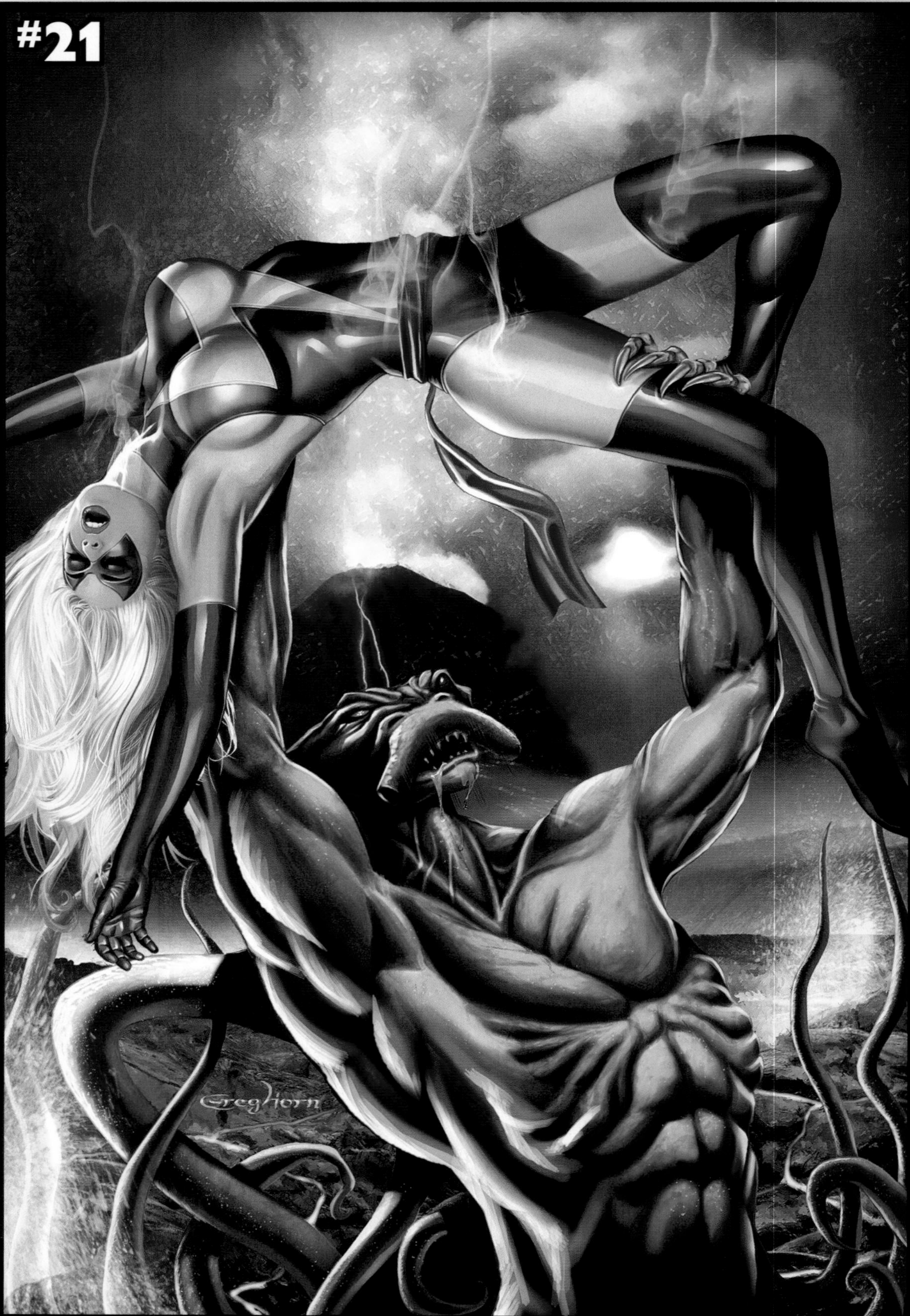
#21
GregHorn

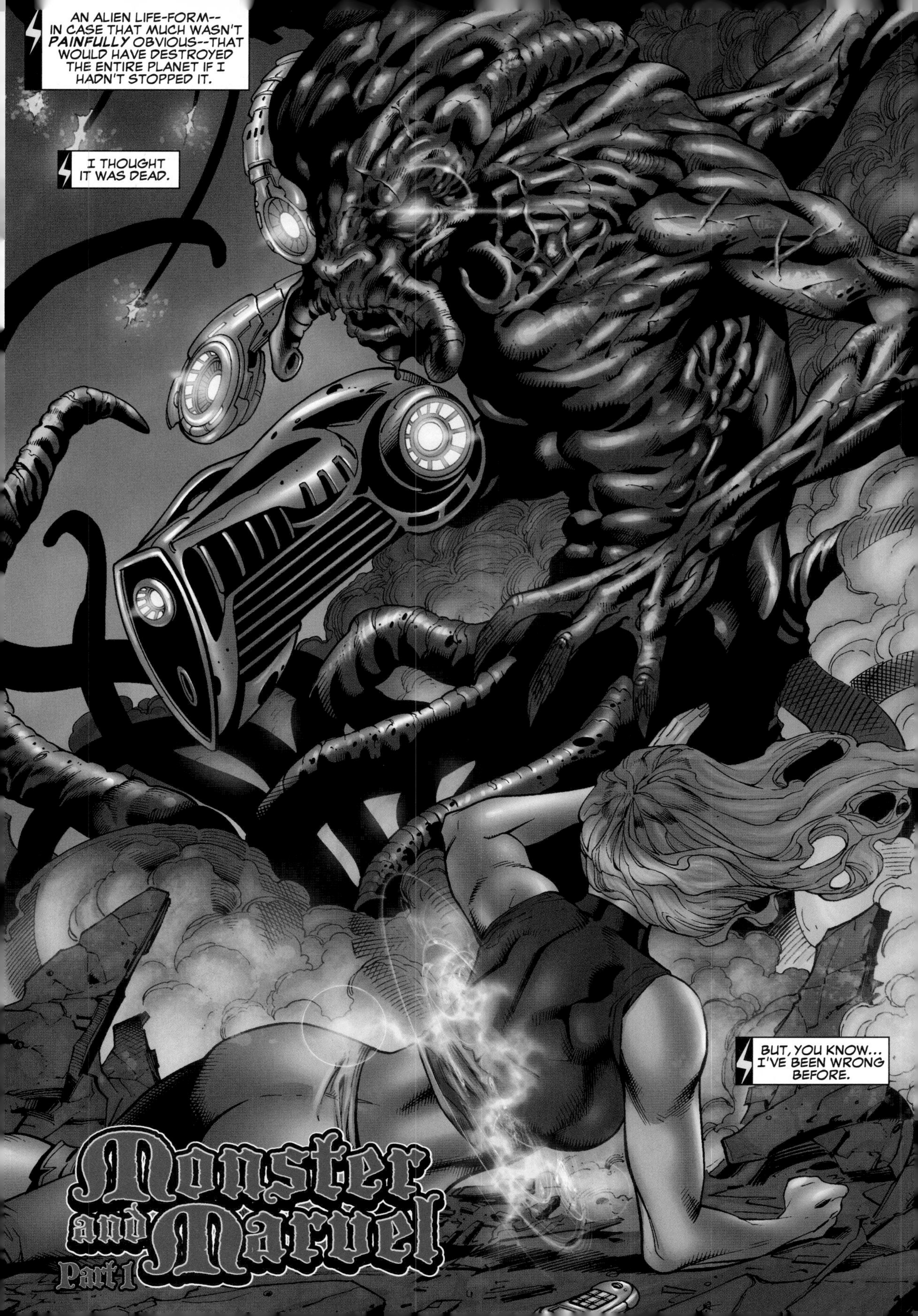
AN ALIEN LIFE-FORM-- IN CASE THAT MUCH WASN'T *PAINFULLY* OBVIOUS--THAT WOULD HAVE DESTROYED THE ENTIRE PLANET IF I HADN'T STOPPED IT.
I THOUGHT IT WAS DEAD.
BUT, YOU KNOW... I'VE BEEN WRONG BEFORE.
Monster and Marvel Part 1

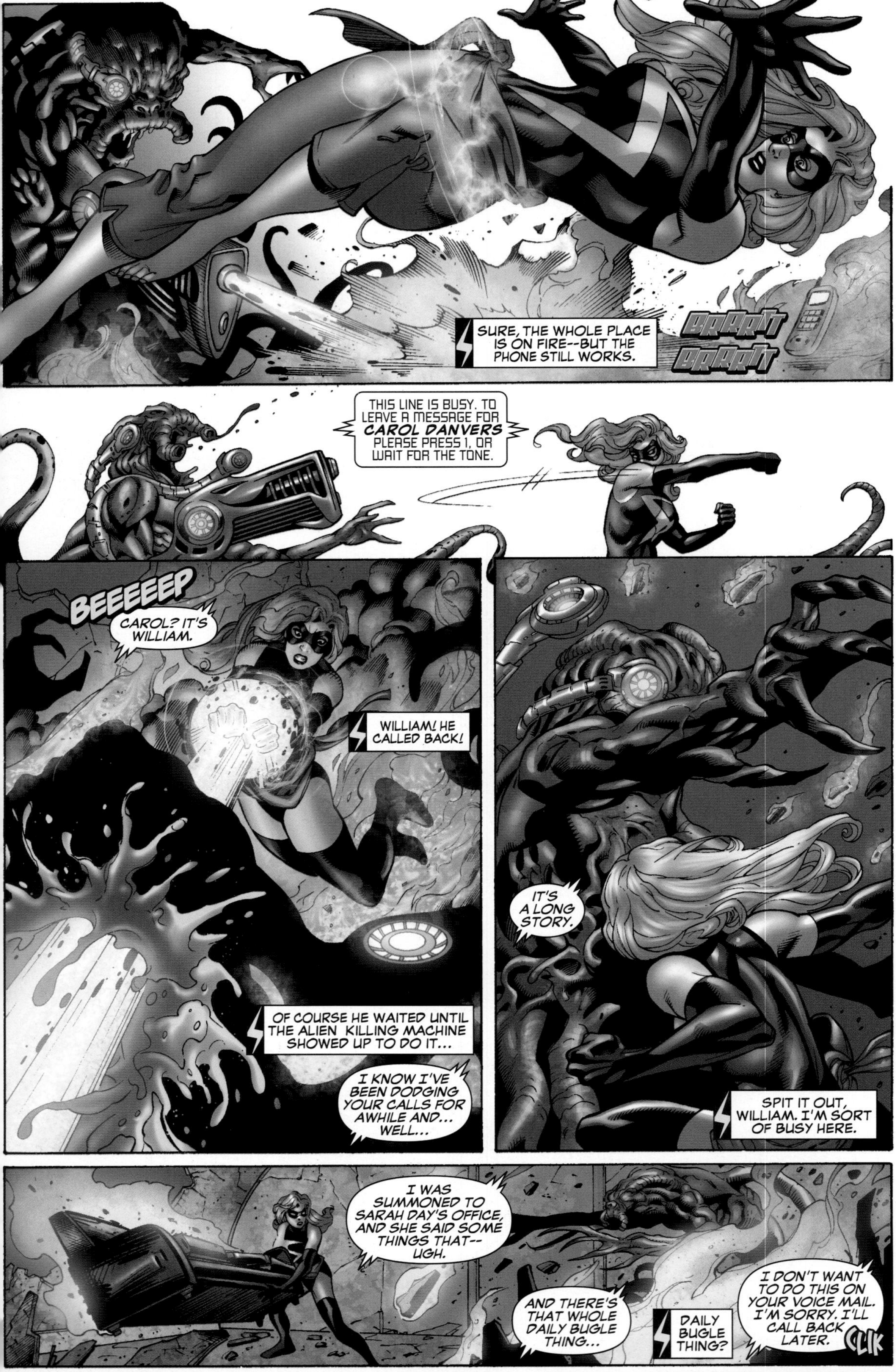

SURE, THE WHOLE PLACE IS ON FIRE--BUT THE PHONE STILL WORKS.
BRRRTT BRRRTT
THIS LINE IS BUSY. TO LEAVE A MESSAGE FOR CAROL DANVERS PLEASE PRESS 1, OR WAIT FOR THE TONE.
BEEEEEP
CAROL? IT'S WILLIAM.
WILLIAM! HE CALLED BACK!
OF COURSE HE WAITED UNTIL THE ALIEN KILLING MACHINE SHOWED UP TO DO IT...
I KNOW I'VE BEEN DODGING YOUR CALLS FOR AWHILE AND... WELL...
IT'S A LONG STORY.
SPIT IT OUT, WILLIAM. I'M SORT OF BUSY HERE.
I WAS SUMMONED TO SARAH DAY'S OFFICE, AND SHE SAID SOME THINGS THAT-- UGH.
AND THERE'S THAT WHOLE DAILY BUGLE THING...
DAILY BUGLE THING?
I DON'T WANT TO DO THIS ON YOUR VOICE MAIL. I'M SORRY. I'LL CALL BACK LATER.
CLIK

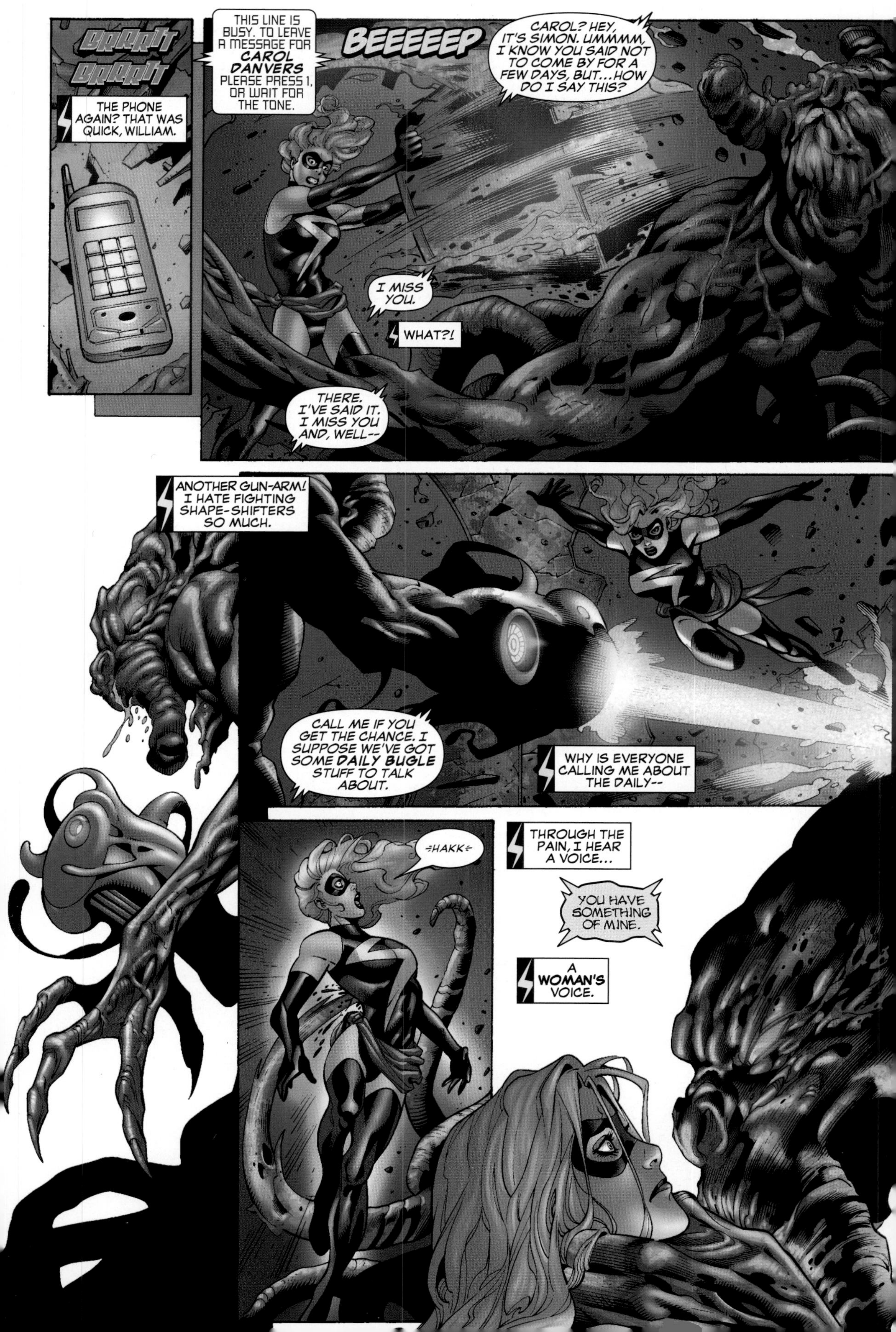
BRRRIT
BRRRIT
THE PHONE AGAIN? THAT WAS QUICK, WILLIAM.
THIS LINE IS BUSY. TO LEAVE A MESSAGE FOR CAROL DANVERS PLEASE PRESS 1, OR WAIT FOR THE TONE.
BEEEEEP
CAROL? HEY, IT'S SIMON. UMMMM, I KNOW YOU SAID NOT TO COME BY FOR A FEW DAYS, BUT...HOW DO I SAY THIS?
I MISS YOU.
WHAT?!
THERE. I'VE SAID IT. I MISS YOU AND, WELL--
ANOTHER GUN-ARM! I HATE FIGHTING SHAPE-SHIFTERS SO MUCH.
CALL ME IF YOU GET THE CHANCE. I SUPPOSE WE'VE GOT SOME DAILY BUGLE STUFF TO TALK ABOUT.
WHY IS EVERYONE CALLING ME ABOUT THE DAILY--
HAKK
THROUGH THE PAIN, I HEAR A VOICE...
YOU HAVE SOMETHING OF MINE.
A WOMAN'S VOICE.

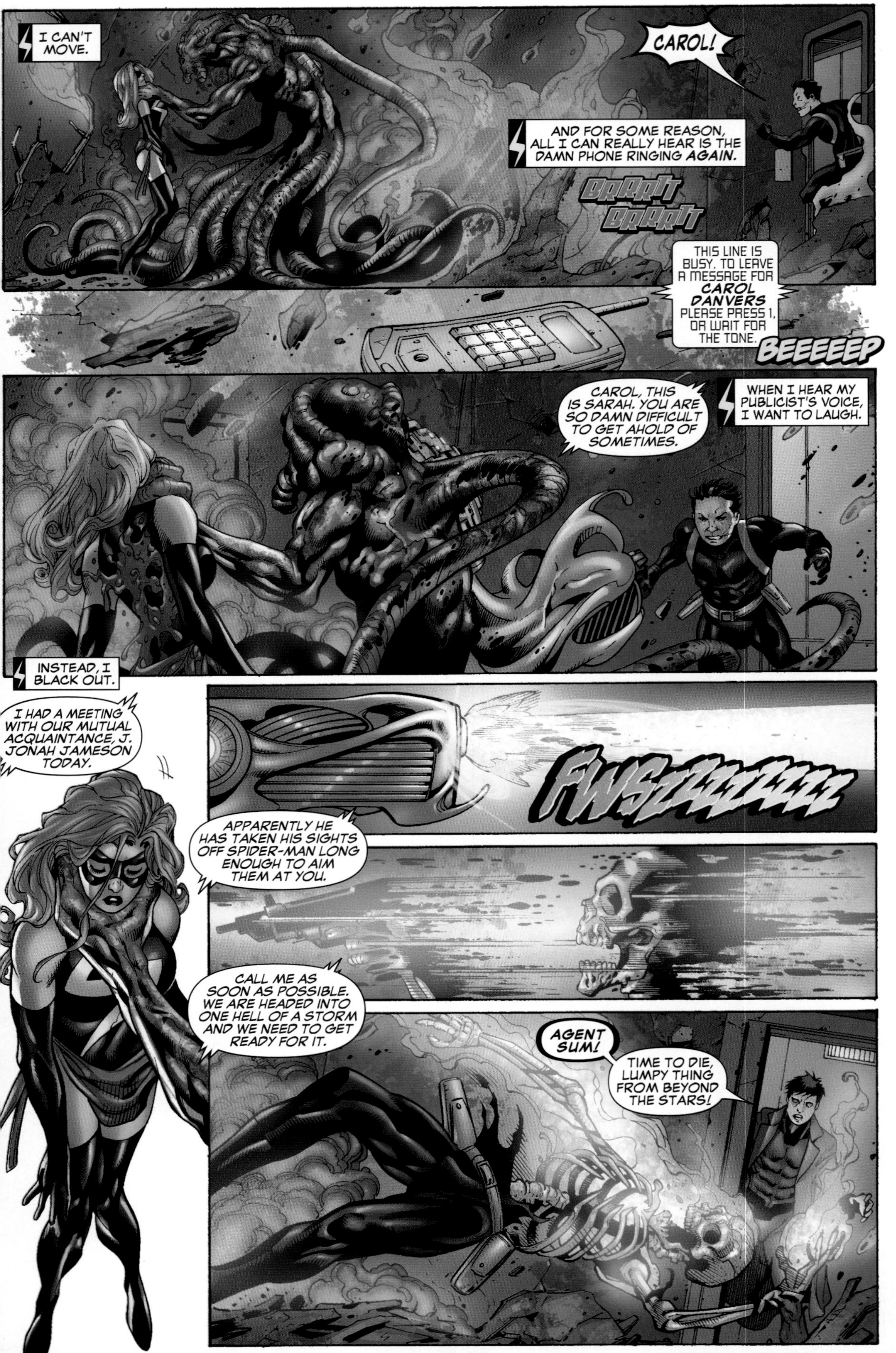
I CAN'T MOVE.
CAROL!
AND FOR SOME REASON, ALL I CAN REALLY HEAR IS THE DAMN PHONE RINGING AGAIN.
BRRRIT BRRRIT
THIS LINE IS BUSY. TO LEAVE A MESSAGE FOR CAROL DANVERS PLEASE PRESS 1, OR WAIT FOR THE TONE.
BEEEEEP
CAROL, THIS IS SARAH. YOU ARE SO DAMN DIFFICULT TO GET AHOLD OF SOMETIMES.
WHEN I HEAR MY PUBLICIST'S VOICE, I WANT TO LAUGH.
INSTEAD, I BLACK OUT.
I HAD A MEETING WITH OUR MUTUAL ACQUAINTANCE, J. JONAH JAMESON TODAY.
FWSZZZZZZZZ
APPARENTLY HE HAS TAKEN HIS SIGHTS OFF SPIDER-MAN LONG ENOUGH TO AIM THEM AT YOU.
CALL ME AS SOON AS POSSIBLE. WE ARE HEADED INTO ONE HELL OF A STORM AND WE NEED TO GET READY FOR IT.
AGENT SUM!
TIME TO DIE, LUMPY THING FROM BEYOND THE STARS!

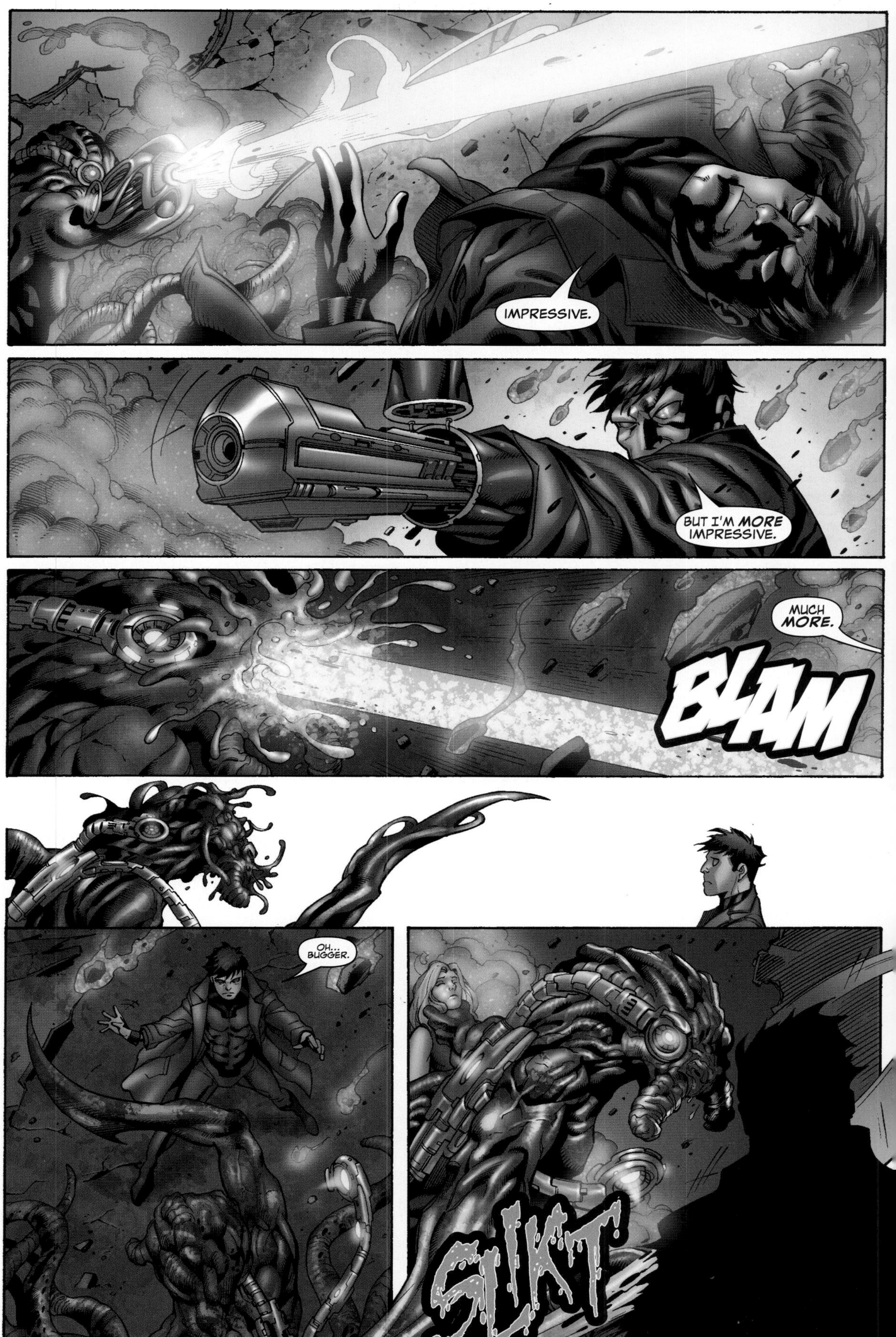

IMPRESSIVE.
BUT I'M MORE IMPRESSIVE.
MUCH MORE.
BLAM
OH... BUGGER.
SLIKT

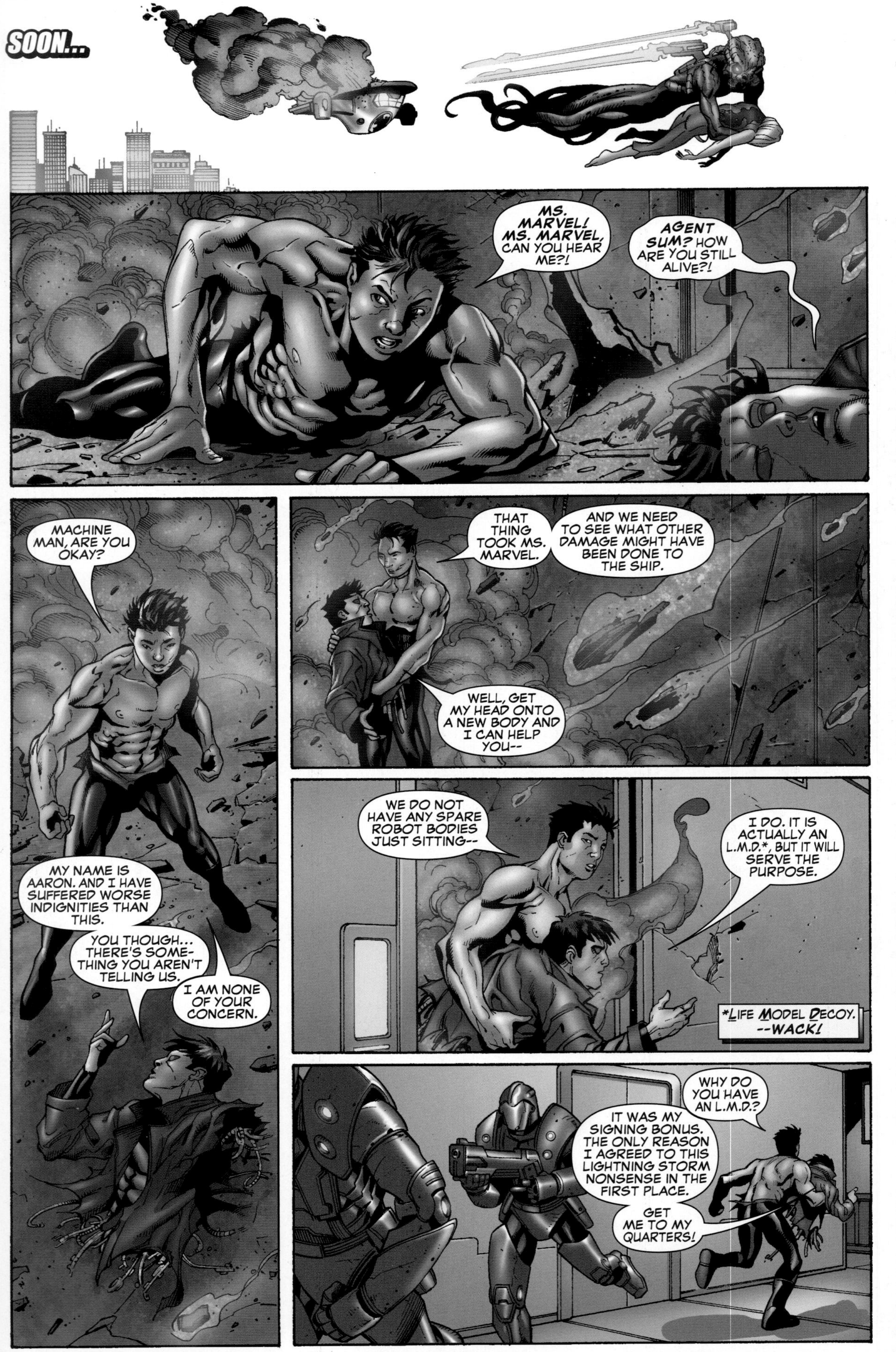
SOON...
MS. MARVEL! MS. MARVEL, CAN YOU HEAR ME?!
AGENT SUM? HOW ARE YOU STILL ALIVE?!
MACHINE MAN, ARE YOU OKAY?
MY NAME IS AARON. AND I HAVE SUFFERED WORSE INDIGNITIES THAN THIS.
YOU THOUGH... THERE'S SOMETHING YOU AREN'T TELLING US.
I AM NONE OF YOUR CONCERN.
THAT THING TOOK MS. MARVEL.
AND WE NEED TO SEE WHAT OTHER DAMAGE MIGHT HAVE BEEN DONE TO THE SHIP.
WELL, GET MY HEAD ONTO A NEW BODY AND I CAN HELP YOU--
WE DO NOT HAVE ANY SPARE ROBOT BODIES JUST SITTING--
I DO. IT IS ACTUALLY AN L.M.D.*, BUT IT WILL SERVE THE PURPOSE.
*LIFE MODEL DECOY. --WACK!
WHY DO YOU HAVE AN L.M.D.?
IT WAS MY SIGNING BONUS. THE ONLY REASON I AGREED TO THIS LIGHTNING STORM NONSENSE IN THE FIRST PLACE.
GET ME TO MY QUARTERS!

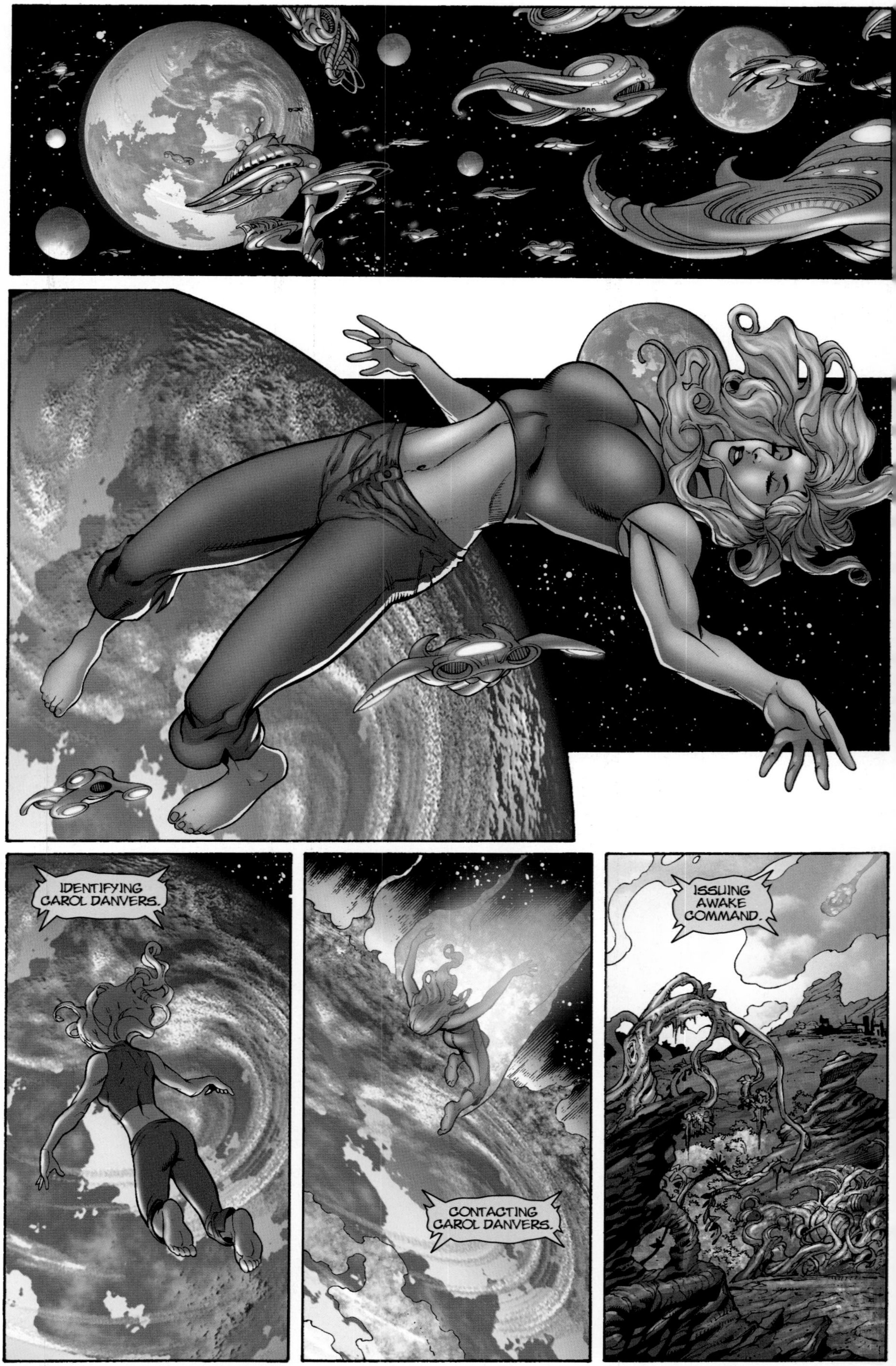
IDENTIFYING CAROL DANVERS.
CONTACTING CAROL DANVERS.
ISSUING AWAKE COMMAND.

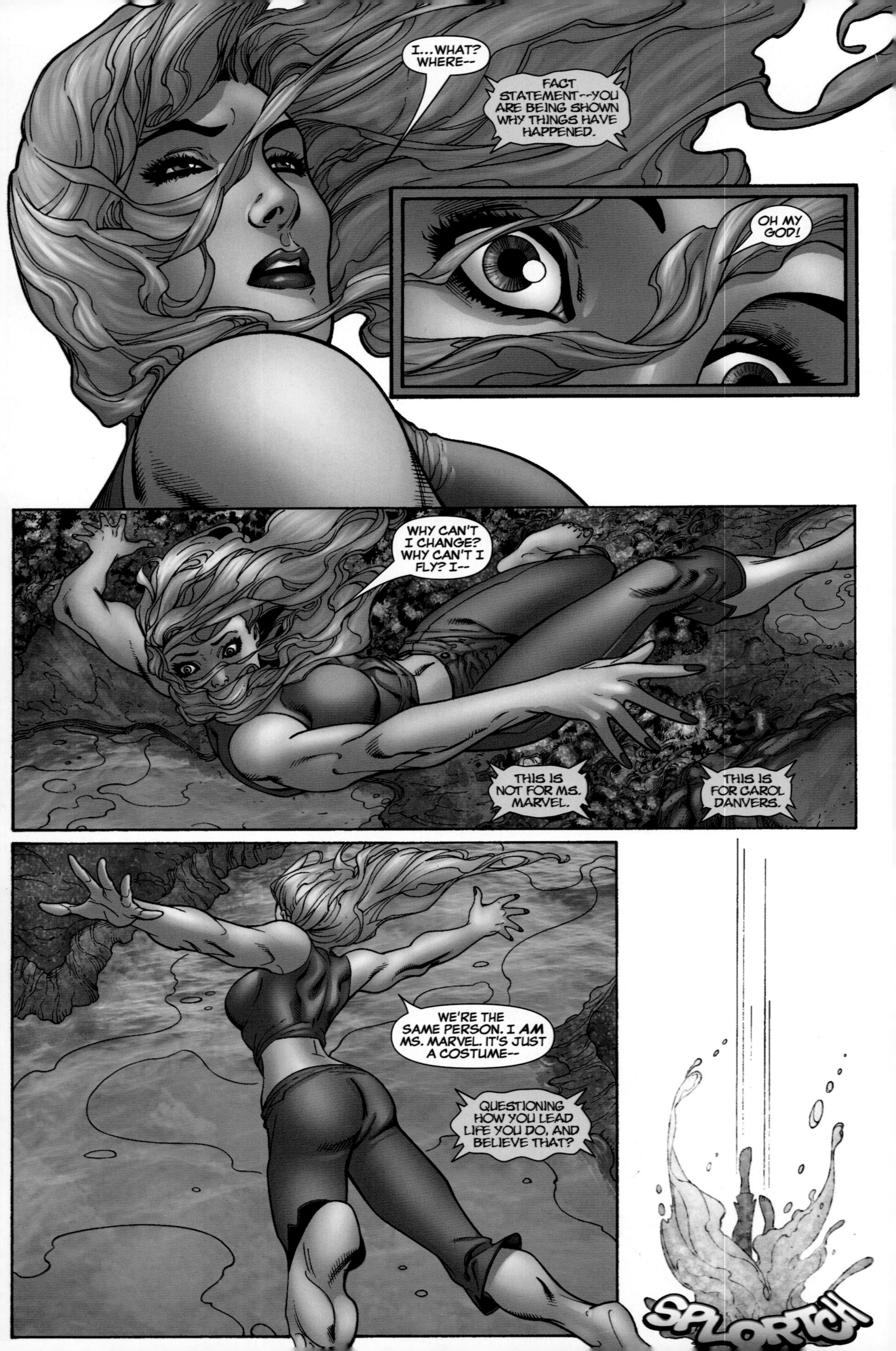
I... WHAT? WHERE--
FACT STATEMENT--YOU ARE BEING SHOWN WHY THINGS HAVE HAPPENED.
OH MY GOD!
WHY CAN'T I CHANGE? WHY CAN'T I FLY? I--
THIS IS NOT FOR MS. MARVEL.
THIS IS FOR CAROL DANVERS.
WE'RE THE SAME PERSON. I AM MS. MARVEL. IT'S JUST A COSTUME--
QUESTIONING HOW YOU LEAD LIFE YOU DO, AND BELIEVE THAT?
SPLORTCH

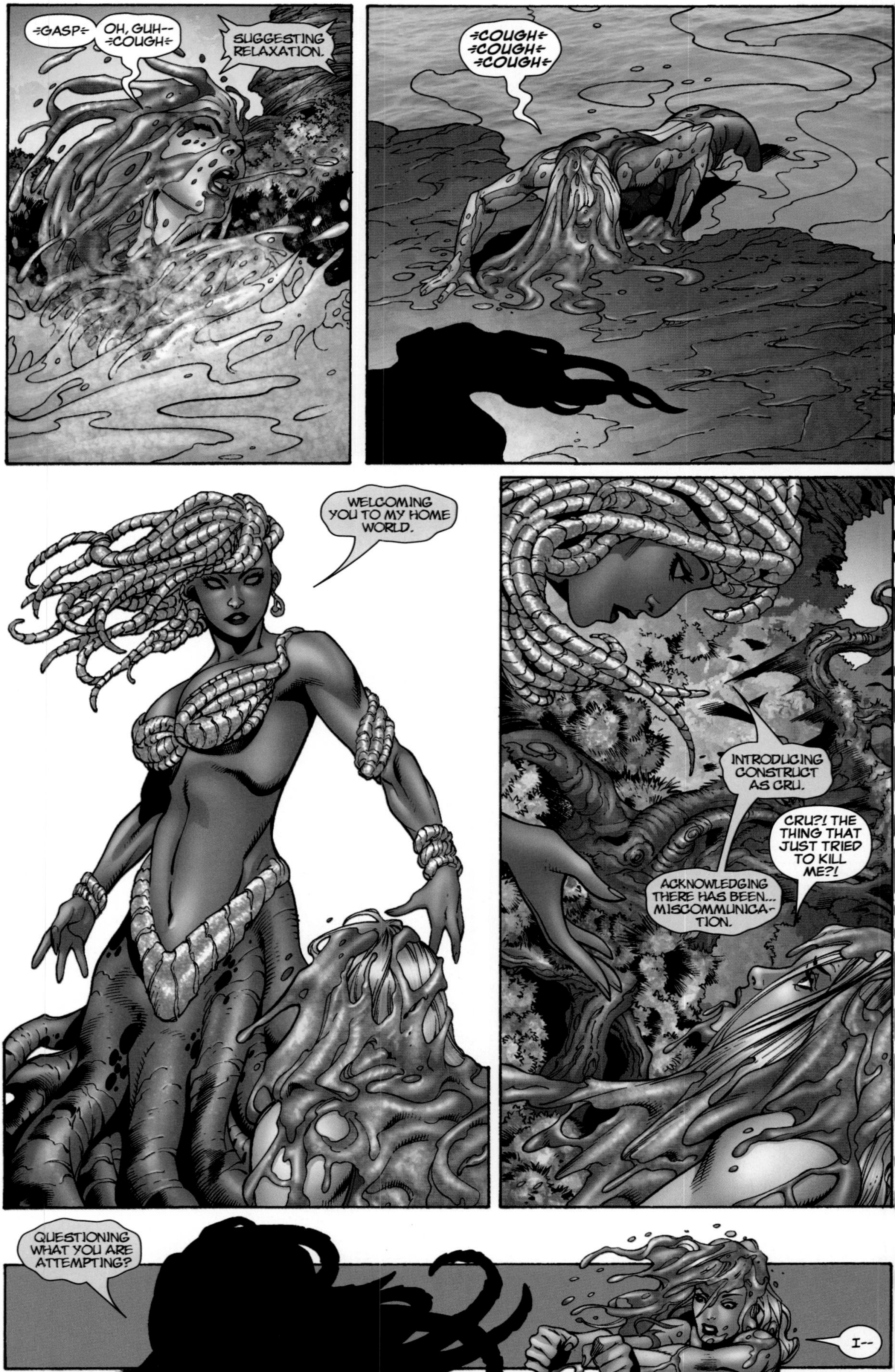

GASP
OH, GUH-- COUGH
SUGGESTING RELAXATION.
COUGH COUGH COUGH
WELCOMING YOU TO MY HOME WORLD.
INTRODUCING CONSTRUCT AS CRU.
CRU?! THE THING THAT JUST TRIED TO KILL ME?!
ACKNOWLEDGING THERE HAS BEEN... MISCOMMUNICATION.
QUESTIONING WHAT YOU ARE ATTEMPTING?
I--

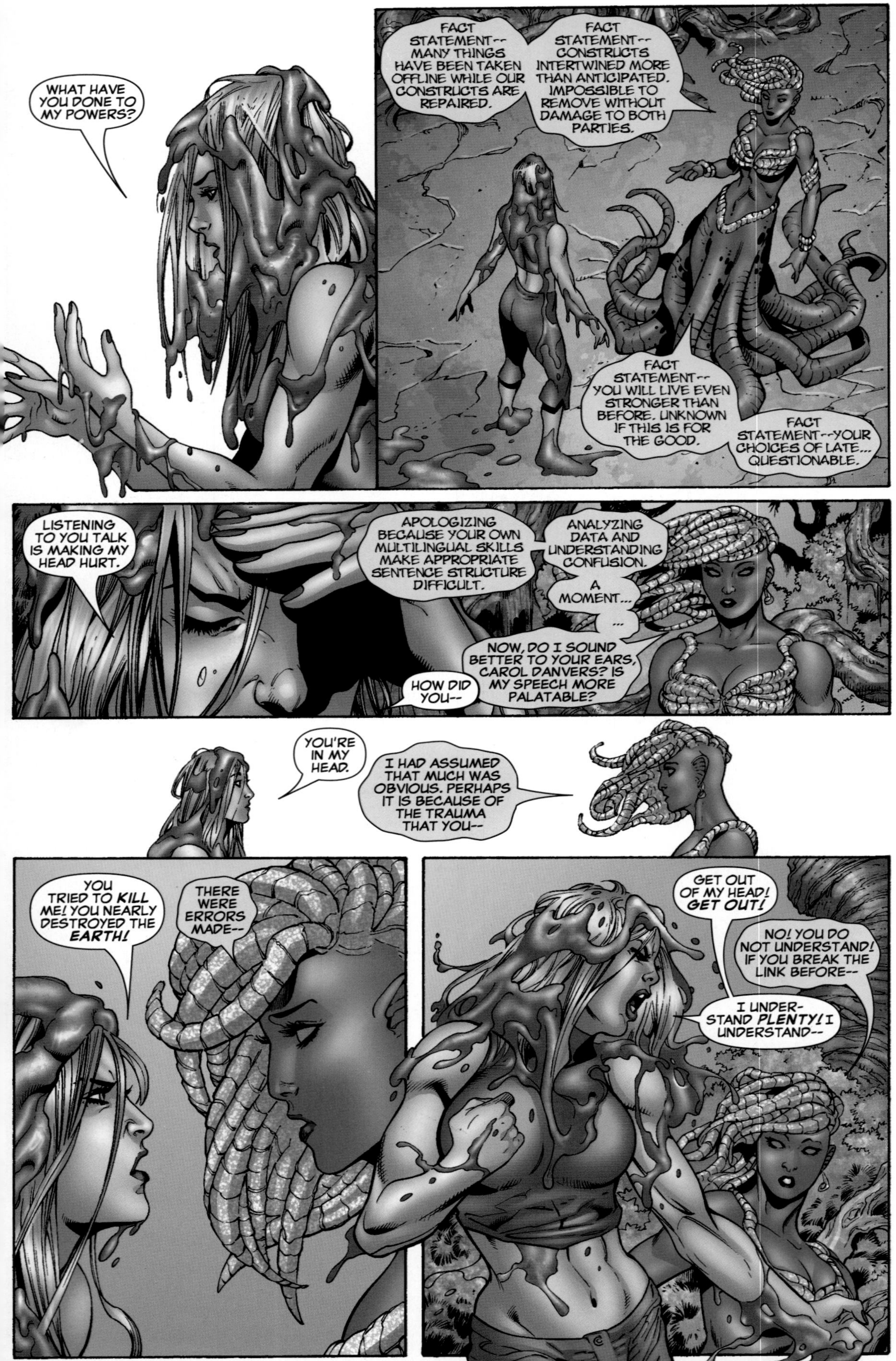
WHAT HAVE YOU DONE TO MY POWERS?
FACT STATEMENT-- MANY THINGS HAVE BEEN TAKEN OFFLINE WHILE OUR CONSTRUCTS ARE REPAIRED.
FACT STATEMENT-- CONSTRUCTS INTERTWINED MORE THAN ANTICIPATED. IMPOSSIBLE TO REMOVE WITHOUT DAMAGE TO BOTH PARTIES.
FACT STATEMENT-- YOU WILL LIVE EVEN STRONGER THAN BEFORE. UNKNOWN IF THIS IS FOR THE GOOD.
FACT STATEMENT--YOUR CHOICES OF LATE... QUESTIONABLE.
LISTENING TO YOU TALK IS MAKING MY HEAD HURT.
APOLOGIZING BECAUSE YOUR OWN MULTILINGUAL SKILLS MAKE APPROPRIATE SENTENCE STRUCTURE DIFFICULT.
ANALYZING DATA AND UNDERSTANDING CONFUSION.
A MOMENT...
...
NOW, DO I SOUND BETTER TO YOUR EARS, CAROL DANVERS? IS MY SPEECH MORE PALATABLE?
HOW DID YOU--
YOU'RE IN MY HEAD.
I HAD ASSUMED THAT MUCH WAS OBVIOUS. PERHAPS IT IS BECAUSE OF THE TRAUMA THAT YOU--
YOU TRIED TO KILL ME! YOU NEARLY DESTROYED THE EARTH!
THERE WERE ERRORS MADE--
GET OUT OF MY HEAD! GET OUT!
NO! YOU DO NOT UNDERSTAND! IF YOU BREAK THE LINK BEFORE--
I UNDER-STAND PLENTY! I UNDERSTAND--

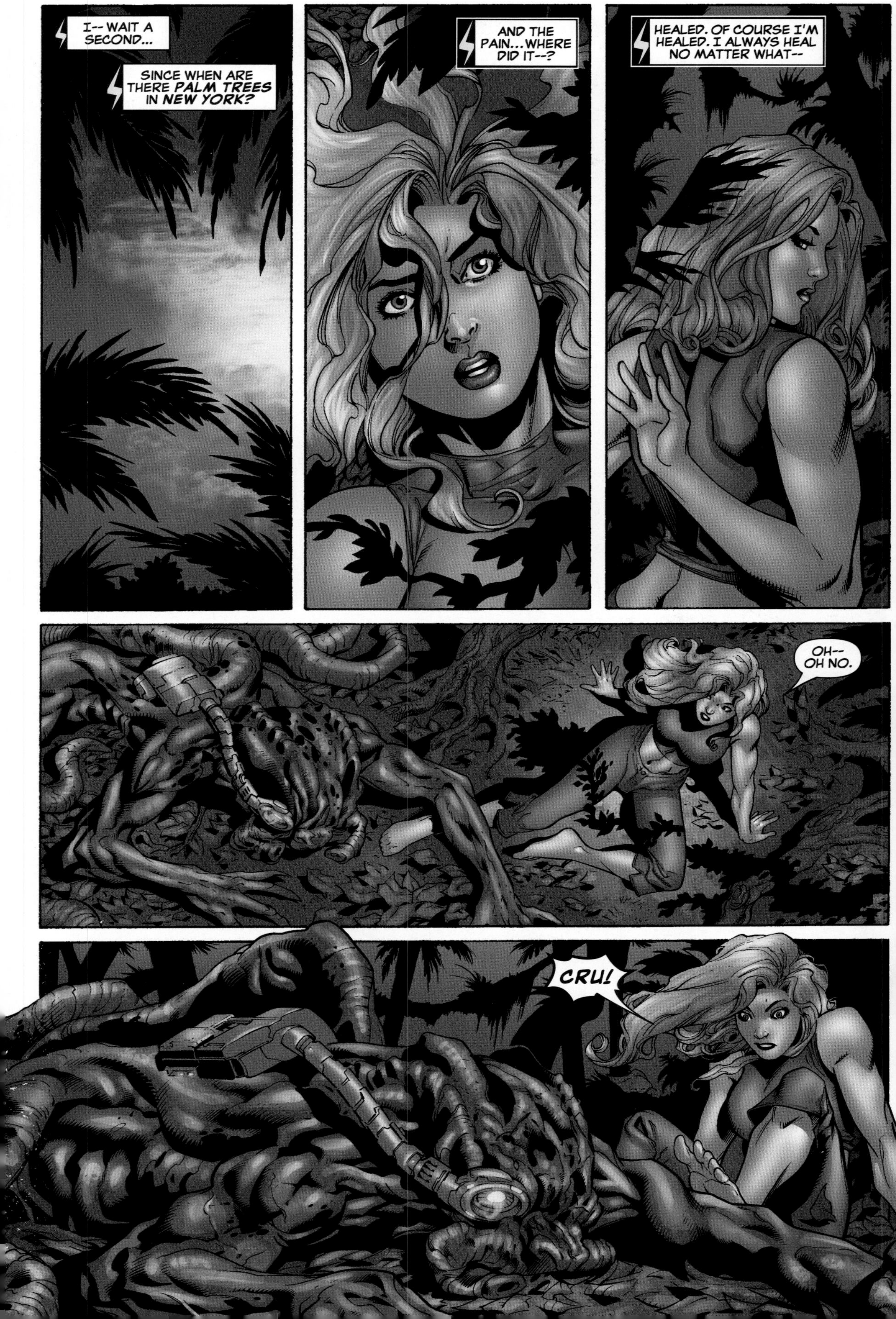
I-- WAIT A SECOND...
SINCE WHEN ARE THERE PALM TREES IN NEW YORK?
AND THE PAIN...WHERE DID IT--?
HEALED. OF COURSE I'M HEALED. I ALWAYS HEAL NO MATTER WHAT--
OH-- OH NO.
CRU!

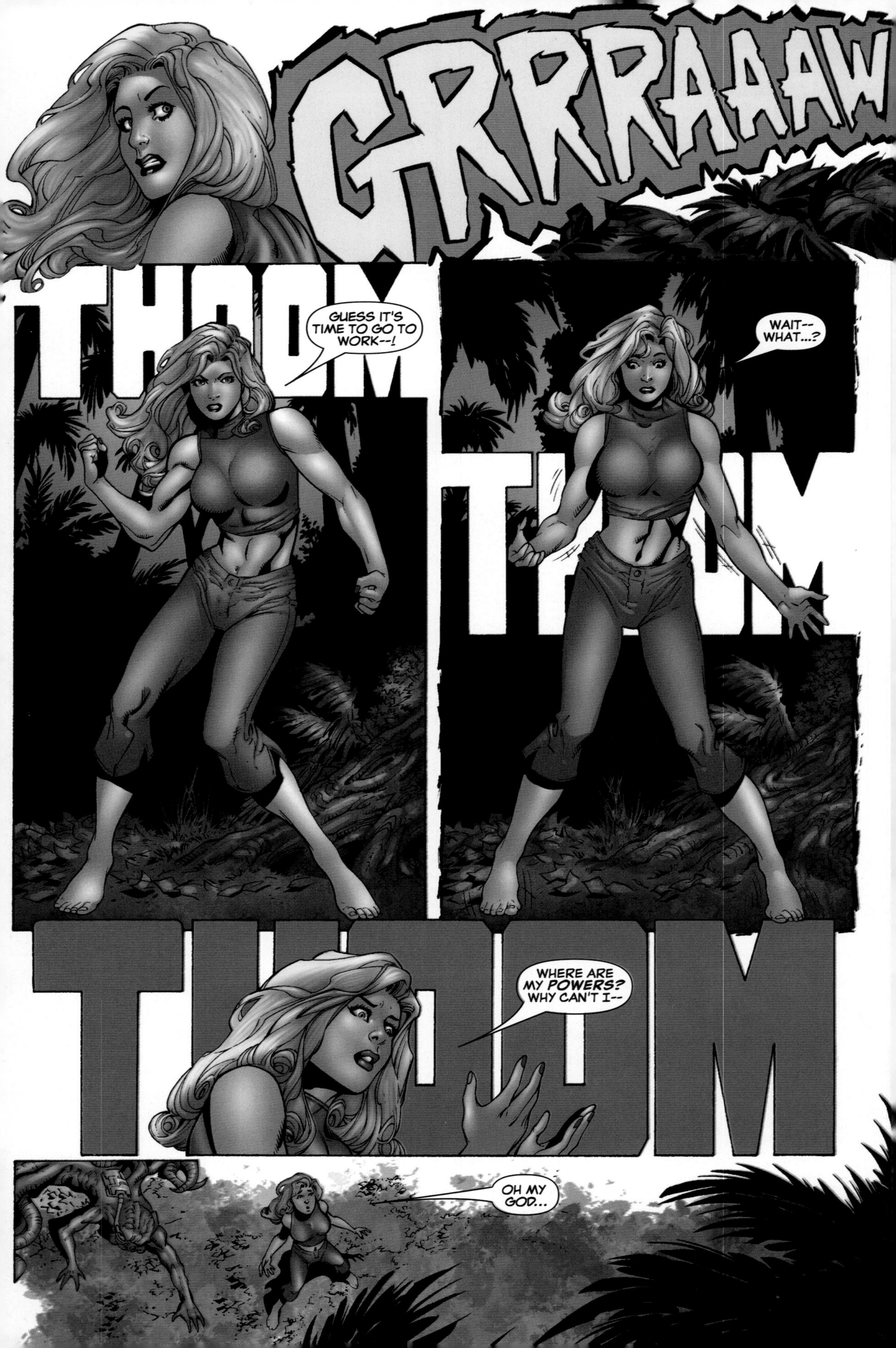
GRRRAAAW
THOOM
GUESS IT'S TIME TO GO TO WORK--!
WAIT-- WHAT...?
WHERE ARE MY *POWERS?* WHY CAN'T I--
OH MY GOD...

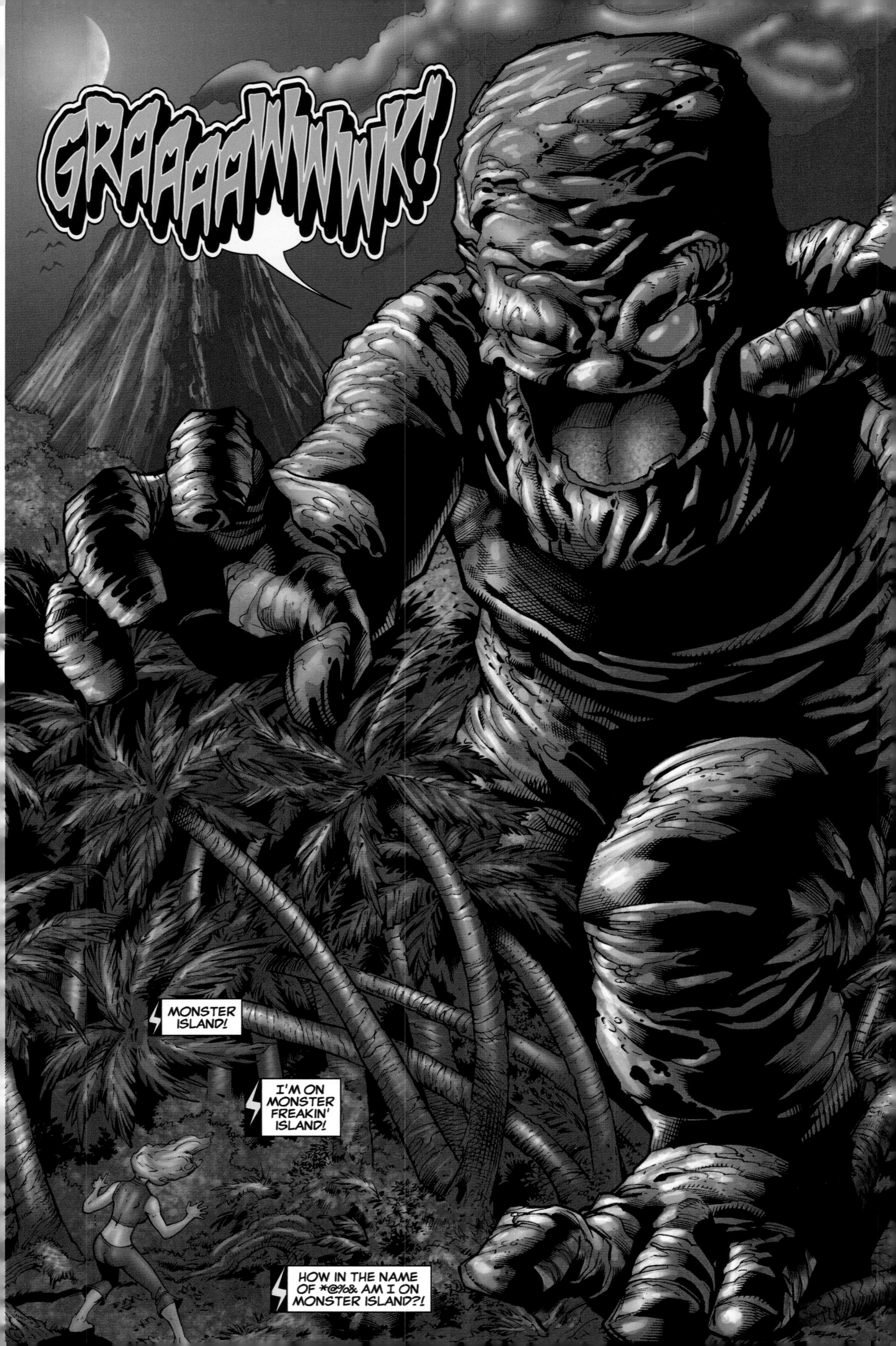
GRAAAAWWWWK!
MONSTER ISLAND!
I'M ON MONSTER FREAKIN' ISLAND!
HOW IN THE NAME OF *@%& AM I ON MONSTER ISLAND?!

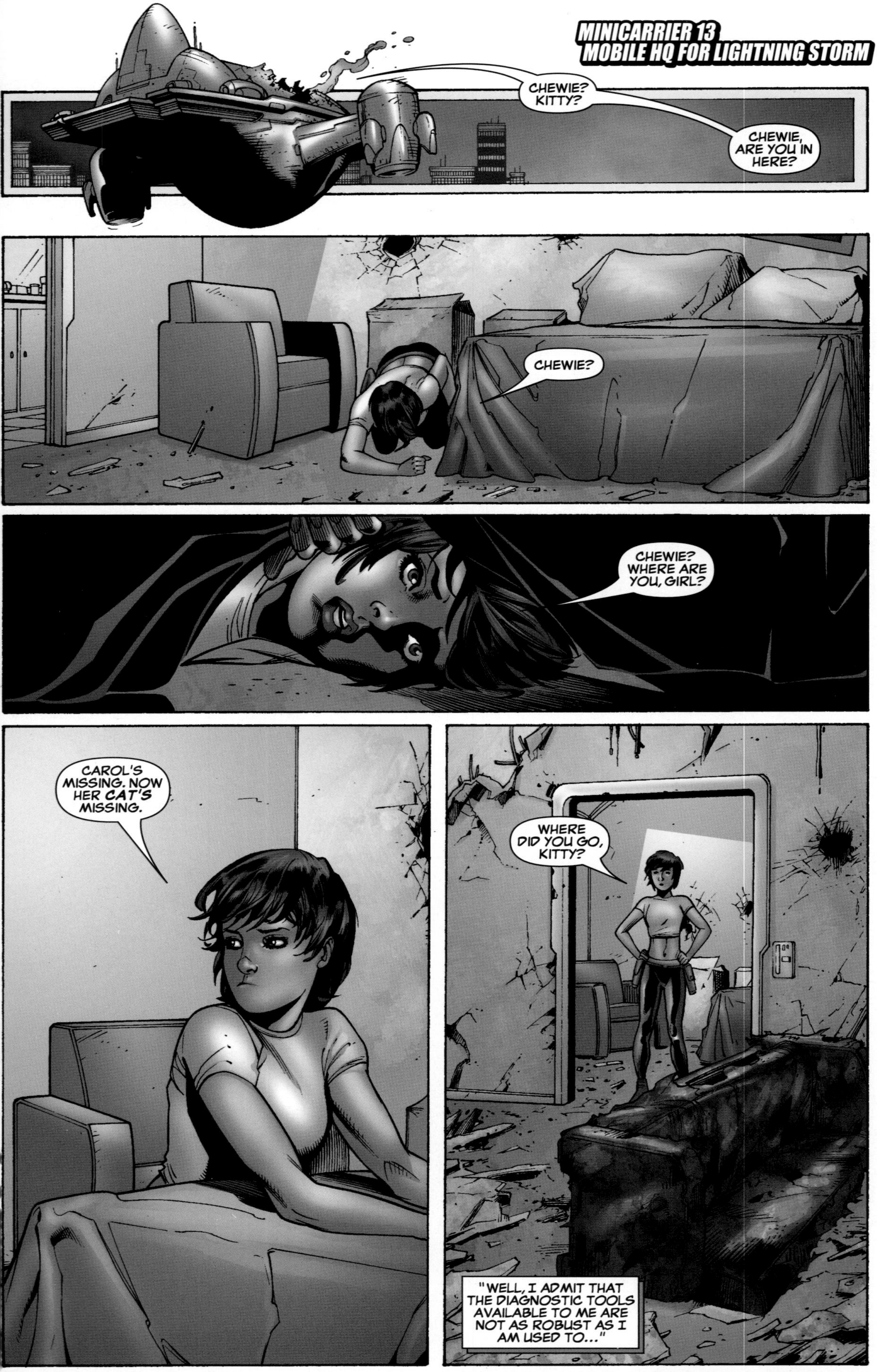
MINICARRIER 13
MOBILE HQ FOR LIGHTNING STORM
CHEWIE? KITTY?
CHEWIE, ARE YOU IN HERE?
CHEWIE?
CHEWIE? WHERE ARE YOU, GIRL?
CAROL'S MISSING. NOW HER CAT'S MISSING.
WHERE DID YOU GO, KITTY?
"WELL, I ADMIT THAT THE DIAGNOSTIC TOOLS AVAILABLE TO ME ARE NOT AS ROBUST AS I AM USED TO..."

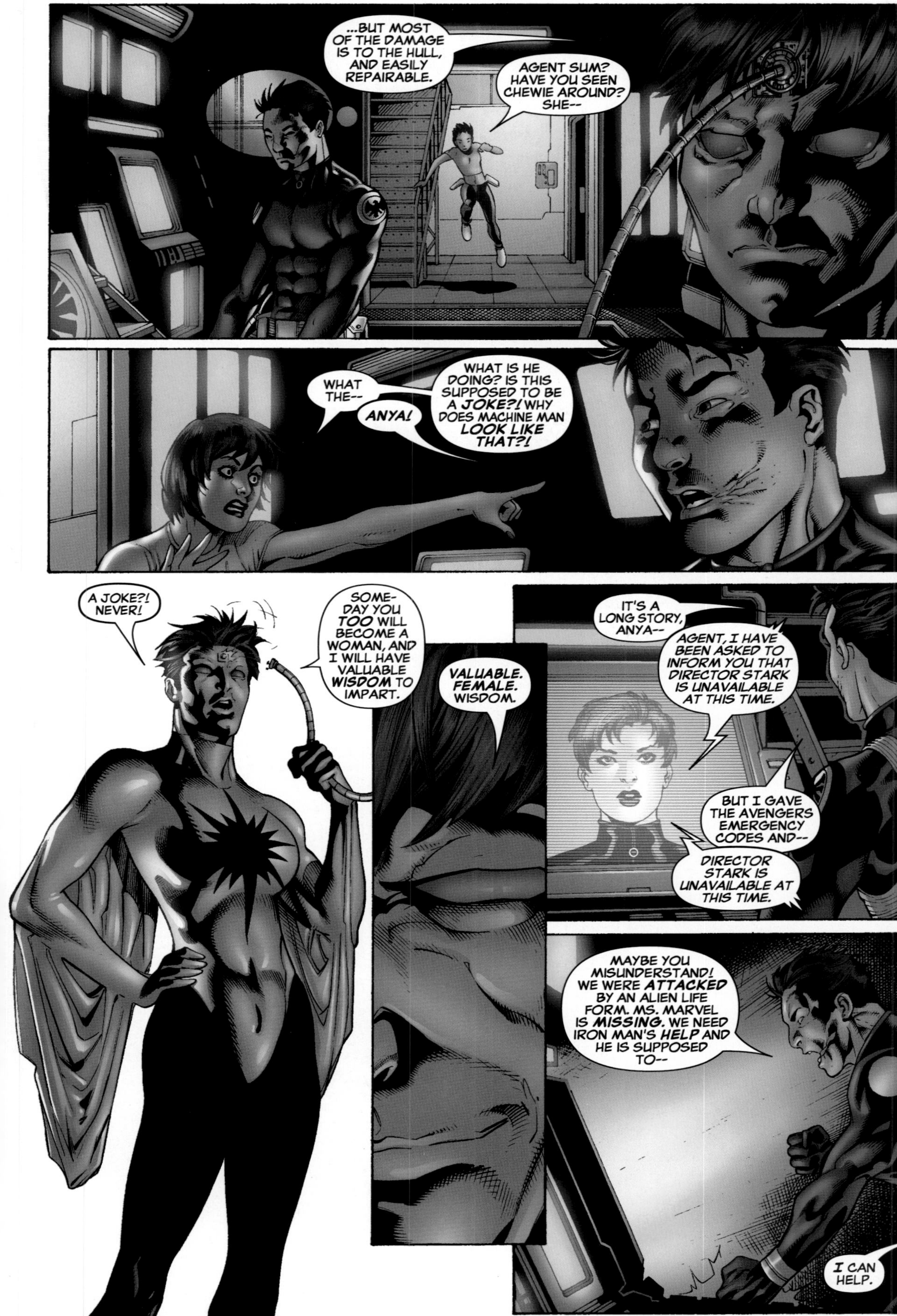
...BUT MOST OF THE DAMAGE IS TO THE HULL, AND EASILY REPAIRABLE.
AGENT SUM? HAVE YOU SEEN CHEWIE AROUND? SHE--
WHAT THE--
ANYA!
WHAT IS HE DOING? IS THIS SUPPOSED TO BE A JOKE?! WHY DOES MACHINE MAN LOOK LIKE THAT?!
A JOKE?! NEVER!
SOME-DAY YOU TOO WILL BECOME A WOMAN, AND I WILL HAVE VALUABLE WISDOM TO IMPART.
VALUABLE. FEMALE. WISDOM.
IT'S A LONG STORY, ANYA--
AGENT, I HAVE BEEN ASKED TO INFORM YOU THAT DIRECTOR STARK IS UNAVAILABLE AT THIS TIME.
BUT I GAVE THE AVENGERS EMERGENCY CODES AND--
DIRECTOR STARK IS UNAVAILABLE AT THIS TIME.
MAYBE YOU MISUNDERSTAND! WE WERE ATTACKED BY AN ALIEN LIFE FORM. MS. MARVEL IS MISSING. WE NEED IRON MAN'S HELP AND HE IS SUPPOSED TO--
I CAN HELP.

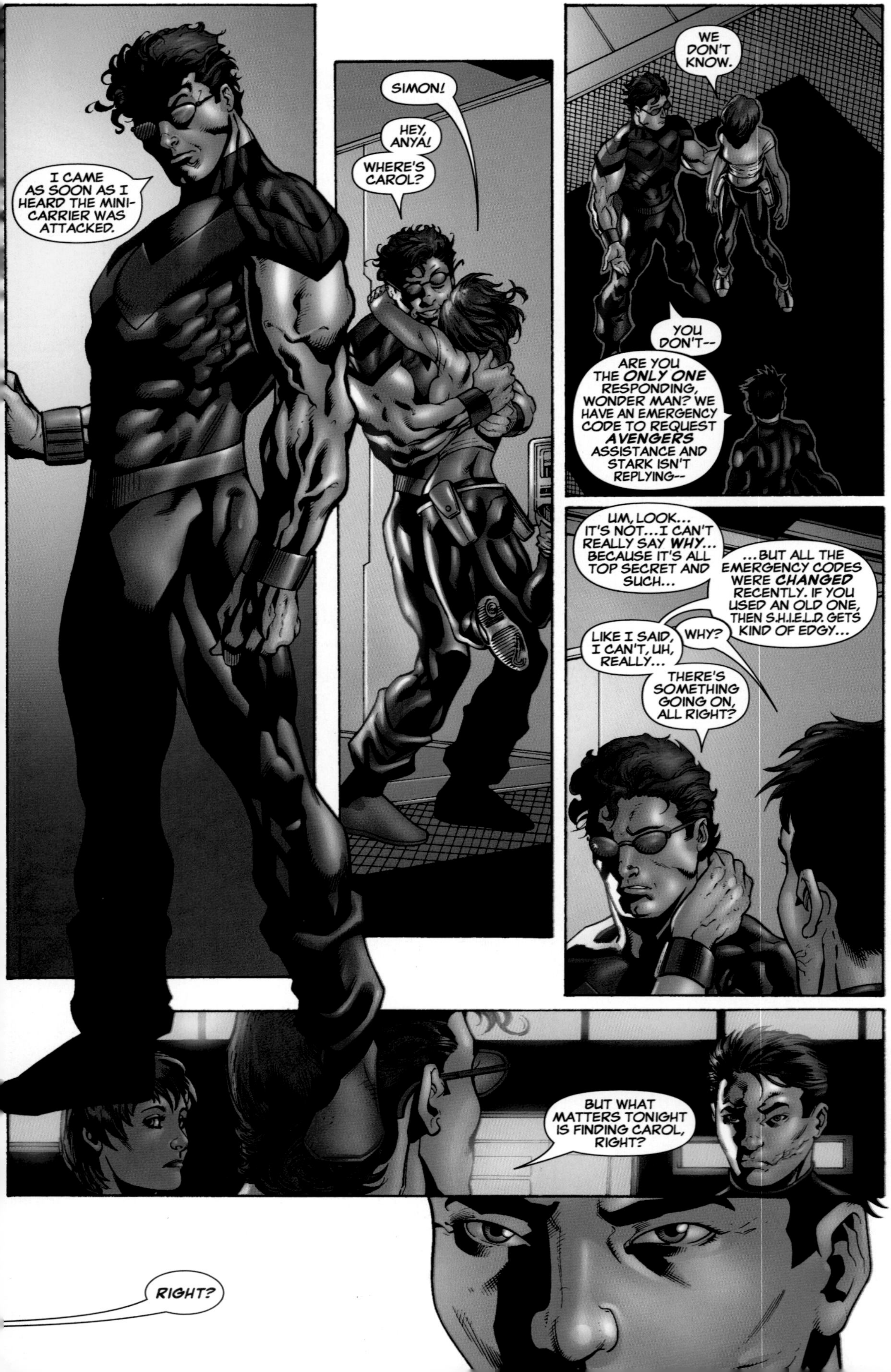
I CAME AS SOON AS I HEARD THE MINI-CARRIER WAS ATTACKED.
SIMON!
HEY, ANYA!
WHERE'S CAROL?
WE DON'T KNOW.
YOU DON'T--
ARE YOU THE ONLY ONE RESPONDING, WONDER MAN? WE HAVE AN EMERGENCY CODE TO REQUEST AVENGERS ASSISTANCE AND STARK ISN'T REPLYING--
UM, LOOK... IT'S NOT...I CAN'T REALLY SAY WHY... BECAUSE IT'S ALL TOP SECRET AND SUCH...
...BUT ALL THE EMERGENCY CODES WERE CHANGED RECENTLY. IF YOU USED AN OLD ONE, THEN S.H.I.E.L.D. GETS KIND OF EDGY...
WHY?
LIKE I SAID, I CAN'T, UH, REALLY...
THERE'S SOMETHING GOING ON, ALL RIGHT?
BUT WHAT MATTERS TONIGHT IS FINDING CAROL, RIGHT?
RIGHT?

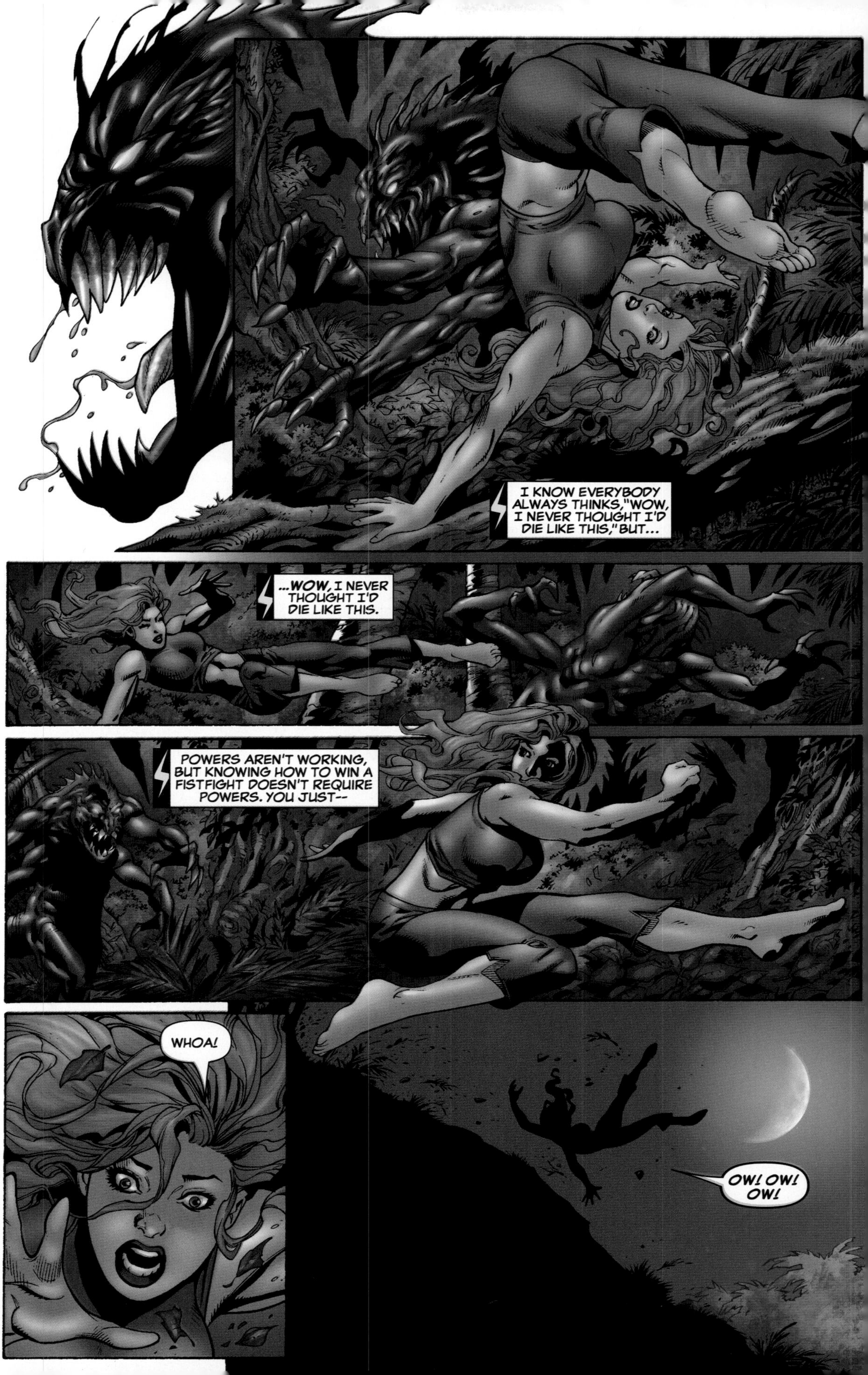
I KNOW EVERYBODY ALWAYS THINKS, "WOW, I NEVER THOUGHT I'D DIE LIKE THIS," BUT...
...WOW, I NEVER THOUGHT I'D DIE LIKE THIS.
POWERS AREN'T WORKING, BUT KNOWING HOW TO WIN A FISTFIGHT DOESN'T REQUIRE POWERS. YOU JUST--
WHOA!
OW! OW! OW!

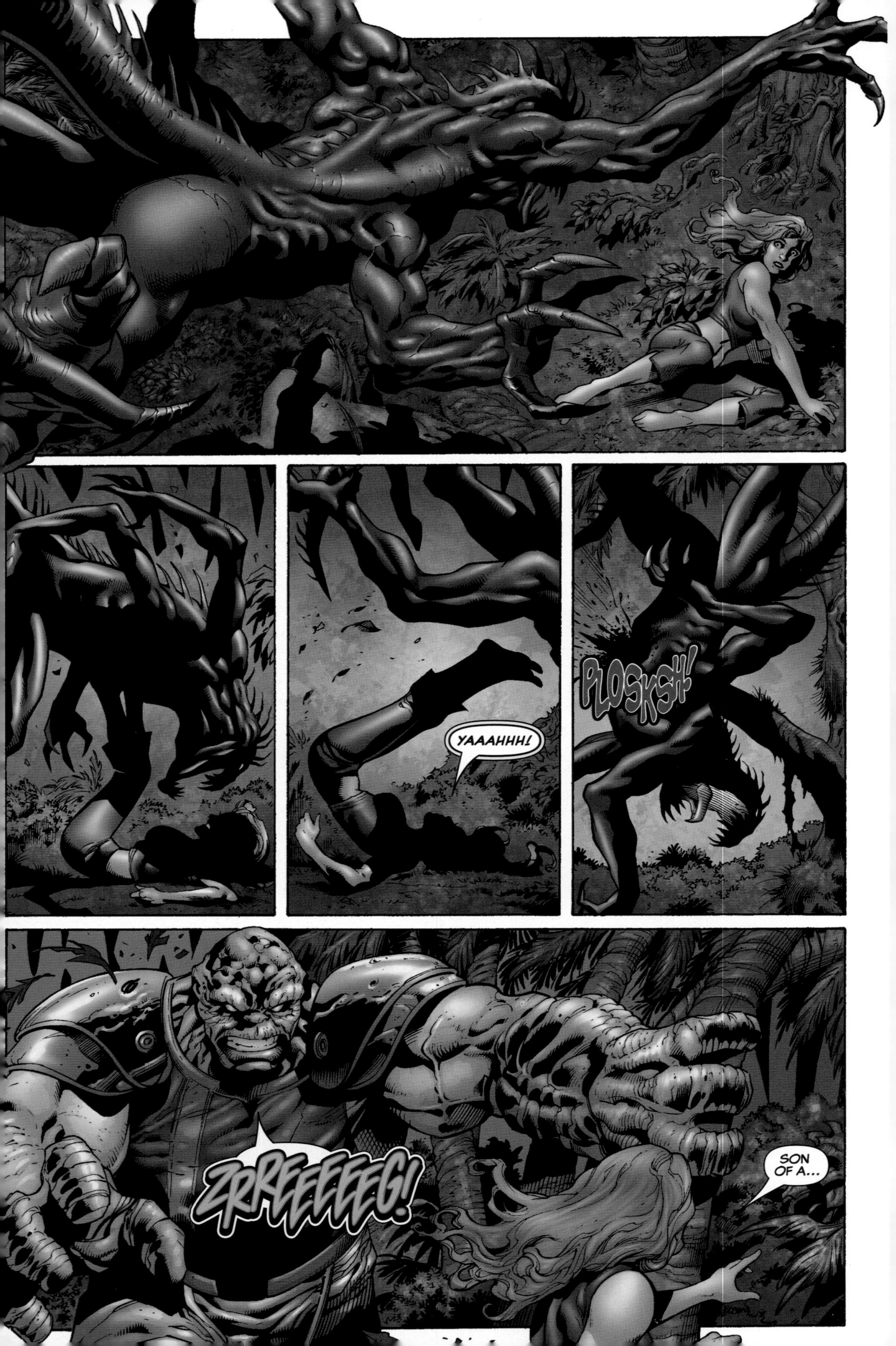
YAAAHHH!
PLOSKSH!
ZRREEEEEG!
SON OF A...

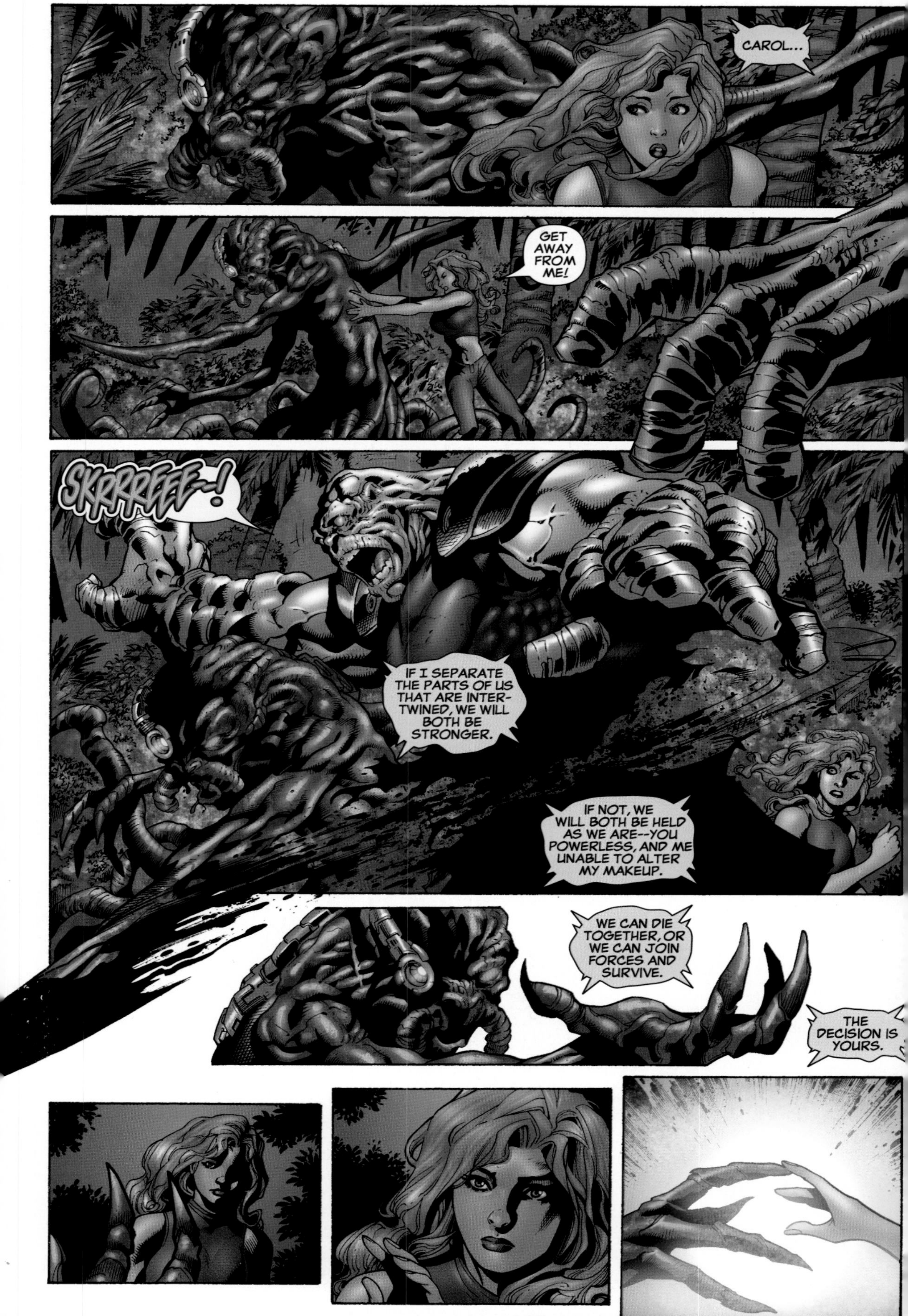
CAROL...
GET AWAY FROM ME!
SKRRRREEE--!
IF I SEPARATE THE PARTS OF US THAT ARE INTER-TWINED, WE WILL BOTH BE STRONGER.
IF NOT, WE WILL BOTH BE HELD AS WE ARE--YOU POWERLESS, AND ME UNABLE TO ALTER MY MAKEUP.
WE CAN DIE TOGETHER, OR WE CAN JOIN FORCES AND SURVIVE.
THE DECISION IS YOURS.

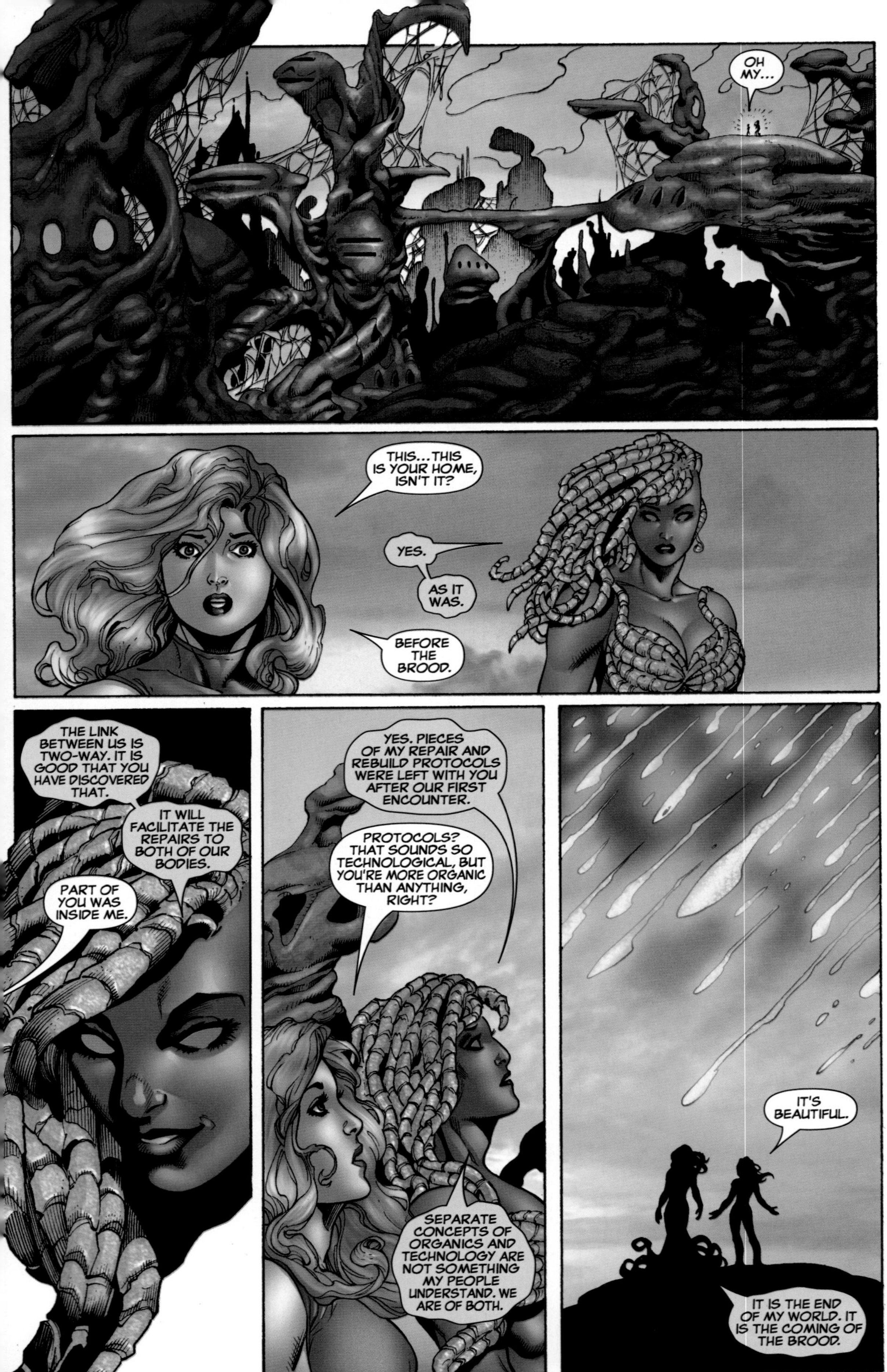
OH MY...
THIS...THIS IS YOUR HOME, ISN'T IT?
YES.
AS IT WAS.
BEFORE THE BROOD.
THE LINK BETWEEN US IS TWO-WAY. IT IS GOOD THAT YOU HAVE DISCOVERED THAT.
IT WILL FACILITATE THE REPAIRS TO BOTH OF OUR BODIES.
PART OF YOU WAS INSIDE ME.
YES. PIECES OF MY REPAIR AND REBUILD PROTOCOLS WERE LEFT WITH YOU AFTER OUR FIRST ENCOUNTER.
PROTOCOLS? THAT SOUNDS SO TECHNOLOGICAL, BUT YOU'RE MORE ORGANIC THAN ANYTHING, RIGHT?
SEPARATE CONCEPTS OF ORGANICS AND TECHNOLOGY ARE NOT SOMETHING MY PEOPLE UNDERSTAND. WE ARE OF BOTH.
IT'S BEAUTIFUL.
IT IS THE END OF MY WORLD. IT IS THE COMING OF THE BROOD.

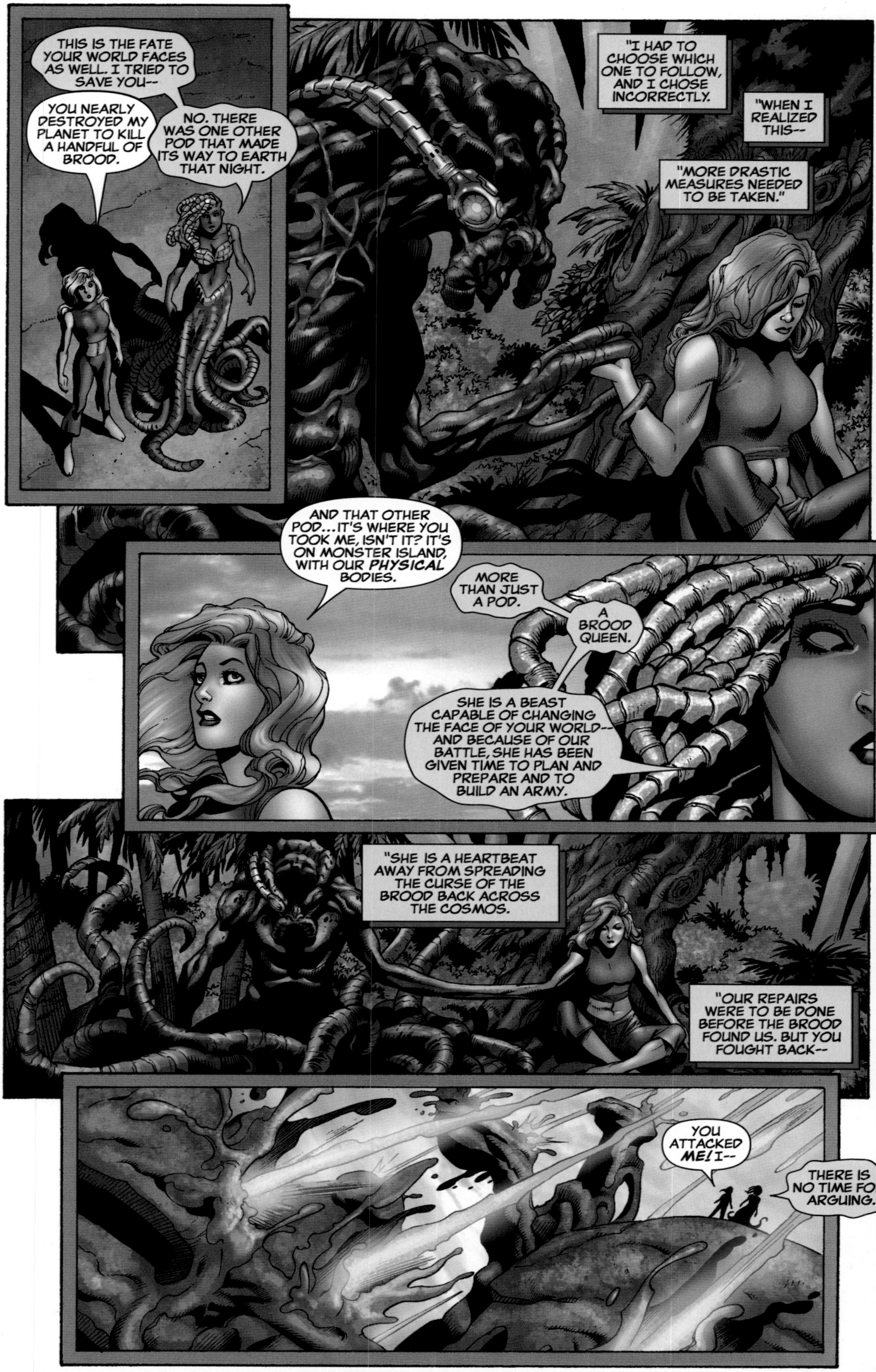
THIS IS THE FATE YOUR WORLD FACES AS WELL. I TRIED TO SAVE YOU--
YOU NEARLY DESTROYED MY PLANET TO KILL A HANDFUL OF BROOD.
NO. THERE WAS ONE OTHER POD THAT MADE ITS WAY TO EARTH THAT NIGHT.
"I HAD TO CHOOSE WHICH ONE TO FOLLOW, AND I CHOSE INCORRECTLY.
"WHEN I REALIZED THIS--
"MORE DRASTIC MEASURES NEEDED TO BE TAKEN."
AND THAT OTHER POD... IT'S WHERE YOU TOOK ME, ISN'T IT? IT'S ON MONSTER ISLAND, WITH OUR PHYSICAL BODIES.
MORE THAN JUST A POD.
A BROOD QUEEN.
SHE IS A BEAST CAPABLE OF CHANGING THE FACE OF YOUR WORLD-- AND BECAUSE OF OUR BATTLE, SHE HAS BEEN GIVEN TIME TO PLAN AND PREPARE AND TO BUILD AN ARMY.
"SHE IS A HEARTBEAT AWAY FROM SPREADING THE CURSE OF THE BROOD BACK ACROSS THE COSMOS.
"OUR REPAIRS WERE TO BE DONE BEFORE THE BROOD FOUND US. BUT YOU FOUGHT BACK--
YOU ATTACKED ME! I--
THERE IS NO TIME FOR ARGUING.

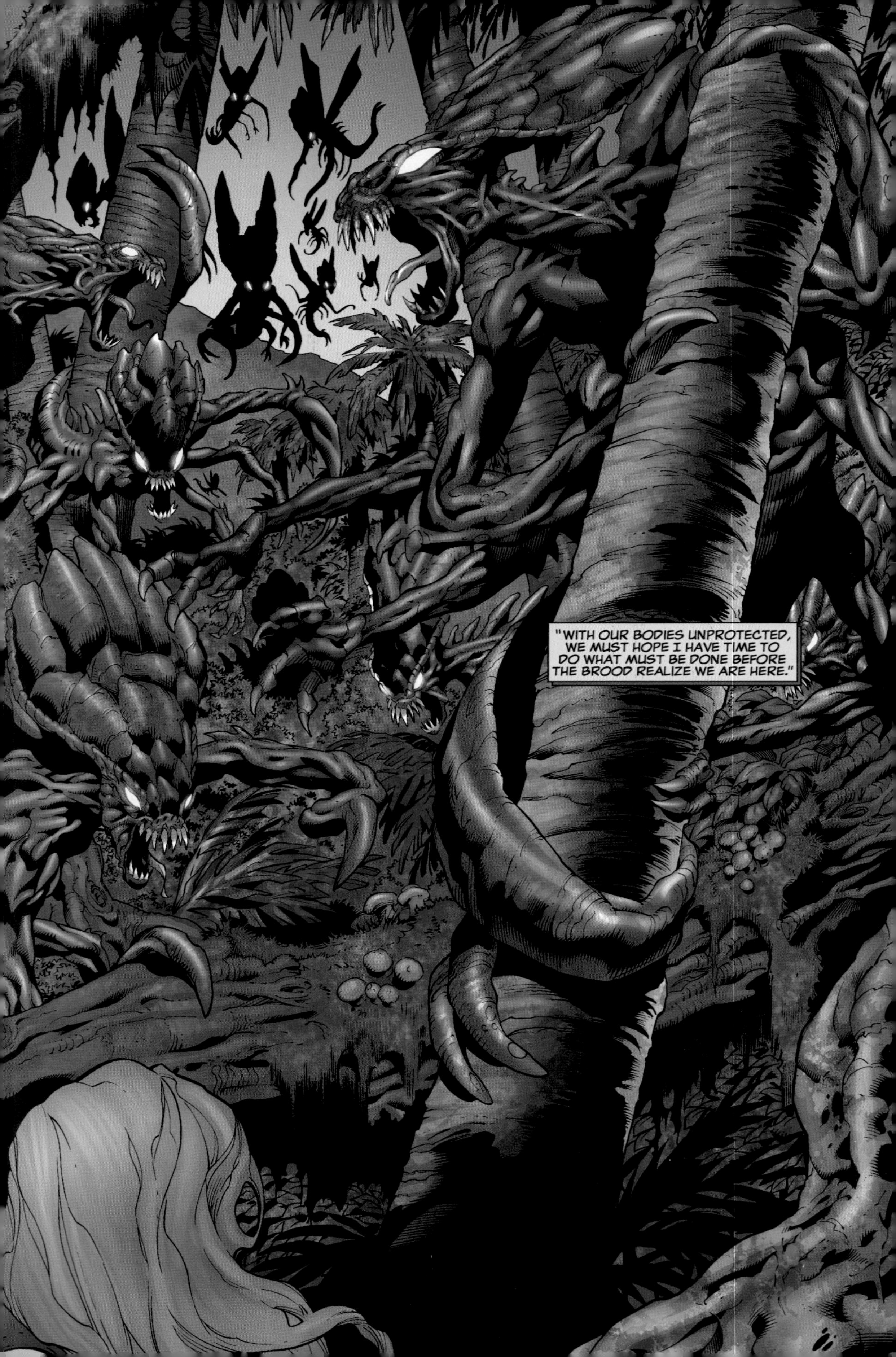
"WITH OUR BODIES UNPROTECTED, WE MUST HOPE I HAVE TIME TO DO WHAT MUST BE DONE BEFORE THE BROOD REALIZE WE ARE HERE."

#22

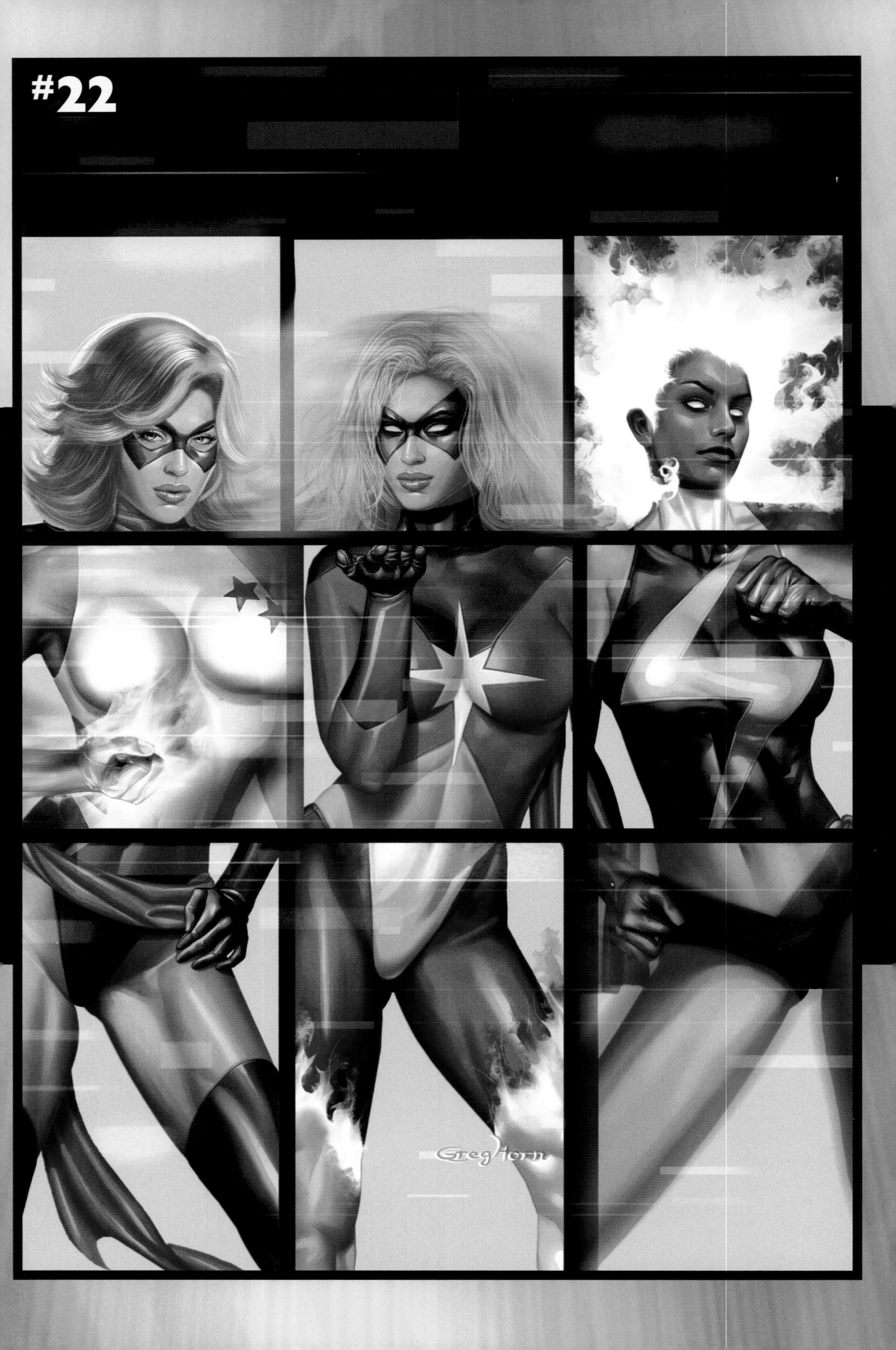
Greg Horn

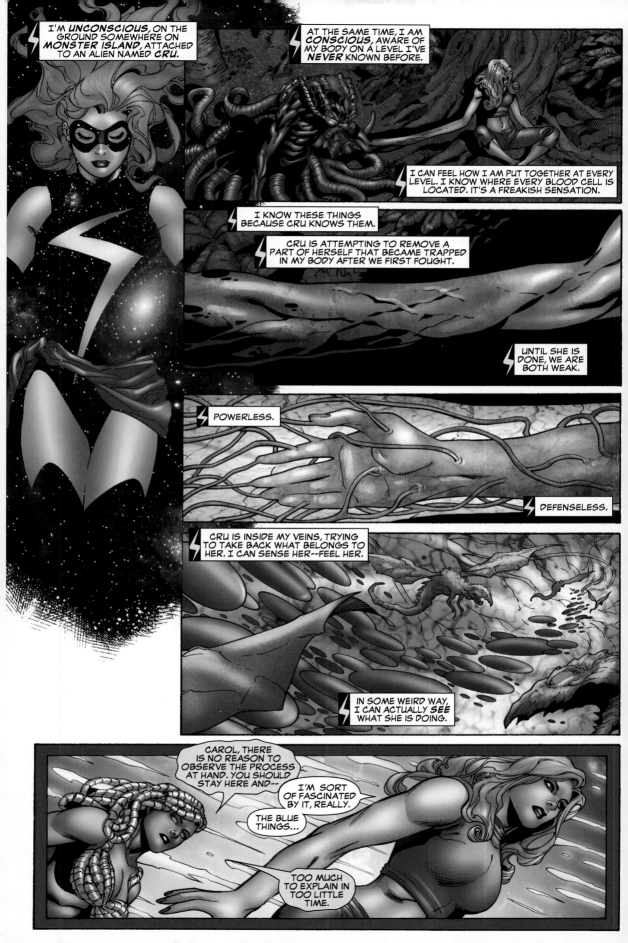

I'M **UNCONSCIOUS**, ON THE GROUND SOMEWHERE ON **MONSTER ISLAND**, ATTACHED TO AN ALIEN NAMED **CRU**.

AT THE SAME TIME, I AM **CONSCIOUS**, AWARE OF MY BODY ON A LEVEL I'VE **NEVER** KNOWN BEFORE.

I CAN FEEL HOW I AM PUT TOGETHER AT EVERY LEVEL. I KNOW WHERE EVERY BLOOD CELL IS LOCATED. IT'S A FREAKISH SENSATION.

I KNOW THESE THINGS BECAUSE CRU KNOWS THEM.

CRU IS ATTEMPTING TO REMOVE A PART OF HERSELF THAT BECAME TRAPPED IN MY BODY AFTER WE FIRST FOUGHT.

UNTIL SHE IS DONE, WE ARE BOTH WEAK.

POWERLESS.

DEFENSELESS.

CRU IS INSIDE MY VEINS, TRYING TO TAKE BACK WHAT BELONGS TO HER. I CAN SENSE HER--FEEL HER.

IN SOME WEIRD WAY, I CAN ACTUALLY **SEE** WHAT SHE IS DOING.

CAROL, THERE IS NO REASON TO OBSERVE THE PROCESS AT HAND. YOU SHOULD STAY HERE AND--

I'M SORT OF FASCINATED BY IT, REALLY.

THE BLUE THINGS...

TOO MUCH TO EXPLAIN IN TOO LITTLE TIME.

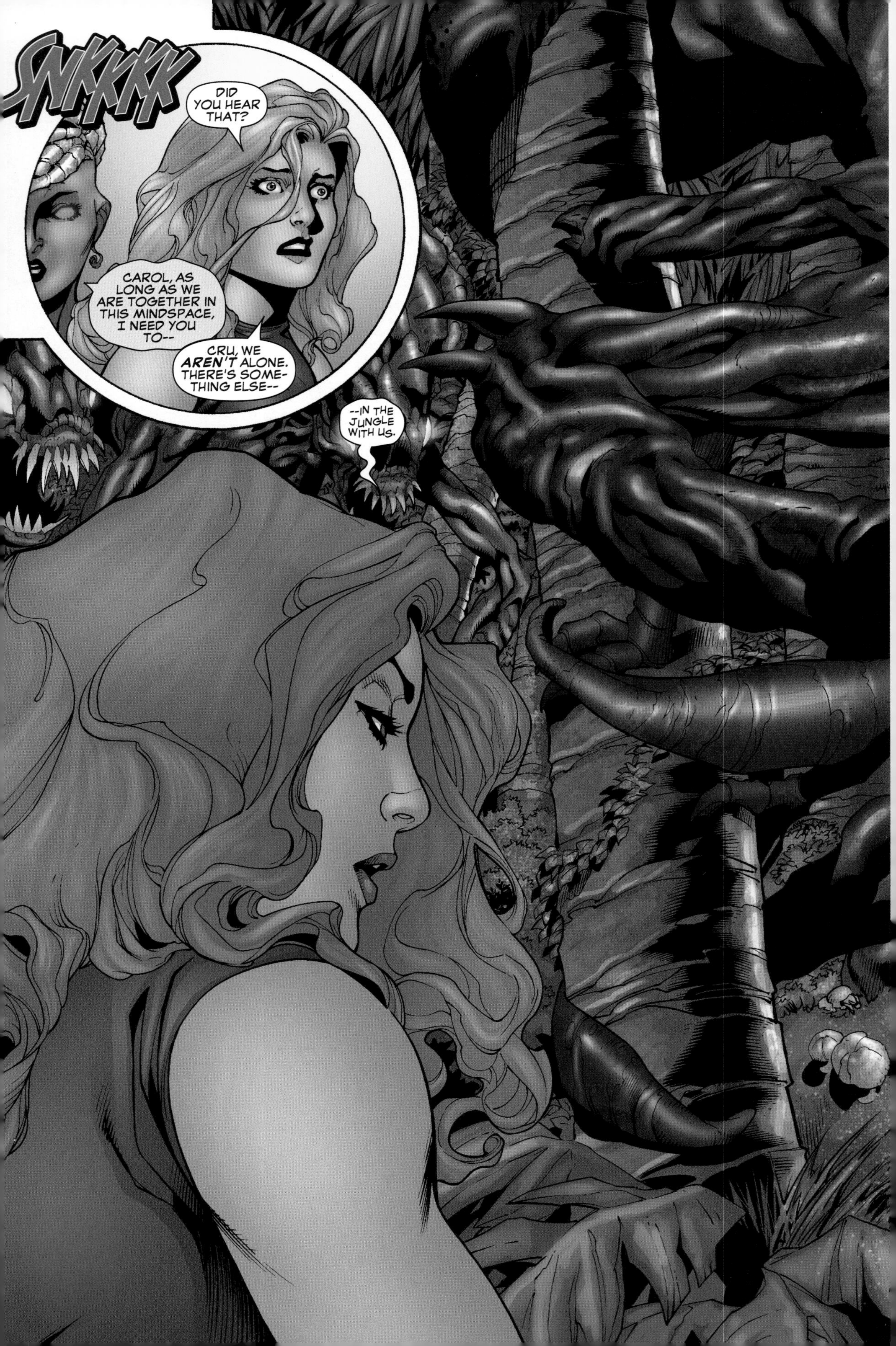
SNKKKK
DID YOU HEAR THAT?
CAROL, AS LONG AS WE ARE TOGETHER IN THIS MINDSPACE, I NEED YOU TO--
CRU, WE AREN'T ALONE. THERE'S SOME-THING ELSE--
--IN THE JUNGLE WITH US.

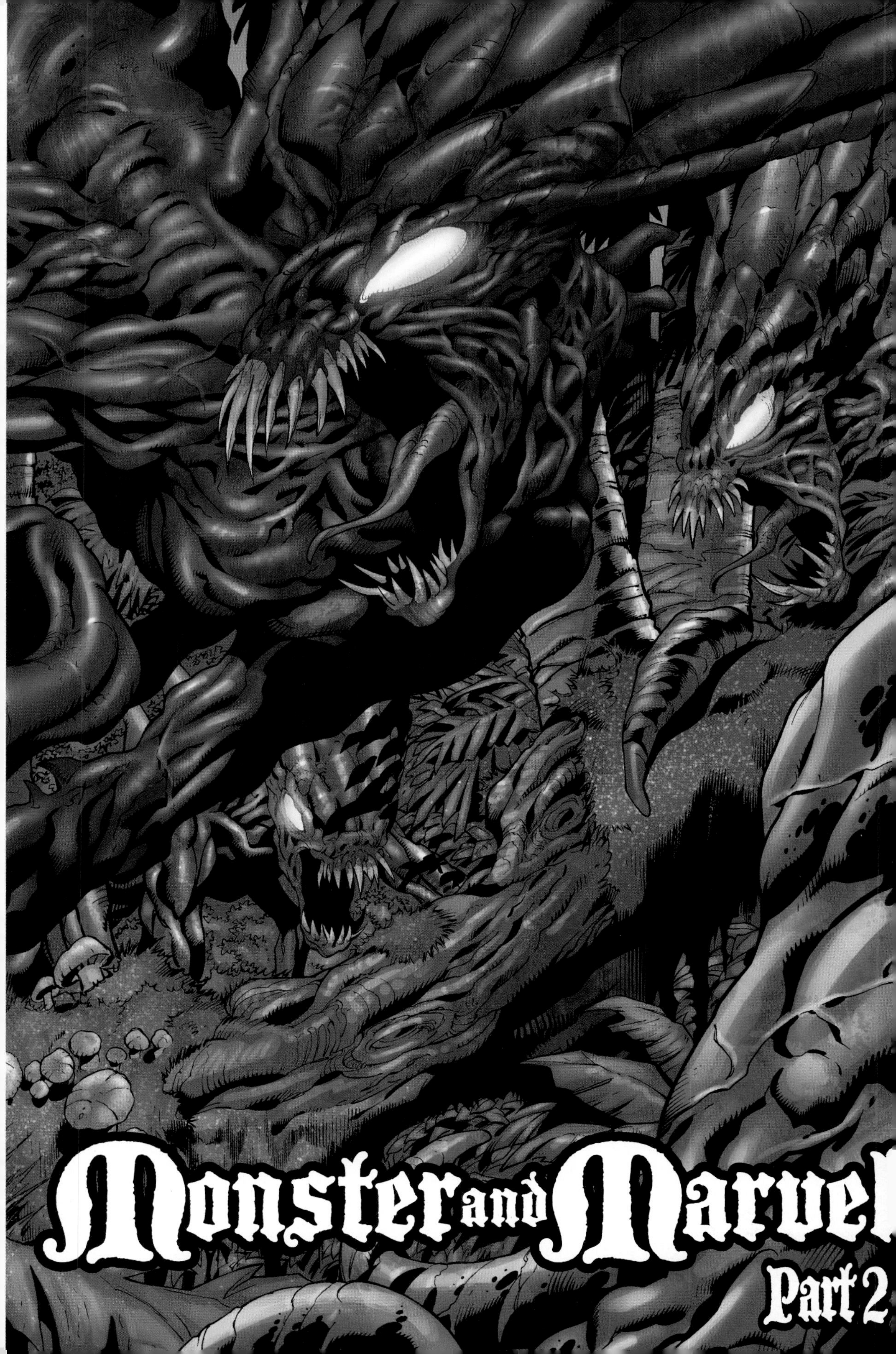
Monster and Marvel
Part 2

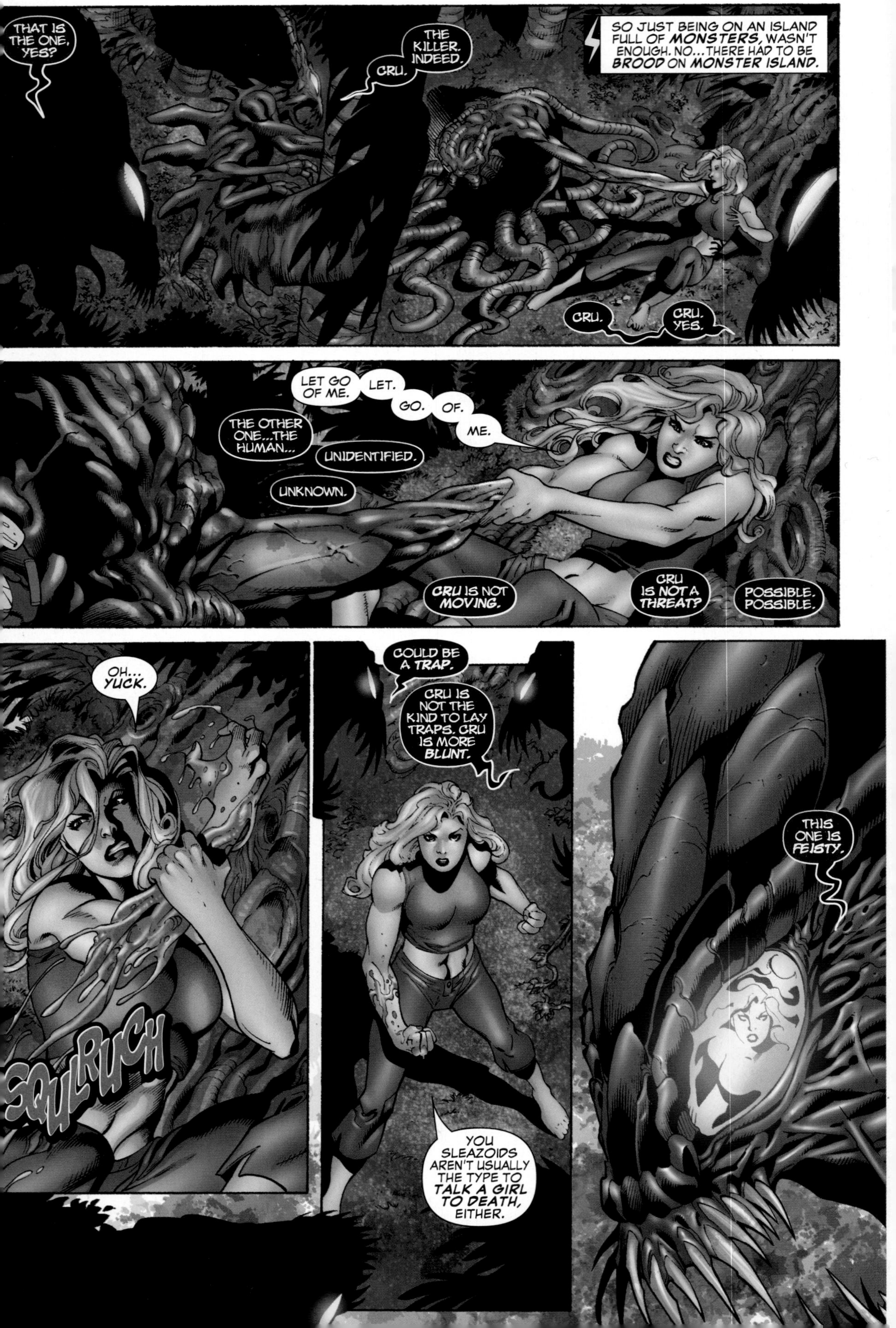

SO JUST BEING ON AN ISLAND FULL OF MONSTERS, WASN'T ENOUGH. NO...THERE HAD TO BE BROOD ON MONSTER ISLAND.
THAT IS THE ONE, YES?
CRU.
THE KILLER. INDEED.
CRU.
CRU. YES.
THE OTHER ONE...THE HUMAN...
UNIDENTIFIED.
UNKNOWN.
LET GO OF ME.
LET.
GO.
OF.
ME.
CRU IS NOT MOVING.
CRU IS NOT A THREAT?
POSSIBLE. POSSIBLE.
OH... YUCK.
SQULRUCH
COULD BE A TRAP.
CRU IS NOT THE KIND TO LAY TRAPS. CRU IS MORE BLUNT.
YOU SLEAZOIDS AREN'T USUALLY THE TYPE TO TALK A GIRL TO DEATH, EITHER.
THIS ONE IS FEISTY.

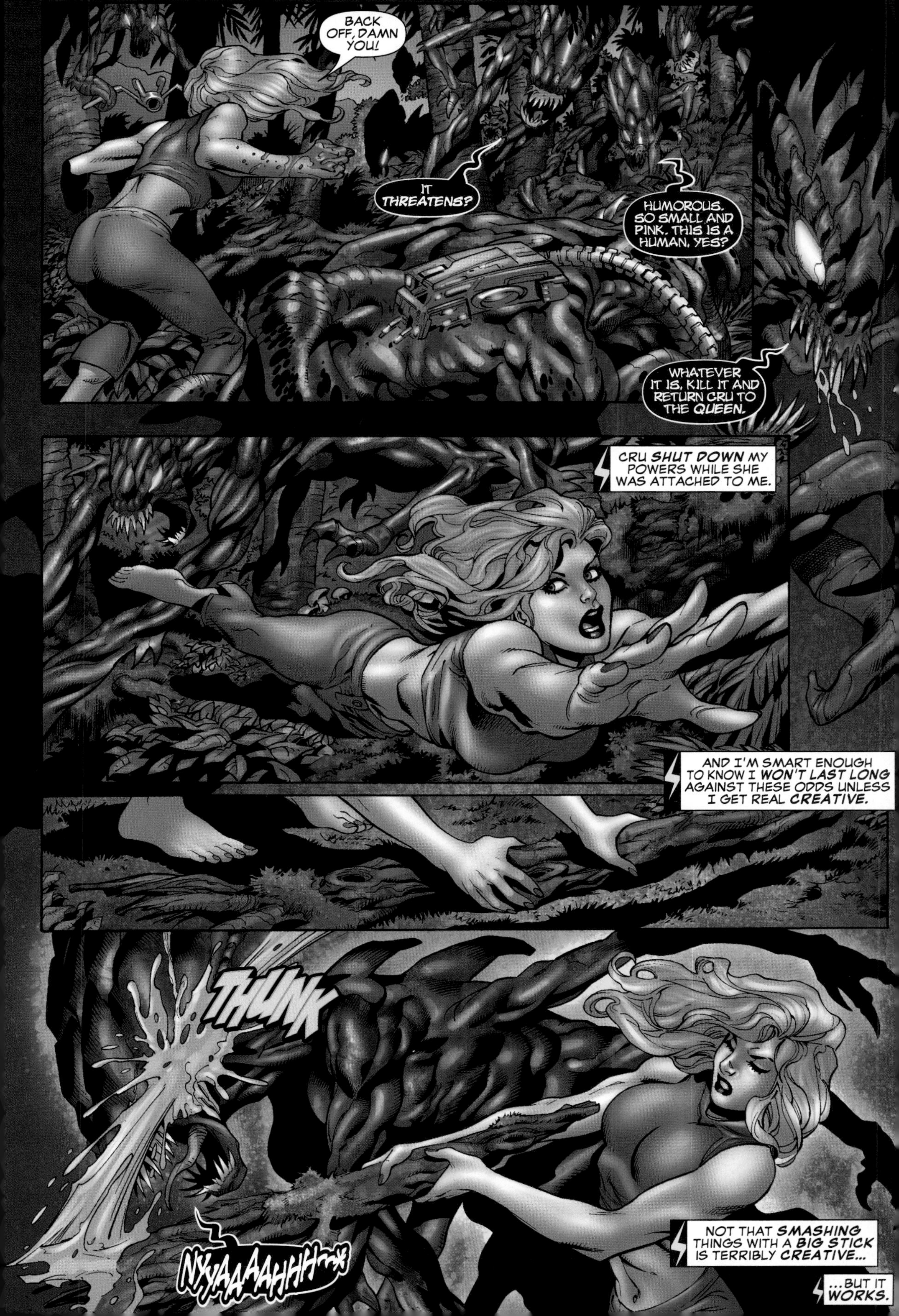
BACK OFF, DAMN YOU!
IT THREATENS?
HUMOROUS. SO SMALL AND PINK. THIS IS A HUMAN, YES?
WHATEVER IT IS, KILL IT AND RETURN CRU TO THE QUEEN.
CRU SHUT DOWN MY POWERS WHILE SHE WAS ATTACHED TO ME.
AND I'M SMART ENOUGH TO KNOW I WON'T LAST LONG AGAINST THESE ODDS UNLESS I GET REAL CREATIVE.
THUNK
NYYAAAAHHH
NOT THAT SMASHING THINGS WITH A BIG STICK IS TERRIBLY CREATIVE...
...BUT IT WORKS.

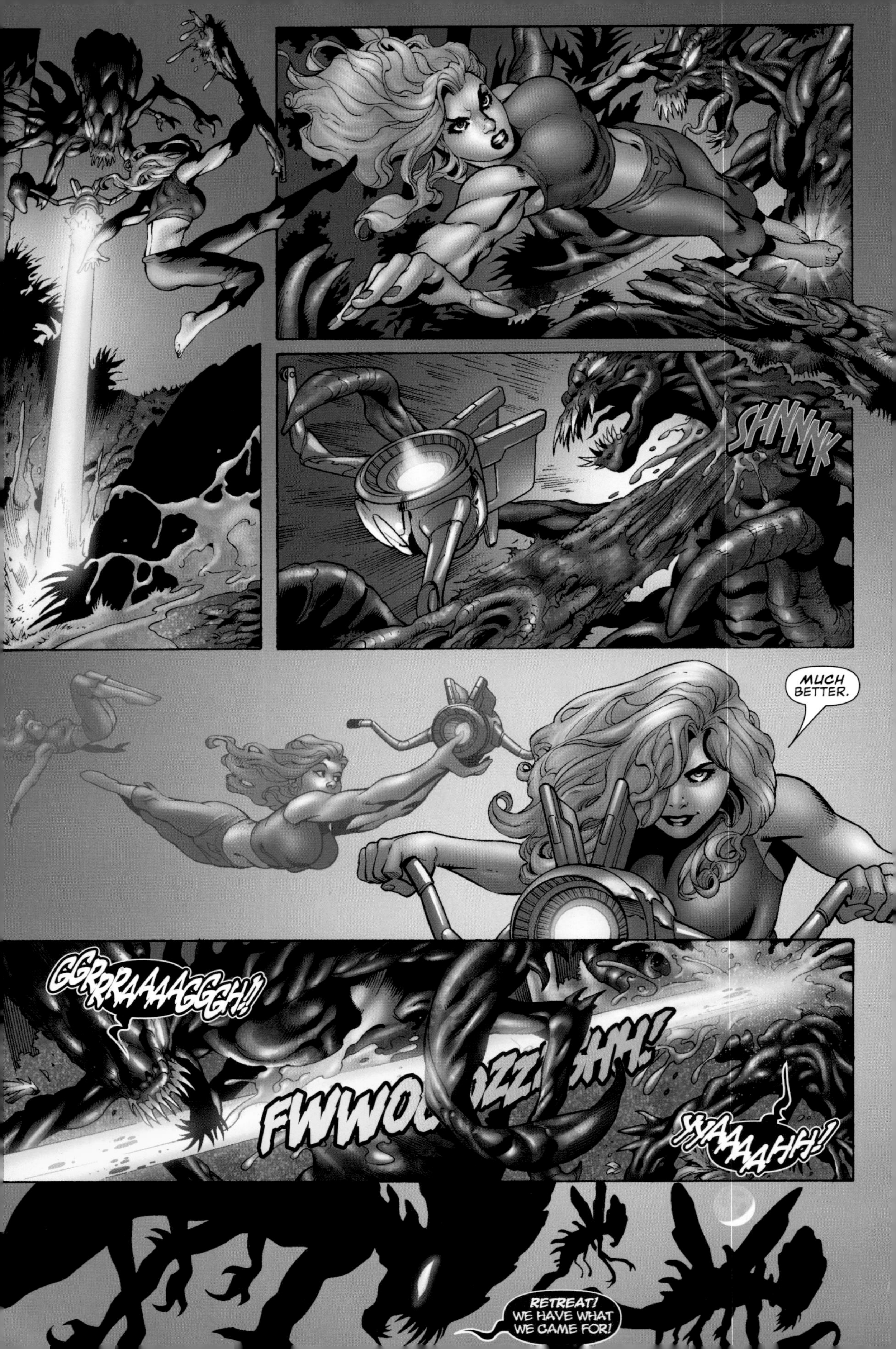
SHNNNK
MUCH BETTER.
GGRRRAAAAGGGH!!
FWWOOOOZZZHHH!
YYAAAAAHH!
RETREAT! WE HAVE WHAT WE CAME FOR!

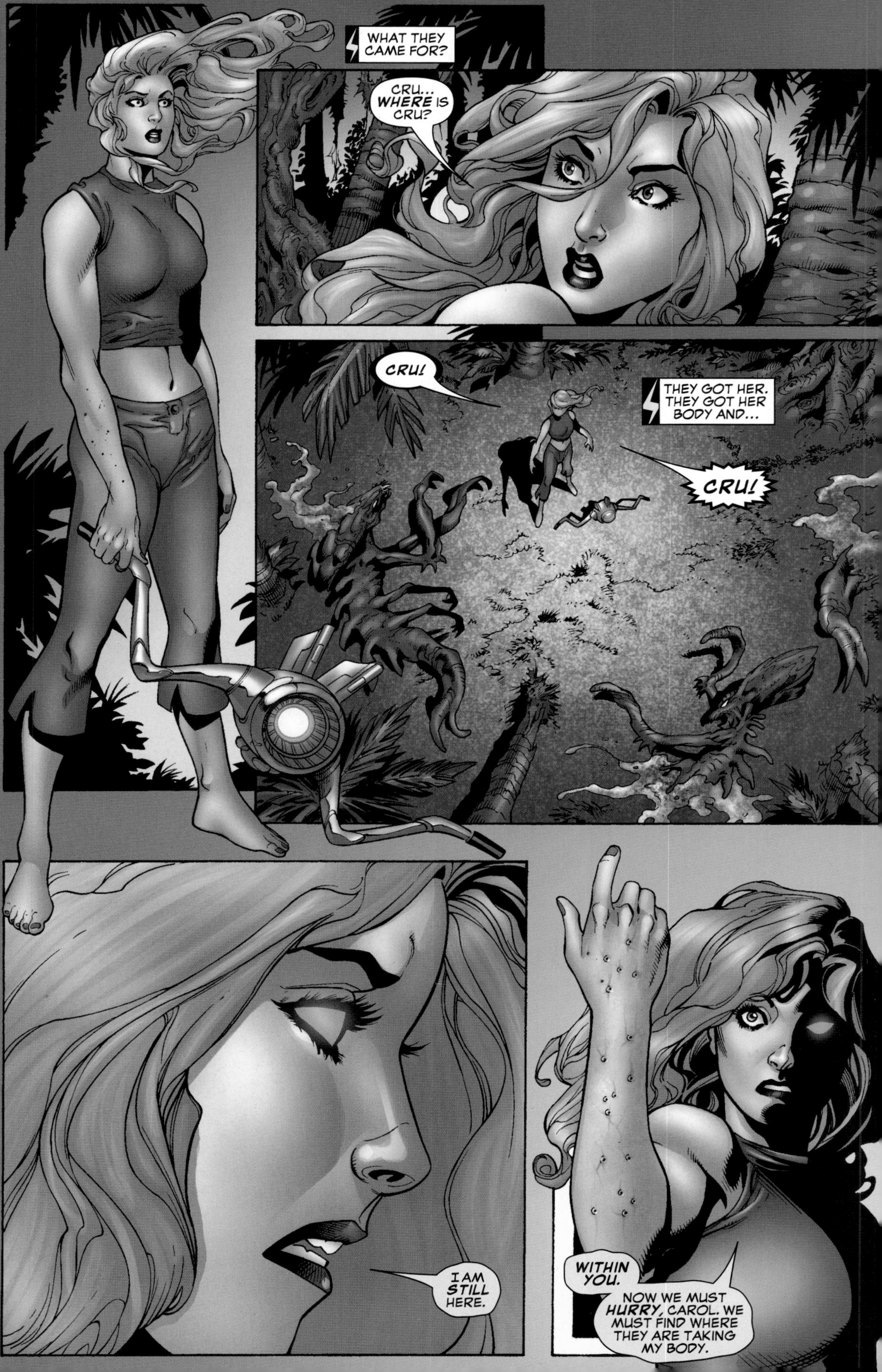
WHAT THEY CAME FOR?
CRU... WHERE IS CRU?
CRU!
THEY GOT HER. THEY GOT HER BODY AND...
CRU!
I AM STILL HERE.
WITHIN YOU.
NOW WE MUST HURRY, CAROL. WE MUST FIND WHERE THEY ARE TAKING MY BODY.

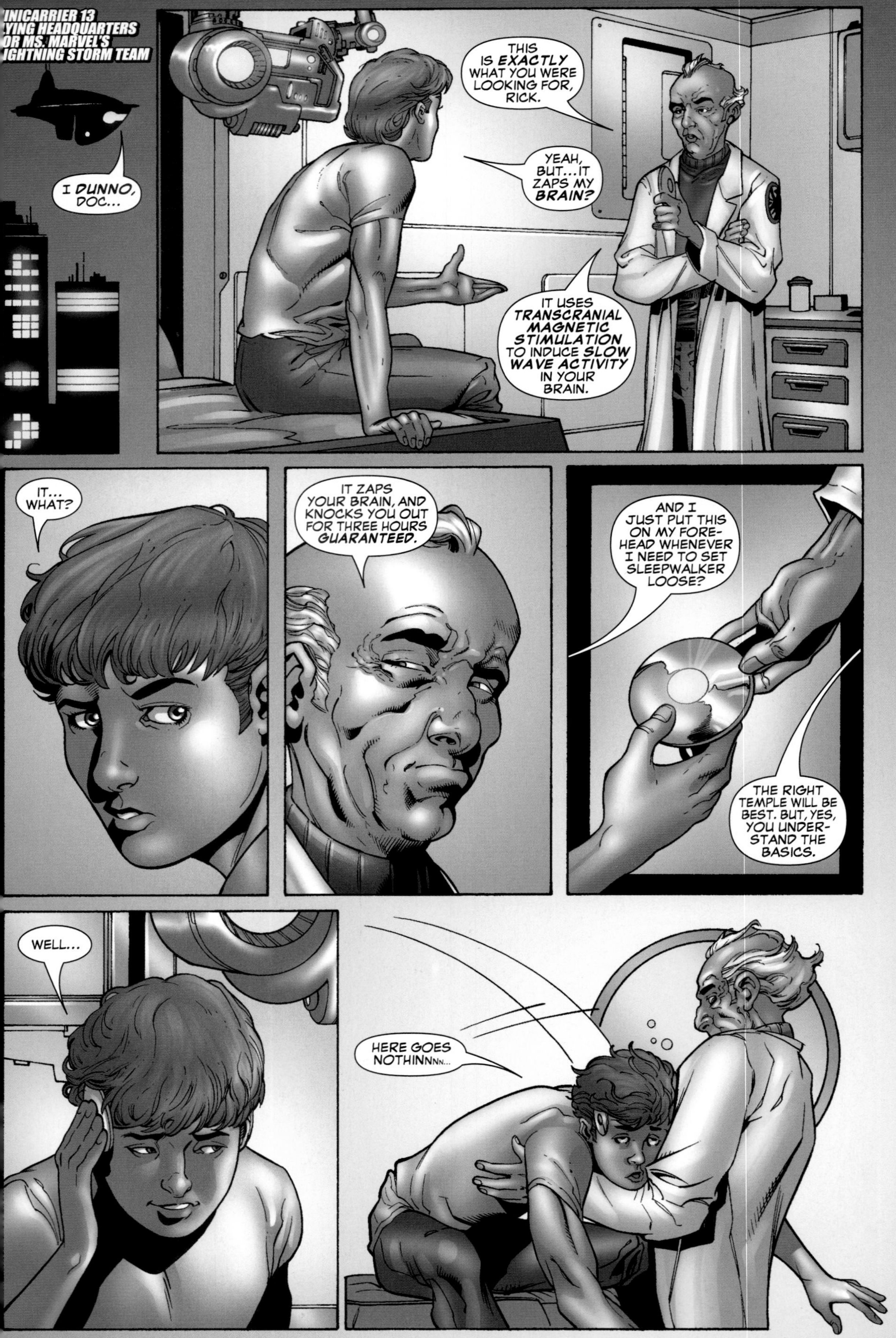

HELICARRIER 13
FLYING HEADQUARTERS
FOR MS. MARVEL'S
LIGHTNING STORM TEAM
I DUNNO, DOC...
THIS IS EXACTLY WHAT YOU WERE LOOKING FOR, RICK.
YEAH, BUT...IT ZAPS MY BRAIN?
IT USES TRANSCRANIAL MAGNETIC STIMULATION TO INDUCE SLOW WAVE ACTIVITY IN YOUR BRAIN.
IT... WHAT?
IT ZAPS YOUR BRAIN, AND KNOCKS YOU OUT FOR THREE HOURS GUARANTEED.
AND I JUST PUT THIS ON MY FOREHEAD WHENEVER I NEED TO SET SLEEPWALKER LOOSE?
THE RIGHT TEMPLE WILL BE BEST. BUT, YES, YOU UNDERSTAND THE BASICS.
WELL...
HERE GOES NOTHINNNNN...

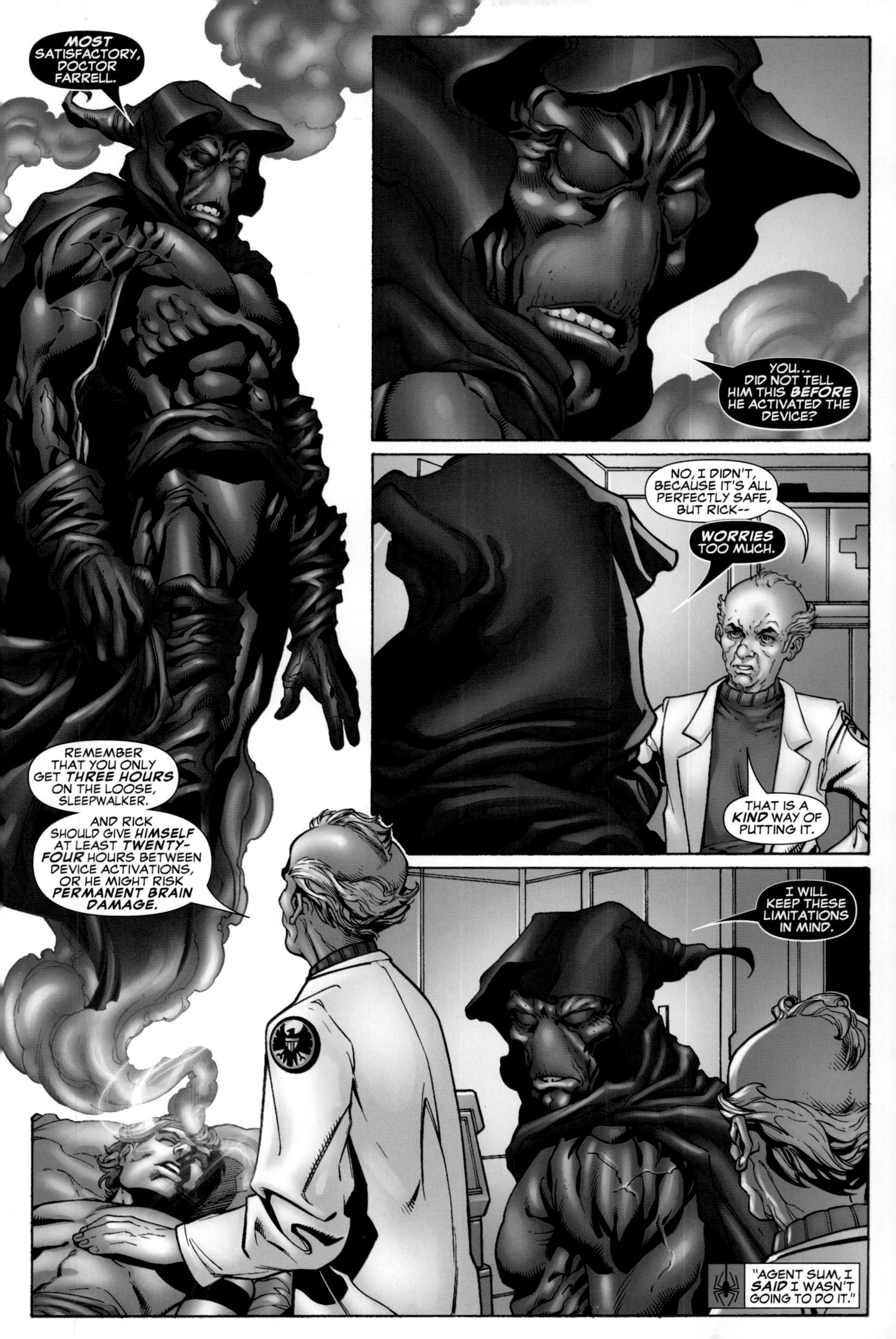
MOST SATISFACTORY, DOCTOR FARRELL.
YOU... DID NOT TELL HIM THIS BEFORE HE ACTIVATED THE DEVICE?
NO, I DIDN'T, BECAUSE IT'S ALL PERFECTLY SAFE, BUT RICK--
WORRIES TOO MUCH.
THAT IS A KIND WAY OF PUTTING IT.
REMEMBER THAT YOU ONLY GET THREE HOURS ON THE LOOSE, SLEEPWALKER.
AND RICK SHOULD GIVE HIMSELF AT LEAST TWENTY-FOUR HOURS BETWEEN DEVICE ACTIVATIONS, OR HE MIGHT RISK PERMANENT BRAIN DAMAGE.
I WILL KEEP THESE LIMITATIONS IN MIND.
"AGENT SUM, I SAID I WASN'T GOING TO DO IT."

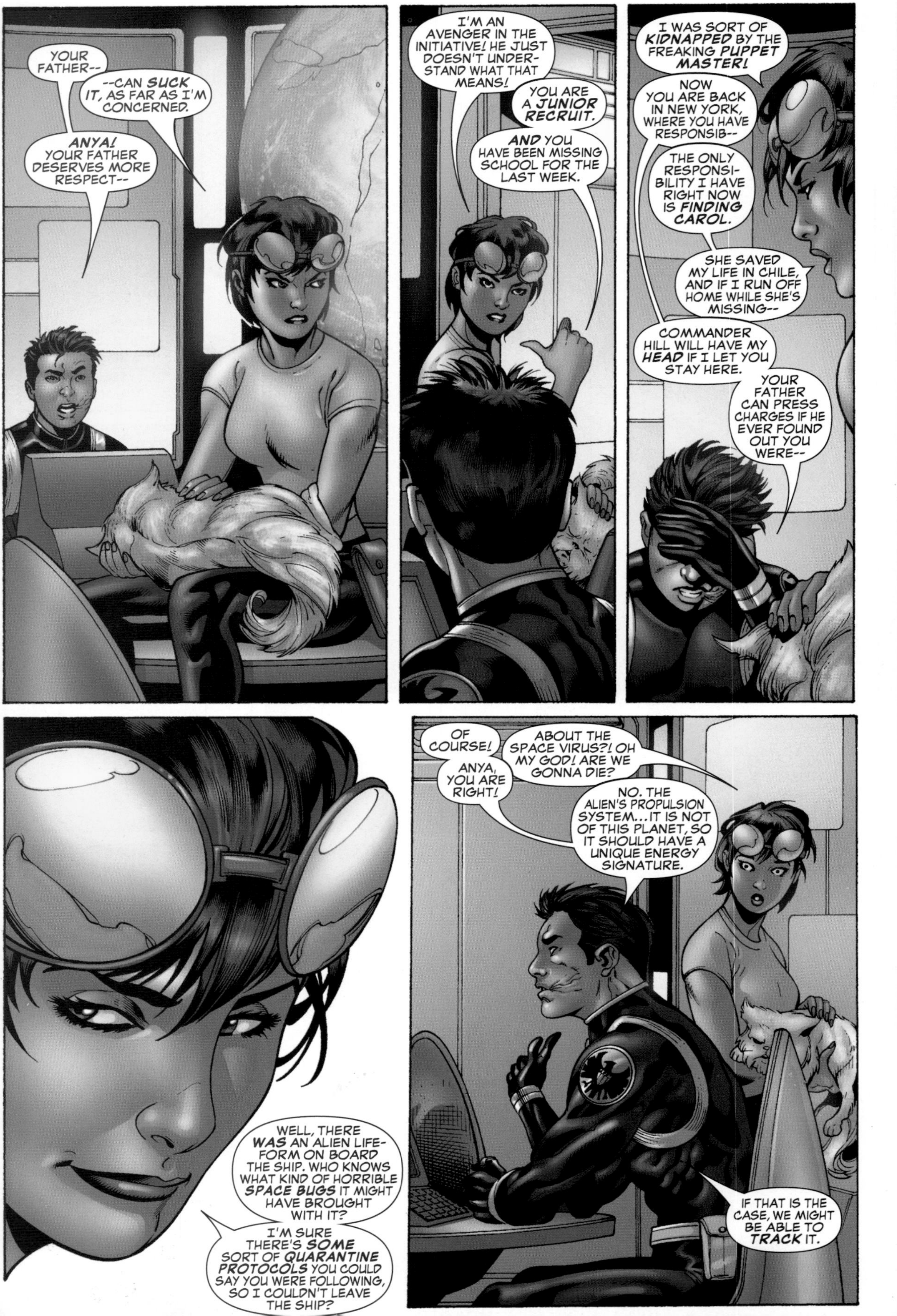
YOUR FATHER--
--CAN SUCK IT, AS FAR AS I'M CONCERNED.
ANYA! YOUR FATHER DESERVES MORE RESPECT--
I'M AN AVENGER IN THE INITIATIVE! HE JUST DOESN'T UNDERSTAND WHAT THAT MEANS!
YOU ARE A JUNIOR RECRUIT.
AND YOU HAVE BEEN MISSING SCHOOL FOR THE LAST WEEK.
I WAS SORT OF KIDNAPPED BY THE FREAKING PUPPET MASTER!
NOW YOU ARE BACK IN NEW YORK, WHERE YOU HAVE RESPONSIB--
THE ONLY RESPONSIBILITY I HAVE RIGHT NOW IS FINDING CAROL.
SHE SAVED MY LIFE IN CHILE, AND IF I RUN OFF HOME WHILE SHE'S MISSING--
COMMANDER HILL WILL HAVE MY HEAD IF I LET YOU STAY HERE.
YOUR FATHER CAN PRESS CHARGES IF HE EVER FOUND OUT YOU WERE--
WELL, THERE WAS AN ALIEN LIFE-FORM ON BOARD THE SHIP. WHO KNOWS WHAT KIND OF HORRIBLE SPACE BUGS IT MIGHT HAVE BROUGHT WITH IT?
I'M SURE THERE'S SOME SORT OF QUARANTINE PROTOCOLS YOU COULD SAY YOU WERE FOLLOWING, SO I COULDN'T LEAVE THE SHIP?
OF COURSE!
ANYA, YOU ARE RIGHT!
ABOUT THE SPACE VIRUS?! OH MY GOD! ARE WE GONNA DIE?
NO. THE ALIEN'S PROPULSION SYSTEM...IT IS NOT OF THIS PLANET, SO IT SHOULD HAVE A UNIQUE ENERGY SIGNATURE.
IF THAT IS THE CASE, WE MIGHT BE ABLE TO TRACK IT.

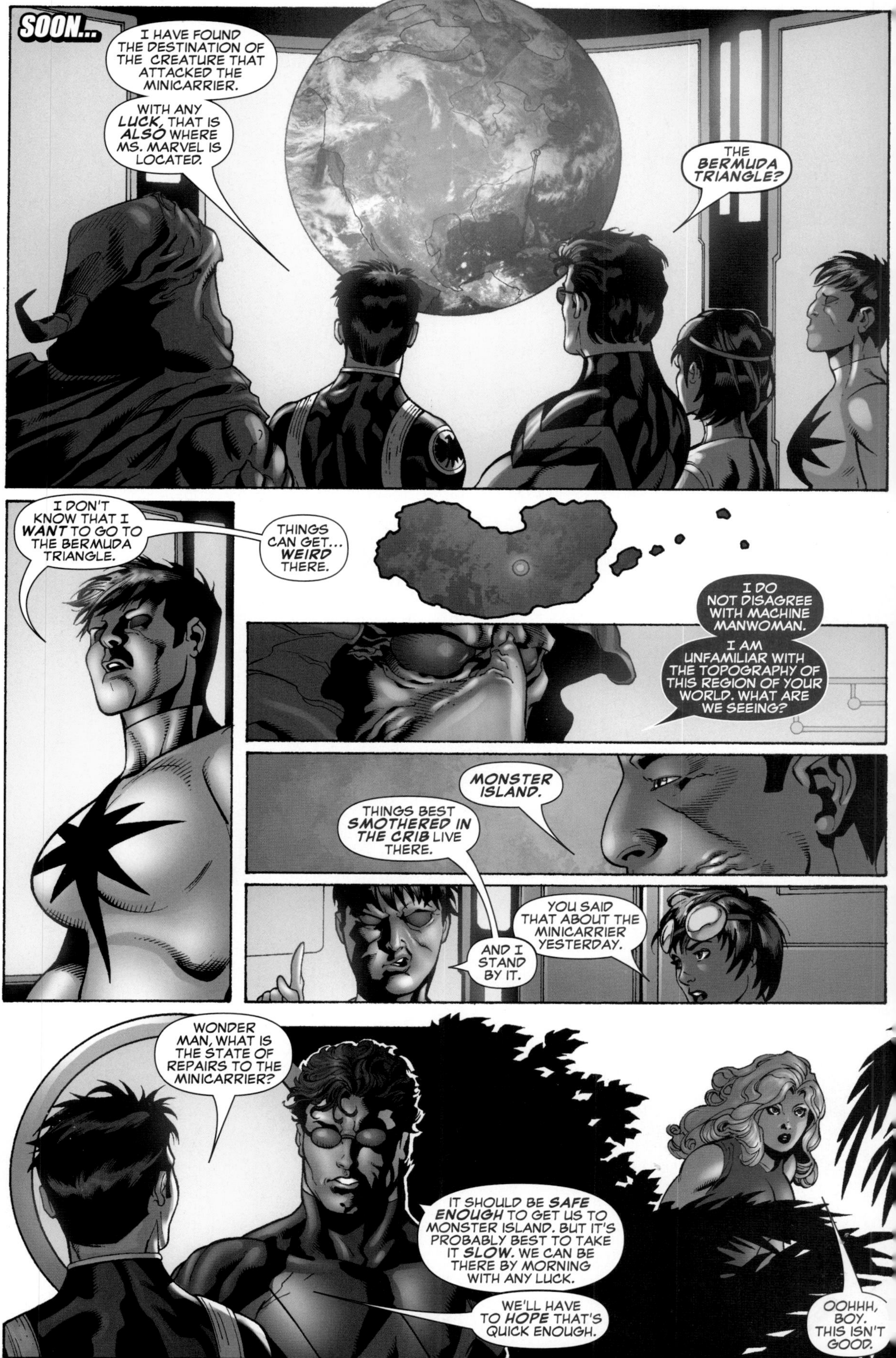
SOON...
I HAVE FOUND THE DESTINATION OF THE CREATURE THAT ATTACKED THE MINICARRIER.
WITH ANY LUCK, THAT IS ALSO WHERE MS. MARVEL IS LOCATED.
THE BERMUDA TRIANGLE?
I DON'T KNOW THAT I WANT TO GO TO THE BERMUDA TRIANGLE.
THINGS CAN GET... WEIRD THERE.
I DO NOT DISAGREE WITH MACHINE MANWOMAN.
I AM UNFAMILIAR WITH THE TOPOGRAPHY OF THIS REGION OF YOUR WORLD. WHAT ARE WE SEEING?
MONSTER ISLAND.
THINGS BEST SMOTHERED IN THE CRIB LIVE THERE.
YOU SAID THAT ABOUT THE MINICARRIER YESTERDAY.
AND I STAND BY IT.
WONDER MAN, WHAT IS THE STATE OF REPAIRS TO THE MINICARRIER?
IT SHOULD BE SAFE ENOUGH TO GET US TO MONSTER ISLAND. BUT IT'S PROBABLY BEST TO TAKE IT SLOW. WE CAN BE THERE BY MORNING WITH ANY LUCK.
WE'LL HAVE TO HOPE THAT'S QUICK ENOUGH.
OOHHH, BOY. THIS ISN'T GOOD.

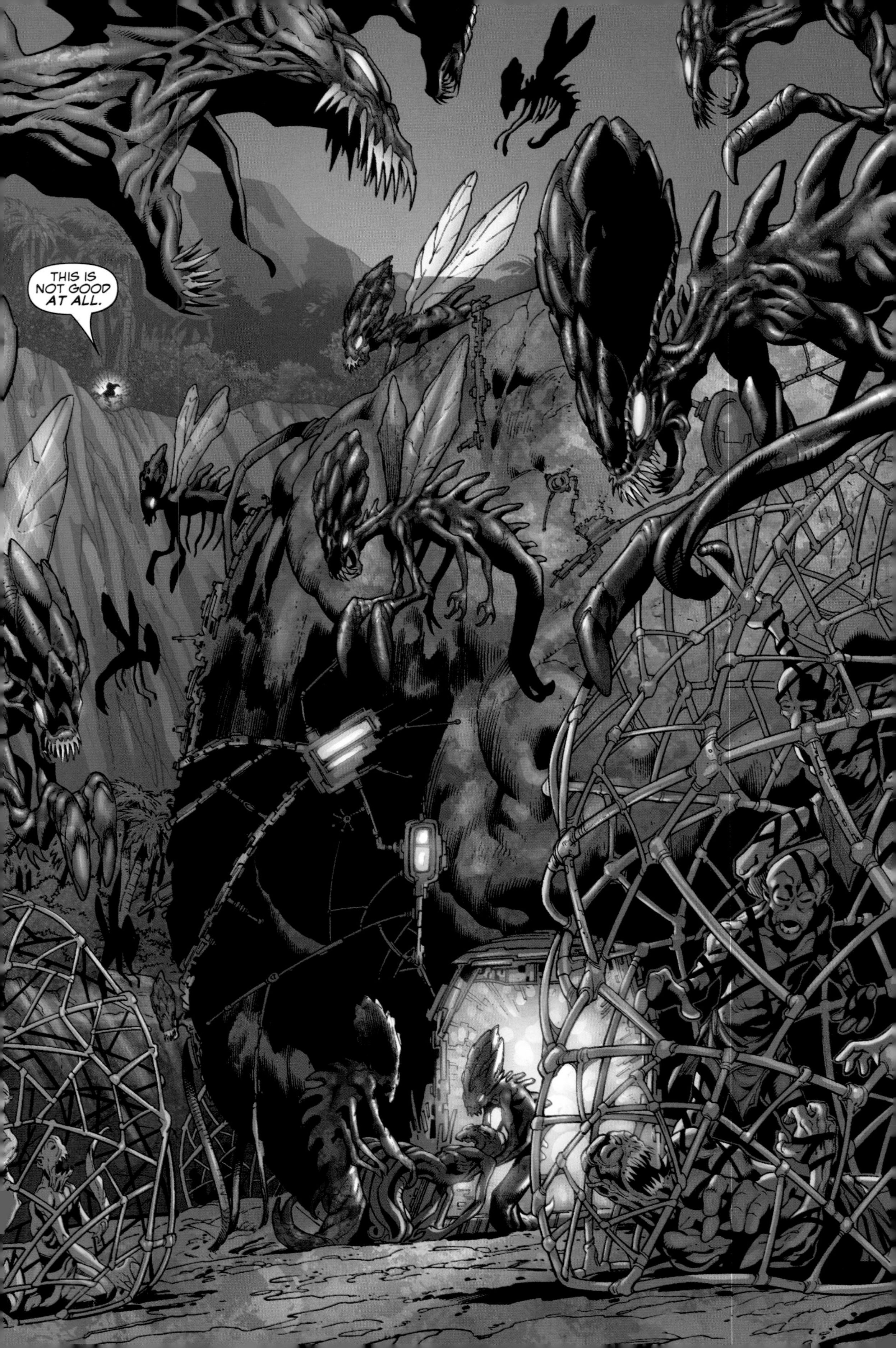
THIS IS NOT GOOD AT ALL.

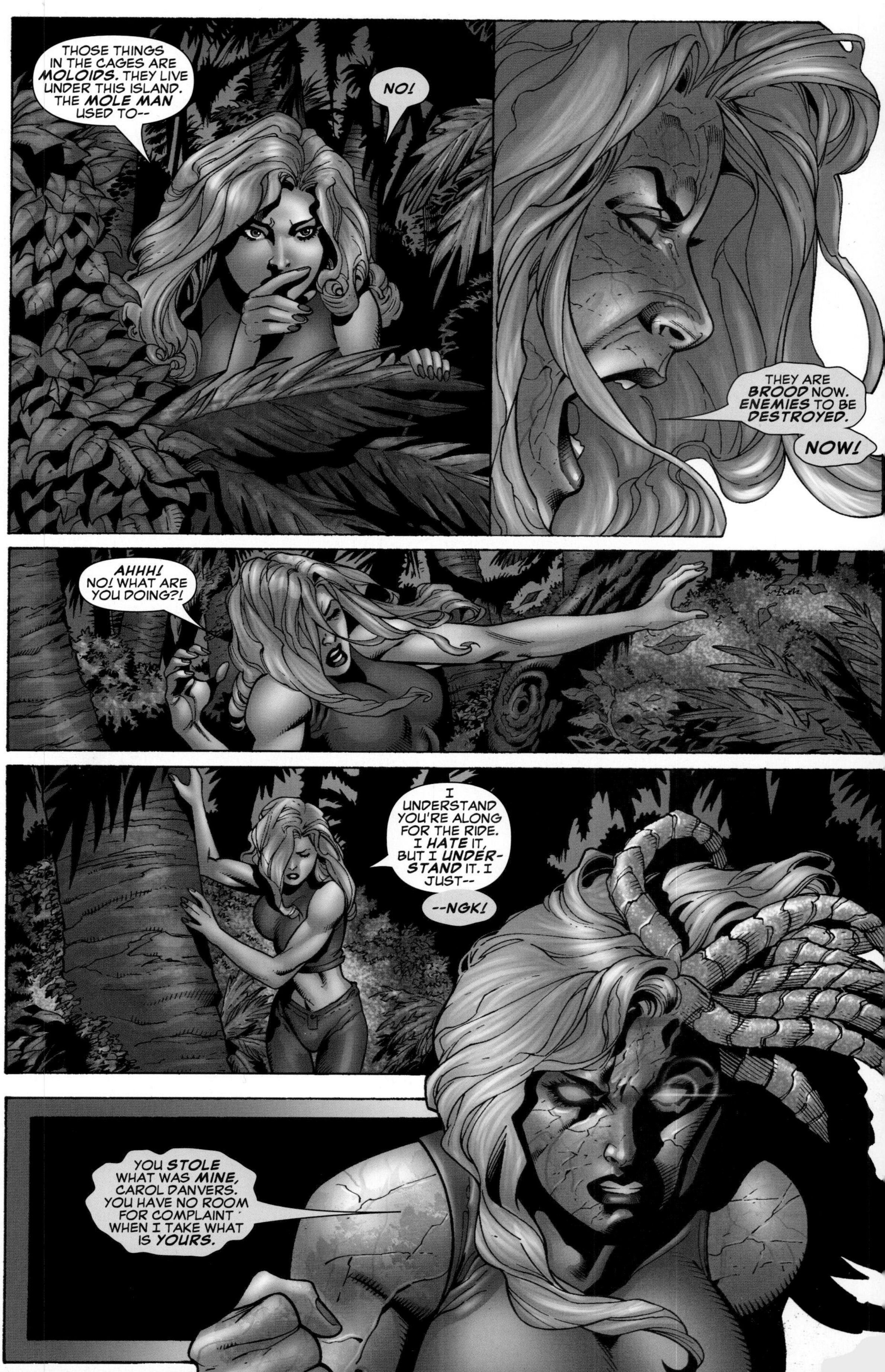
THOSE THINGS IN THE CAGES ARE MOLOIDS. THEY LIVE UNDER THIS ISLAND. THE MOLE MAN USED TO--
NO!
THEY ARE BROOD NOW. ENEMIES TO BE DESTROYED.
NOW!
AHHH! NO! WHAT ARE YOU DOING?!
I UNDERSTAND YOU'RE ALONG FOR THE RIDE. I HATE IT, BUT I UNDERSTAND IT. I JUST--
--NGK!
YOU STOLE WHAT WAS MINE, CAROL DANVERS. YOU HAVE NO ROOM FOR COMPLAINT WHEN I TAKE WHAT IS YOURS.

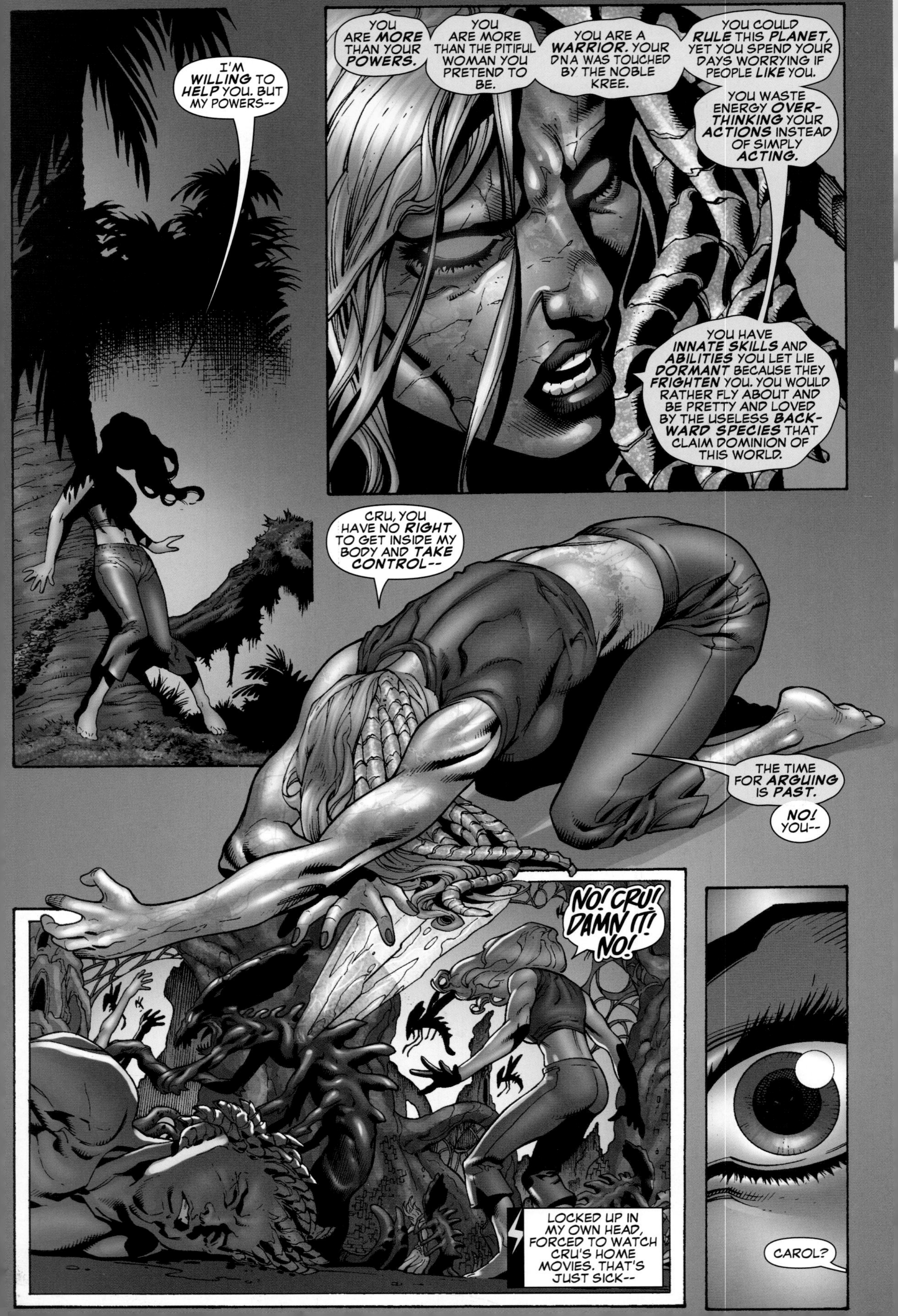
I'M WILLING TO HELP YOU. BUT MY POWERS--
YOU ARE MORE THAN YOUR POWERS.
YOU ARE MORE THAN THE PITIFUL WOMAN YOU PRETEND TO BE.
YOU ARE A WARRIOR. YOUR DNA WAS TOUCHED BY THE NOBLE KREE.
YOU COULD RULE THIS PLANET, YET YOU SPEND YOUR DAYS WORRYING IF PEOPLE LIKE YOU.
YOU WASTE ENERGY OVER-THINKING YOUR ACTIONS INSTEAD OF SIMPLY ACTING.
YOU HAVE INNATE SKILLS AND ABILITIES YOU LET LIE DORMANT BECAUSE THEY FRIGHTEN YOU. YOU WOULD RATHER FLY ABOUT AND BE PRETTY AND LOVED BY THE USELESS BACK-WARD SPECIES THAT CLAIM DOMINION OF THIS WORLD.
CRU, YOU HAVE NO RIGHT TO GET INSIDE MY BODY AND TAKE CONTROL--
THE TIME FOR ARGUING IS PAST.
NO! YOU--
NO! CRU! DAMN IT! NO!
LOCKED UP IN MY OWN HEAD, FORCED TO WATCH CRU'S HOME MOVIES. THAT'S JUST SICK--
CAROL?

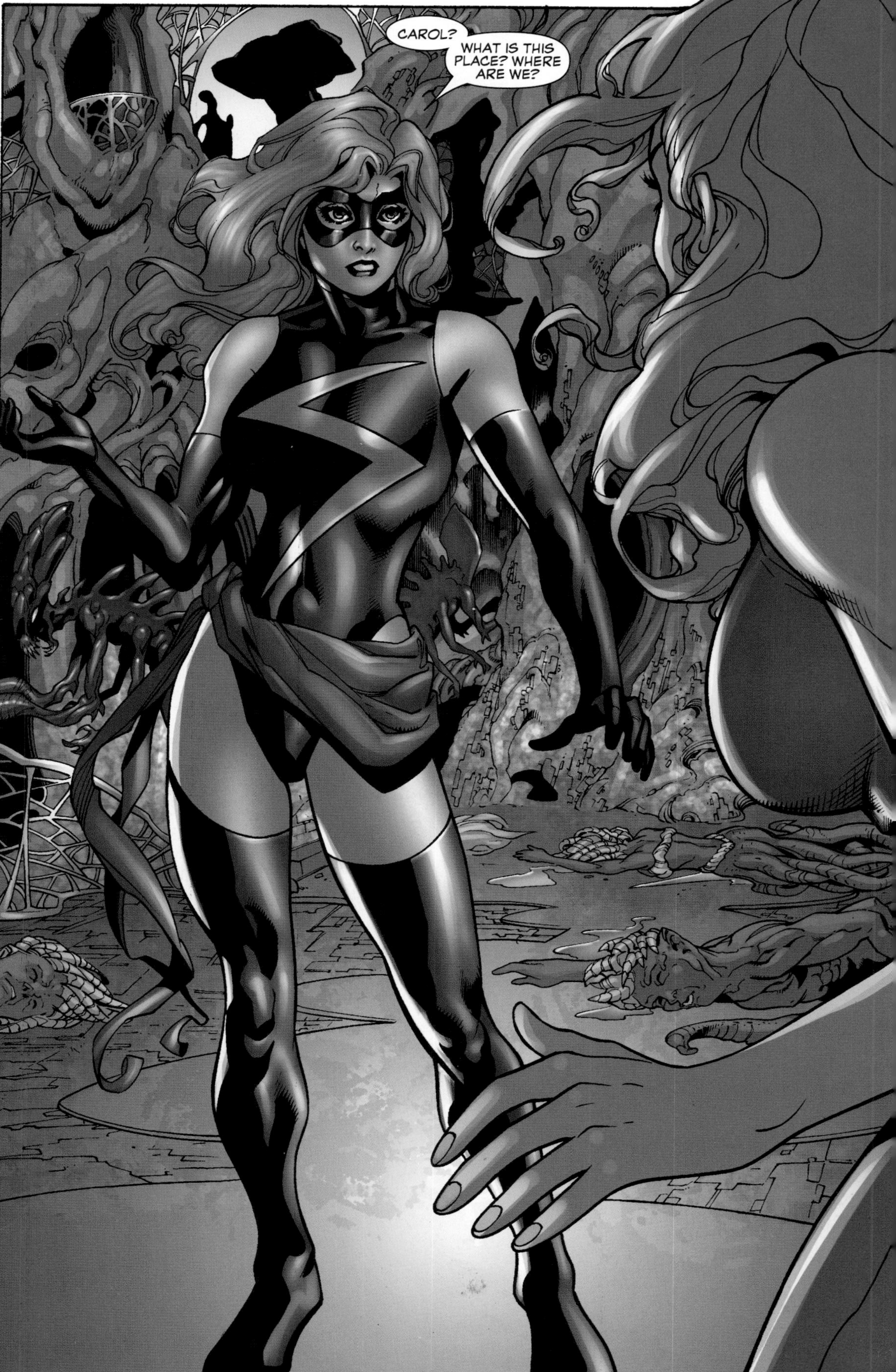
CAROL?
WHAT IS THIS PLACE? WHERE ARE WE?

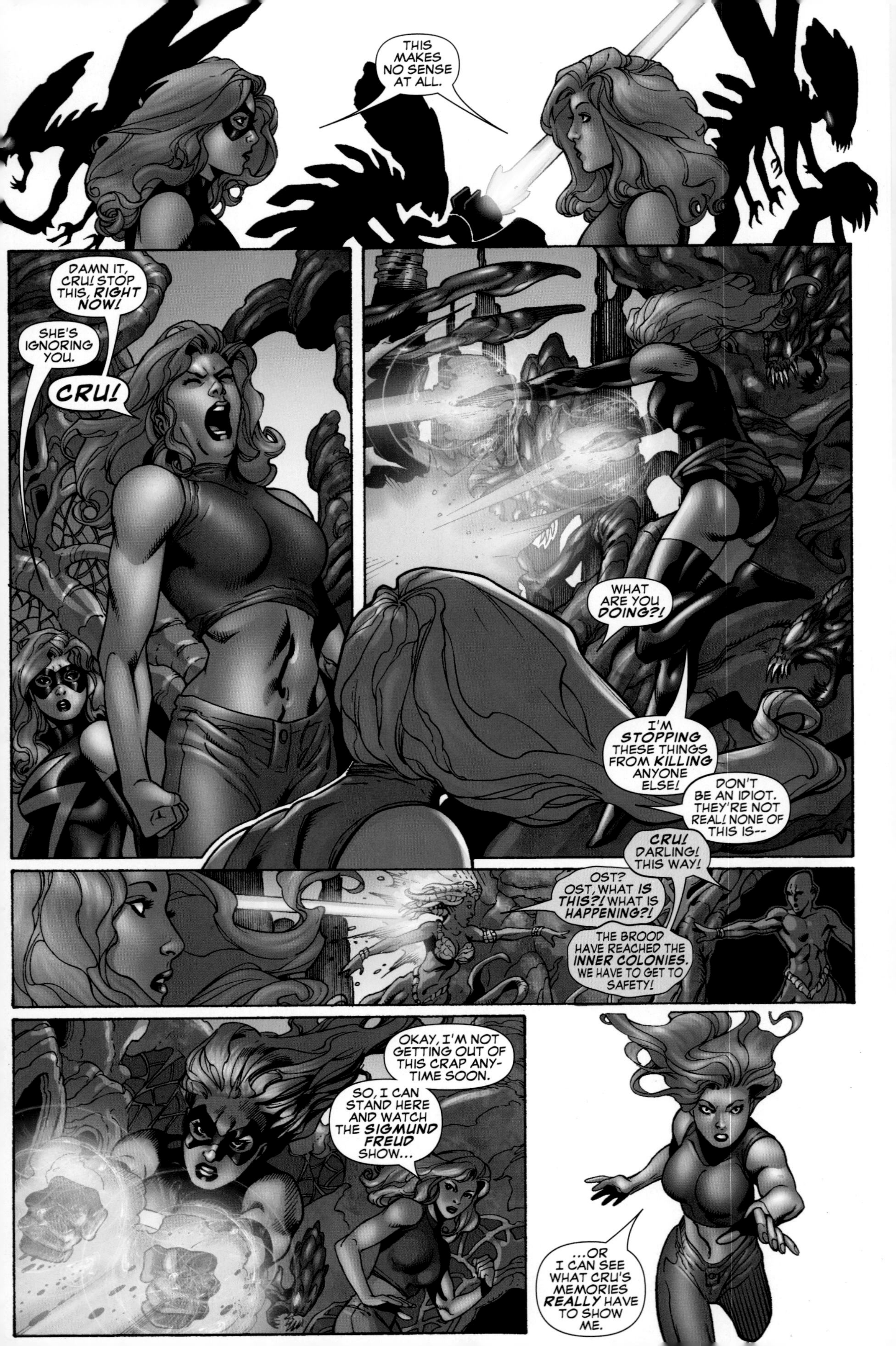
THIS MAKES NO SENSE AT ALL.
DAMN IT, CRU! STOP THIS, RIGHT NOW!
SHE'S IGNORING YOU.
CRU!
WHAT ARE YOU DOING?!
I'M STOPPING THESE THINGS FROM KILLING ANYONE ELSE!
DON'T BE AN IDIOT. THEY'RE NOT REAL! NONE OF THIS IS--
CRU! DARLING! THIS WAY!
OST? OST, WHAT IS THIS?! WHAT IS HAPPENING?!
THE BROOD HAVE REACHED THE INNER COLONIES. WE HAVE TO GET TO SAFETY!
OKAY, I'M NOT GETTING OUT OF THIS CRAP ANY-TIME SOON.
SO, I CAN STAND HERE AND WATCH THE SIGMUND FREUD SHOW...
...OR I CAN SEE WHAT CRU'S MEMORIES REALLY HAVE TO SHOW ME.

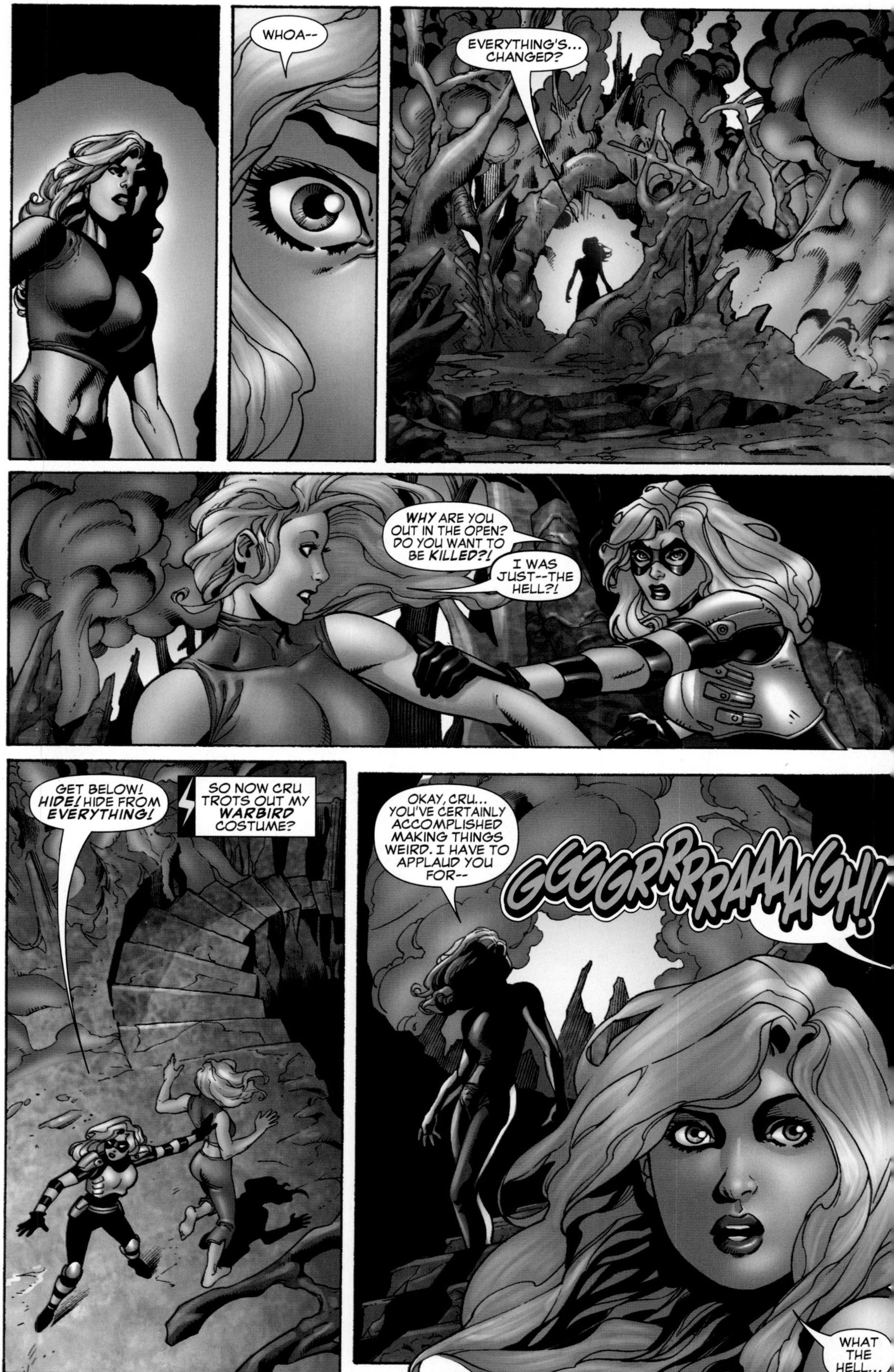

WHOA--
EVERYTHING'S... CHANGED?
WHY ARE YOU OUT IN THE OPEN? DO YOU WANT TO BE KILLED?!
I WAS JUST--THE HELL?!
GET BELOW! HIDE! HIDE FROM EVERYTHING!
SO NOW CRU TROTS OUT MY WARBIRD COSTUME?
OKAY, CRU... YOU'VE CERTAINLY ACCOMPLISHED MAKING THINGS WEIRD. I HAVE TO APPLAUD YOU FOR--
GGGGRRRRAAAAAGH!
WHAT THE HELL...

PLEAAASE! STOOONNNYYYAAA!

FAMILIAR, YES?

BINARY?! WHAT IS THIS? WHAT'S *HAPPENING?* WHY AM I GETTING THE OLD COSTUME TOUR?

CRU IS BEING... AUGMENTED.

SHE *VOLUNTEERED* FOR THIS PROCEDURE, HOPING TO AVENGE THE BROOD MURDER OF HER *HUSBAND,* OST, AND THEIR *CHILDREN.*

SHE *VOLUNTEERED?*

UNLIKE YOU AND I.

BUT THE RESULT IS THE *SAME,* YES? A *BEAUTIFUL WOMAN* HAS BEEN TURNED INTO A *MONSTER.*

A *KILLING MACHINE.*

I'M *NOT* LIKE THAT. I WAS NEVER--NOT EVEN WHEN I WAS *YOU.*

IF YOU LEARN *NOTHING ELSE* IN THIS LIFE, CAROL, YOU NEED TO LEARN *THIS* ONE LESSON.

WE ARE *EXACTLY* LIKE THAT.

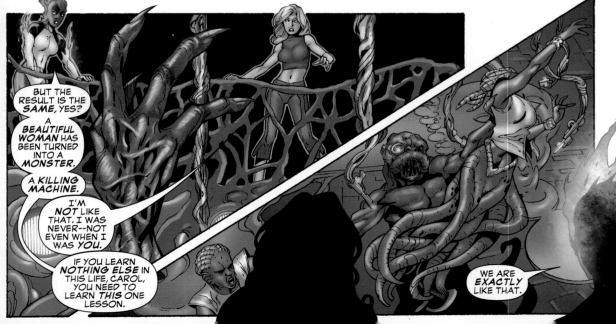

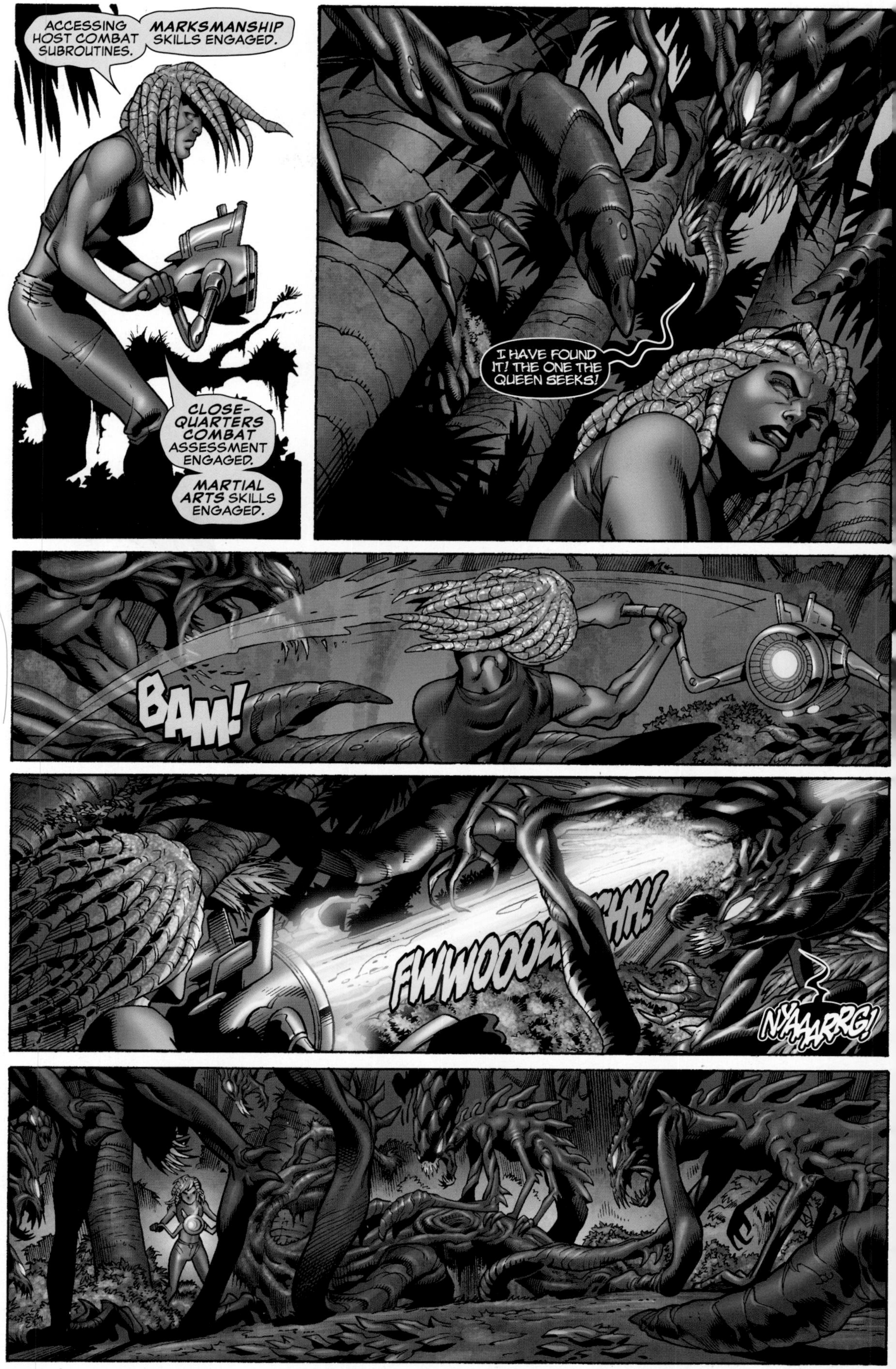
ACCESSING HOST COMBAT SUBROUTINES.
MARKSMANSHIP SKILLS ENGAGED.
CLOSE-QUARTERS COMBAT ASSESSMENT ENGAGED.
MARTIAL ARTS SKILLS ENGAGED.
I HAVE FOUND IT! THE ONE THE QUEEN SEEKS!
BAM!
NYAAARRG!

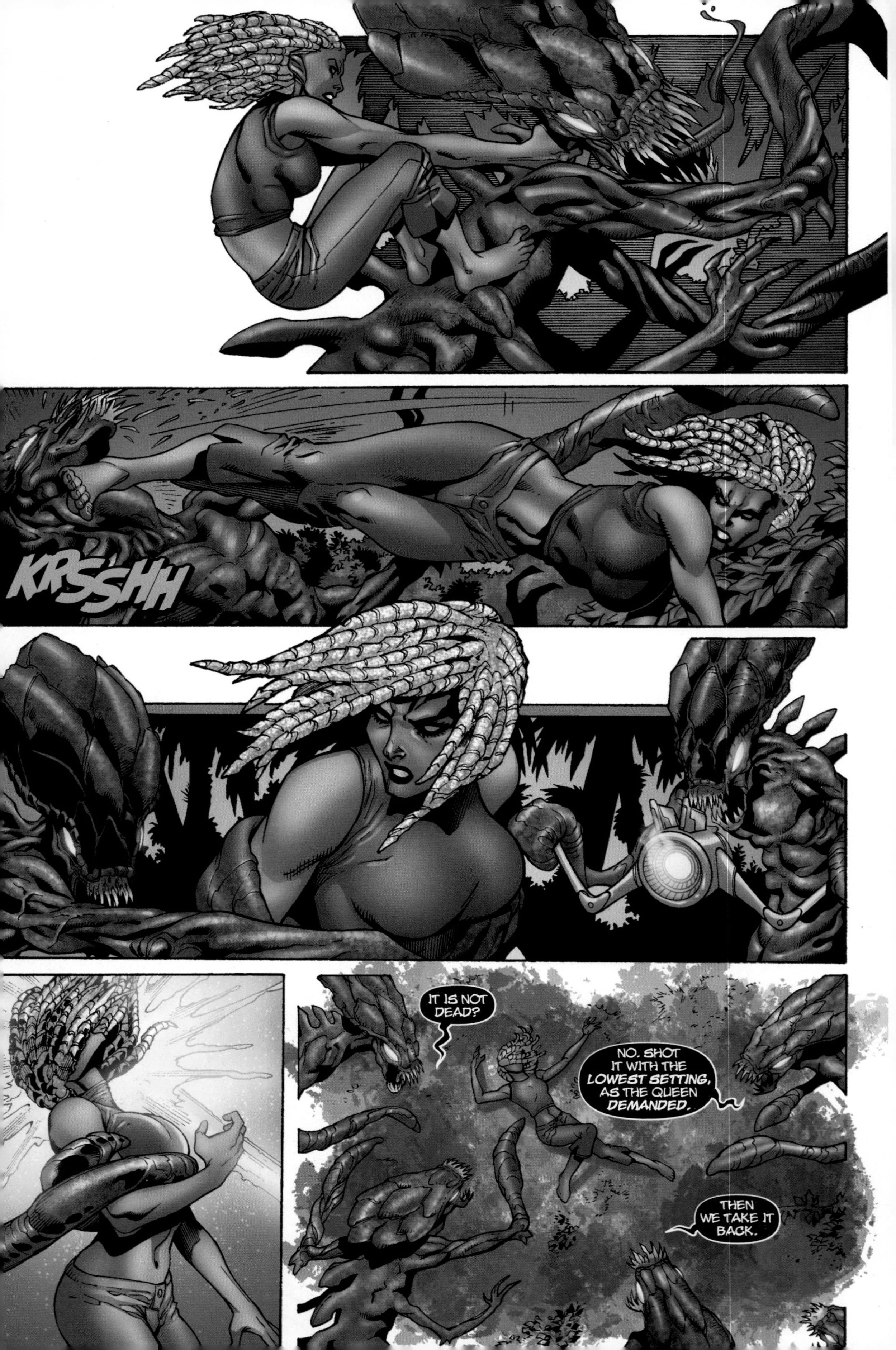
KRSSHH
IT IS NOT DEAD?
NO. SHOT IT WITH THE LOWEST SETTING, AS THE QUEEN DEMANDED.
THEN WE TAKE IT BACK.

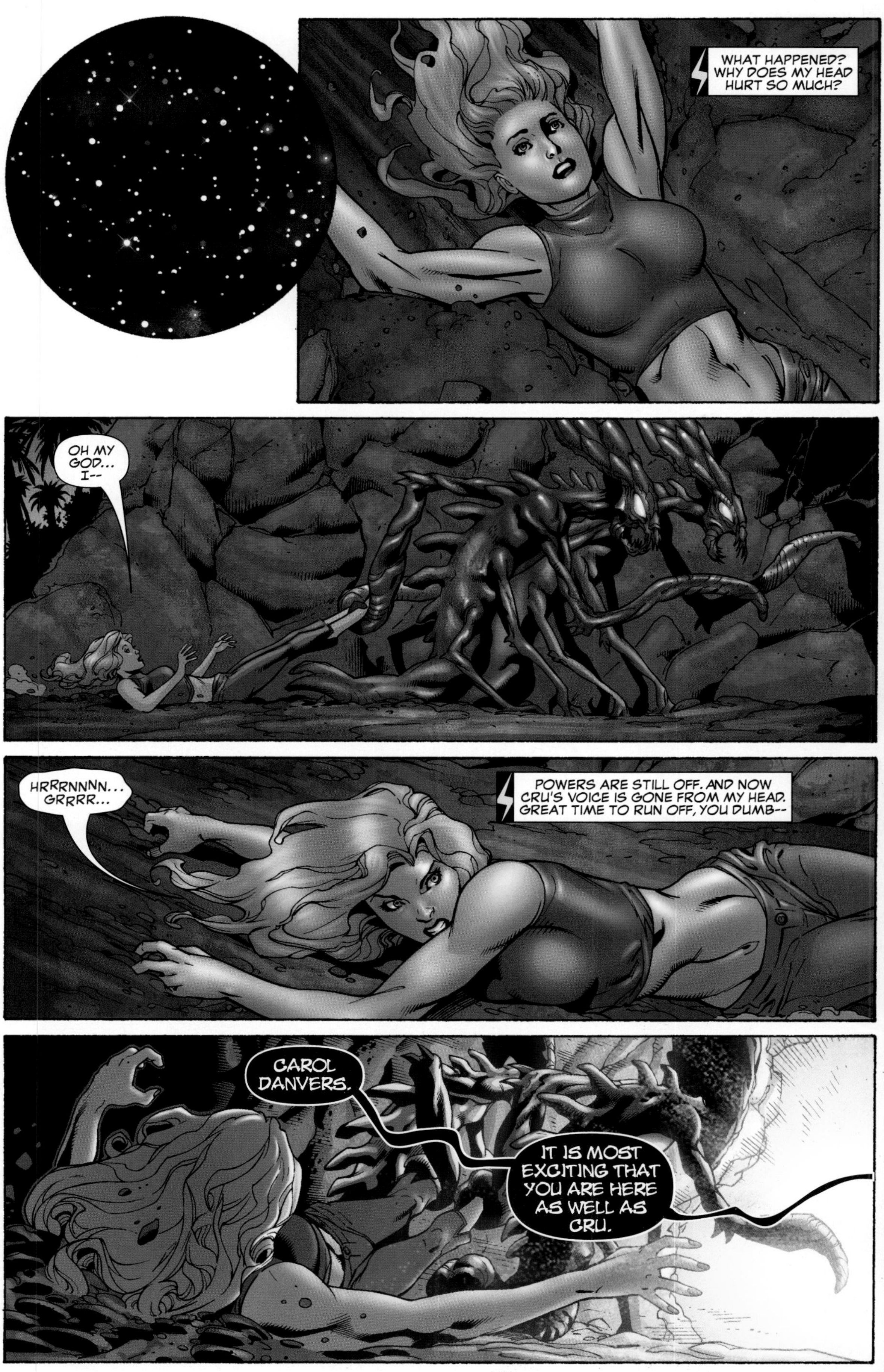

WHAT HAPPENED? WHY DOES MY HEAD HURT SO MUCH?
OH MY GOD... I--
HRRRNNNN... GRRRR...
POWERS ARE STILL OFF. AND NOW CRU'S VOICE IS GONE FROM MY HEAD. GREAT TIME TO RUN OFF, YOU DUMB--
CAROL DANVERS.
IT IS MOST EXCITING THAT YOU ARE HERE AS WELL AS CRU.

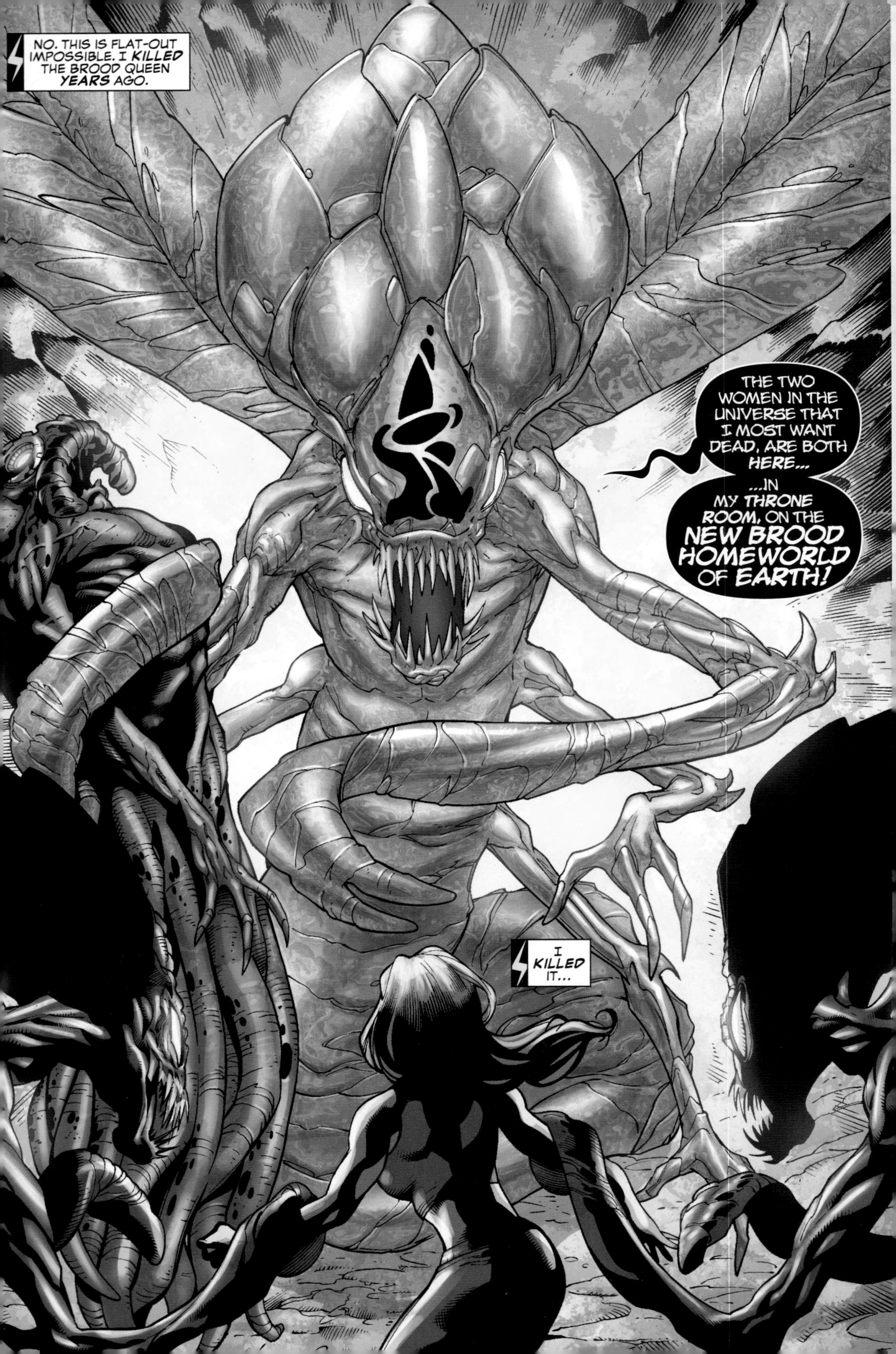
NO. THIS IS FLAT-OUT IMPOSSIBLE. I KILLED THE BROOD QUEEN YEARS AGO.
THE TWO WOMEN IN THE UNIVERSE THAT I MOST WANT DEAD, ARE BOTH HERE...
...IN MY THRONE ROOM, ON THE NEW BROOD HOMEWORLD OF EARTH!
I KILLED IT...

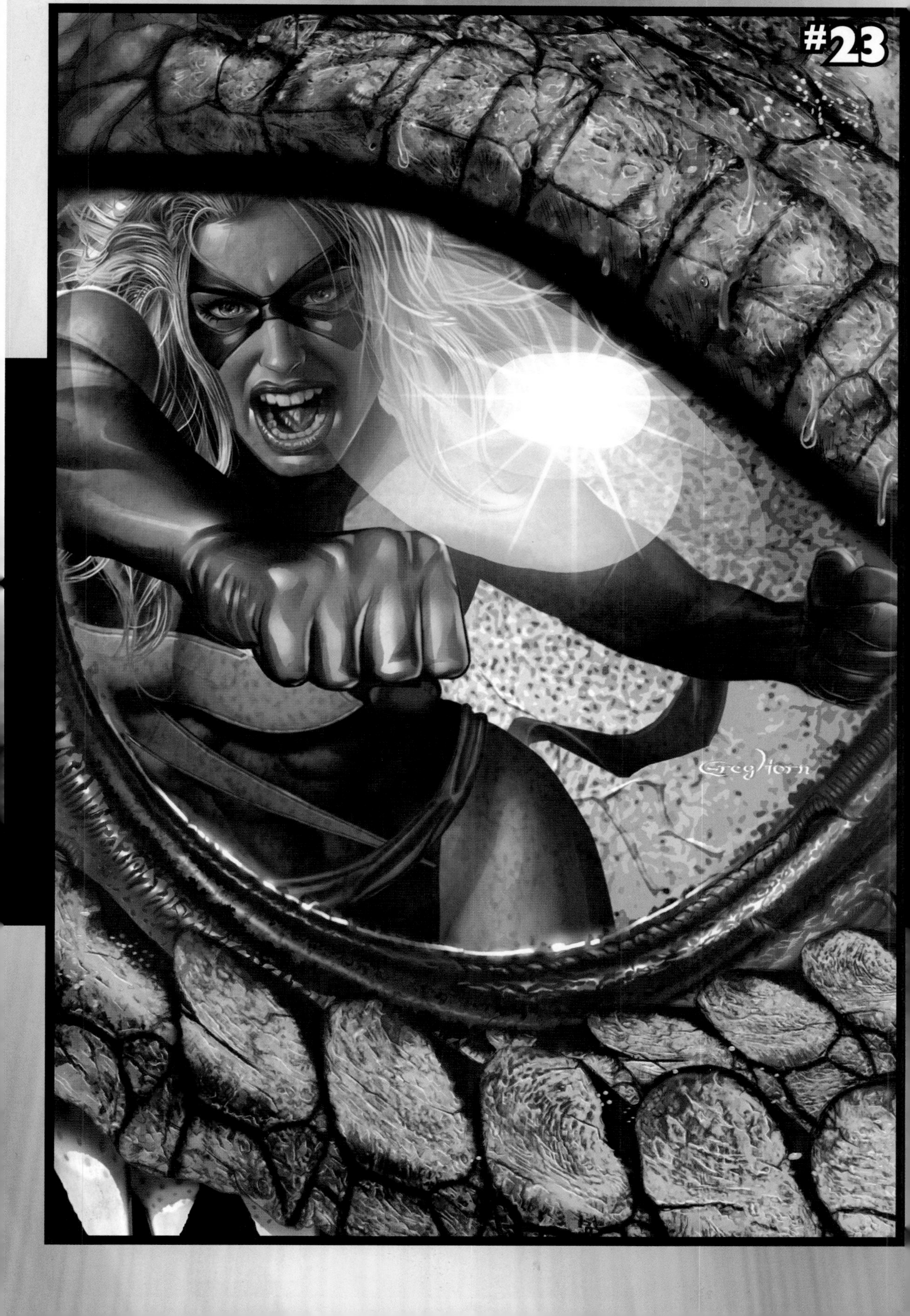
#23
Greg Horn

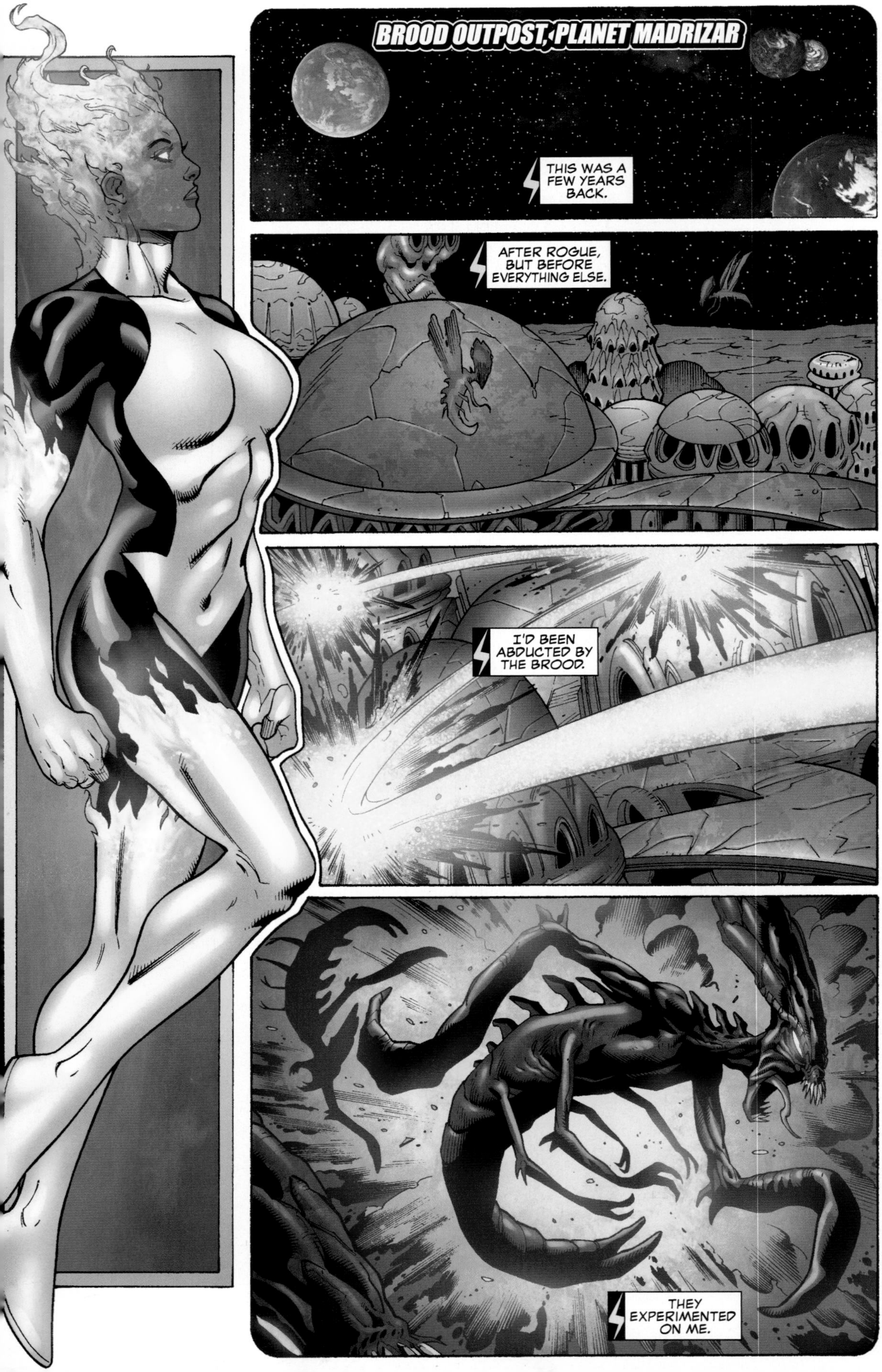
BROOD OUTPOST, PLANET MADRIZAR
THIS WAS A FEW YEARS BACK.
AFTER ROGUE, BUT BEFORE EVERYTHING ELSE.
I'D BEEN ABDUCTED BY THE BROOD.
THEY EXPERIMENTED ON ME.

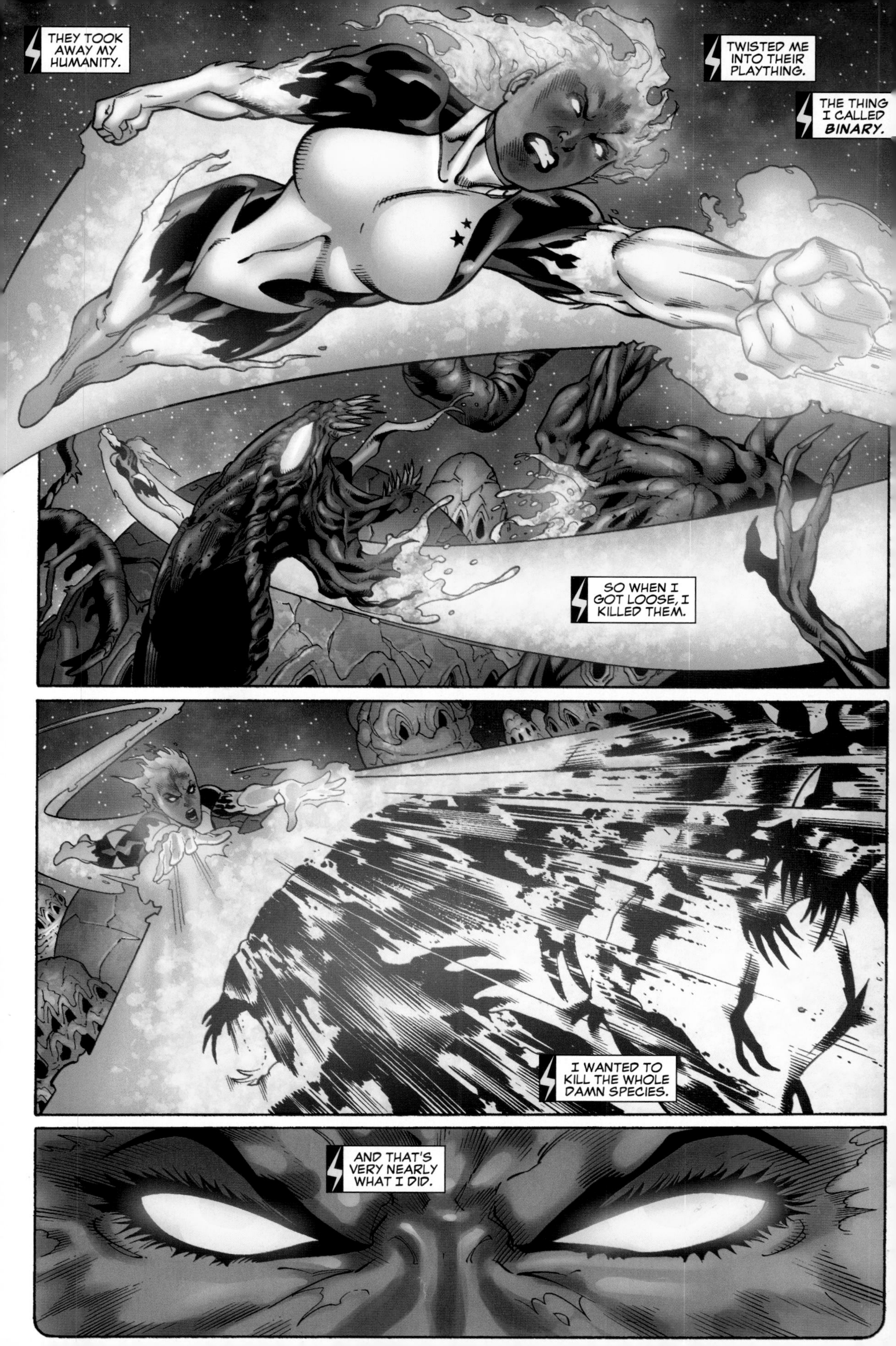
THEY TOOK AWAY MY HUMANITY.
TWISTED ME INTO THEIR PLAYTHING.
THE THING I CALLED BINARY.
SO WHEN I GOT LOOSE, I KILLED THEM.
I WANTED TO KILL THE WHOLE DAMN SPECIES.
AND THAT'S VERY NEARLY WHAT I DID.

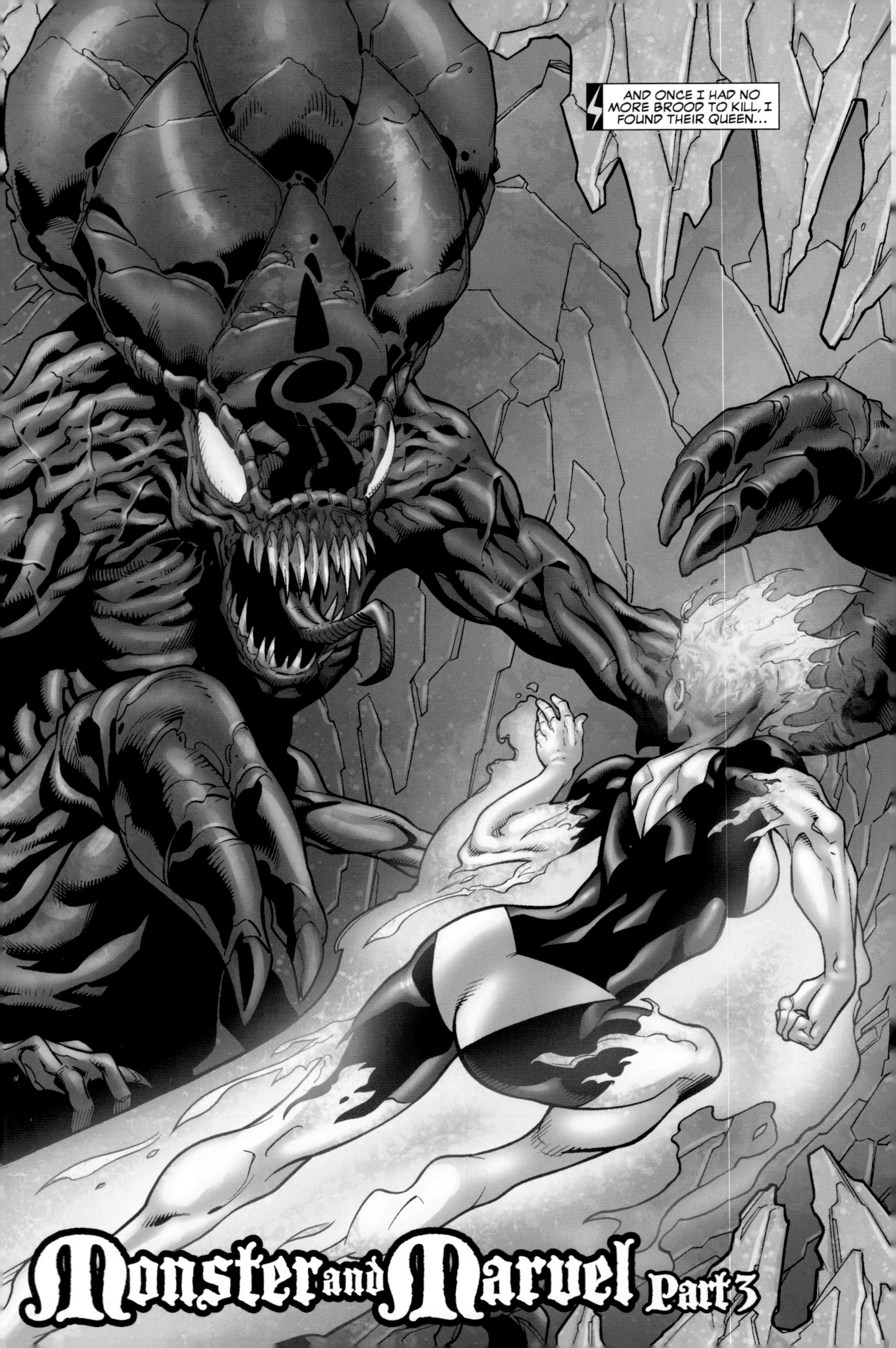
AND ONCE I HAD NO MORE BROOD TO KILL, I FOUND THEIR QUEEN...
Monster and Marvel Part 3

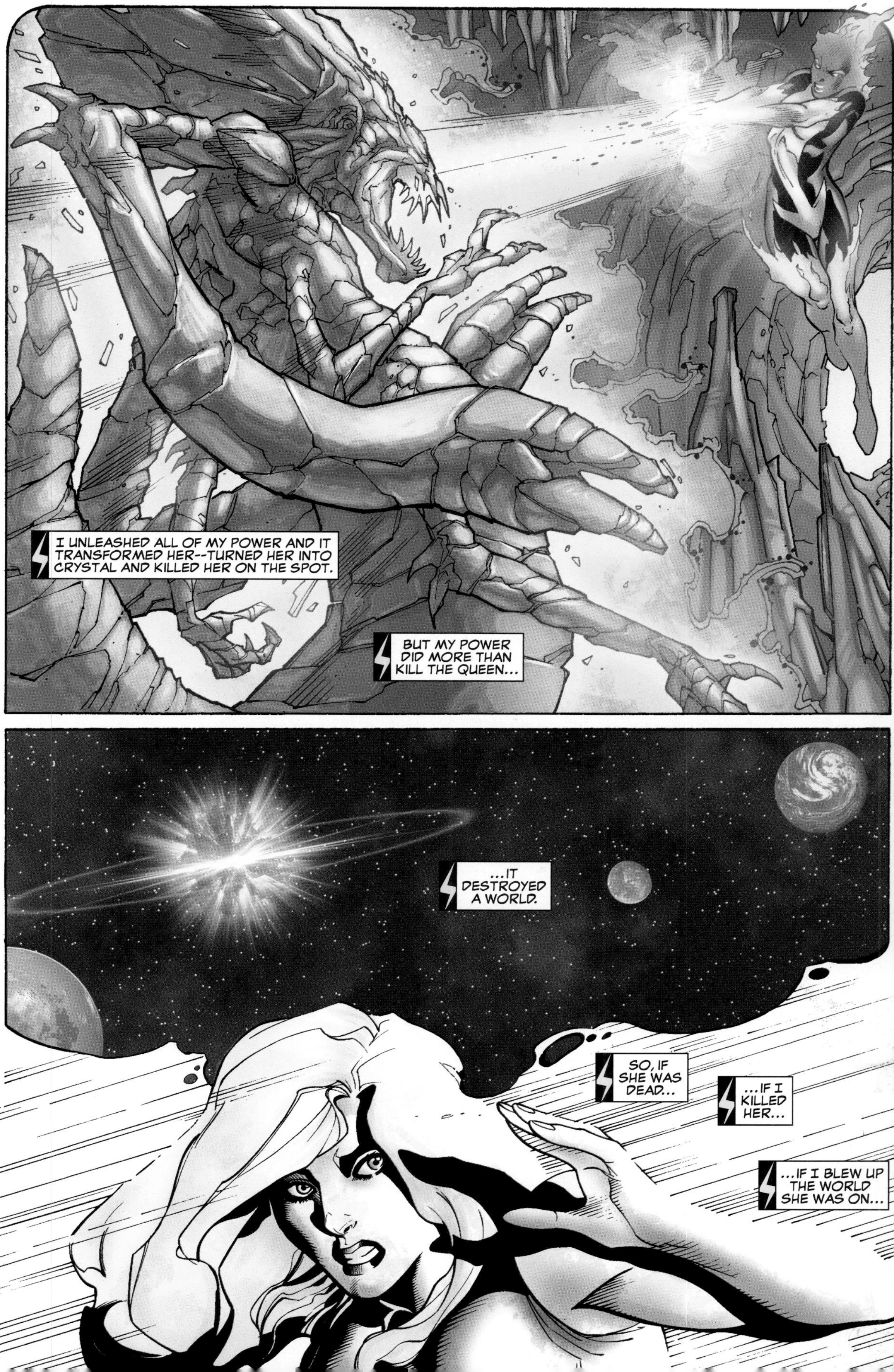
I UNLEASHED ALL OF MY POWER AND IT TRANSFORMED HER--TURNED HER INTO CRYSTAL AND KILLED HER ON THE SPOT.
BUT MY POWER DID MORE THAN KILL THE QUEEN...
...IT DESTROYED A WORLD.
SO, IF SHE WAS DEAD...
...IF I KILLED HER...
...IF I BLEW UP THE WORLD SHE WAS ON...

...HOW CAN SHE BE HERE? ON EARTH?

CAROL DANVERS...

...I'VE THOUGHT ABOUT YOU FOR A LONG, LONG TIME, SWEET ONE.

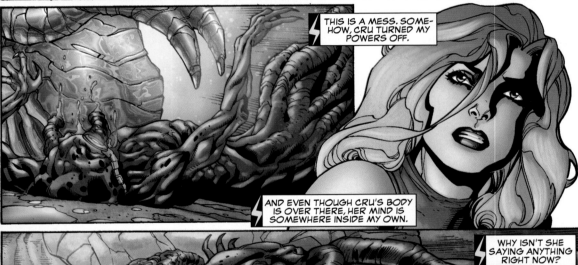

THIS IS A MESS. SOMEHOW, CRU TURNED MY POWERS OFF.

AND EVEN THOUGH CRU'S BODY IS OVER THERE, HER MIND IS SOMEWHERE INSIDE MY OWN.

WHY ISN'T SHE SAYING ANYTHING RIGHT NOW?

I NEVER THOUGHT I'D WORRY ABOUT NOT HEARING VOICES IN MY HEAD.

I AM SO VERY EXCITED THAT YOU ARE HERE.

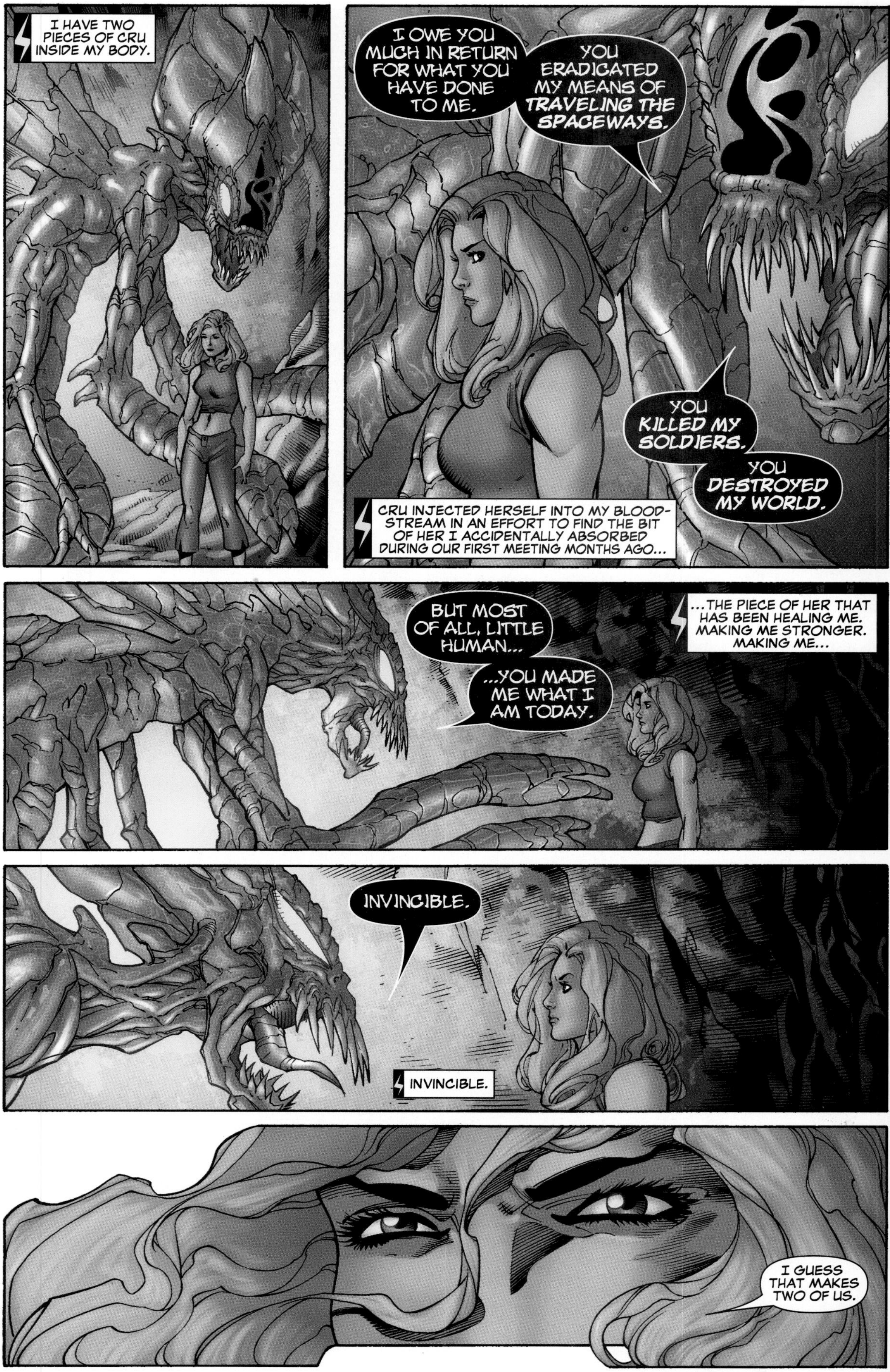
I HAVE TWO PIECES OF CRU INSIDE MY BODY.
I OWE YOU MUCH IN RETURN FOR WHAT YOU HAVE DONE TO ME.
YOU ERADICATED MY MEANS OF TRAVELING THE SPACEWAYS.
YOU KILLED MY SOLDIERS.
YOU DESTROYED MY WORLD.
CRU INJECTED HERSELF INTO MY BLOOD-STREAM IN AN EFFORT TO FIND THE BIT OF HER I ACCIDENTALLY ABSORBED DURING OUR FIRST MEETING MONTHS AGO...
BUT MOST OF ALL, LITTLE HUMAN...
...YOU MADE ME WHAT I AM TODAY.
...THE PIECE OF HER THAT HAS BEEN HEALING ME. MAKING ME STRONGER. MAKING ME...
INVINCIBLE.
INVINCIBLE.
I GUESS THAT MAKES TWO OF US.

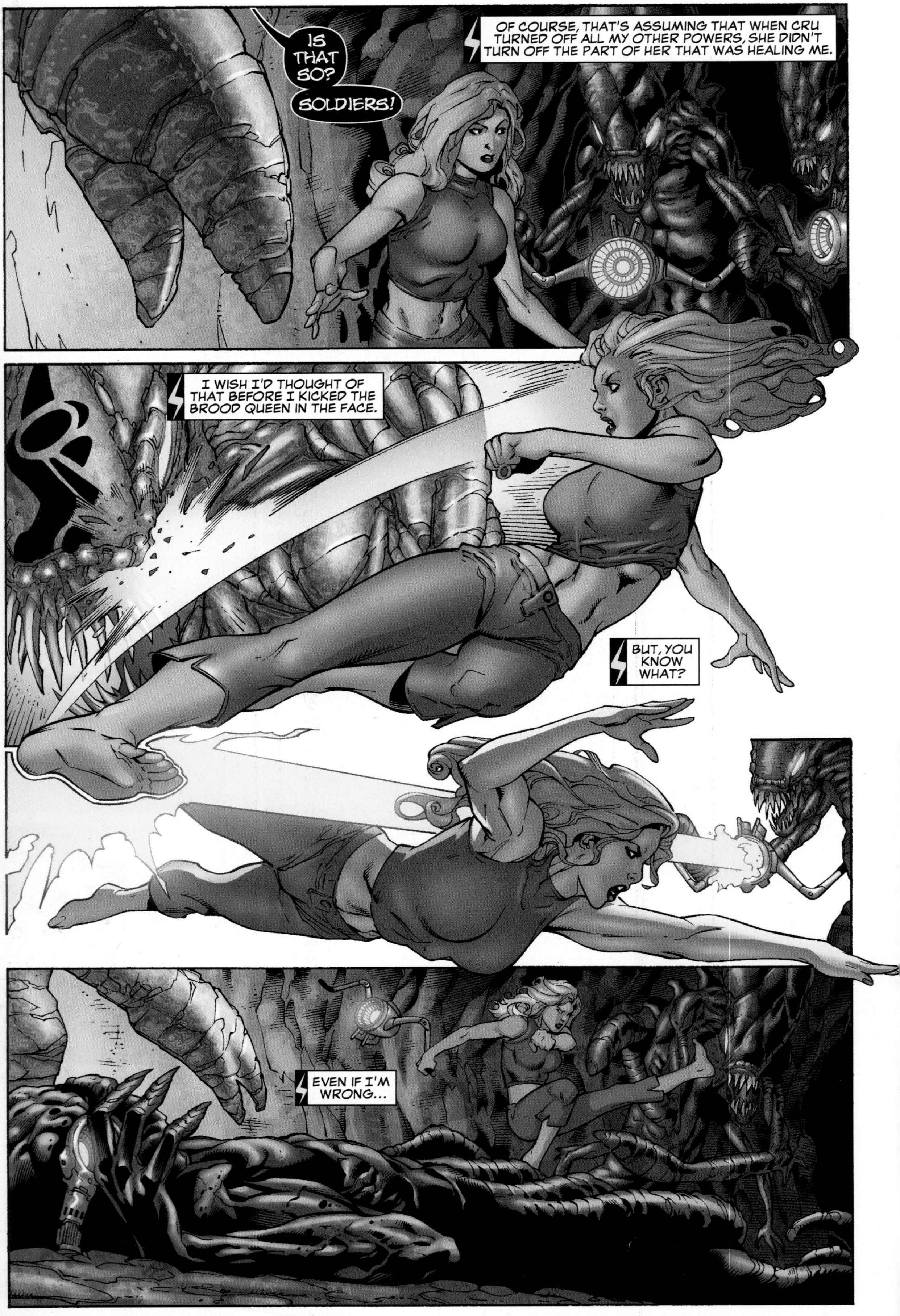

IS THAT SO?
SOLDIERS!
OF COURSE, THAT'S ASSUMING THAT WHEN CRU TURNED OFF ALL MY OTHER POWERS, SHE DIDN'T TURN OFF THE PART OF HER THAT WAS HEALING ME.
I WISH I'D THOUGHT OF THAT BEFORE I KICKED THE BROOD QUEEN IN THE FACE.
BUT, YOU KNOW WHAT?
EVEN IF I'M WRONG...

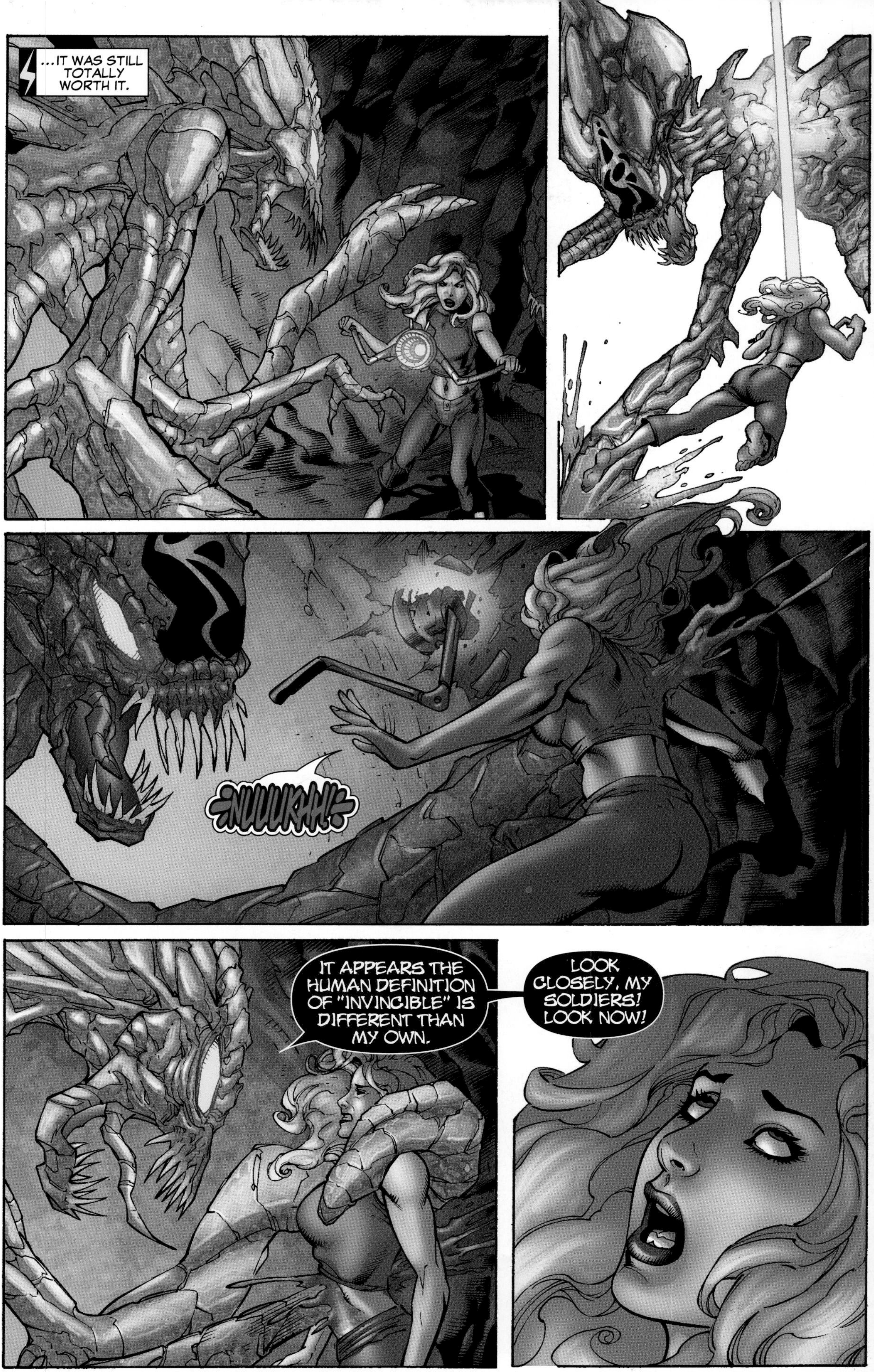

...IT WAS STILL TOTALLY WORTH IT.
NUUUKAH!
IT APPEARS THE HUMAN DEFINITION OF "INVINCIBLE" IS DIFFERENT THAN MY OWN.
LOOK CLOSELY, MY SOLDIERS! LOOK NOW!

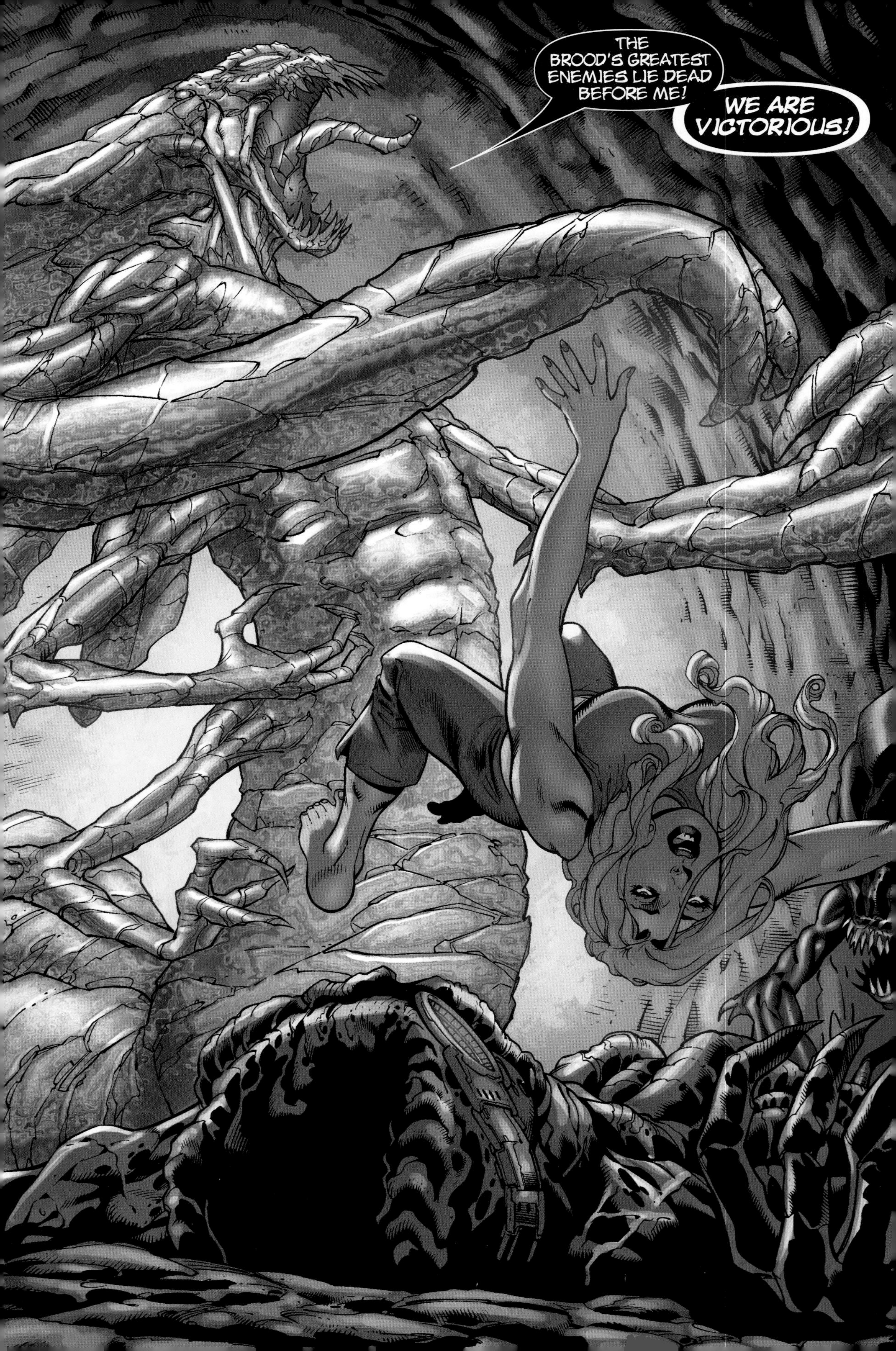
THE BROOD'S GREATEST ENEMIES LIE DEAD BEFORE ME!
WE ARE VICTORIOUS!

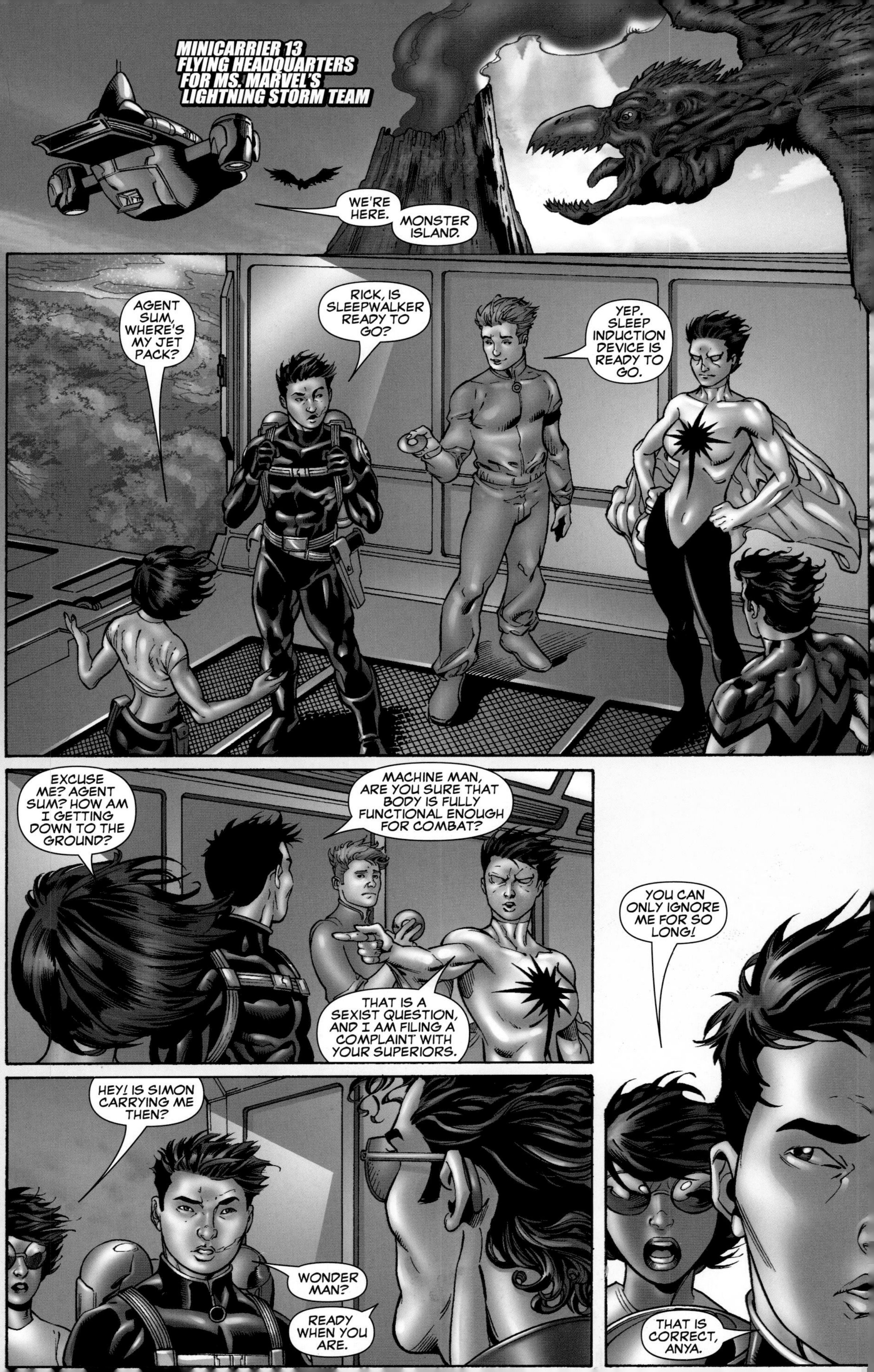
MINICARRIER 13
FLYING HEADQUARTERS
FOR MS. MARVEL'S
LIGHTNING STORM TEAM
WE'RE HERE.
MONSTER ISLAND.
AGENT SUM, WHERE'S MY JET PACK?
RICK, IS SLEEPWALKER READY TO GO?
YEP. SLEEP INDUCTION DEVICE IS READY TO GO.
EXCUSE ME? AGENT SUM? HOW AM I GETTING DOWN TO THE GROUND?
MACHINE MAN, ARE YOU SURE THAT BODY IS FULLY FUNCTIONAL ENOUGH FOR COMBAT?
THAT IS A SEXIST QUESTION, AND I AM FILING A COMPLAINT WITH YOUR SUPERIORS.
YOU CAN ONLY IGNORE ME FOR SO LONG!
HEY! IS SIMON CARRYING ME THEN?
WONDER MAN?
READY WHEN YOU ARE.
THAT IS CORRECT, ANYA.

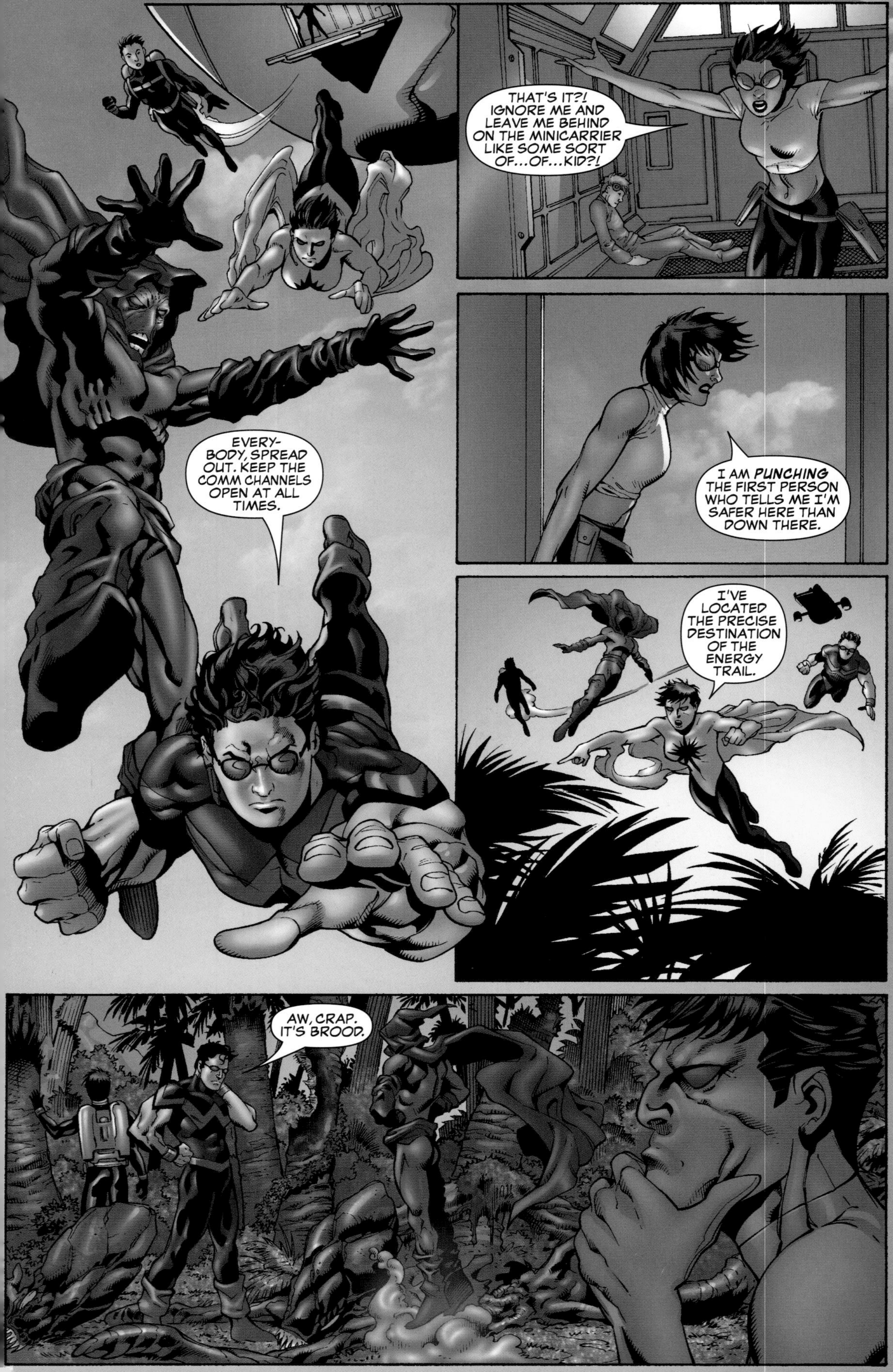
THAT'S IT?! IGNORE ME AND LEAVE ME BEHIND ON THE MINICARRIER LIKE SOME SORT OF...OF...KID?!
I AM PUNCHING THE FIRST PERSON WHO TELLS ME I'M SAFER HERE THAN DOWN THERE.
EVERY-BODY, SPREAD OUT. KEEP THE COMM CHANNELS OPEN AT ALL TIMES.
I'VE LOCATED THE PRECISE DESTINATION OF THE ENERGY TRAIL.
AW, CRAP. IT'S BROOD.

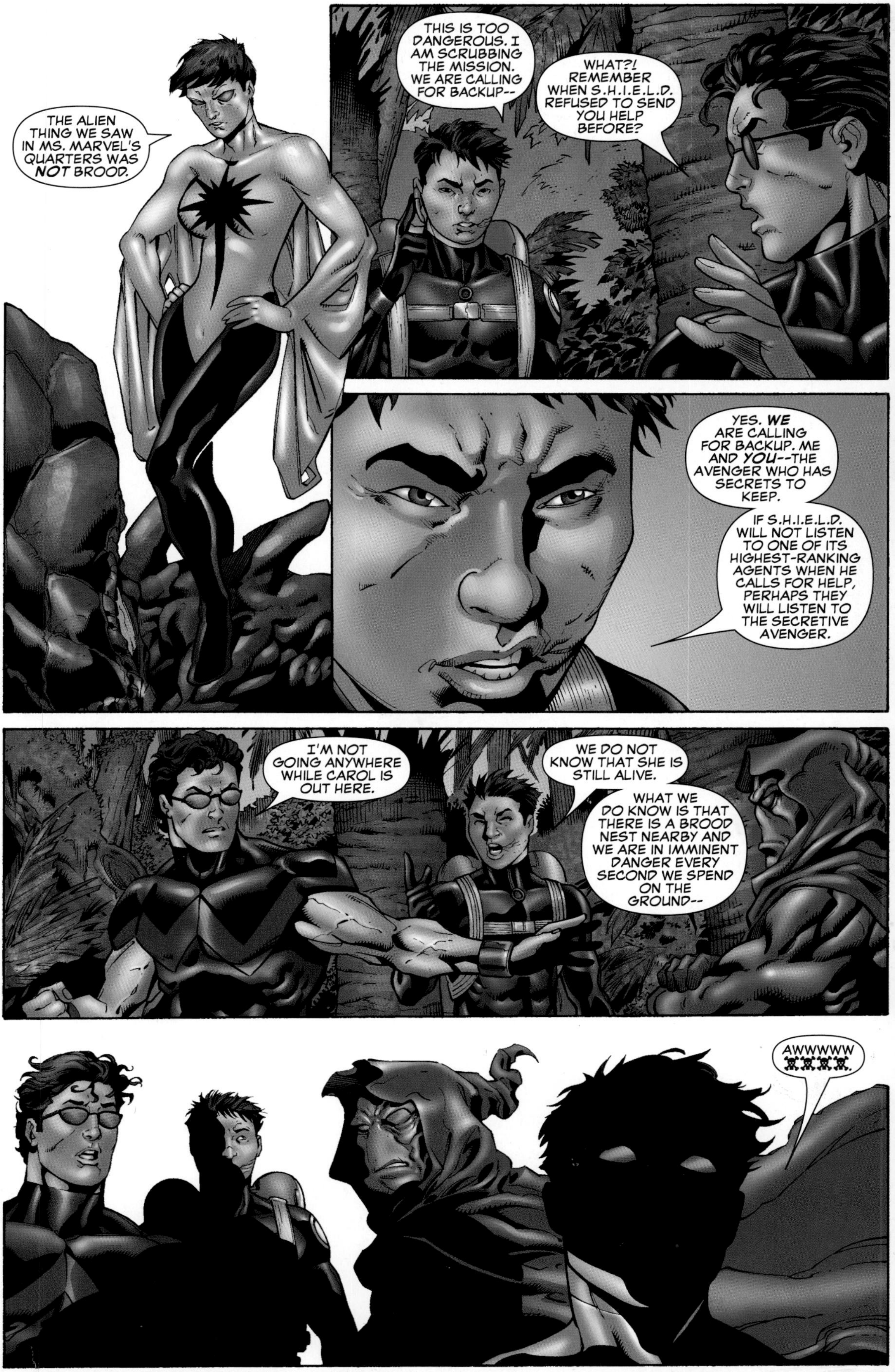
THE ALIEN THING WE SAW IN MS. MARVEL'S QUARTERS WAS NOT BROOD.
THIS IS TOO DANGEROUS. I AM SCRUBBING THE MISSION. WE ARE CALLING FOR BACKUP--
WHAT?! REMEMBER WHEN S.H.I.E.L.D. REFUSED TO SEND YOU HELP BEFORE?
YES. WE ARE CALLING FOR BACKUP. ME AND YOU--THE AVENGER WHO HAS SECRETS TO KEEP.
IF S.H.I.E.L.D. WILL NOT LISTEN TO ONE OF ITS HIGHEST-RANKING AGENTS WHEN HE CALLS FOR HELP, PERHAPS THEY WILL LISTEN TO THE SECRETIVE AVENGER.
I'M NOT GOING ANYWHERE WHILE CAROL IS OUT HERE.
WE DO NOT KNOW THAT SHE IS STILL ALIVE.
WHAT WE DO KNOW IS THAT THERE IS A BROOD NEST NEARBY AND WE ARE IN IMMINENT DANGER EVERY SECOND WE SPEND ON THE GROUND--
AWWWWW

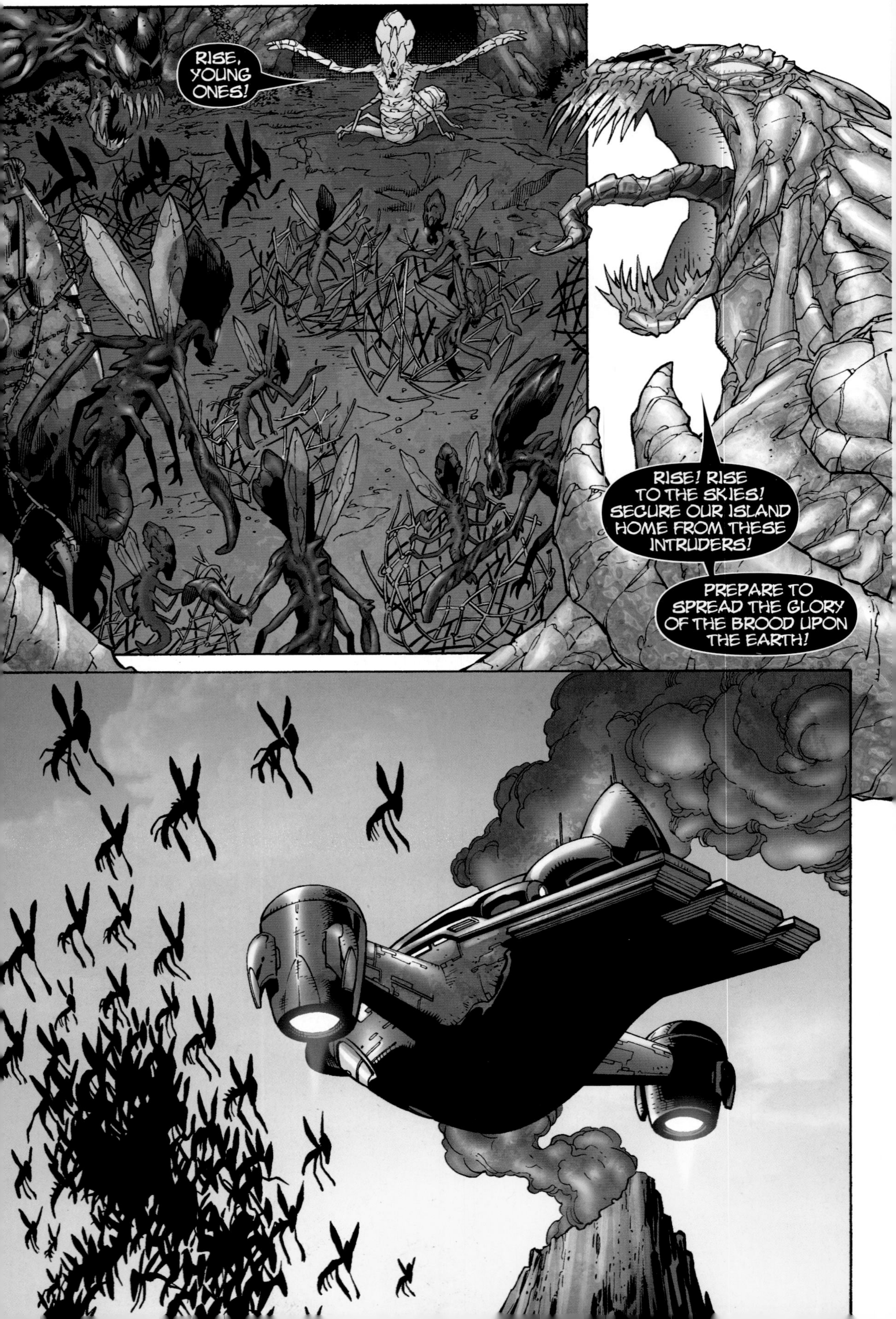
RISE, YOUNG ONES!
RISE! RISE TO THE SKIES! SECURE OUR ISLAND HOME FROM THESE INTRUDERS!
PREPARE TO SPREAD THE GLORY OF THE BROOD UPON THE EARTH!

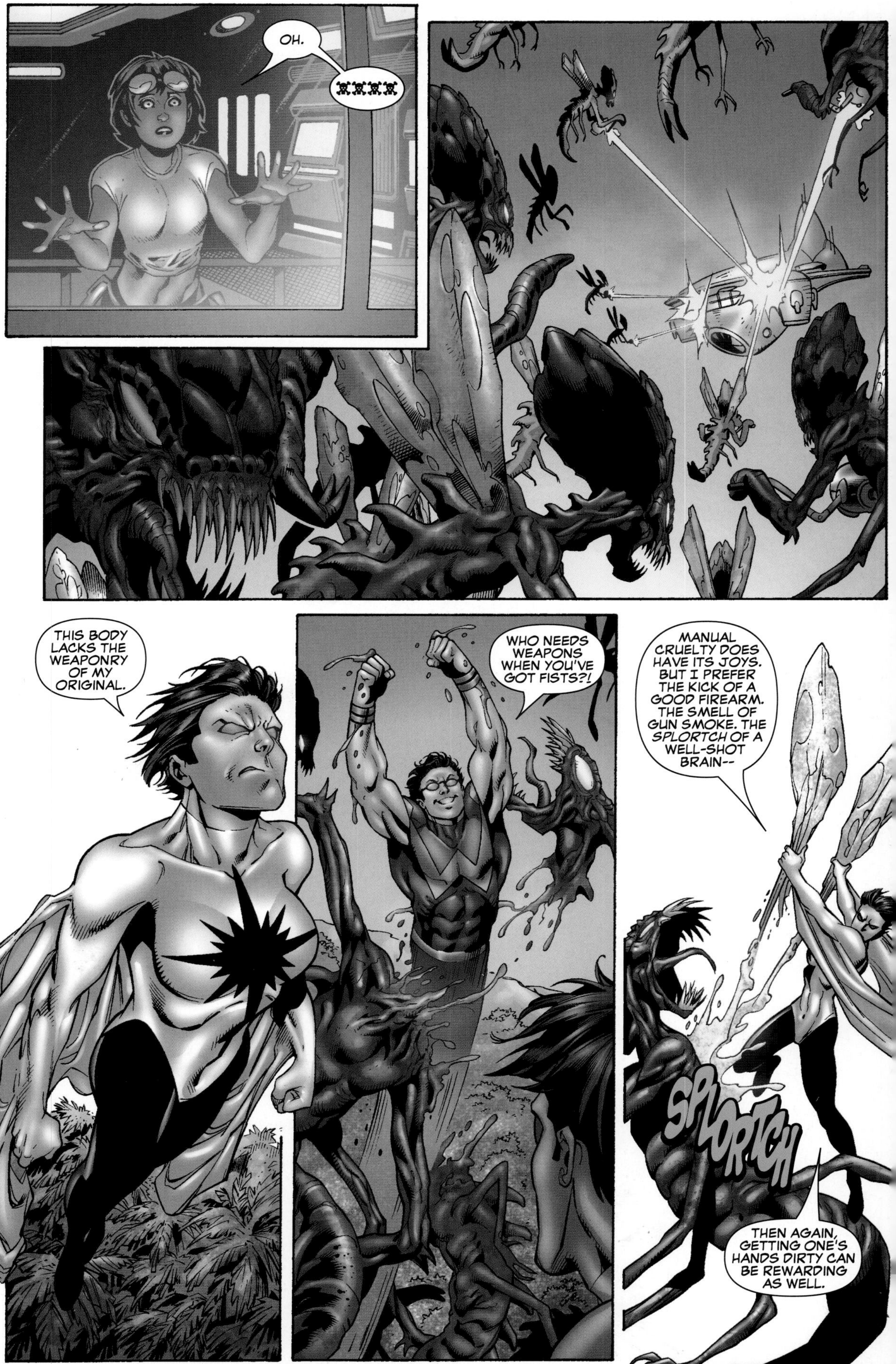
OH.
☠☠☠☠
THIS BODY LACKS THE WEAPONRY OF MY ORIGINAL.
WHO NEEDS WEAPONS WHEN YOU'VE GOT FISTS?!
MANUAL CRUELTY DOES HAVE ITS JOYS. BUT I PREFER THE KICK OF A GOOD FIREARM. THE SMELL OF GUN SMOKE. THE SPLORTCH OF A WELL-SHOT BRAIN--
SPLORTCH
THEN AGAIN, GETTING ONE'S HANDS DIRTY CAN BE REWARDING AS WELL.

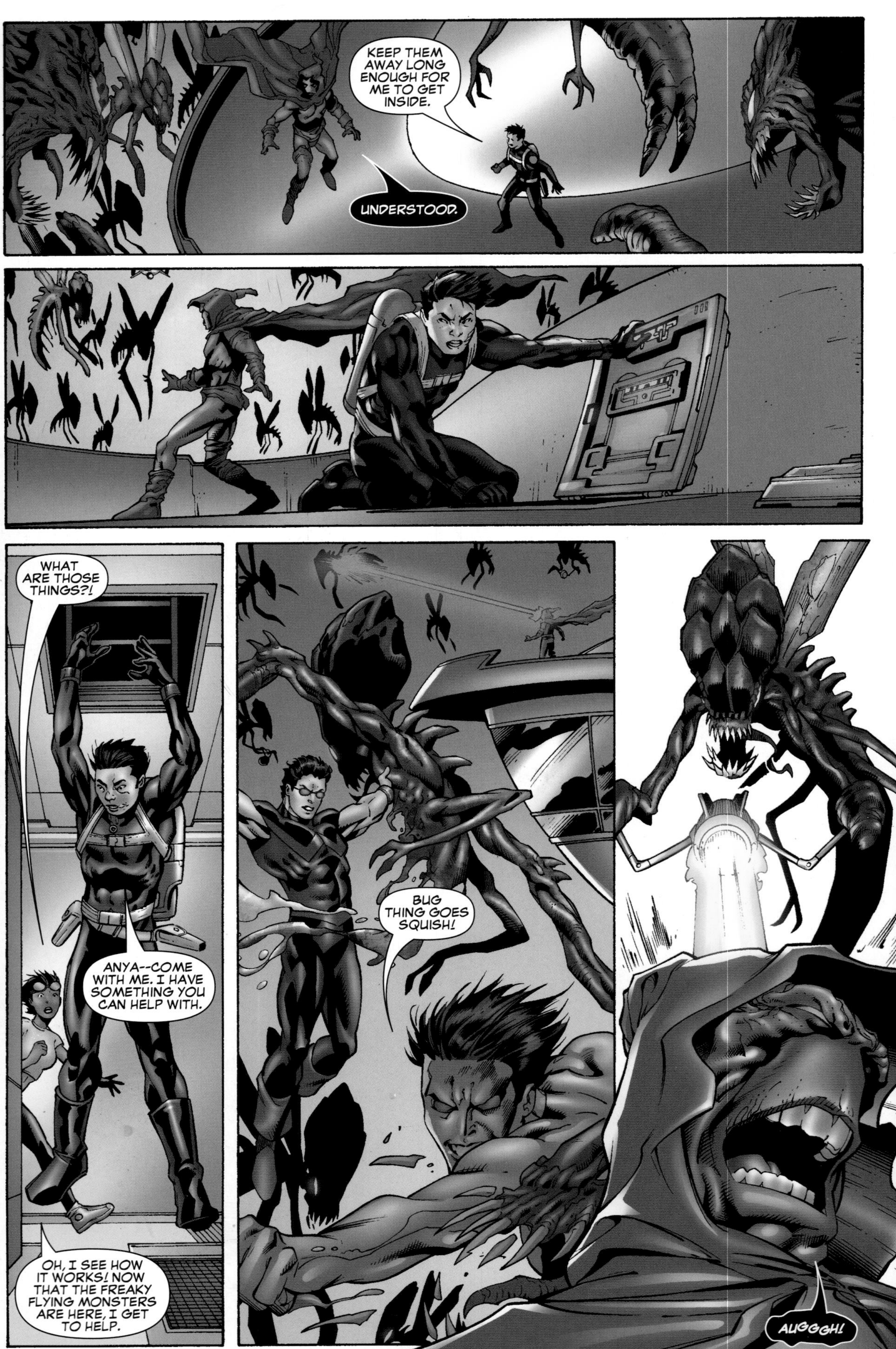
KEEP THEM AWAY LONG ENOUGH FOR ME TO GET INSIDE.
UNDERSTOOD.
WHAT ARE THOSE THINGS?!
ANYA--COME WITH ME. I HAVE SOMETHING YOU CAN HELP WITH.
OH, I SEE HOW IT WORKS! NOW THAT THE FREAKY FLYING MONSTERS ARE HERE, I GET TO HELP.
BUG THING GOES SQUISH!
AUGGGH!

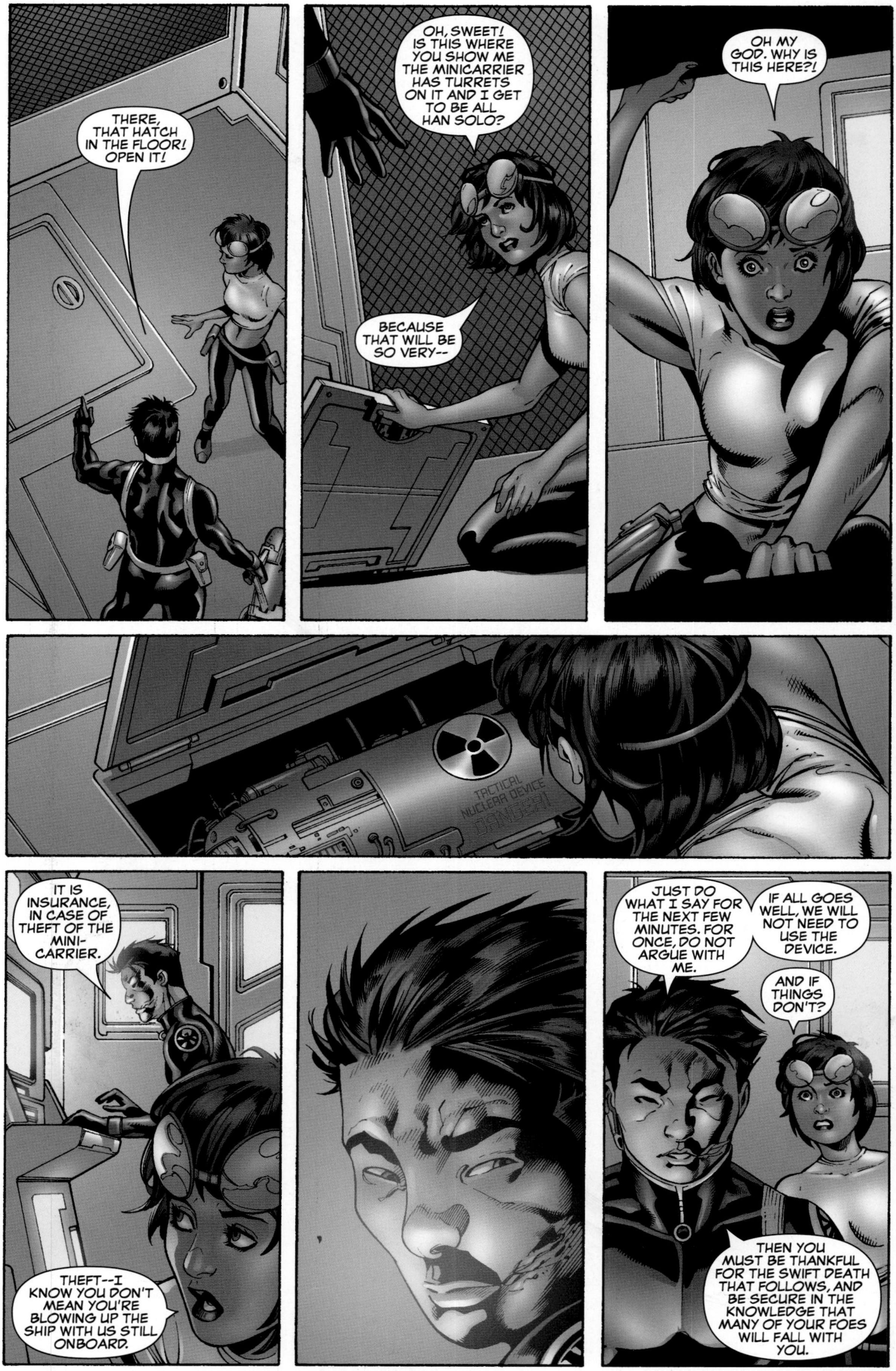
THERE, THAT HATCH IN THE FLOOR! OPEN IT!
OH, SWEET! IS THIS WHERE YOU SHOW ME THE MINICARRIER HAS TURRETS ON IT AND I GET TO BE ALL HAN SOLO?
BECAUSE THAT WILL BE SO VERY--
OH MY GOD. WHY IS THIS HERE?!
TACTICAL NUCLEAR DEVICE DANGER!
IT IS INSURANCE, IN CASE OF THEFT OF THE MINI-CARRIER.
THEFT--I KNOW YOU DON'T MEAN YOU'RE BLOWING UP THE SHIP WITH US STILL ONBOARD.
JUST DO WHAT I SAY FOR THE NEXT FEW MINUTES. FOR ONCE, DO NOT ARGUE WITH ME.
IF ALL GOES WELL, WE WILL NOT NEED TO USE THE DEVICE.
AND IF THINGS DON'T?
THEN YOU MUST BE THANKFUL FOR THE SWIFT DEATH THAT FOLLOWS, AND BE SECURE IN THE KNOWLEDGE THAT MANY OF YOUR FOES WILL FALL WITH YOU.

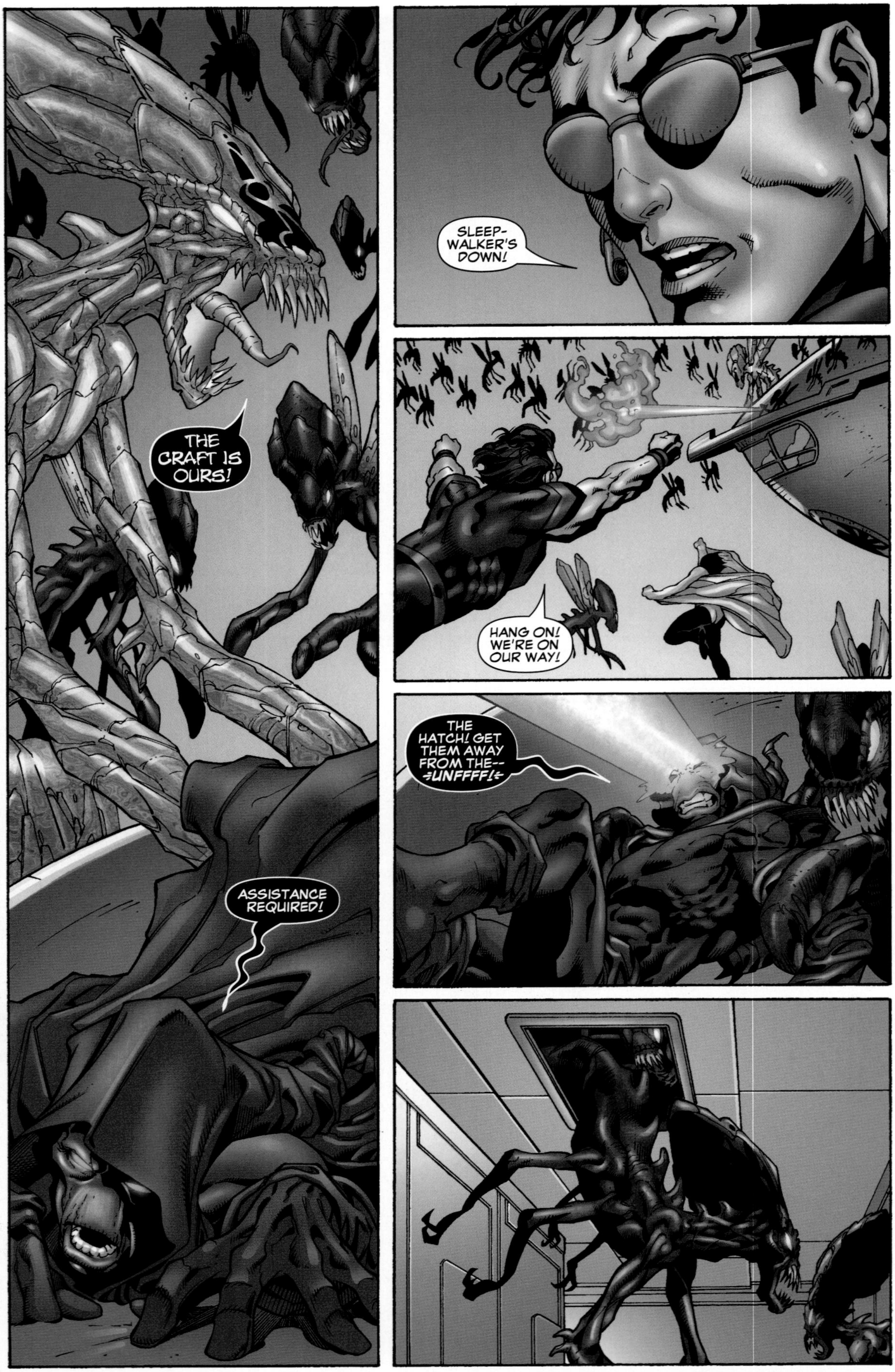
THE CRAFT IS OURS!
ASSISTANCE REQUIRED!
SLEEP-WALKER'S DOWN!
HANG ON! WE'RE ON OUR WAY!
THE HATCH! GET THEM AWAY FROM THE-- UNFFFF!

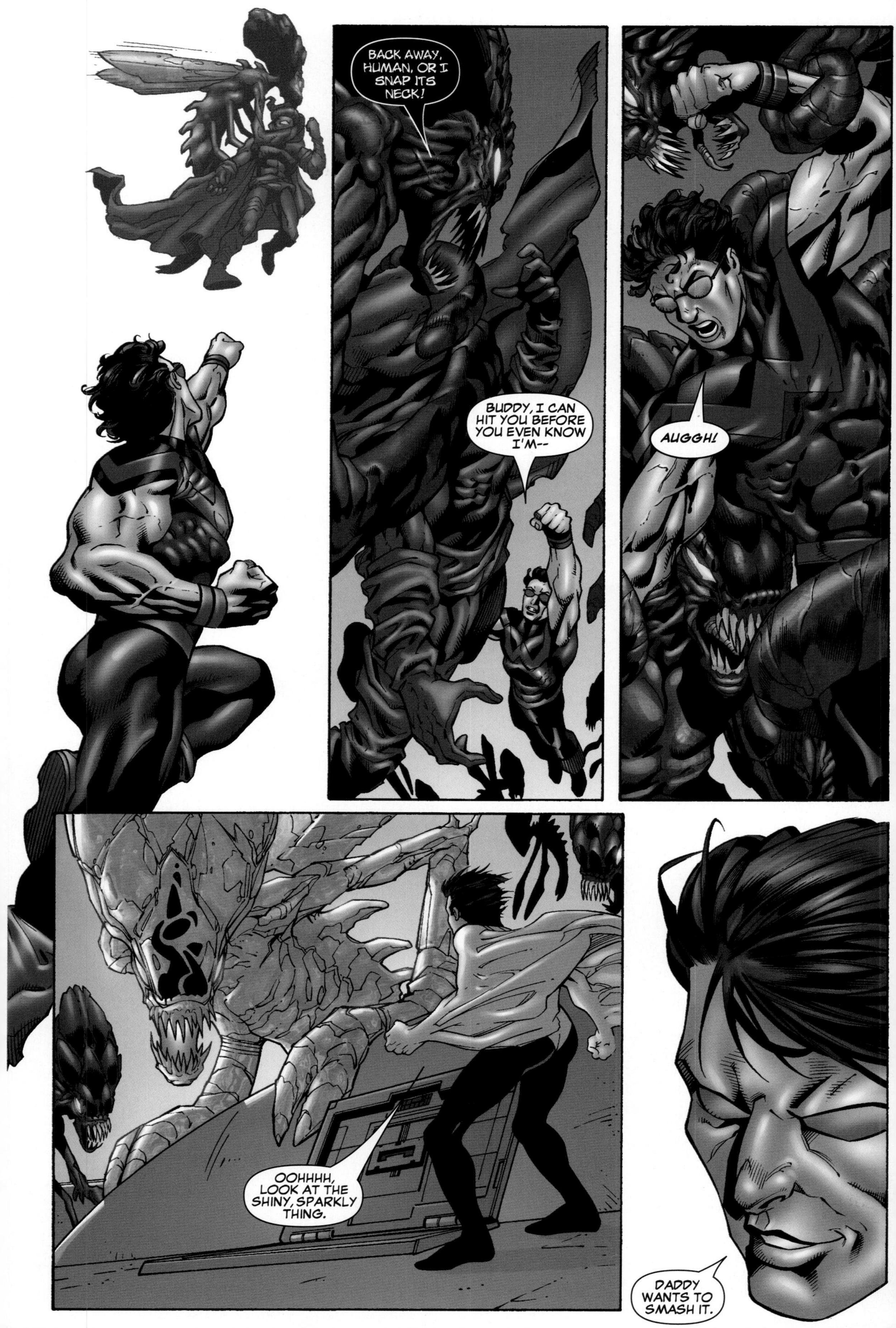
BACK AWAY, HUMAN, OR I SNAP ITS NECK!
BUDDY, I CAN HIT YOU BEFORE YOU EVEN KNOW I'M--
AUGGH!
OOHHHH, LOOK AT THE SHINY, SPARKLY THING.
DADDY WANTS TO SMASH IT.

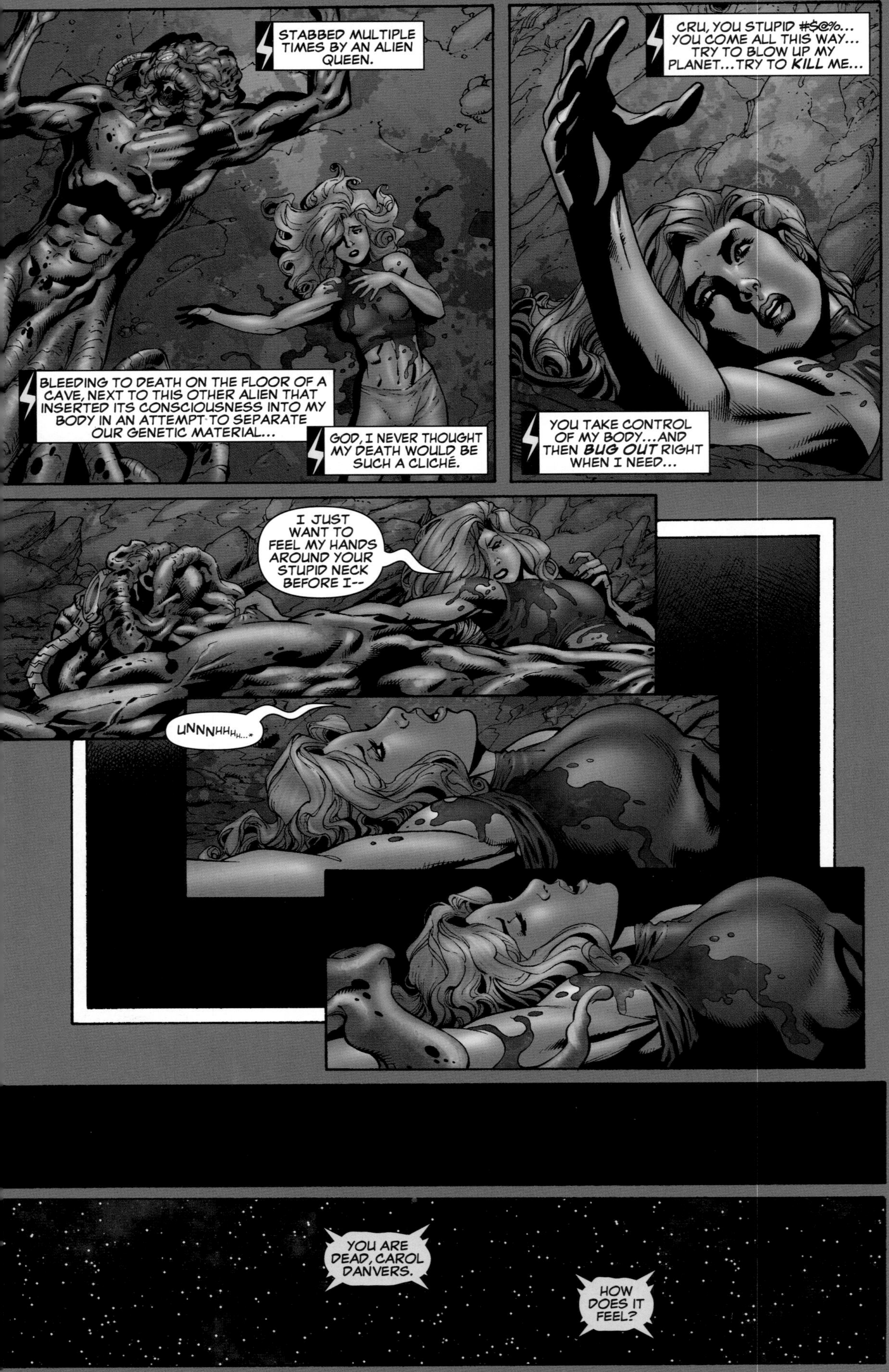
STABBED MULTIPLE TIMES BY AN ALIEN QUEEN.
BLEEDING TO DEATH ON THE FLOOR OF A CAVE, NEXT TO THIS OTHER ALIEN THAT INSERTED ITS CONSCIOUSNESS INTO MY BODY IN AN ATTEMPT TO SEPARATE OUR GENETIC MATERIAL...
GOD, I NEVER THOUGHT MY DEATH WOULD BE SUCH A CLICHÉ.
CRU, YOU STUPID #$@%... YOU COME ALL THIS WAY... TRY TO BLOW UP MY PLANET...TRY TO KILL ME...
YOU TAKE CONTROL OF MY BODY...AND THEN BUG OUT RIGHT WHEN I NEED...
I JUST WANT TO FEEL MY HANDS AROUND YOUR STUPID NECK BEFORE I--
UNNNHHHH...*
YOU ARE DEAD, CAROL DANVERS.
HOW DOES IT FEEL?

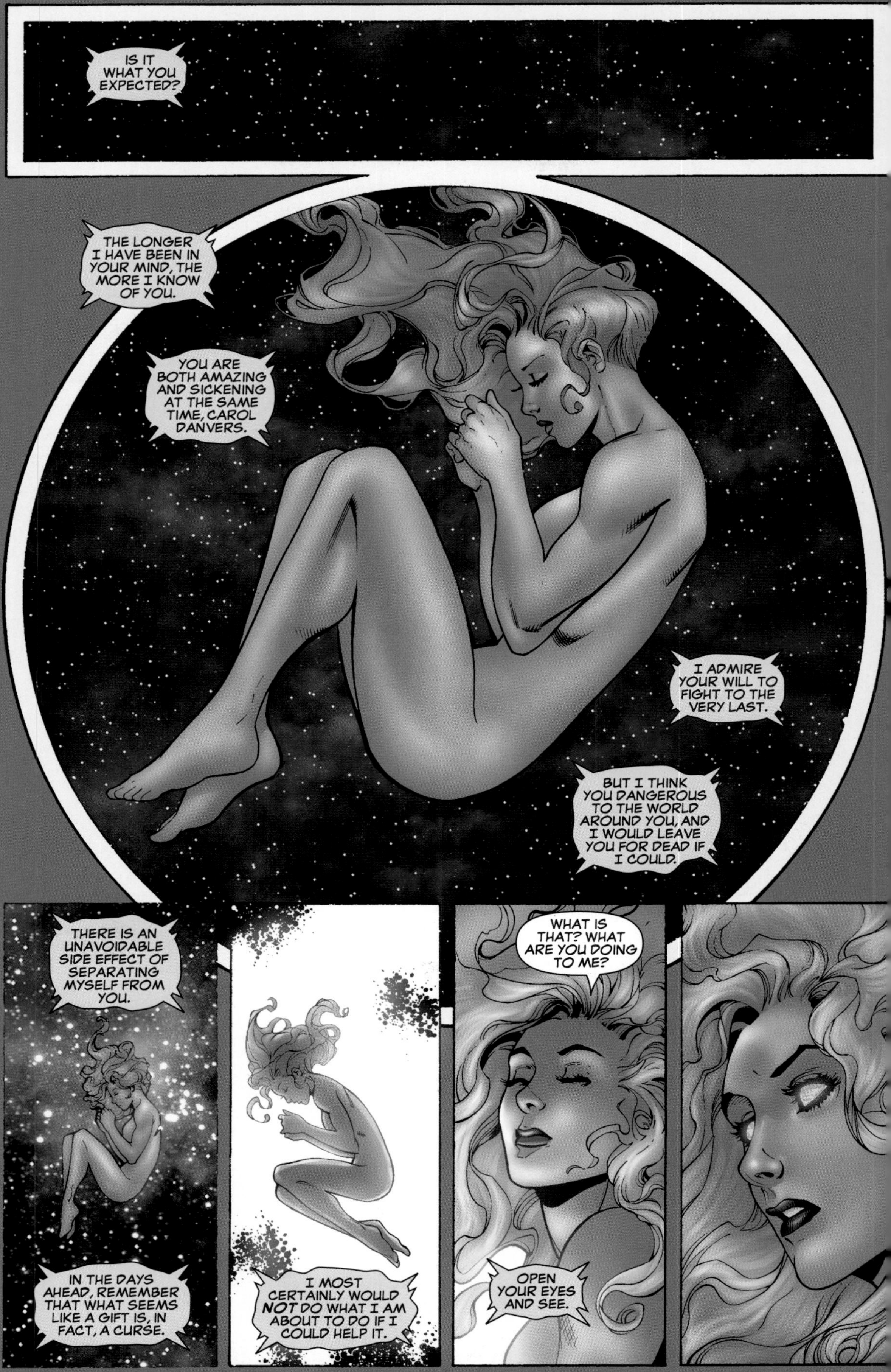
IS IT WHAT YOU EXPECTED?
THE LONGER I HAVE BEEN IN YOUR MIND, THE MORE I KNOW OF YOU.
YOU ARE BOTH AMAZING AND SICKENING AT THE SAME TIME, CAROL DANVERS.
I ADMIRE YOUR WILL TO FIGHT TO THE VERY LAST.
BUT I THINK YOU DANGEROUS TO THE WORLD AROUND YOU, AND I WOULD LEAVE YOU FOR DEAD IF I COULD.
THERE IS AN UNAVOIDABLE SIDE EFFECT OF SEPARATING MYSELF FROM YOU.
IN THE DAYS AHEAD, REMEMBER THAT WHAT SEEMS LIKE A GIFT IS, IN FACT, A CURSE.
I MOST CERTAINLY WOULD NOT DO WHAT I AM ABOUT TO DO IF I COULD HELP IT.
WHAT IS THAT? WHAT ARE YOU DOING TO ME?
OPEN YOUR EYES AND SEE.

STUPID L.M.D. BODY MALFUNCTION! I'LL WRITE A NASTY LETTER TO THE MANUFACTURER, I WILL--

OW.

THUUUD

WHAT IN THE NAME OF...

YOU LOOK DIFFERENT.

I LOOK DIFFERENT?! WHAT THE HELL HAPPENED TO YOU?!

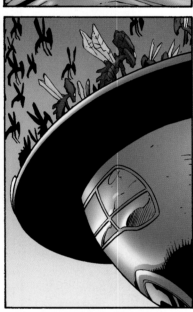

MY QUEEN! DANGER!

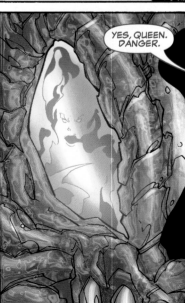

YES, QUEEN. DANGER.

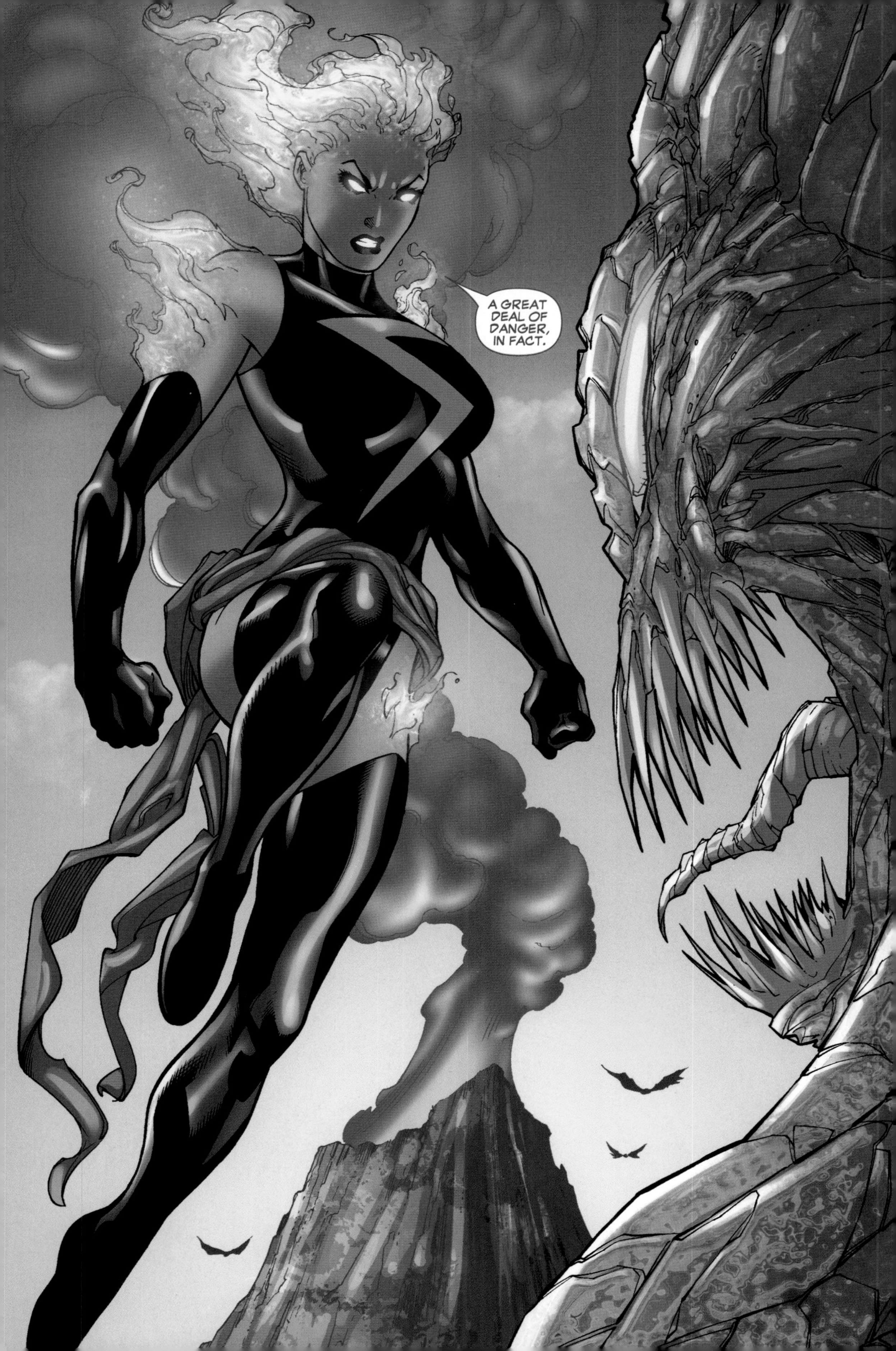
A GREAT DEAL OF DANGER, IN FACT.

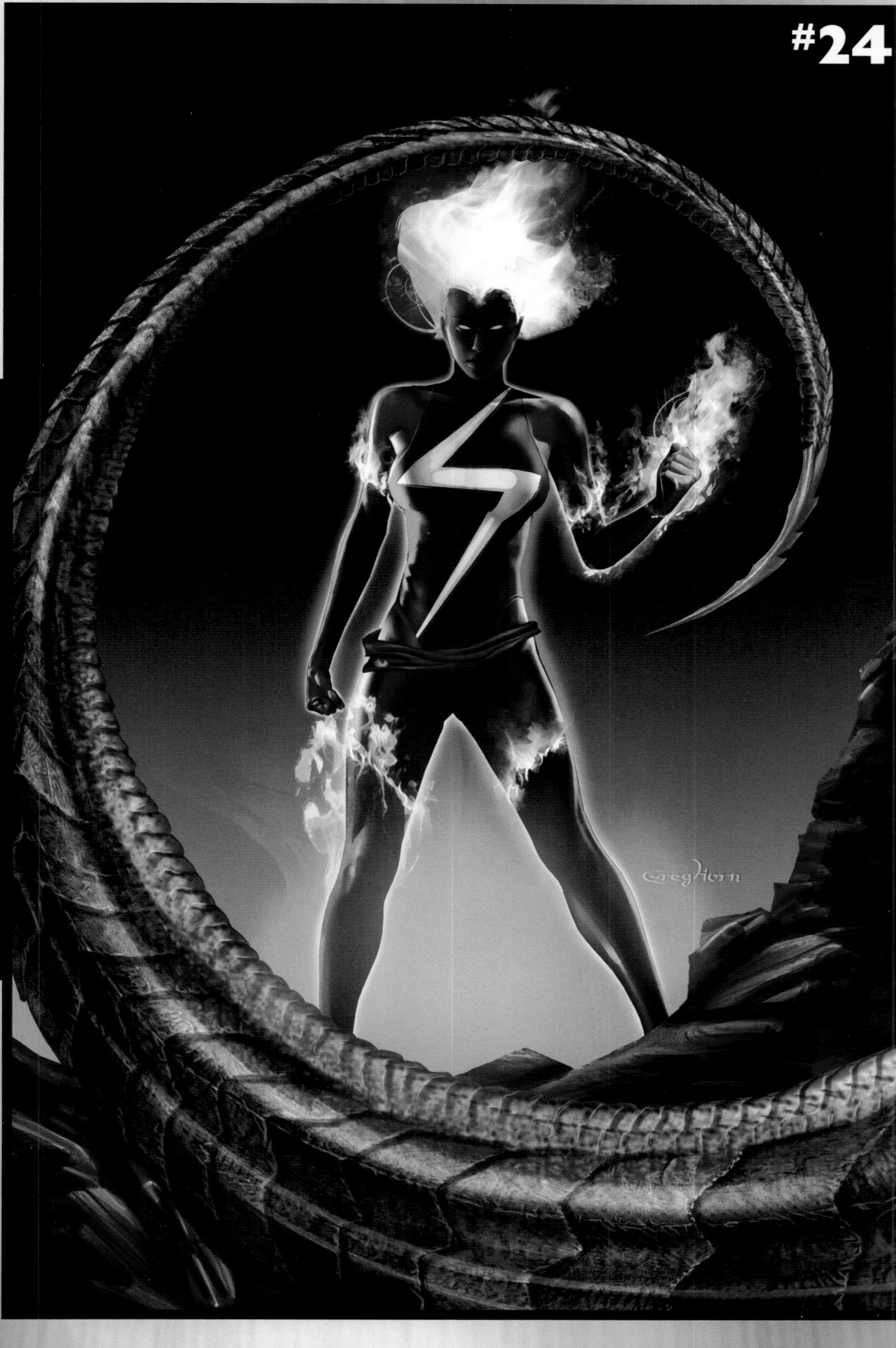
#24
Greg Horn

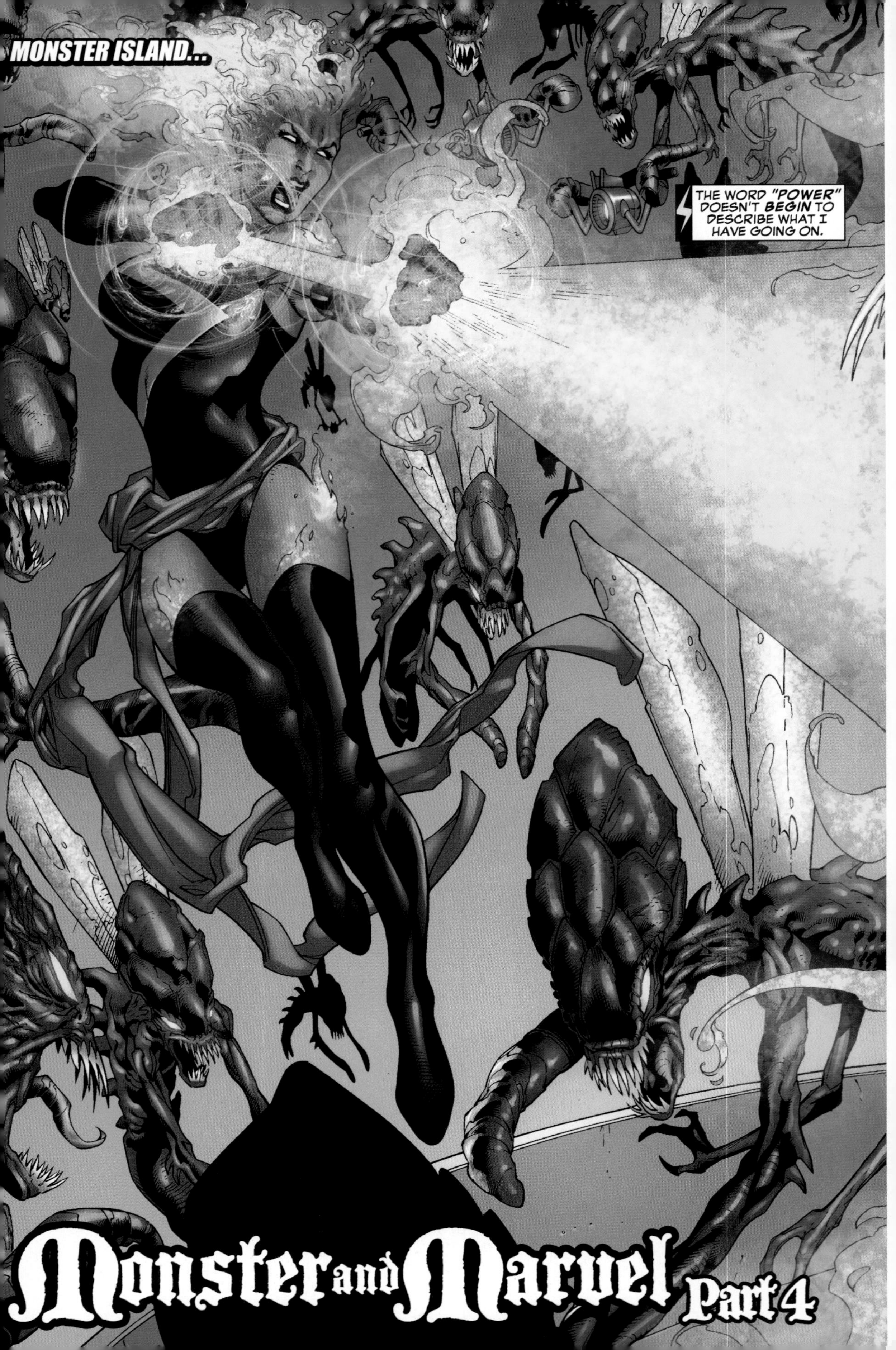
MONSTER ISLAND...
THE WORD "POWER" DOESN'T BEGIN TO DESCRIBE WHAT I HAVE GOING ON.
Monster and Marvel Part 4

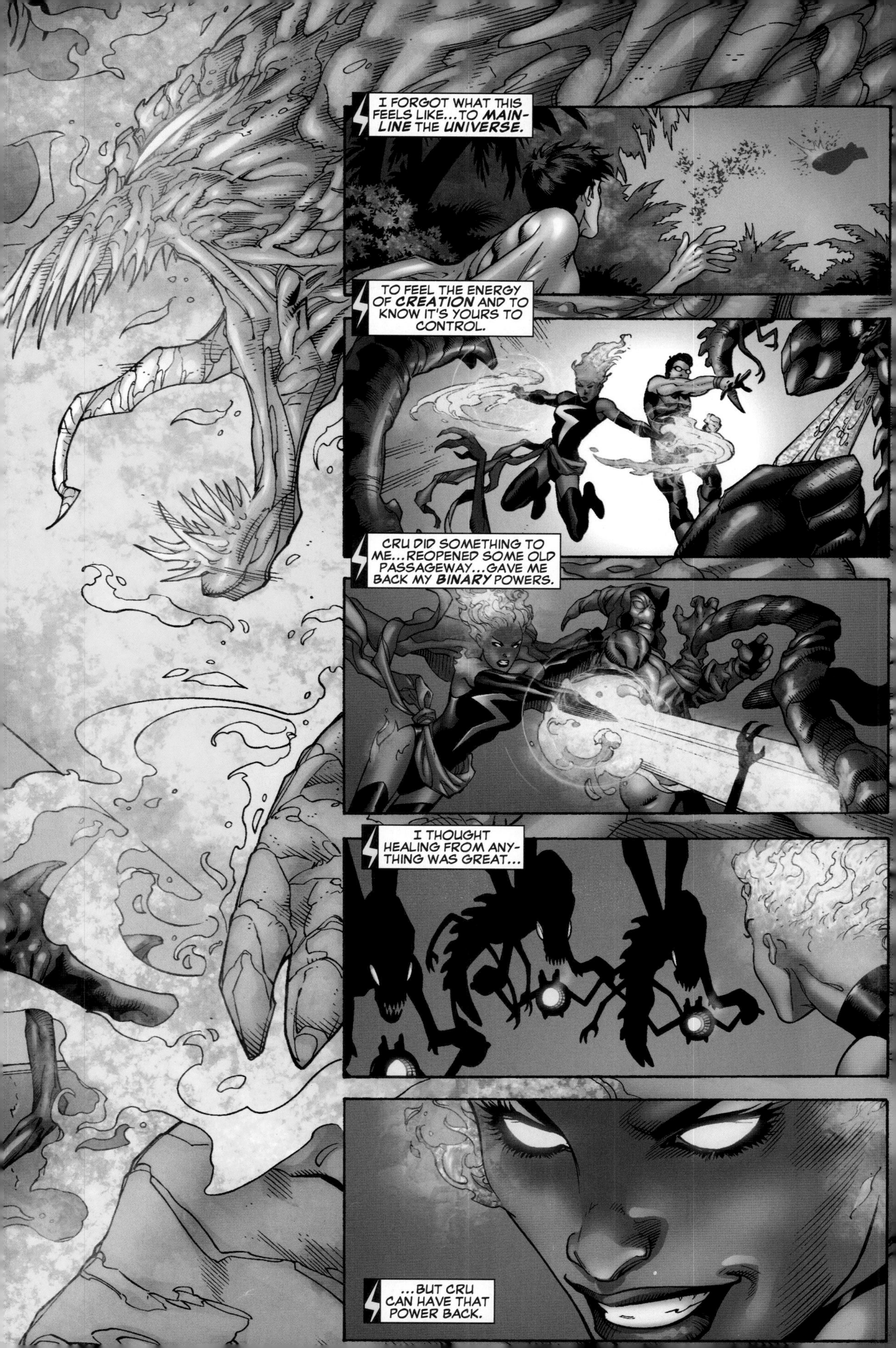

I FORGOT WHAT THIS FEELS LIKE...TO MAIN-LINE THE UNIVERSE.
TO FEEL THE ENERGY OF CREATION AND TO KNOW IT'S YOURS TO CONTROL.
CRU DID SOMETHING TO ME...REOPENED SOME OLD PASSAGEWAY...GAVE ME BACK MY BINARY POWERS.
I THOUGHT HEALING FROM ANY-THING WAS GREAT...
...BUT CRU CAN HAVE THAT POWER BACK.

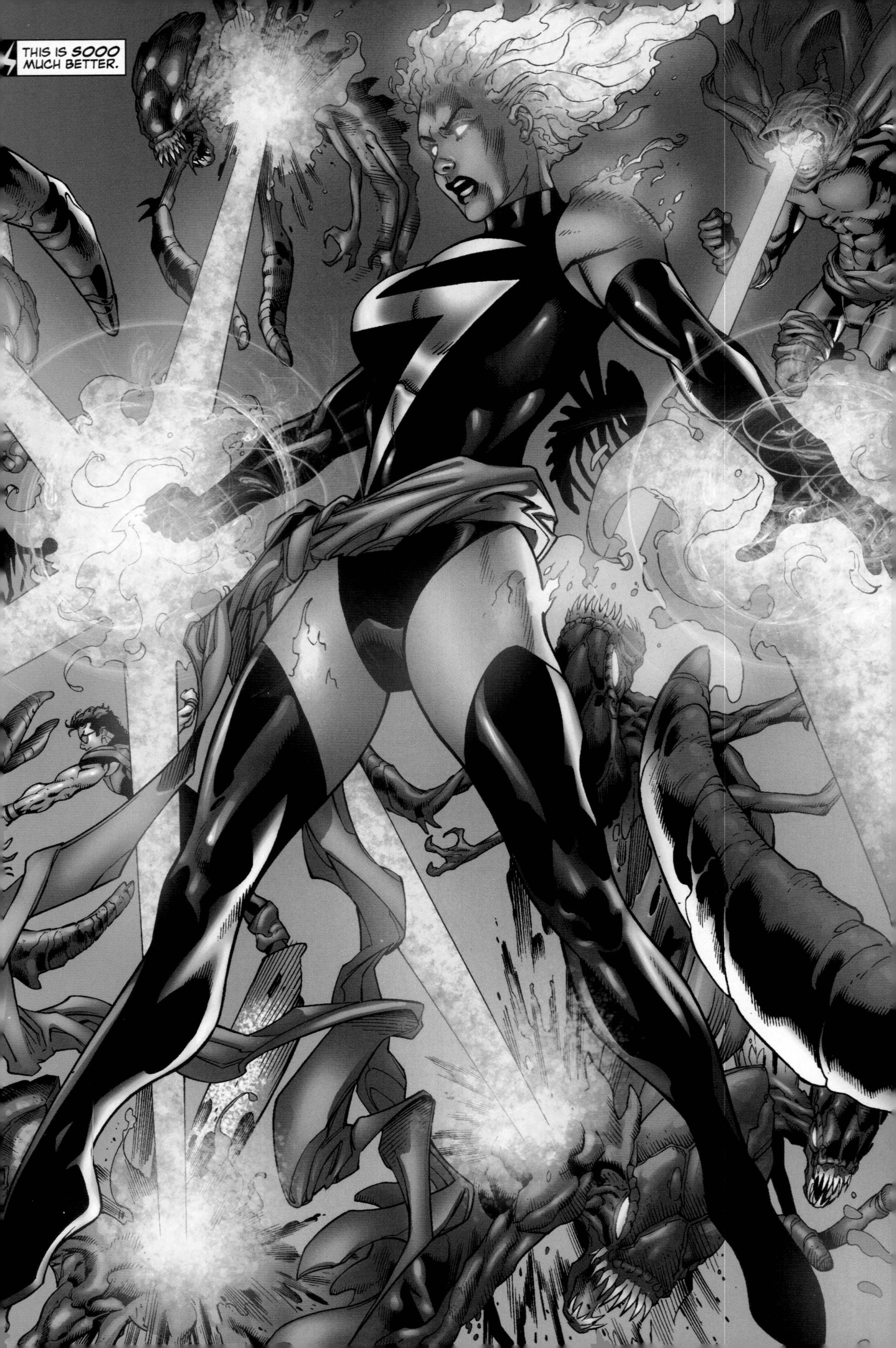
THIS IS SOOO MUCH BETTER.

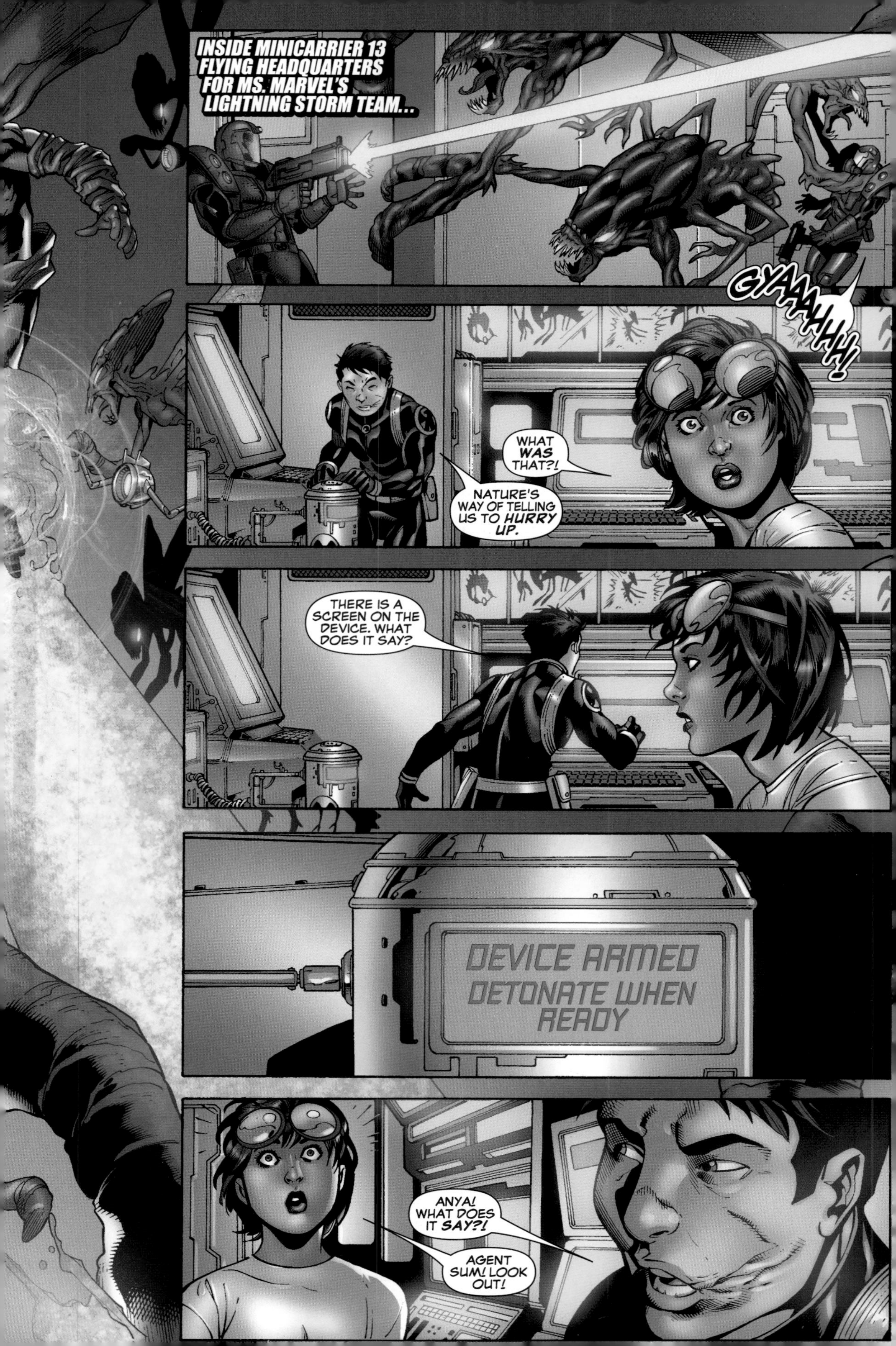
INSIDE MINICARRIER 13 FLYING HEADQUARTERS FOR MS. MARVEL'S LIGHTNING STORM TEAM...
GYAAAHHH!
WHAT WAS THAT?!
NATURE'S WAY OF TELLING US TO HURRY UP.
THERE IS A SCREEN ON THE DEVICE. WHAT DOES IT SAY?
DEVICE ARMED
DETONATE WHEN READY
ANYA! WHAT DOES IT SAY?!
AGENT SUM! LOOK OUT!

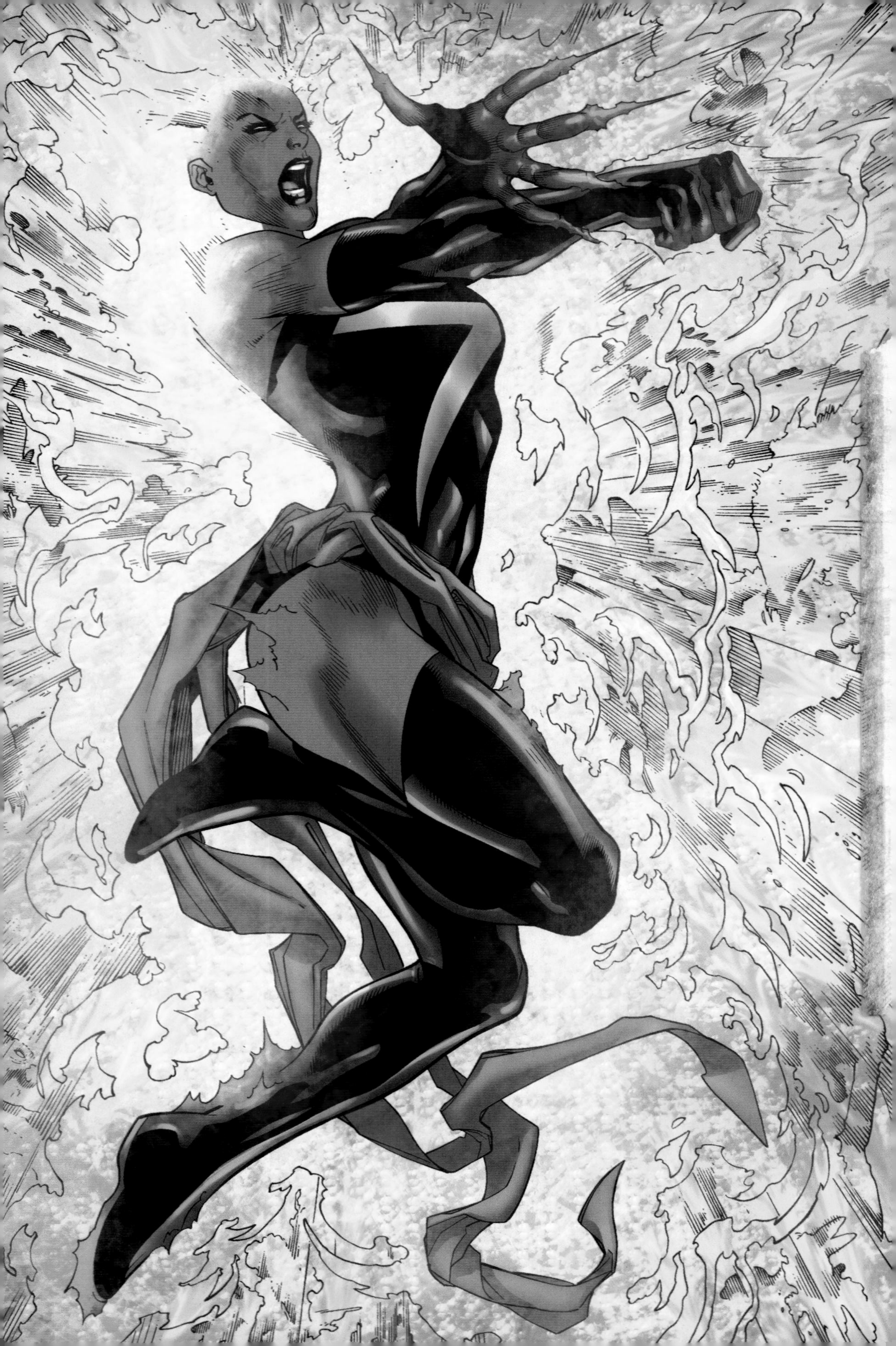

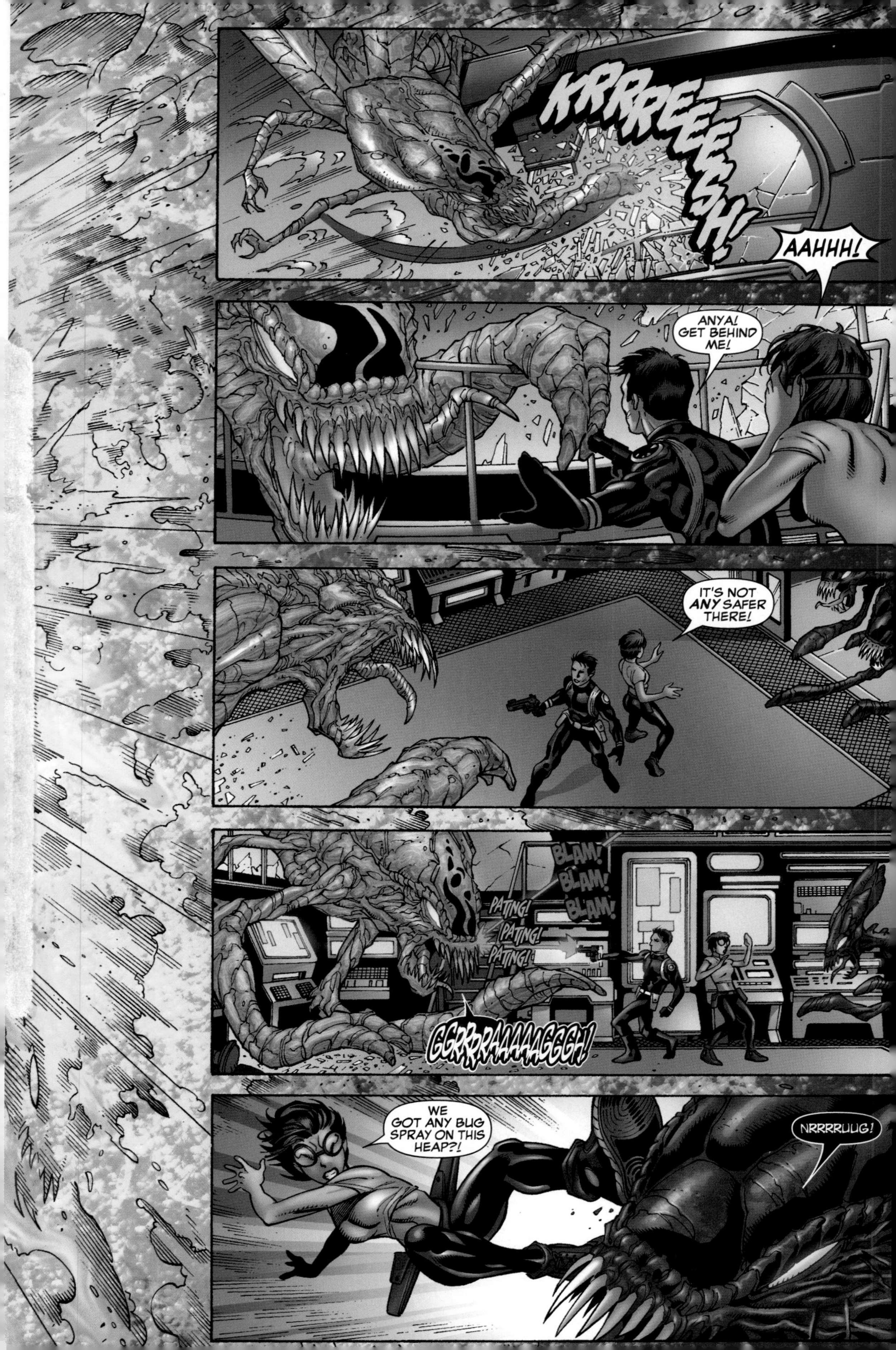
KRRREEESH!
AAHHH!
ANYA! GET BEHIND ME!
IT'S NOT ANY SAFER THERE!
BLAM! BLAM! BLAM!
PATING! PATING! PATING!
GGRRRRAAAAAGGGH!
WE GOT ANY BUG SPRAY ON THIS HEAP?!
NRRRRUUG!

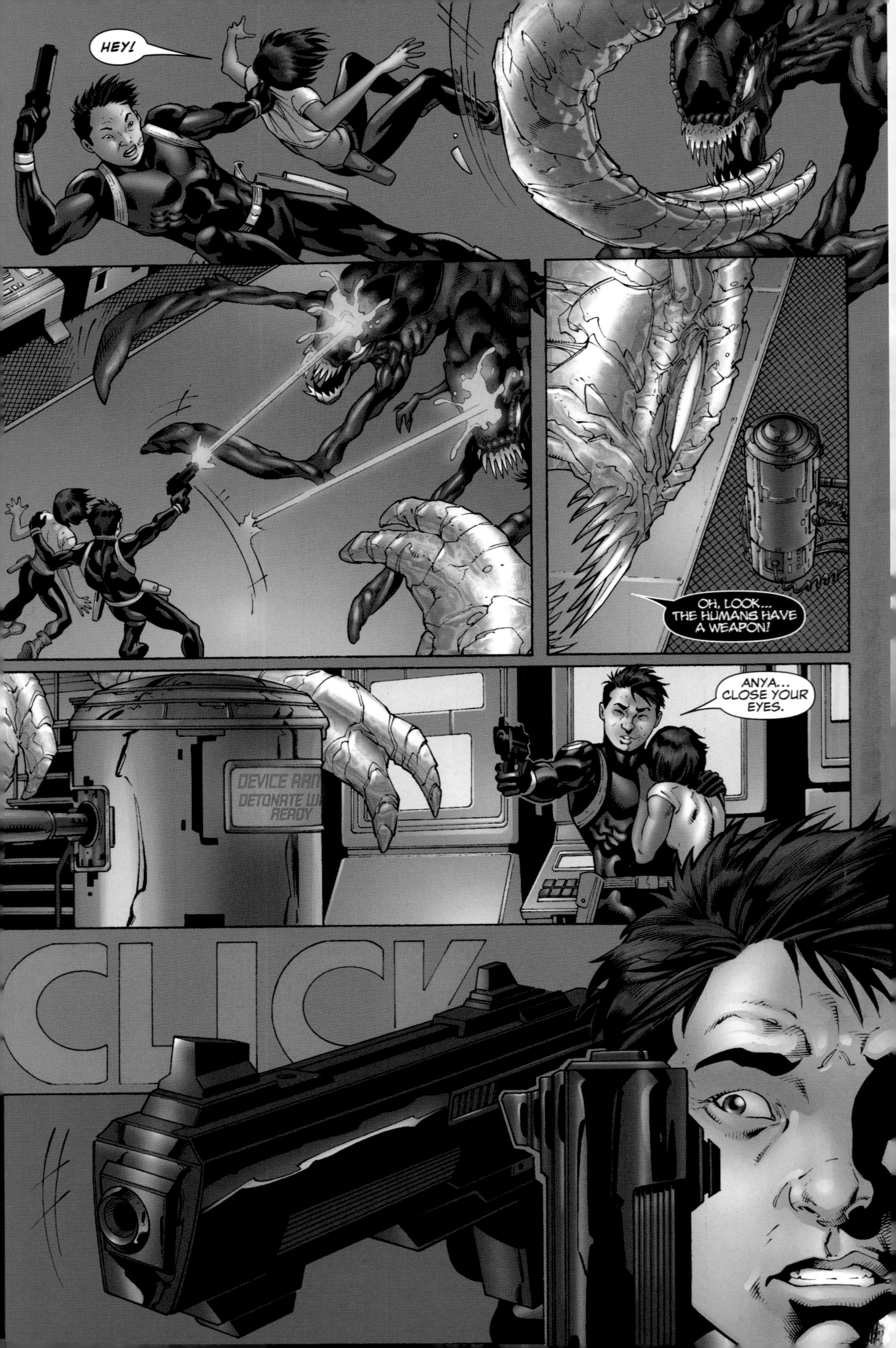
HEY!
OH, LOOK... THE HUMANS HAVE A WEAPON!
ANYA... CLOSE YOUR EYES.
CLICK

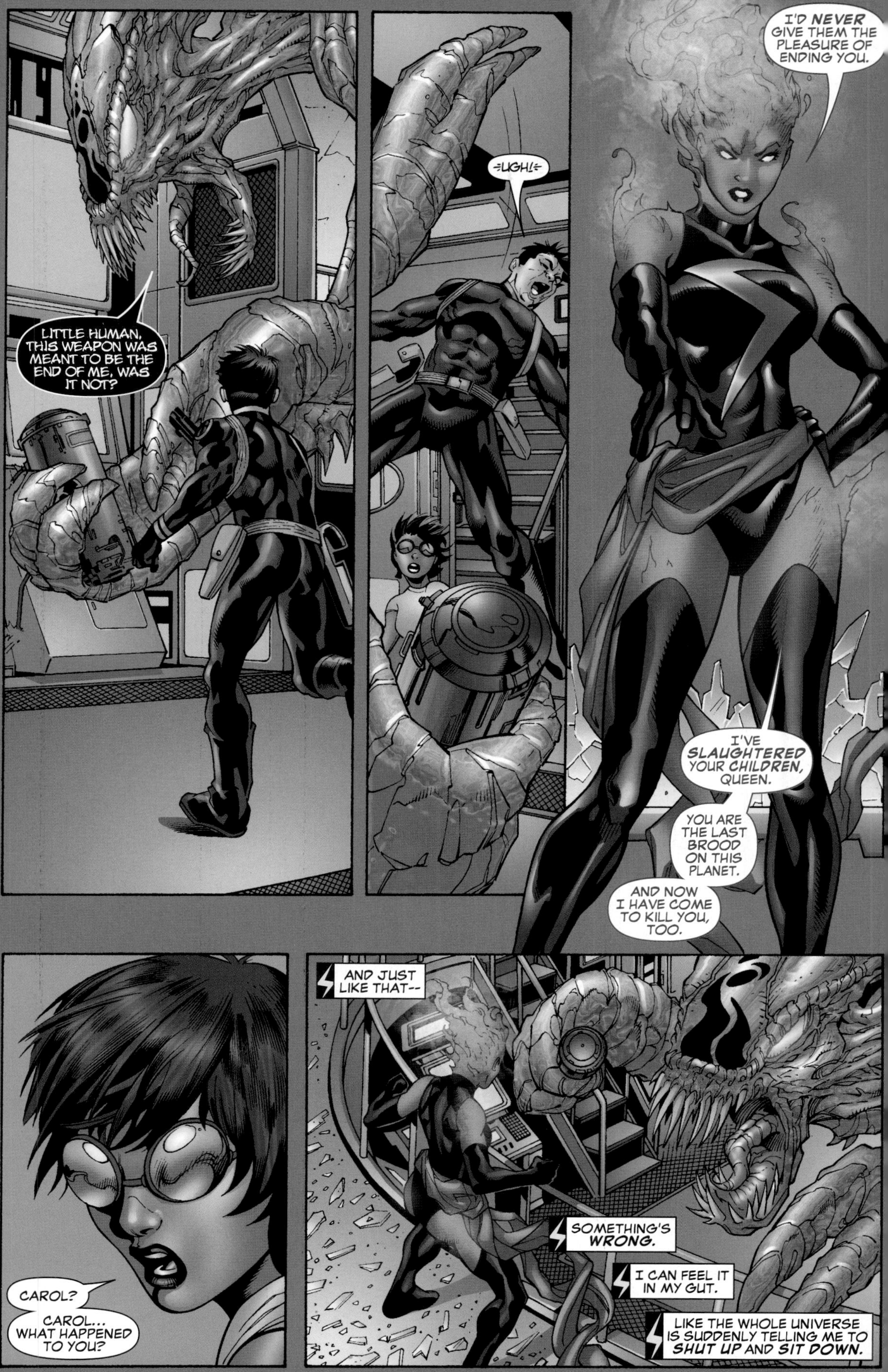
LITTLE HUMAN, THIS WEAPON WAS MEANT TO BE THE END OF ME, WAS IT NOT?
=UGH!=
I'D NEVER GIVE THEM THE PLEASURE OF ENDING YOU.
I'VE SLAUGHTERED YOUR CHILDREN, QUEEN.
YOU ARE THE LAST BROOD ON THIS PLANET.
AND NOW I HAVE COME TO KILL YOU, TOO.
CAROL?
CAROL... WHAT HAPPENED TO YOU?
AND JUST LIKE THAT--
SOMETHING'S WRONG.
I CAN FEEL IT IN MY GUT.
LIKE THE WHOLE UNIVERSE IS SUDDENLY TELLING ME TO SHUT UP AND SIT DOWN.

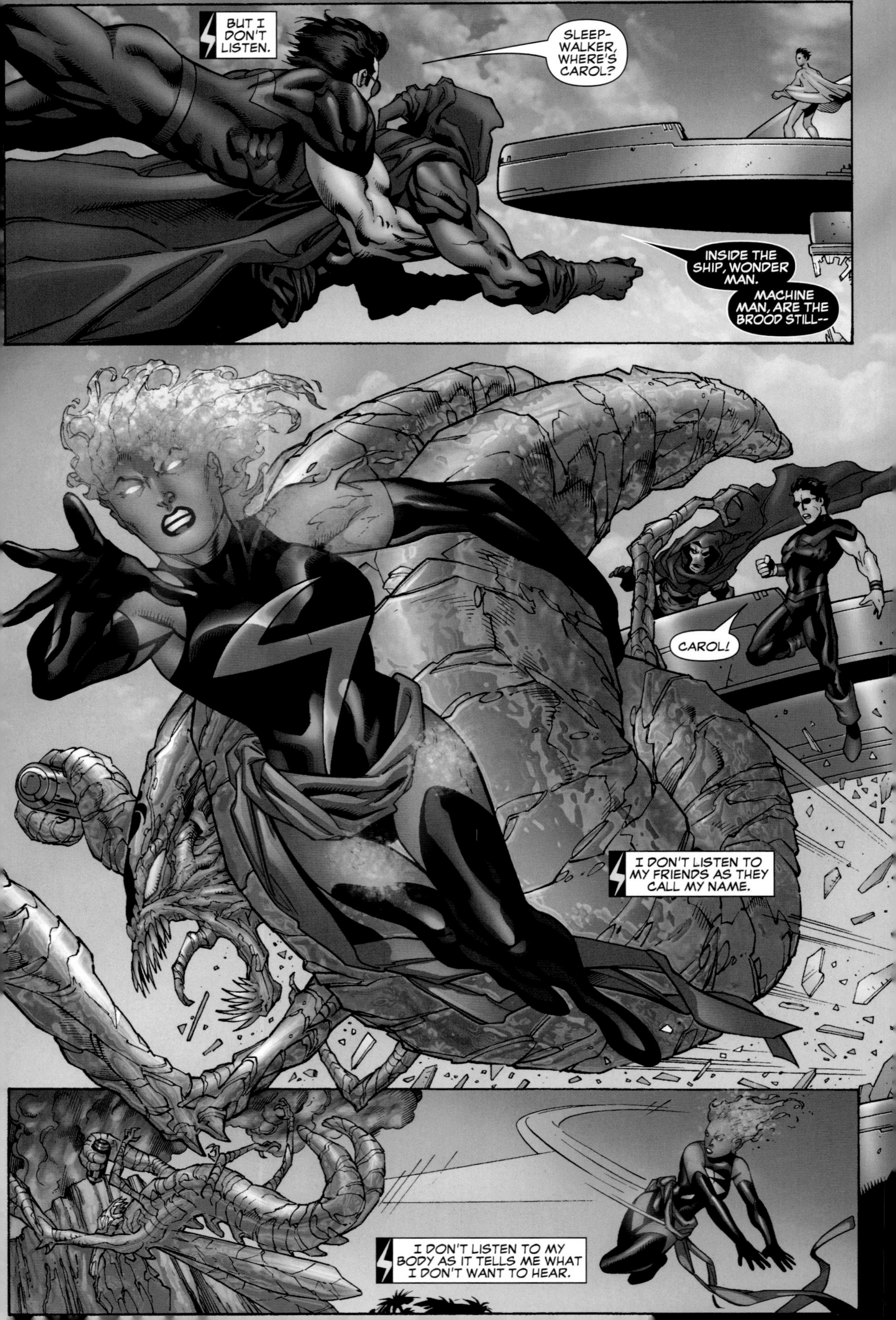
BUT I DON'T LISTEN.
SLEEP-WALKER, WHERE'S CAROL?
INSIDE THE SHIP, WONDER MAN.
MACHINE MAN, ARE THE BROOD STILL--
CAROL!
I DON'T LISTEN TO MY FRIENDS AS THEY CALL MY NAME.
I DON'T LISTEN TO MY BODY AS IT TELLS ME WHAT I DON'T WANT TO HEAR.

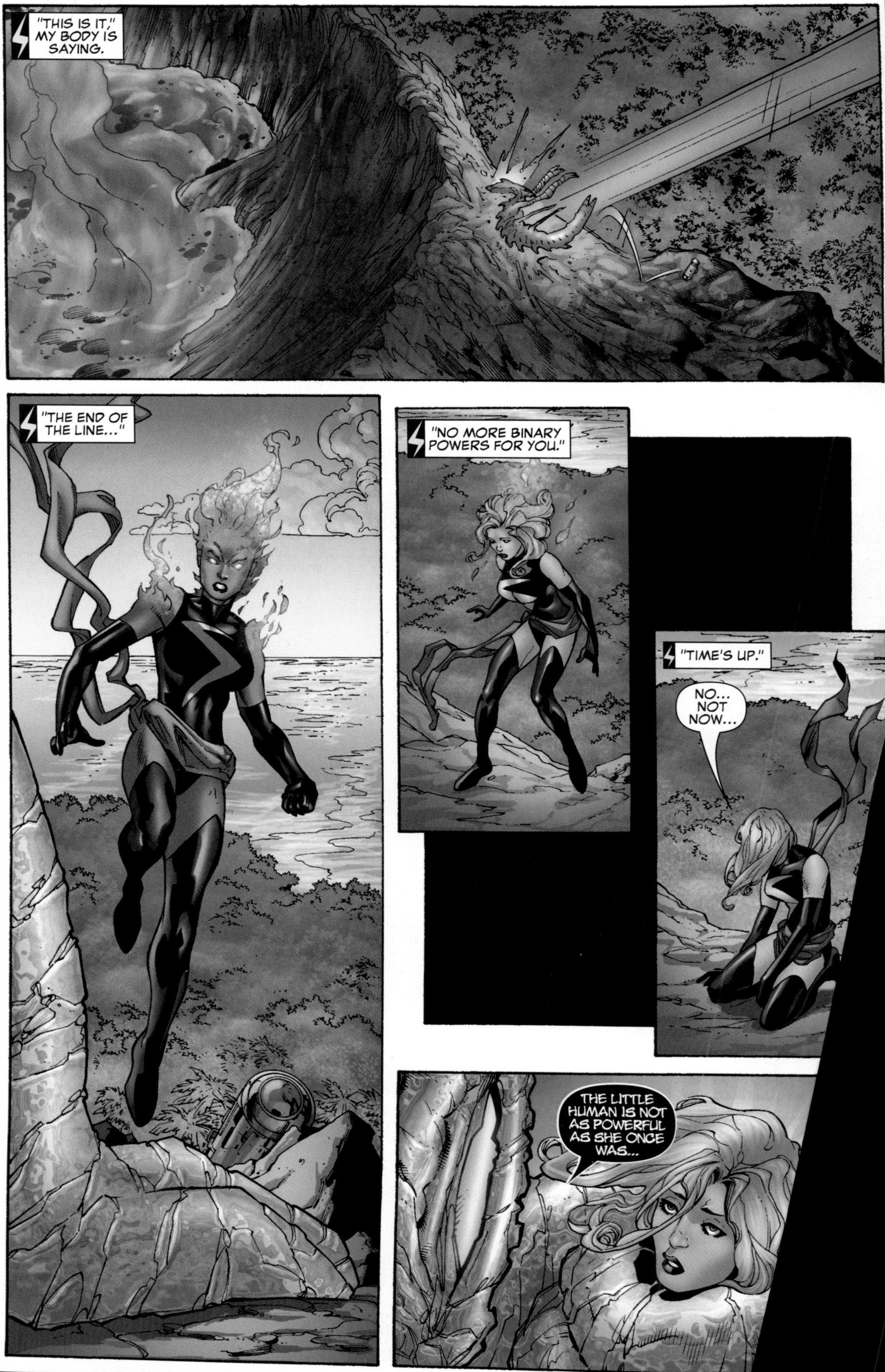
"THIS IS IT," MY BODY IS SAYING.
"THE END OF THE LINE..."
"NO MORE BINARY POWERS FOR YOU."
"TIME'S UP."
NO... NOT NOW...
THE LITTLE HUMAN IS NOT AS POWERFUL AS SHE ONCE WAS...

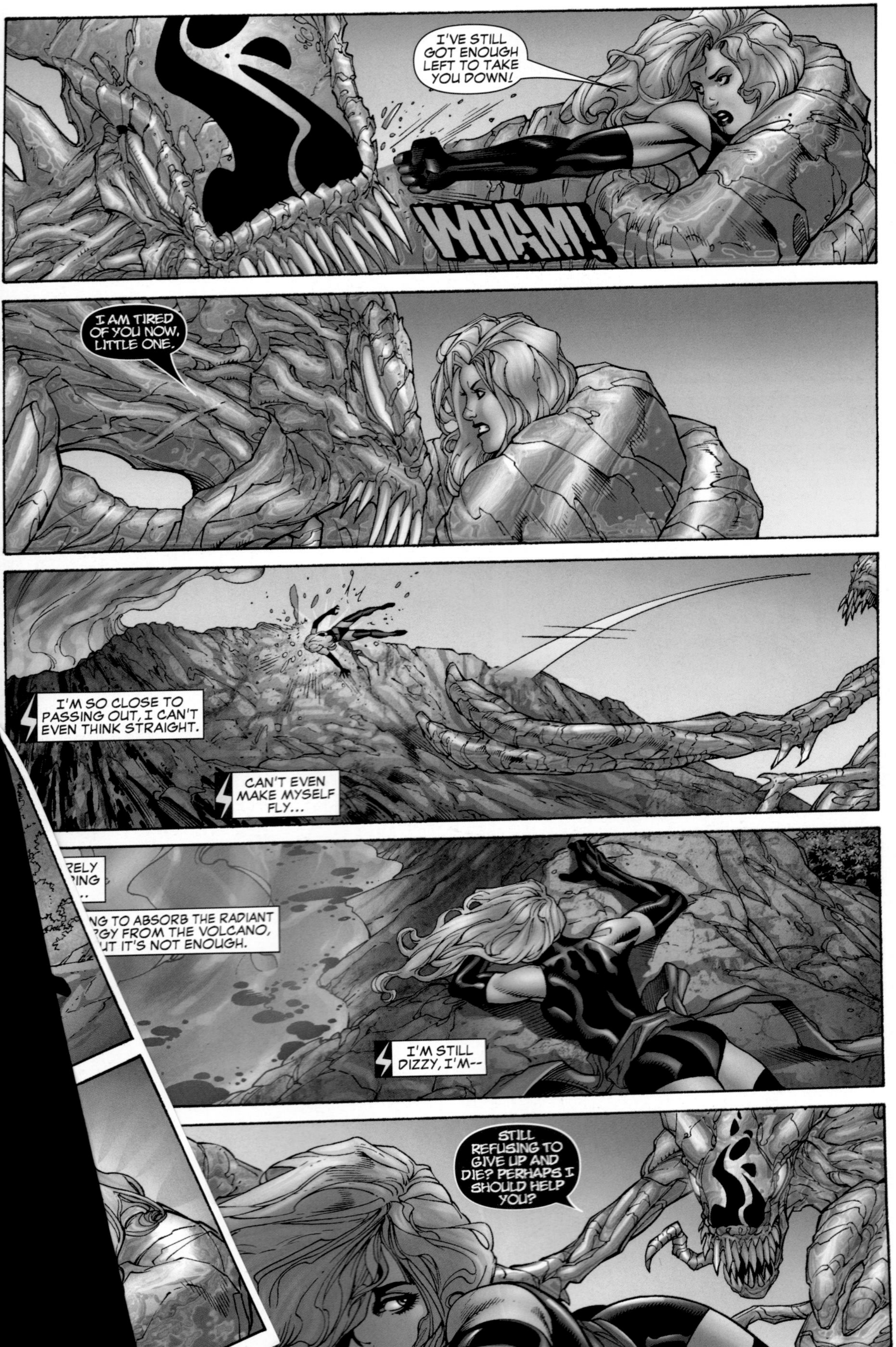
I'VE STILL GOT ENOUGH LEFT TO TAKE YOU DOWN!
WHAM!
I AM TIRED OF YOU NOW, LITTLE ONE.
I'M SO CLOSE TO PASSING OUT, I CAN'T EVEN THINK STRAIGHT.
CAN'T EVEN MAKE MYSELF FLY...
TO ABSORB THE RADIANT
FROM THE VOLCANO,
IT'S NOT ENOUGH.
I'M STILL DIZZY, I'M--
STILL REFUSING TO GIVE UP AND DIE? PERHAPS I SHOULD HELP YOU?

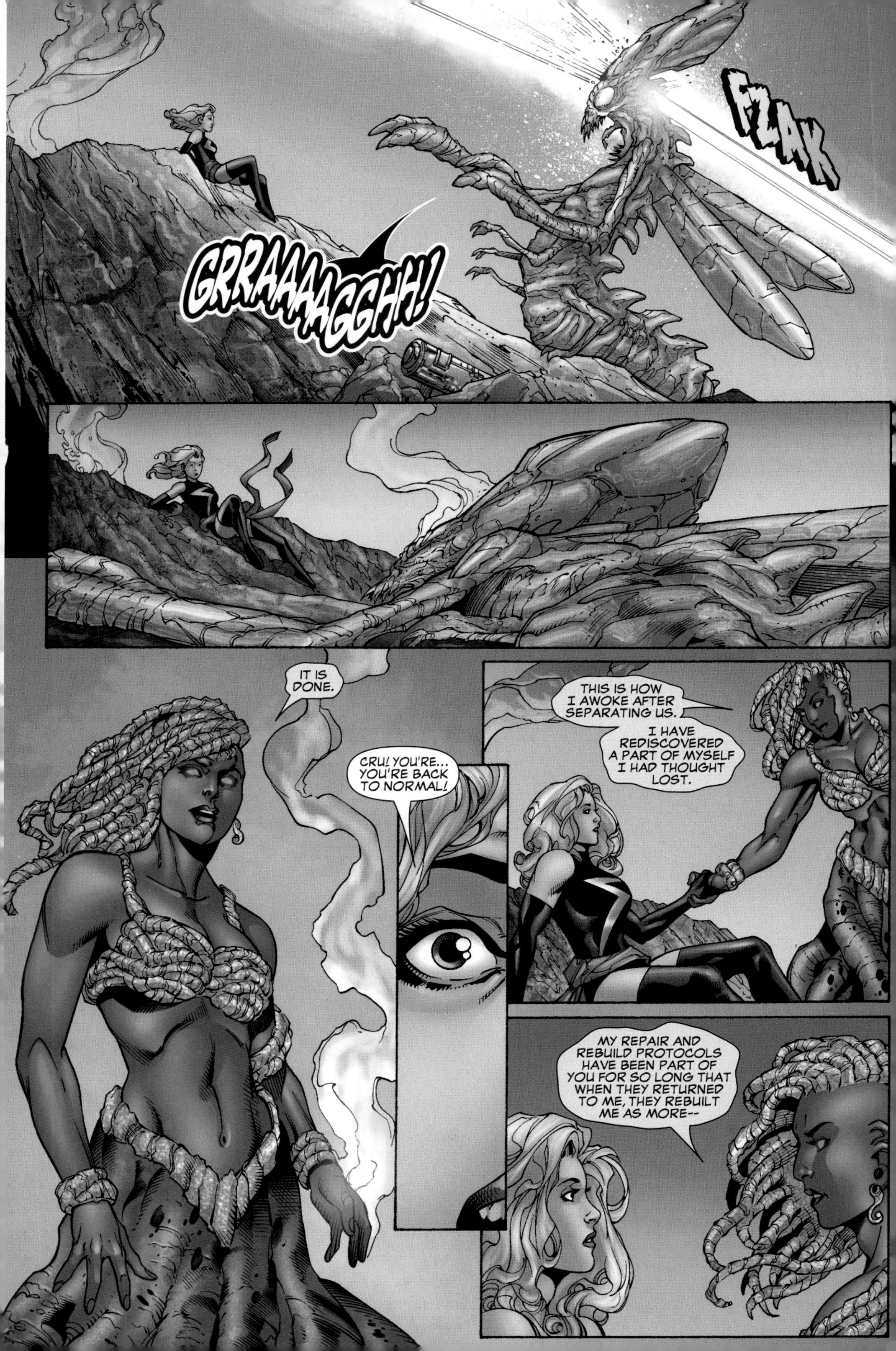

FZZAK
GRRAAAAAGGHH!
IT IS DONE.
CRU! YOU'RE... YOU'RE BACK TO NORMAL!
THIS IS HOW I AWOKE AFTER SEPARATING US.
I HAVE REDISCOVERED A PART OF MYSELF I HAD THOUGHT LOST.
MY REPAIR AND REBUILD PROTOCOLS HAVE BEEN PART OF YOU FOR SO LONG THAT WHEN THEY RETURNED TO ME, THEY REBUILT ME AS MORE--

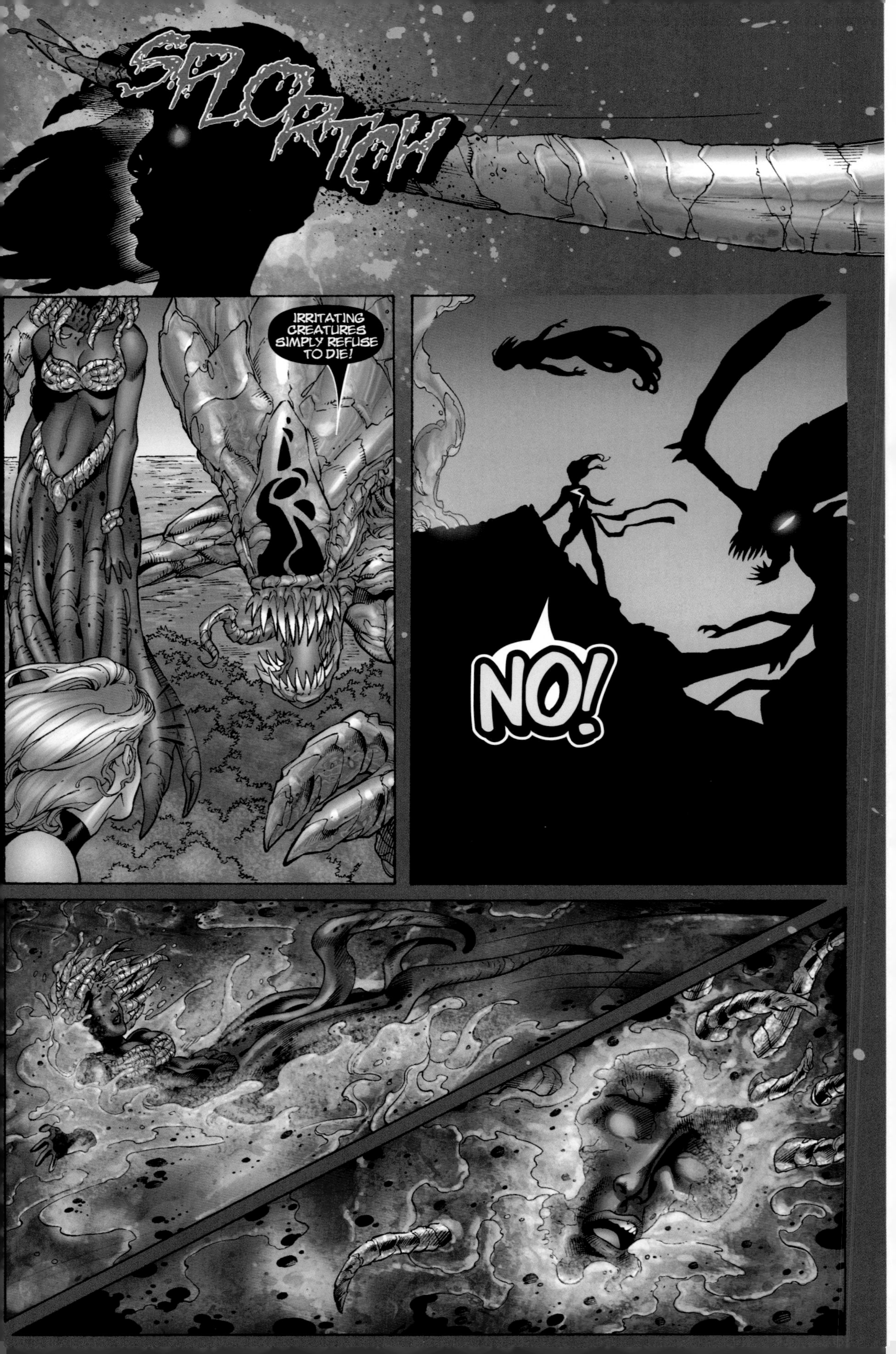
SPLORTCH
IRRITATING CREATURES SIMPLY REFUSE TO DIE!
NO!

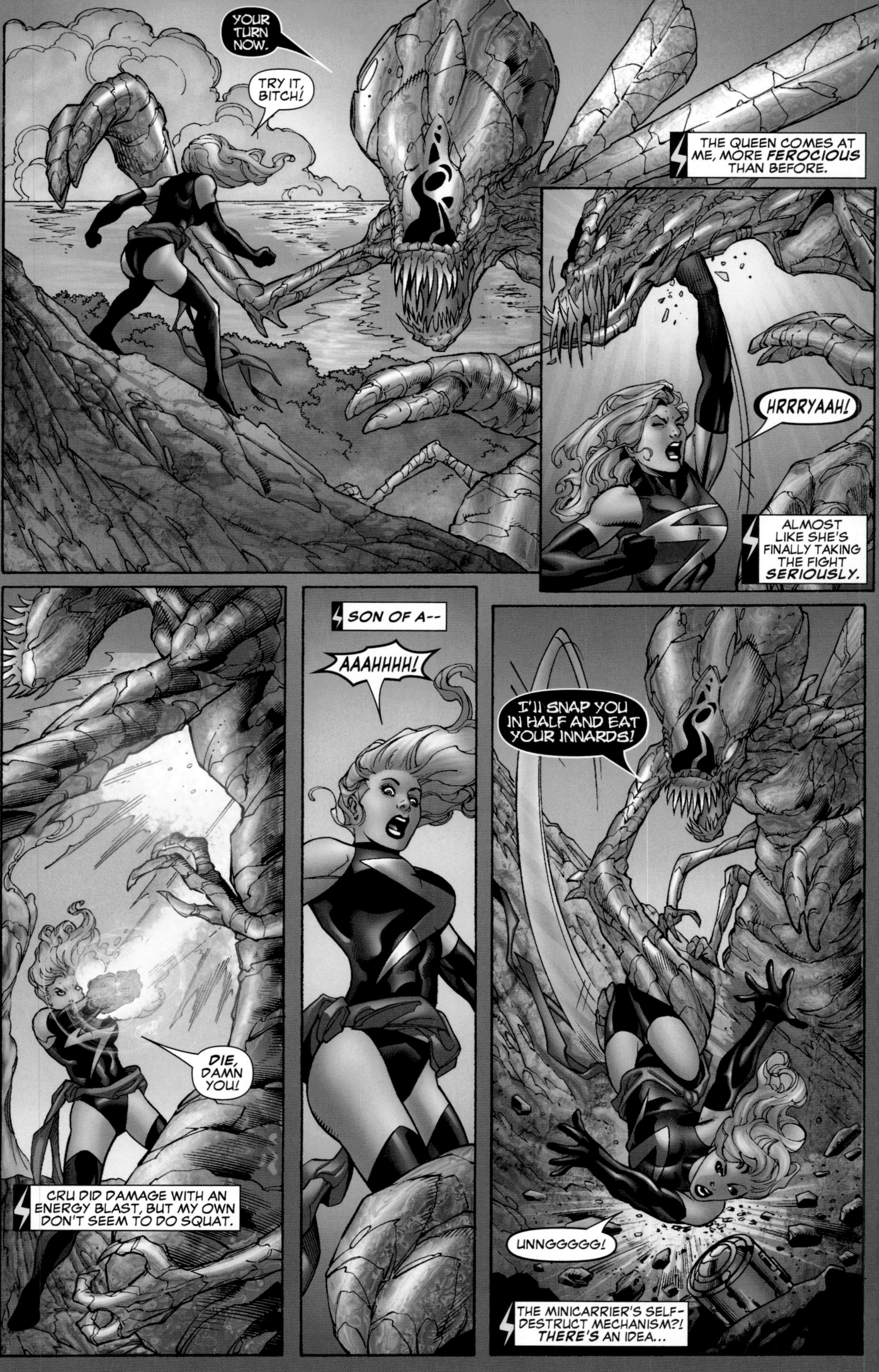
YOUR TURN NOW.
TRY IT, BITCH!
THE QUEEN COMES AT ME, MORE FEROCIOUS THAN BEFORE.
HRRRYAAH!
ALMOST LIKE SHE'S FINALLY TAKING THE FIGHT SERIOUSLY.
DIE, DAMN YOU!
CRU DID DAMAGE WITH AN ENERGY BLAST, BUT MY OWN DON'T SEEM TO DO SQUAT.
SON OF A--
AAAHHHH!
I'LL SNAP YOU IN HALF AND EAT YOUR INNARDS!
UNNGGGGG!
THE MINICARRIER'S SELF-DESTRUCT MECHANISM?! THERE'S AN IDEA...

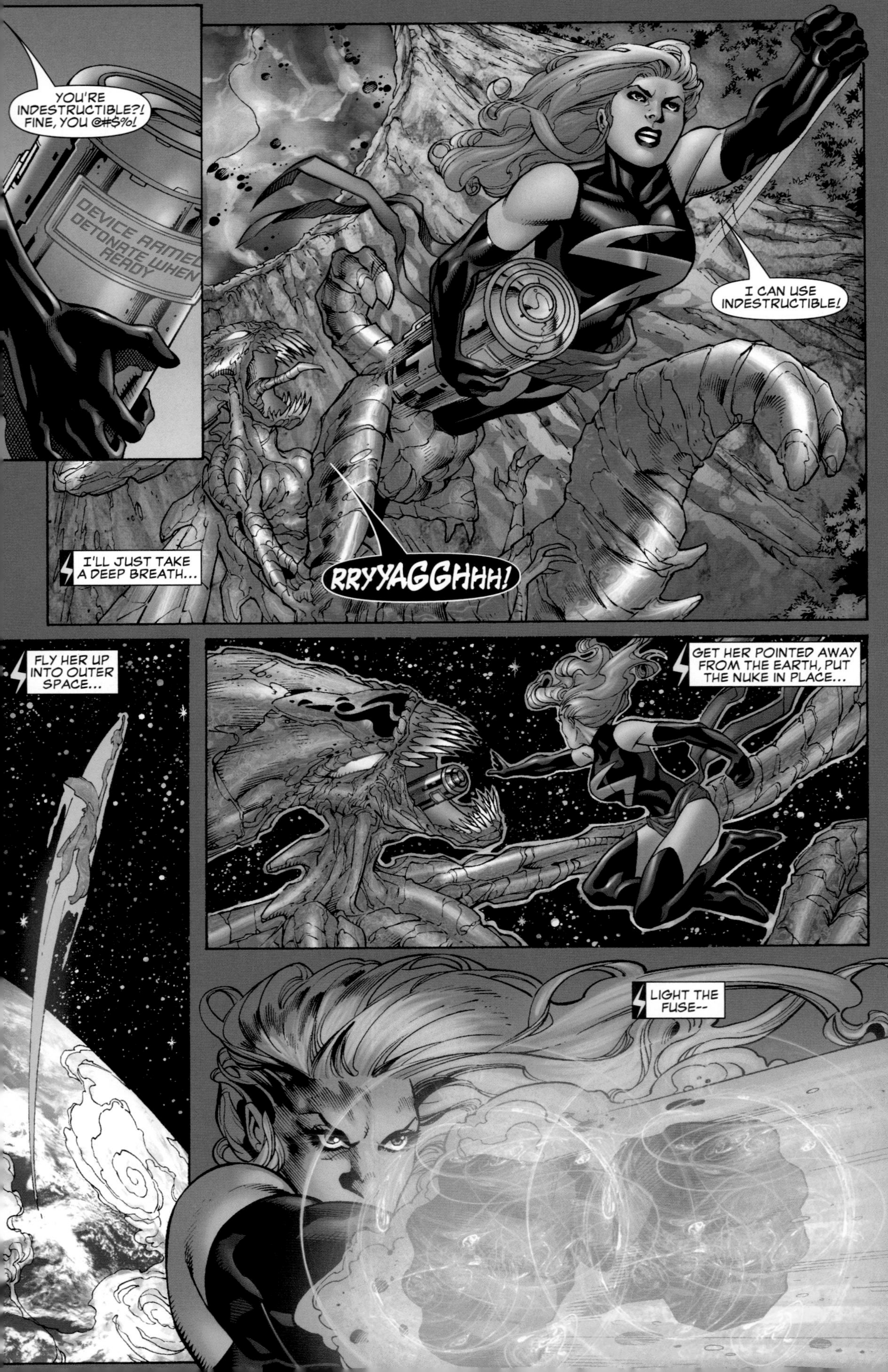
YOU'RE INDESTRUCTIBLE?! FINE, YOU @#$%!
DEVICE ARMED DETONATE WHEN READY
I CAN USE INDESTRUCTIBLE!
I'LL JUST TAKE A DEEP BREATH...
RRYYAGGHHH!
FLY HER UP INTO OUTER SPACE...
GET HER POINTED AWAY FROM THE EARTH, PUT THE NUKE IN PLACE...
LIGHT THE FUSE--

--AND SAY
A PRAYER.

IF I'M RIGHT, SHE SHOULD FLY
FOR A LONG, LONG TIME BEFORE
SHE RUNS INTO ANYTHING.

IF ONLY I
COULD BE
SO LUCKY.

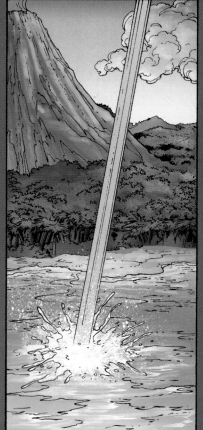

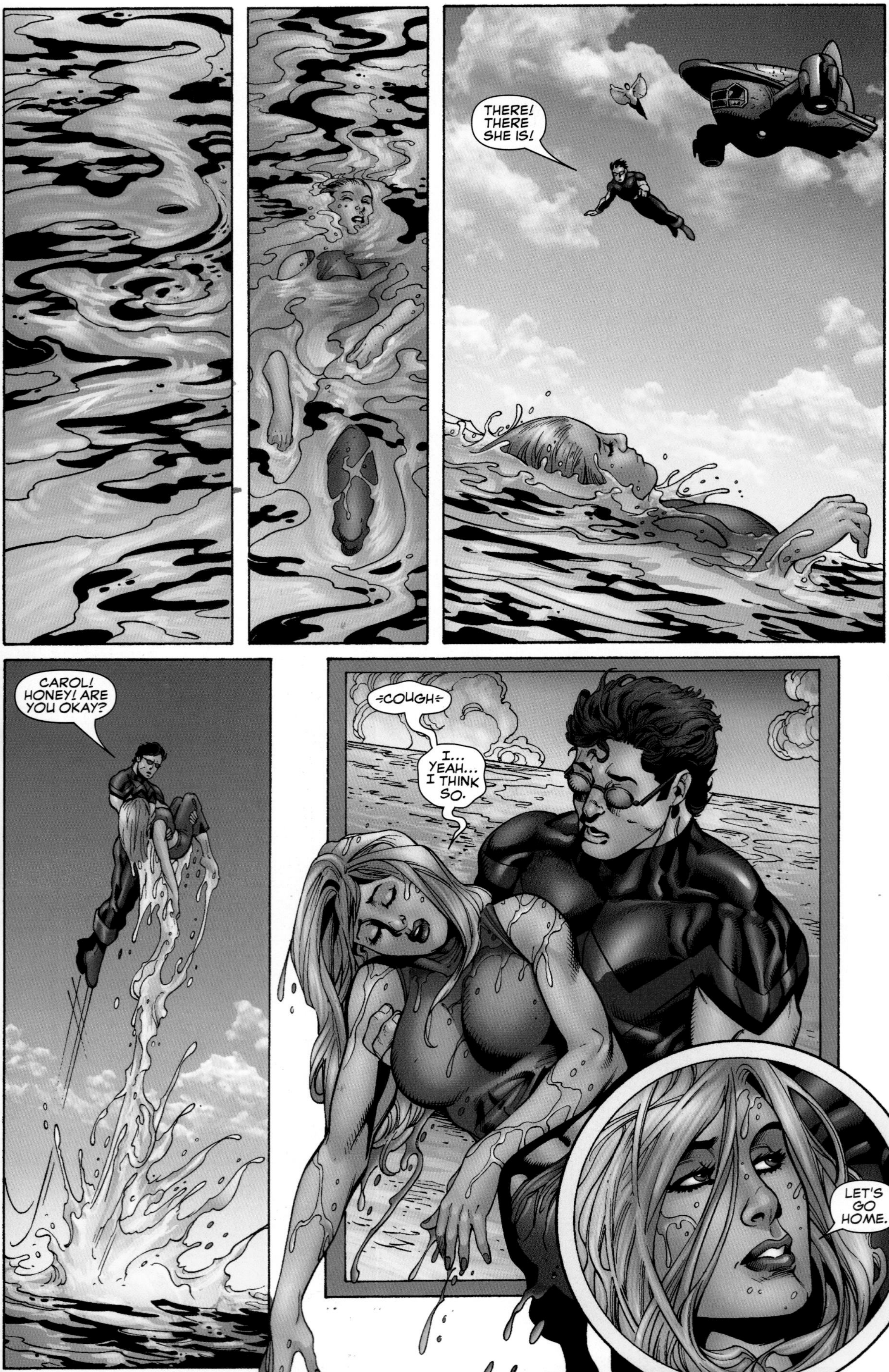
THERE! THERE SHE IS!
CAROL! HONEY! ARE YOU OKAY?
-COUGH-
I... YEAH... I THINK SO.
LET'S GO HOME.

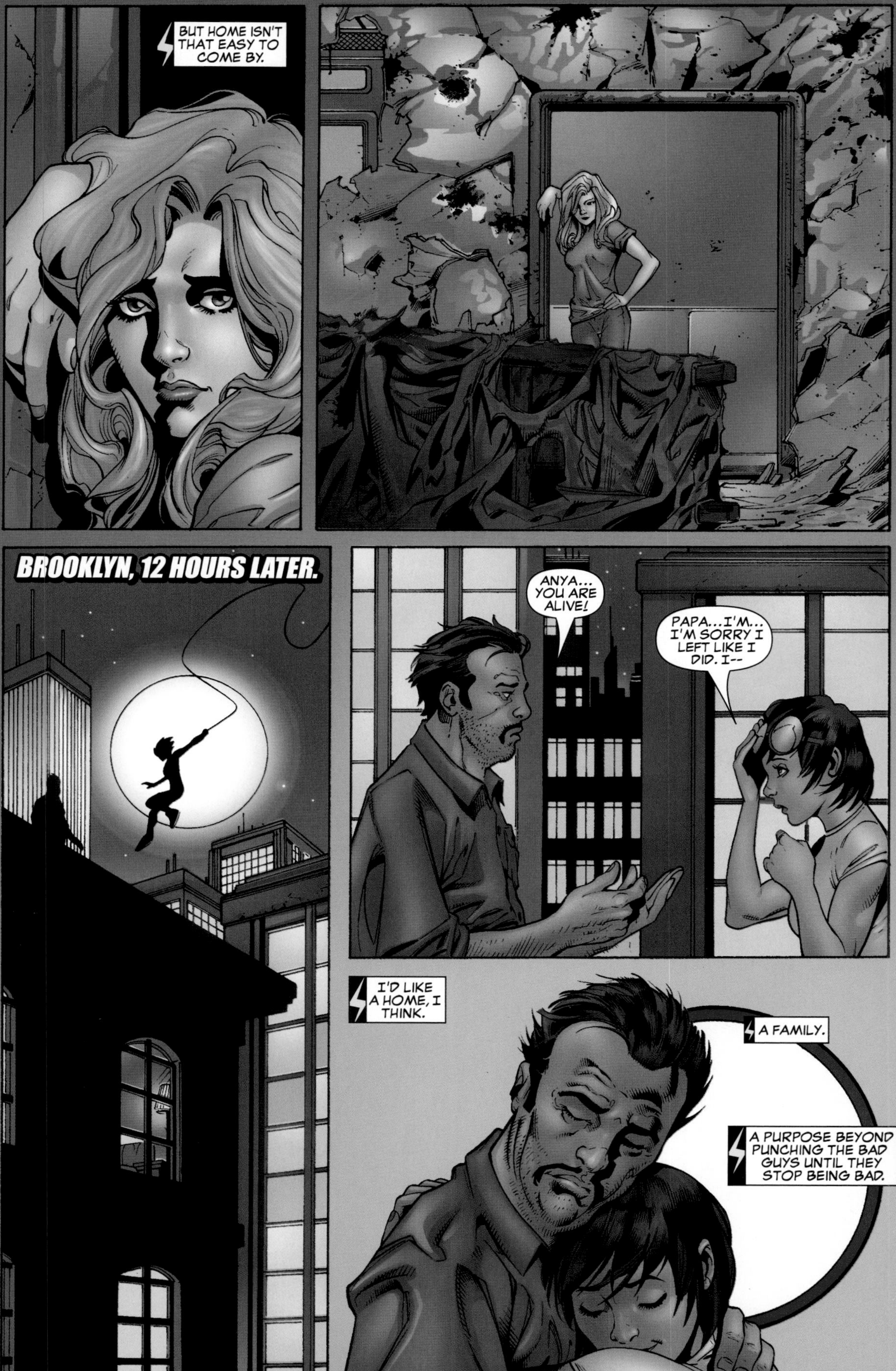

BUT HOME ISN'T THAT EASY TO COME BY.
BROOKLYN, 12 HOURS LATER.
ANYA... YOU ARE ALIVE!
PAPA...I'M... I'M SORRY I LEFT LIKE I DID. I--
I'D LIKE A HOME, I THINK.
A FAMILY.
A PURPOSE BEYOND PUNCHING THE BAD GUYS UNTIL THEY STOP BEING BAD.

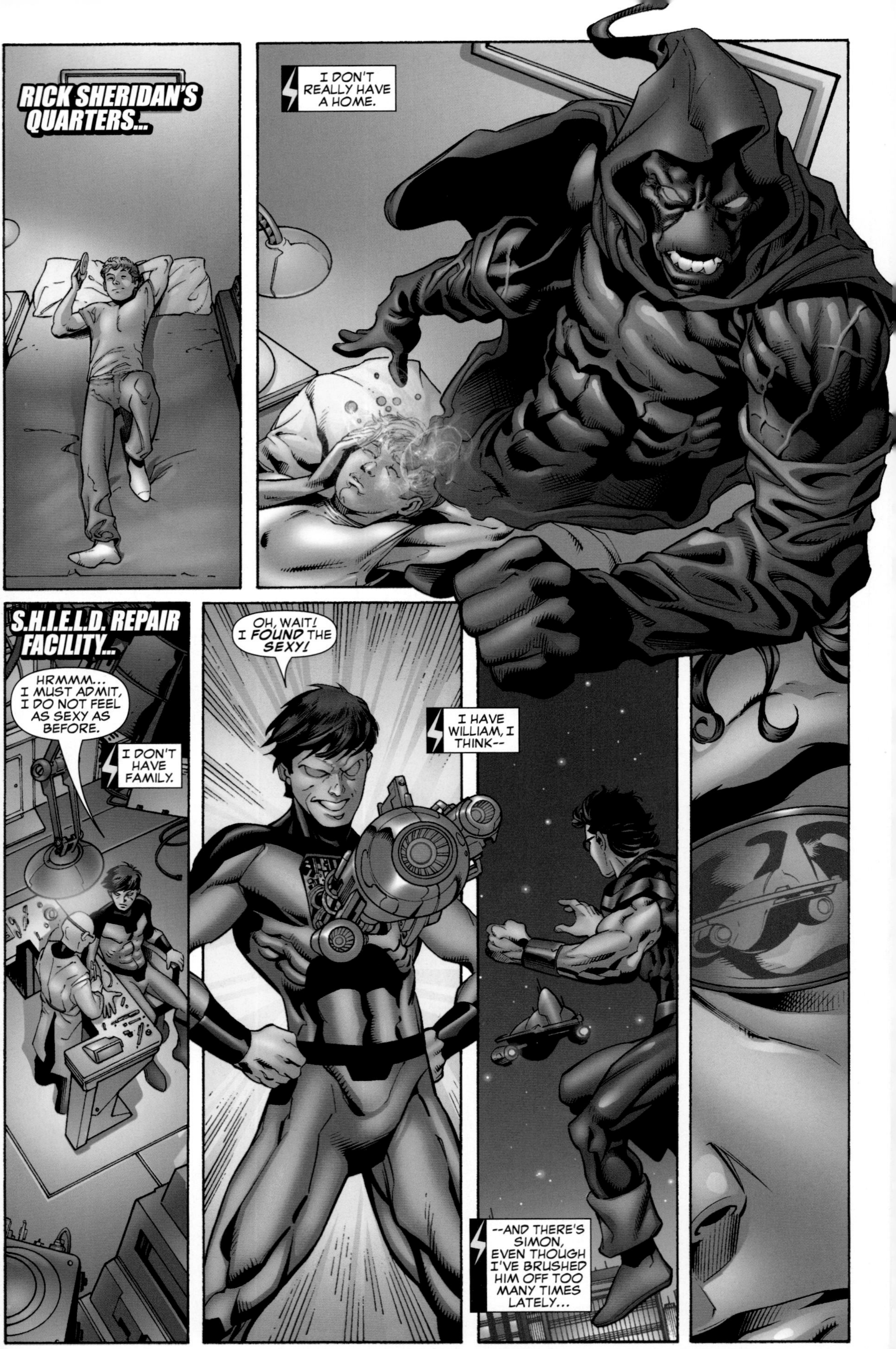

RICK SHERIDAN'S QUARTERS...
I DON'T REALLY HAVE A HOME.
S.H.I.E.L.D. REPAIR FACILITY...
HRMMM... I MUST ADMIT, I DO NOT FEEL AS SEXY AS BEFORE.
I DON'T HAVE FAMILY.
OH, WAIT! I FOUND THE SEXY!
I HAVE WILLIAM, I THINK--
--AND THERE'S SIMON, EVEN THOUGH I'VE BRUSHED HIM OFF TOO MANY TIMES LATELY...

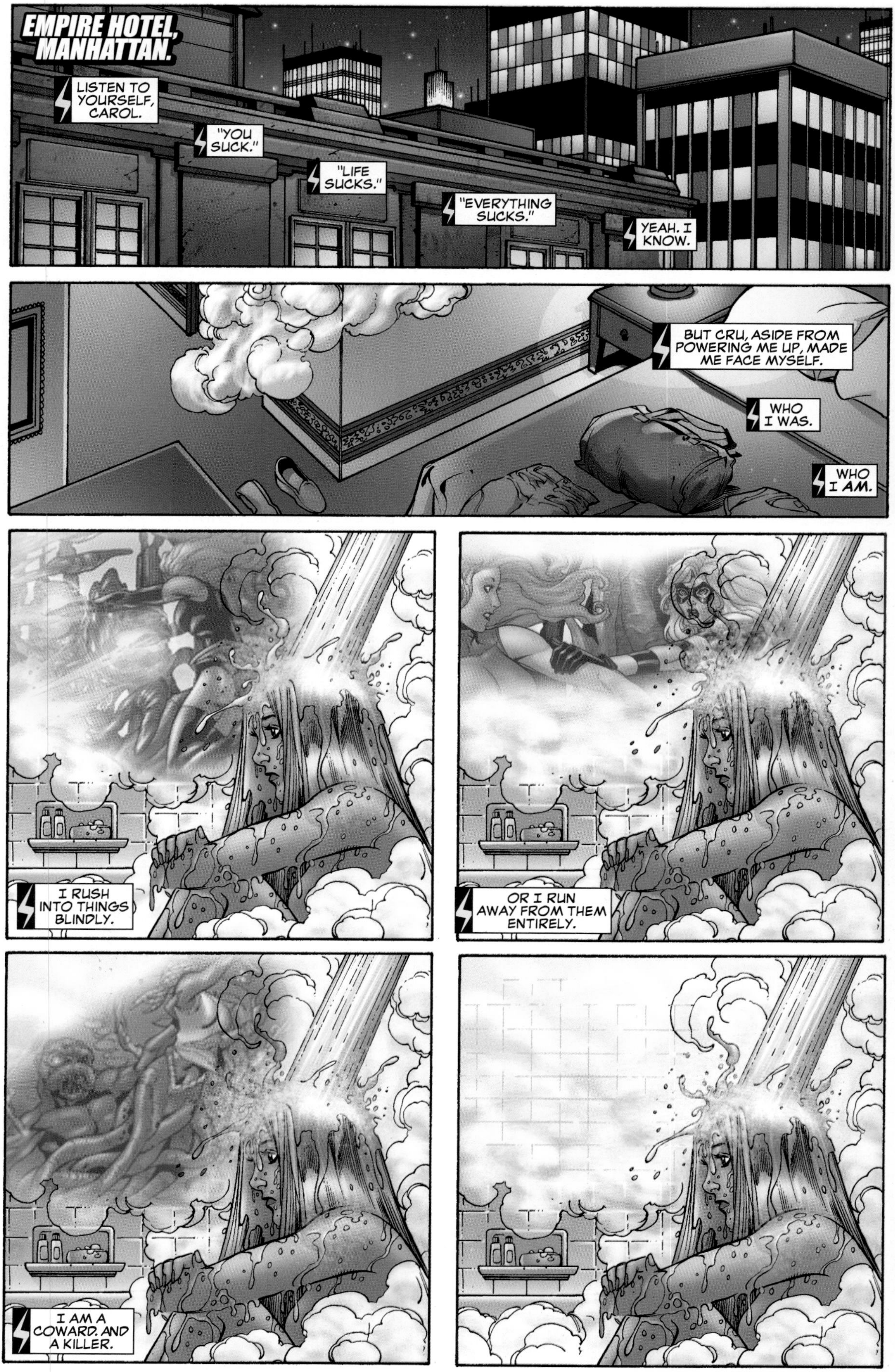
EMPIRE HOTEL, MANHATTAN.
LISTEN TO YOURSELF, CAROL.
"YOU SUCK."
"LIFE SUCKS."
"EVERYTHING SUCKS."
YEAH. I KNOW.
BUT CRU, ASIDE FROM POWERING ME UP, MADE ME FACE MYSELF.
WHO I WAS.
WHO I AM.
I RUSH INTO THINGS BLINDLY.
OR I RUN AWAY FROM THEM ENTIRELY.
I AM A COWARD. AND A KILLER.

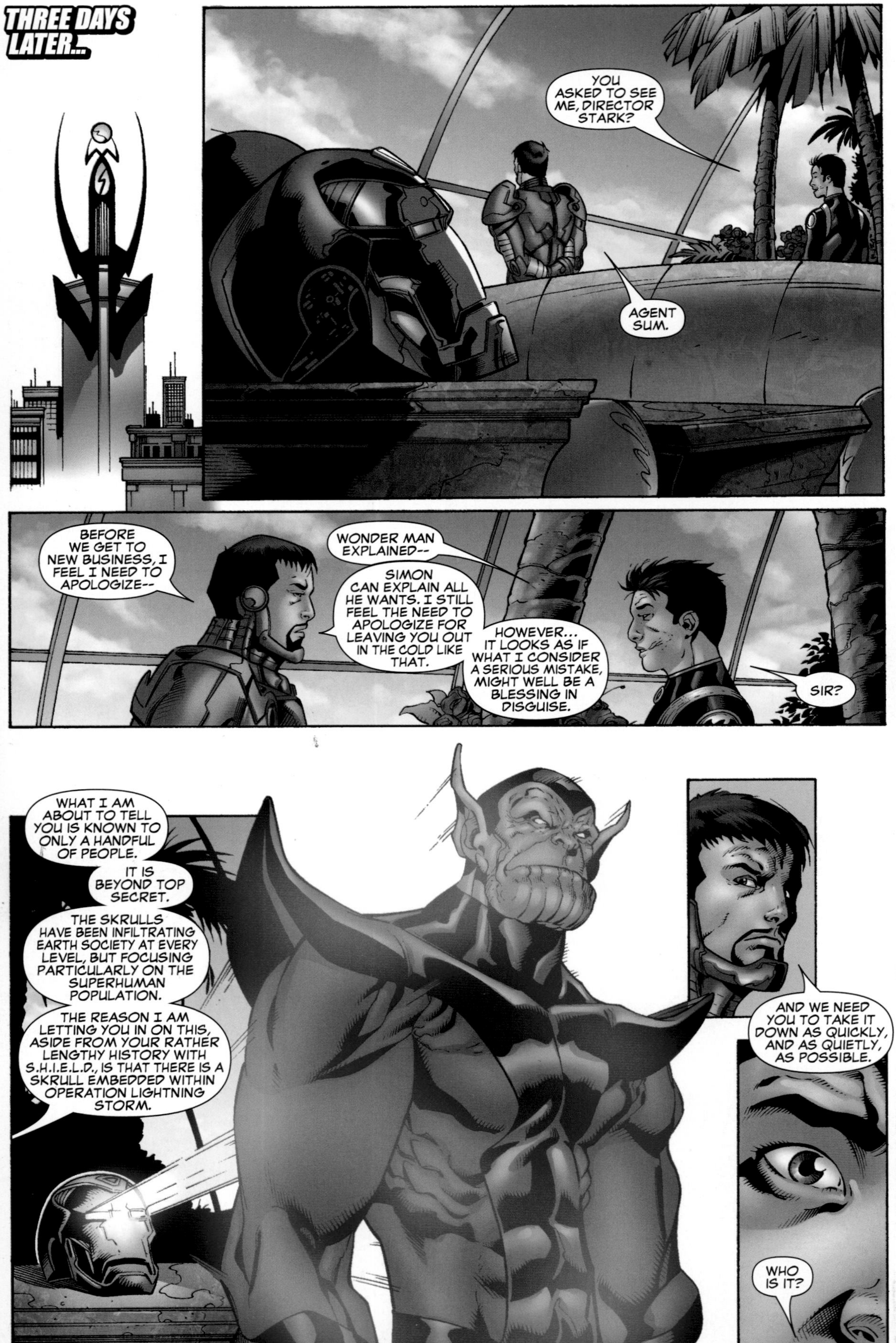
THREE DAYS LATER...
YOU ASKED TO SEE ME, DIRECTOR STARK?
AGENT SUM.
BEFORE WE GET TO NEW BUSINESS, I FEEL I NEED TO APOLOGIZE--
WONDER MAN EXPLAINED--
SIMON CAN EXPLAIN ALL HE WANTS. I STILL FEEL THE NEED TO APOLOGIZE FOR LEAVING YOU OUT IN THE COLD LIKE THAT.
HOWEVER... IT LOOKS AS IF WHAT I CONSIDER A SERIOUS MISTAKE, MIGHT WELL BE A BLESSING IN DISGUISE.
SIR?
WHAT I AM ABOUT TO TELL YOU IS KNOWN TO ONLY A HANDFUL OF PEOPLE.
IT IS BEYOND TOP SECRET.
THE SKRULLS HAVE BEEN INFILTRATING EARTH SOCIETY AT EVERY LEVEL, BUT FOCUSING PARTICULARLY ON THE SUPERHUMAN POPULATION.
THE REASON I AM LETTING YOU IN ON THIS, ASIDE FROM YOUR RATHER LENGTHY HISTORY WITH S.H.I.E.L.D., IS THAT THERE IS A SKRULL EMBEDDED WITHIN OPERATION LIGHTNING STORM.
AND WE NEED YOU TO TAKE IT DOWN AS QUICKLY, AND AS QUIETLY, AS POSSIBLE.
WHO IS IT?

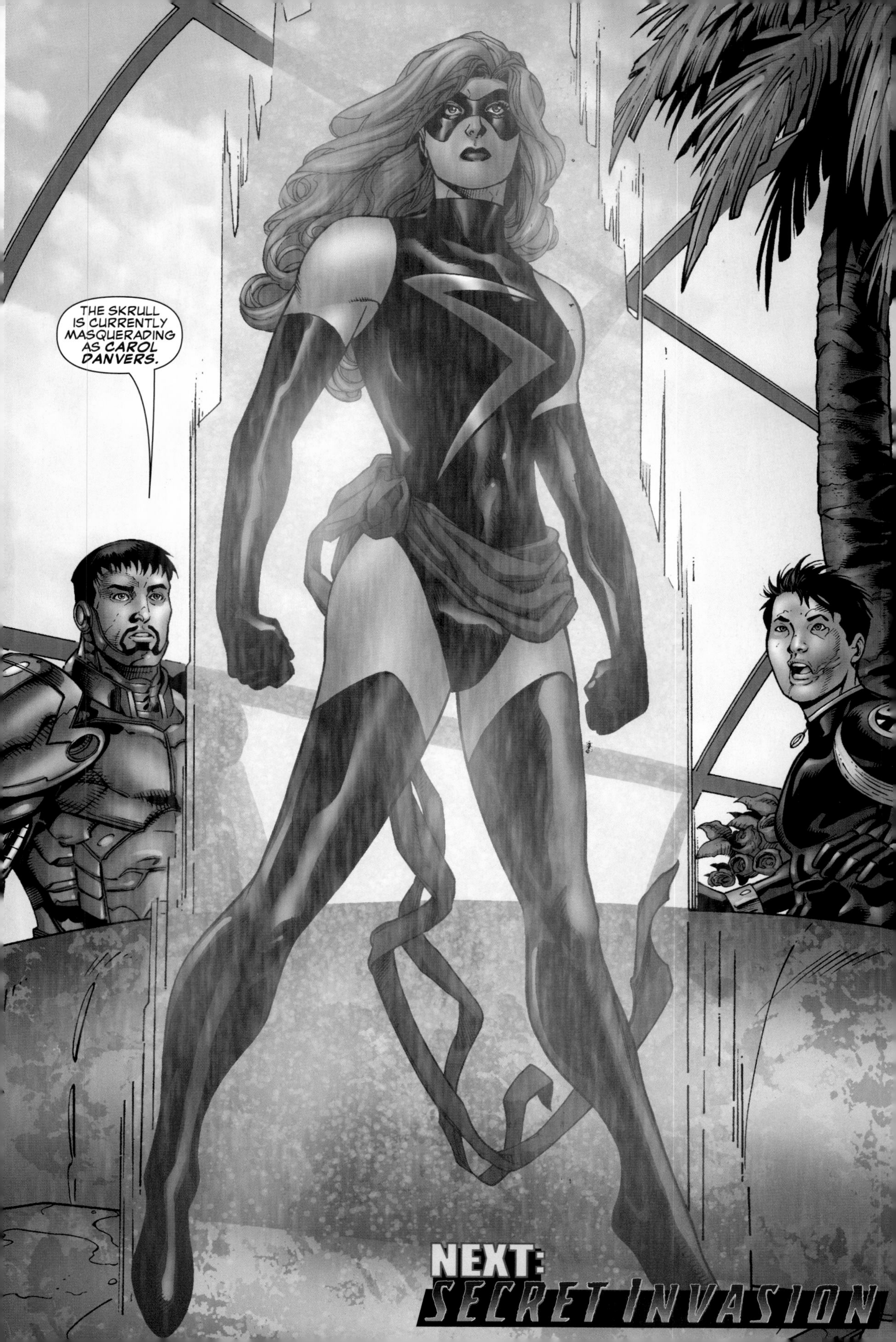
THE SKRULL IS CURRENTLY MASQUERADING AS CAROL DANVERS.
NEXT: SECRET INVASION

#20 VARIANT
BY AARON LOPRESTI

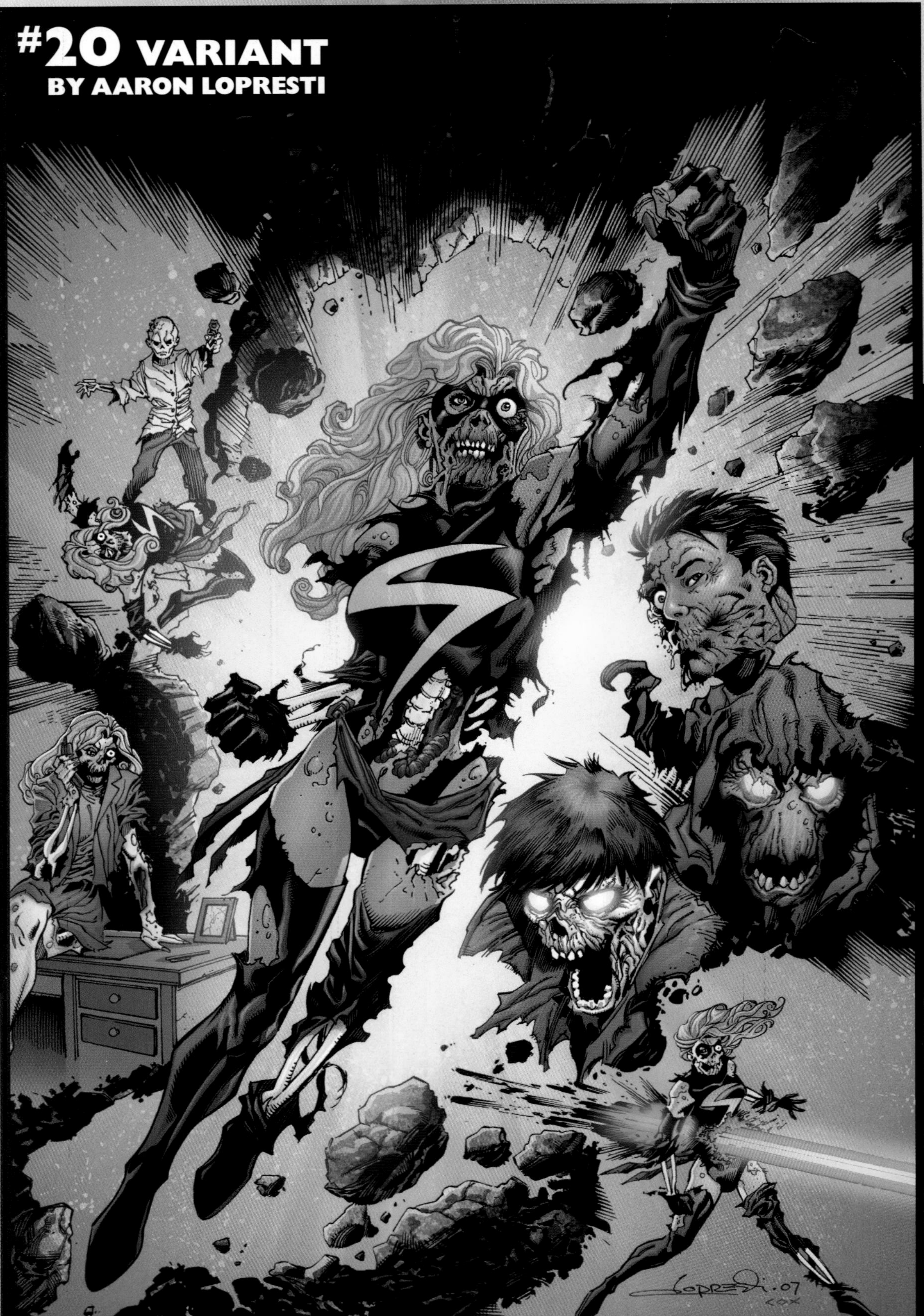